Enterprise Systems and Technological Convergence

A volume in
Emerging Information Technologies: Applications, Innovations, and Research
Sam Goundar, *Series Editor*

Enterprise Systems and Technological Convergence

Research and Practice

edited by

Sam Goundar

The University of the South Pacific, Fiji

INFORMATION AGE PUBLISHING, INC.
Charlotte, NC • www.infoagepub.com

Library of Congress Cataloging-in-Publication Data

A CIP record for this book is available from the Library of Congress
http://www.loc.gov

ISBN: 978-1-64802-341-5 (Paperback)
       978-1-64802-342-2 (Hardcover)
       978-1-64802-343-9 (E-Book)

CONTENTS

CHAPTER 1

INTRODUCTION TO ENTERPRISE SYSTEMS AND TECHNOLOGICAL CONVERGENCE

Sam Goundar
The University of the South Pacific

Enterprise systems, namely enterprise resource planning (ERP), have existed for decades and enabled organizations to gain a competitive advantage while integrating their functions and streamlining their operations. Over the years, enterprise systems have evolved with developments in technology and new ways of doing business. Technologies like cloud computing, in particular, have made access to enterprise systems ubiquitous. Such technologies were needed to cater for new business models like e-commerce that resulted in a different business environment. This rapid acceleration of technological diffusion has changed the way we work, do business, and live. The business and research community took this interplay of work, technology, and peoples into serious consideration which generated many researches and publications on socio-technical systems. The current enterprise systems that we have are results of these research and development efforts.

Enterprise Systems and Technological Convergence, pages 1–21
Copyright © 2021 by Information Age Publishing

1

Today's fourth industrial revolution (4IR) is building on the third (the digital revolution), and future work is all about automation, machine learning, and artificial intelligence. The first industrial revolution introduced mechanization, which saved us from mundane tasks such as fetching water from the well and collecting firewood. The second industrial revolution used electrification to power factories into mass production and its products again assisted us for washing clothes, keeping our drinks cold, and heating our food. The third industrial revolution was about information communications technology to automate office work and business processes. However, we were still required to start the computers, run the programs, check the results, monitor processes, and take corrective action. With the fourth industrial revolution, the intention is to completely automate, let machines handle everything, and totally free ourselves.

In terms of technology, we initially started off by doing our own developments and isolating ourselves from others because we were out to compete, and taking market share as the bottom line was vital. For example, we started off with different and incompatible computer hardware in the form of distinct models where work done on one computer could not be used on another. Then, we went through the platform wars of Microsoft vs. Apple vs. Linux, and so on. And the same is being witnessed in the mobile platforms with Apple and Android. However, we have come to our senses and realized it is more profitable to become compatible, interoperable, and converge. Technologies have converged, likewise. Every existing and new technology needs to be able to converge with others for survival. The Internet became the platform for technological convergence and a one-stop shop to find anything and everything.

Your smartphone is an ideal example of technical convergence. Initially, with a phone, you could only make voice phone calls. Now, with a smartphone, not only can you make a voice phone call, you can also text, email, take photos, record videos, listen to music, make payments, get a ride, do banking, order food, browse the Internet, and the list is endless. Just imagine how many different technologies have converged into your smartphone: phone (voice call), camera (take photos), walkman (listen to music), video recorder (record videos), computer (email, browse, etc.), and the list of technologies that have converged into your smartphone goes on. Similarly, a number of technologies have converged with enterprise systems. For example, blockchains and smart contracts can now be used to converge different supply chains of all the stakeholders of a particular product, ensure transparency and build trust with customers and each other.

Organizations now operate in a global environment, are driven by technology, and need to contend with all demographics. These organizations collect data (very large amounts of data—big data), deal with and process information (information overload) to make decisions. These organizations are now looking for enterprise systems that are smart, intelligent, and capable of analyzing and making fast decisions with big data to be able to survive in a global economy and fickle customers.

ENTERPRISE SYSTEMS

The evolution of enterprise systems started during the early 1990s after decades of using silo-based information systems within business organizations. Enterprise systems, like ERP, is a software-based system that is responsible for making information, reporting, and functions widely available and centrally located within business organizations. ERP systems are comprehensive applications that support and connect all aspects of an organization's business processes. Business processes, such as departments of accounting, human resources, marketing, purchasing, manufacturing, and so forth, are all integrated into one system that shares a common database. This common database enables all departments and functions to share and access real-time information about the organization. ERP systems appeared in the 1990s as a way to provide accessibility, flexibility, and consistency across all the major business functions, unlike its predecessors. Organizations that use ERP systems have a better chance of being sustainable in an ever-changing business environment.

According to Motiwalla and Thompson (2012), the five important components have to work together in order to create an ERP system. These components are hardware, software, information, processes, and people. Hardware consists of the physical equipment such as servers and peripherals. Software is the operating system and/or database that the company or specific department uses. Examples of software today are Windows 10 or Linux. The information component is basically the data that is input to the system by internal or external organizational resources. Processes consist of policies and procedures that create the ways of conducting their business. The people of an ERP system are the end-users and IT staff. End-users can be anyone from the employees to the suppliers of a company. Just like homes and large-scale buildings, ERP systems have an architecture that the implementers must follow. Most of the time, a vendor is the one who creates the ERP architecture when an organization wishes to purchase outside the company (Motiwalla & Thompson, 2012).

Enterprise systems as described above do not exist anymore because they could not keep up with technological, organizational, and management demands of the contemporary workplace. Modern enterprise systems have emerged and taken over. Enterprise systems have now become more intelligent, intuitive, and cloud based. The solution has evolved to more than just processing the back-office tasks. Modern enterprise systems take care of customers (customer relationship management [CRM] systems), suppliers (supply chain management [SCM] systems), employees (human resources information systems [HRIS]), and assists management in making decisions (decision support systems [DSS]). The advent of social media has allowed for more immediate and direct communication that shifts expectations for businesses and consumers alike. Customers are writing about their experiences of dealing with the organizations. The enterprise systems need to capture these reviews, analyze, and report to management what the customer feedback is.

In their article, Vom Brocke et al. (2018) talk about how, in the years ahead, enterprise systems (ES) will be subject to significant changes as they see more applications empowered by artificial intelligence (AI), primarily due to substantial advancements in machine learning algorithms. Areas such as natural language processing, deep neural networks, or self-service analytics are probably some of the prime beneficiaries of machine learning applications. By adding AI capabilities to ES, they are enabled to sense and dynamically respond to their environment as well as continuously learn. The evolving intelligent enterprise systems (IES) will represent a new class of systems and become a key element in the future work environment. The design of IES comes with many interesting challenges for information systems (IS) research. One important area is proposing design principles for interactive IES. One example is the design of conversational interfaces in IES, offering text- and speech-based interaction with its users.

TECHNOLOGICAL CONVERGENCE

Information communications technology (ICT) is the simplest example of technological convergence. Before information technology, information was either disseminated via print media (newspapers), audio media (radios), or audio and video (TV). To consume this information, an individual was required to pay for and access three different technologies on three different mediums or devices. Now, via the Internet, on a webpage, a consumer can access all three media at once with a single technology. Therefore, the print, audio, and voice and audio technologies have all converged on a single web page and accessed via a single device. With this convergence, the user has control in terms of when, for how long, and how many times, the user can access this information, with the option of archiving it for future retrieval and reference. With this simple example, we can say that the integration of different technologies into one and the provision of them as a single service is technological convergence.

Similar statements were echoed in an essay written by Papadakis (2007), for the International Telecommunications Union. He defines the term technological convergence as, "a process by which telecommunications, information technology and the media, sectors that originally operated largely independent of one another, are growing together" (p. 1). He adds, "Technological convergence has both a technical and a functional side. The technical side refers to the ability of any infrastructure to transport any type of data, while the functional side means the consumers may be able to integrate in a seamless way the functions of computation, entertainment, and voice in a unique device able to execute a multiplicity of tasks" (p. 1). Technological convergence if appropriately managed can play an important role in national economic and social development of every nation. Governments can capitalize on the opportunity to stimulate market development and meet previous unmet society communication needs (Papadakis, 2007).

In an organization, analog phone lines, fax machines, duplicating machines, and other stand-alone office equipment have converged into a computer network connected via digital data lines. Now, from one device, a number of different services on different technologies can be accessed. VoIP has replaced phone line communications and email attachments have replaced faxes and postal. Technological convergence results in greater benefits from increased diversity in products and services in an organization. Using networking technology that connects all information and communications services with a single network, companies can add services to their previous ones, without new investments in infrastructure. The ability to integrate different technologies (technological convergence) seamlessly has resulted in disruptive technologies like Uber, Netflix, 3D printing, self-driving cars, drone deliveries, and the list is not exhaustive. Technological convergence emerged as a savior for all of us during the time of the COVID-19 pandemic.

Already converged technologies like AI, blockchains, robotics, bioinformatics, data science, are converging again to provide totally automated and intelligent services that did not exist before. The article, "The Technological Convergence Innovation" authored by Adams, Taricani, and Pitasi (2018), discusses the acceleration and integration of everything (AIE), that is, of all forms of electronic devices into a distributed communications grid that will, inexorably, ubiquitously change the way we exist towards a convergent singularity of robotics, informatics, genetics, and nanotechnology. The changes may be more than the collective or individual human psyche is prepared to engage and will require that societies get used to these changes and incorporate them. The use of communication and information technology is also as important for sociology as it is for any other subject as it influences and is influenced by different kinds of policy, about citizenship (Adams, Taricani, & Pitasi, 2018). This research article indicates that technological convergence still has a long way to go and there will be further disruptions.

ENTERPRISE SYSTEMS AND TECHNOLOGICAL CONVERGENCE

Organizations and its enterprise systems did not have any other alternative. Internally, to effortlessly integrate different divisions, functions, operations, departments and their diverse systems and technologies, technological convergence was the only option. For organizations that were geographically dispersed, converged technologies like cloud computing and services on the web was the alternative. Externally, for supply chain management (SCM), it meant finding ways to converge different organizations, its systems, networks, processes, and everything else with each other. This meant finding a technology that was compatible or that could integrate the different technologies and systems used by all the different organizations in the supply chain. Connecting with customers and external users with systems like customer relationship management (CRM) meant finding a platform that was compatible with all devices, operating systems, browsers, networks, and whatever else exists in the ecosystem.

Vom Brocke et al. (2018) in their research paper titled "Future Work and Enterprise Systems" write about what they call *intelligent enterprise systems* (IES). According to them, "A large part of current AI projects addresses the optimization of existing business tasks" (p. 3). Exemplary are chat bot projects to optimize customer contact in call centers. The often mentioned predictive maintenance projects also target the reduction of maintenance costs. Industry 4.0 is above all a transformational approach which changes mass production into individual production. Examples of innovative transformation initiatives include the Internet of Things (IoT) platforms by multinational enterprises. By AI-based transformation initiatives, these companies start to explore novel business models with unforeseeable repercussions on traditional business models (Vom Brocke et al., 2018). Data Science, another converged technology is gaining quite a traction with enterprise systems as well by analyzing big data for better decisions.

Apart from the converged technologies mentioned above, there are many other technological convergence examples used in businesses today. For example, cloud computing technologies have enabled businesses to access all services from different technologies as a one-stop shop. Many businesses, instead of developing and deploying in-house enterprise systems now outsource it from cloud service providers. Whether you need different software (software as a service), different platforms (platform as a service), different infrastructure (infrastructure as a service), or any combination of technology at all, you can get it from the cloud. Fog computing or mobile edge computing technologies are pushing all the converged technologies and services from the cloud to the users on the edge (mobile devices users). These users are able to access whatever technology they need, wherever they are, and whenever. And the next generation network, namely, 5G, is going to make this faster, smarter, and pervasive.

Rapid advances in industrial information integration methods have spurred tremendous growth in the use of enterprise systems (Da Xu, 2011). Consequently, a variety of techniques have been used for probing enterprise systems. These techniques include business process management, work flow management, enterprise application integration (EAI), service-oriented architecture (SOA), grid computing, and others. Many applications require a combination of these techniques, which is giving rise to the emergence of enterprise systems. Development of the techniques has originated from different disciplines and has the potential to significantly improve the performance of enterprise systems. However, the lack of powerful tools still poses a major hindrance to exploiting the full potential of enterprise systems. In particular, formal methods and systems methods are crucial for modeling complex enterprise systems, which poses unique challenges. Enterprise systems has emerged as a promising tool used for integrating and extending business processes across the boundaries at both intraorganizational and interorganizational levels (Da Xu, 2011).

ENTERPRISE SYSTEMS AND TECHNOLOGICAL CONVERGENCE: RESEARCH AND PRACTICE

A search on Google Scholar using the keywords, "enterprise systems and technological convergence: research and practice," produces hundreds of published research papers. Most of these are recently published papers in reputable journals with a good number of citations. This is evidence enough that the domain of enterprise systems and technological convergence is a hot and trending topic of research. As a professor, I teach a graduate course, code named "Enterprise Systems," but I have found it necessary to make technological convergence part of the course content. In fact, research and writing a term paper on enterprise systems and technological convergence is a major assessment of the course. ERP vendors like SAP, Oracle ERP Cloud, Microsoft Dynamics 365 Business Central, Infor Cloudsuite, and others have all made technological convergence a priority in their implementation. The fact that articles are published weekly in computer magazines denotes the popularity of its practice.

Highlights of some popular research within the last 3 years are as follows:

- Pei Breivold (2020). "Towards Factories of the Future: Migration of Industrial Legacy Automation Systems in the Cloud Computing and Internet-of-Things Context"
- Ahmad and Mehmood (2020). "Enterprise Systems for Networked Smart Cities"
- Usman, Mehmood, and Katib (2020). "Big Data and HPC Convergence for Smart Infrastructures: A Review and Proposed Architecture"
- Secundo et al. (2019). "Creativity and Stakeholders' Engagement in Open Innovation: Design for Knowledge Translation in Technology-Intensive Enterprises"
- Ebert and Dubey (2019). "Convergence of Enterprise IT and Embedded Systems"
- Walther et al. (2018). "Should We Stay, or Should We Go? Analysing Continuance of Cloud Enterprise Systems"
- Oghazi et al. (2018). "RFID and ERP Systems in Supply Chain Management"
- Tsiatsis, Karnouskos, Höller, Boyle, & Mulligan (2018). "Internet of Things: Technologies and Applications for a New Age of Intelligence"
- Perona, Saccani, and Bacchetti (2017). "Research vs. Practice on Manufacturing Firms' Servitization Strategies: A Gap Analysis and Research Agenda"
- Magalhães and Proper (2017). Model-Enabled Design and Engineering of Organizations and Their Enterprises.

In practice, enterprise systems and ERPs are mostly proprietary and vendor-centric. That is, very few enterprise systems have been developed in-house and are maintained internally by the organization. Most ERP implementations are managed by vendors like SAP, Oracle, Microsoft, and so forth. As these vendors are in the forefront of technological innovation and have several proprietary technologies, the practice of technological convergence starts with them and ends up in the hands of the organization, its employees, and customers. One of the major benefits of implementing a technology converged enterprise system is the opportunity to take advantage of best practices designed into the system by the vendors. Most likely, the system was designed by people who saw a gap between what was available, and what could or should be available.

Looking ahead, in a world where everything that can be automated will eventually be automated. It is not a question of "if," but "when," and that when is soon. The automation of work systems through innovative technology marks an avenue for future work systems that may be referred to as "enterprise systems with technological convergence" (ESTC). We have already seen smart contracts on blockchain networks automating transactions, minting new bitcoins, updating the ledger and providing transparent and immutable records of transactions. Expert systems and medical diagnostic systems are already popular with decision makers and doctors.

ABOUT THIS BOOK

Enterprise systems have been used for many years to integrate technology with the management of an organization, but rapid technological disruptions are now creating new challenges and opportunities that require urgent consideration. This book reappraises the implementation and management of enterprise systems in the digital age and investigates the vital link between business processes, information technology, and the Internet for an organization's competitive advantage and success. This book primarily focuses on the implementation, operation, management, and integration of enterprise systems with fast-emerging disruptive technologies such as blockchains, big data, cryptocurrencies, artificial intelligence, cloud computing, data mining, and data analytics. These disruptive technologies are now becoming mainstream and the book proposes several innovations that organizations need to adopt to remain competitive within this rapidly changing landscape. In addition, it examines enterprise systems, their components, architecture, and applications and enlightens readers on the benefits and shortcomings of implementing them.

This book contains primary research on organizations, case studies, and benchmarks ERP implementation against international best practice. It also focuses on convergence of technologies to create the best practices for using enterprise systems and streamlining operations. The target audience for this book will be readers interested in enterprise systems, ERP systems, and management information systems. They will primarily be academics, researchers, and postgraduate level students. This book will also be of interest to industry practitioners such as IT professionals, government officials, and others who are working in this field. Postgraduate students studying enterprise systems can use the book as a reference guide to study the application of enterprise systems in real world organizations. Academics can incorporate the book as a recommended course textbook or as supplementary reading for courses on enterprise systems, ERP systems, and management information systems. Industry practitioners can use the book to benchmark the implementation, operation, and management of enterprise systems in their organizations.

This book publication deals with enterprise systems integration and operation with disruptive technologies like blockchains, cryptocurrencies, big data, artificial intelligence, and edge computing. Enterprise systems have existed for a very long time. The computing landscape architecture has changed from centralized systems to decentralized ones on the web enabled by cloud computing. This book deals with enterprise systems now on mobile devices and Cloud. For a very long time, research and development in enterprise systems has looked at how information communications technology has changed the contemporary workplace. This book provides anecdotal evidence of such research and development through case studies and research. Today, technological innovation happens at a faster pace and reaches users more quickly than ever before. For example, while it took 75 years for the telephone to reach 100 million users, it was 16 years for mobile phones, 7 years for the World Wide Web, 4.5 years for Facebook (Dreischmeier et al., 2015), and only a few weeks for Pokémon GO (Moon, 2016).

The scope of this book was left open to whatever novel ideas, applications, research, and case studies the authors could come up with. The initial scope for the call for chapters included the following: management information systems, enterprise systems, ERP systems information systems, customer relationship management (CRM) systems, supply chain management (SCM) systems, decision support systems, expert systems, knowledge management systems, transaction processing systems, data processing systems, database management systems, and artificial intelligence. In addition to these, chapters on edge computing, blockchains, cryptocurrencies, e-Commerce, educational ERPs, big data were accepted for publication.

ORGANIZATION OF THE BOOK

The chapters in the book are organized as follows:

Chapter 2: An ERP Implementation Framework for Regional Enterprises

This chapter is set out to investigate the best practices for implementing an ERP system by reviewing several related literatures, and to identify the critical success factors. Not only that, but literature review for existing ERP system implementation framework was also carried out. In addition to these literature reviews, this chapter also considered several influencing factors (attributes/aspects) of some of the Pacific countries (Fiji, Tonga, Vanuatu, and Kiribati) enterprises such as their size, budget, business culture, infrastructures, connectivity (network), expertise, type of business, information system, and structure. An ERP system life cycle which is considered an essential topic was covered and was made a basis of this study. With all the information acquired from literature reviews and data collected from the different Pacific Islands enterprises, a relevant framework for an ERP system implementation in the context of the Pacific was developed. The use of IT (information technology) nowadays has been increasing and is still increasing rapidly, becoming a crucial component of every organization in performing their day to day operations.

Chapter 3: ERP Implementation Challenges and Critical Success Factors

One of the most important tools in any organization today is the management information system (MIS) which aims to provide reliable, complete, accessible, and understandable information in a timely manner to the users of the system. The MIS plays a similar role compared to the role of the heart in the body; information is the blood and MIS is the heart. The system ensures that an appropriate amount of data is collected from the various sources, processed, and sent further to all the needy destinations. The system is expected to address the information needs of an individual, a group of individuals, and the management functionaries: the middle managers and executive level management. The objective of this chapter is to present a case study of an enterprise resource planning (ERP) implementation by a beverage company in the manufacturing industry that produces and distributes its products both locally and overseas. ERP software has become a critical tool for businesses to ensure that information is managed in a more centralized and efficient manner, since it is an enterprise-wide application software package that integrates all business functions into a single system with a common database.

Chapter 4: Local ERP Implementation Processes and Standard Methodologies

Local companies in Fiji have implemented and have been trying to implement enterprise resource planning (ERP) systems for decades. While a few have been successful with their implementation, many have seen frequent failures. This chapter will compare the implementation practices used by Fijian companies with the standard methodologies. Regardless of companies achieving a success or failure, the purpose of this research will be to bridge the gap between the practices currently used by Fijian companies with that of the standard methods. This chapter will be one of its first to provide insight to future local companies who are planning to implement ERP, hence its contribution towards the global ERP implementors into designing the best strategy will be vital. Analytical hierarchy process will be used to compare the local practices against those of the standard methods and determine the best for companies projecting to implement ERP in the future. With technology emerging day by day, businesses are trying to keep up with the latest innovations. As such, ERP systems have been a subject of keen interest. An ERP system is an integrated information system that is used to support business processes.

Chapter 5: How Artificial Intelligence is Transforming the ERP Systems

Enterprise Resource Planning (ERP) systems have become a crucial part of every business organization. The need for ERP systems have drastically increased over the past decade and it is a key factor in bringing success to any organization. Keeping in mind the impact of ERP systems, another notable factor to consider in this time and age is the impact of artificial intelligence (AI). The world is currently digitizing every minute and the involvement of AI in that is quite extraordinary.

Artificial intelligence as an integrated part of the ERP system will affect the very essence of daily operations. AI solutions will most likely take over routine tasks currently performed by humans. Therefore, the development of the new technology is also driven by an increasing need to reduce business operating costs by supporting employees' workflows, thus enhancing the efficiency of the organization's operations. The development of artificial intelligence is, in other words, a development the companies must follow if they want to stay efficient and competitive. Artificial intelligence has just begun to appear in ERP applications and the addition of the new technology is still a relatively new phenomenon.

Chapter 6: Using Business Intelligence in Organizations—Benefits and Challenges

Big data, big data analytics, and business intelligence is the buzzword in today's business arena. With the advent of the Internet and in particular the Internet of things, the opportunity that it presents may be too good to pass up. The chance to be able to get to know not just your customers but more so their behavior can help you, in a way, to serve them better. Also, it presents the opportunity to be able to know your competitors and how they are doing in the market given that everything is now connected. Due to the above fact, the team is inspired to find out whether the realization of the opportunity that big data, big data analytics, and therefore business intelligence presence has reached Fiji or not, and if some SME have realized it and successfully made the change to incorporate them into their daily business. It would also be interesting to note whether the challenges and benefits that local SME go through are like those their overseas counterparts encounter or whether there are differences. The first part of this chapter focuses on a literature review to further discuss, "What is Big Data?" "What is Big Data Analytics" and also their contribution to business intelligence.

Chapter 7: e-Commerce and e-Business Innovations With ERP Systems

The continuous advancements in technologies and higher accessibility to new and improved technologies are becoming the enabler and leading to digital transformations in the entire business industry and for the national economy of any country. It opens up opportunities to improve business practices and processes and offers ways to do business in a more dynamic, better, smarter, faster, transparent, and accountable way. It also enables businesses to explore ways to move from cash payment collection systems to cashless, electronic, and digital payment systems. The reason for introducing electronic payment collection solutions is not to remove cash collection systems but to use it as a more transparent and far better option than cash. Digital or e-payment solutions (going cashless) are a very important part of ecommerce and e-business innovations. This chapter aims to study the literature available for electronic payment solutions with the objective to highlight the scope of Fiji's envisioned journey towards a "cashless society." This research is in alignment with the Fijian government's vision and moves towards a cashless society.

Chapter 8: Impact of ERP Systems and ERP Capabilities for Organizational Success

Enterprise resource planning (ERP) systems are crucial for organizations in order to manage and automate its business effortlessly to possess a competitive advantage. This research was conducted with the purpose to understand the relationship between ERP systems. ERP capabilities will contribute towards achieving a competitive advantage. The chapter also examines the impact of ERP capabilities on decision-making efficiencies. The research is based on telecommunication companies in Fiji who have adopted ERP systems for their daily business process. Organization fit perspective and Porter's model will be the key drivers for this research in order to understand the relationship between independent and dependent variables. Lastly, the aim of this chapter is to investigate the impact of ERP capabilities on differentiation and low-cost advantage of competitive advantage. Competition across business environments has increased enormously due to the acceleration of technology evolution. Intense competition among rivalries has made each organization to enhance their competitive advantage in order to survive and compete in the market. An improved and efficient system is capable of leading to more efficient management of business process.

Chapter 9: Extending Educational ERP System's Functionality to Users on the Edge

Enterprise resource planning (ERP) systems provide large organizations with the ability to share information between their cross-functional business units. ERP systems in turn may span over various geographical locations as with the case of multinational organizations. Sharing of information becomes a critical focus for these organizations which may then lead to the implementation of cloud computing services. ERP systems now also have the capability to be hosted on the cloud which enables the information sharing to be available at a central location. However, this gives rise to deficiencies such as availability, speed, and network latency issues especially for developing countries particularly in the south pacific. As an alternate solution, an additional layer between the cloud and the end devices can be introduced to improve service delivery and performance—fog computing layer. The University of the South Pacific is such an organization that can benefit from the amalgamation of its enterprise system with an extension of its student registration process to the edge per se, using the devices and technologies that students have access to.

Chapter 10: Customer Relationship Management Issues and Analysis

Customer relationship management (CRM) is used to manage and analyze customer interactions within an organization. The aim of the research is to identify and analyze CRM problems in a public entity in order to increase value from the CRM functions. The research will run through the information system success model consisting of three influential factors, namely: (a) system characteristics, (b) utility characteristics, and (c) performance. The proposed holistic approach is based on a review of factors and essential elements in order to have a clear understanding on the problems and develop specific evaluation criteria of the three areas of CRM systems. It will then have the survey analysis to be validated and to have a comprehensive indulgent of the feasibility of the model. The management of customer relationships has become a priority factor for many organizations. But the factors behind CRM success and what constitutes CRM is an issue of considerable debate. The research will investigate and identify the problems of CRM at a public entity. Our research is based on a CRM system that was introduced at a public entity.

Chapter 11: Analyzing Human Resource Information System in Organizations

This research was conducted to assess how the use of HRIS affects HR functions of the organization. HRIS research is very limited in Fiji and the Pacific as a whole, therefore there was a need for this study. This chapter uses the DeLone and McLean HRIS success model integrated with some incumbent HRIS factors providing a comprehensive view into vital factors affecting HRIS in the HR department. A standardized questionnaire was used to collect quantitative data. The results from this research showed there were a total of six different factors that affect the use of HRIS in the HR divisions of government organizations. These factors are usefulness, a faster decision-making process, system quality, ease of use, subjective norms such as social and peer pressures, and system unification. The effect of these factors was measured which showed that system quality, service quality, and the ease of use has a positive impact. Further to this, the impact of HRIS on the HR division, in relation to performance and productivity was also investigated with the sample population. It was established that HRIS has a positive and significant effect on the productivity as well as performance of the HR division in government organizations.

Chapter 12: Exploring the Competitive Advantage of ERP in Telecommunications

Over the decades, the growth in the telecommunication and Internet service providers has extended tremendously. The rapid growth has led the telecommunication and Internet service providers to find innovative ways to provide better customer-oriented service to guarantee fast, reliable, efficient, and best customer experience. The South Pacific is no different, the telecommunication industries in the region have invested huge amounts of funds to improve their operational efficiencies to gain competitive advantage over other similar service providers. The key percentage of the funds that each of the service providers spent on is to improve their company profile to upgrade and improve their current business information system to an enterprise resource planning (ERP) system. The value, rarity, imitability, and organization (VRIO) framework and resource-based view (RBV) model has been employed to evaluate if investment into an ERP system improved operational efficiency. Also to check if investment into an ERP software was exploited enough to gain maximum benefit for the future of the company. This chapter aims to illustrate the real competitive advantage with ERP for telecommunications.

Chapter 13: Measuring the Success of ERP With the DeLone & McLean Model

There's a fast-growing use for enterprise resource planning (ERP) systems being done all over by a majority of businesses globally and the measuring of the success of these types of information systems should be done for firms where it is implemented. The firms nowadays invest a large portion of financial resources towards implementation of these information systems (IS), as assessing the success of such IS doesn't happen due to a lot of reasons, including lacking in the knowledge level of what is to be assessed for success determining for an IS such as ERP. The DeLone and McLean (D&M) model development has occurred and majorly been utilized for IS success measuring, therefore the use of this model will be utilized to measure the success of IS. Also there are three main dimensions of the D&M model on which more focused discussion will be done in this chapter which are as follows: user satisfaction, system quality, and information quality. The use of qualitative and quantitative data analysis techniques will be used for various research papers literature review, with structural equation modeling approach being used to examine and summarize the statistical data collected through interviews and questionnaires.

Chapter 14: Analysis of Ethical Issues in HRIS Using the PAPA Model

Information system is an important aspect of the communication industry. It is a storehouse of vital information for the company as well as for the employees. Many companies in Tonga use the information system to retrieve information about the employees' leave history and other personal data for reference and promotion purposes. It is therefore important that the information system in the telecommunications company in Tonga is accurate and that access is secure given the company's heavy dependence on the HRIS information for promotion and other related benefits. In this chapter, we analyzed the ethical issues of the HRIS using the PAPA model, in terms of privacy, accessibility, accuracy, and property. To do this, we reviewed the current policies within the telecommunications company and considered if there is a need for development of standards for accessing information in the human resources department in view of the PAPA model. This chapter is important because it serves to inform those who want to access data in the human resource of the ethical policies and procedures of the company to protect the employee's information.

Chapter 15: An Analysis of a University's ERP Implementation—A Case Study

The main purpose of this chapter is to analyze Fiji National University's legacy information management systems and its related issues. The chapter will summarize FNU's journey towards identifying its issues, documenting the requirements, selecting the right vendor and current project progress. Fiji National University is Fiji's newest university, formed in 2010 after the merger of six major training institutions, which included Fiji Institute of Technology, Fiji School of Medicine, Fiji School of Nursing, Fiji College of Advanced Education, Fiji College of Agriculture and the Lautoka Teachers College. In 2012, the Fiji Maritime Academy and in 2013, the Training and Productivity Authority of Fiji also became part of Fiji National University. When the institutions merged, the challenges related to managing student data multiplied and became more complex. Certain institutions came with their own information systems, while others had only manual records. The library inherited the Horizon Library Management System from the School of Medicine. The finance and HR, two of the other major divisions, inherited Navision and PayGlobal from the Fiji Institute of Technology. In 2013, the software was upgraded.

Chapter 16: Usage and Benefits of Banner ERP System at a University

ERP systems play a vital role in an organization. However, the success of ERP systems is heavily dependent on the structure of the organization and the usage of the ERP system. The benefits of the ERP system implementation is very well reflected on the utilization of the ERP system by the organization. Our team's research is based on the implementation and usage of the Banner ERP system at a university in the South Pacific. The aim of the chapter is to explore the implementation and usage of the ERP Banner system and identify the benefits of it to the university. This chapter will also provide suggestions of ways in which the university could achieve more benefits from the Banner system. The introduction of ERP systems has provided a new direction for all the organizations around the world. With technological advancement at its peak in the 21st century, the increased research into how well ERP systems support the growth of business and organization has allowed ERP systems to make a stance amongst its users. Organizations implement ERP systems to channel their business process in such a way that will boost not only their performance in the market, but also enable them to grow.

Chapter 17: Analyzing the Effectiveness of an ERP's Order Fulfilment Process

The purpose of this chapter is to investigate how an oil company's information system, STRIPES, has assisted in ensuring a competitive advantage for its customers through its operational capabilities. This system systematically examines the processes, from the point where the customer places their order to the time he receives their ordered fuel in their tank. For this chapter, we will be applying the DeLone and McLean information system success model in the context of operational order fulfillment in this oil industry. This study will rely on three research questions to allow us to explain the effectiveness and efficiency of this information system and provide us with a better understanding of how an oil company maintains its competitive advantage. Interviews were conducted and questionnaires were completed as part of the research methodology to collect data from users of the information systems. A structured questionnaire was sent out to 50 operators within the organization which consisted of order fulfillment personnel and delivery analysts to terminal dispatchers and their respective supervisors. In total, we looked at four features: quality of service, deliverables, flexibility, and service for order fulfillment.

Chapter 18: Analyzing the Effectiveness of CRM in a Bank

The current study aims to find out the effectiveness of CRM in banking. It intends to determine the efficiency of how CRM works from a staff and customer perspective. This research is important since CRM has become a leading goal of marketing of every organization. Its outcomes will allow comprehensive understanding of how effective CRM is in this part of the globe. Balanced Scorecard research model was utilized. All the statistical and theoretical data was analyzed through strategy maps and action plans. It was focusing on the four perspectives of financial, customer, internal, and knowledge growth. Once the data was collected through questionnaires and interviews, focus was made based on sub questions reflecting the four perspectives. This study will help test the efficiency and effectiveness of CRM systems used in banks. Thus, allowing room for improvements and further sustainability. The study will provide comprehensive knowledge on how CRM could be best used for productivity and efficient running of banks. According to the financial institution whose key role is to provide its client with banking and financial services, it is essential that the customer is given the power and option to choose the preferred service.

Chapter 19: Human Resources Management System for Integration and Productivity

The focus today has passed from administrative management tasks to becoming a strategic partner of the overall organization strategy, largely with the strong support of information technologies evolution in this field of knowledge area. Two systematic analyses have been carried out to identify the problems. This included an interview and chat with current system users through which it was reported to management. The second one was analyzed through the audit report from the external auditors. The auditor's report highlighted that few of the documents were missing from employee files and recommended the HR division to maintain e-copies of documents. This case study has identified reporting, retrieval of employee documentation, and system integration as the major concerns that need to be resolved. The ways that we are going to resolve the issues identified include:

1. Identify the current challenges presented by the current system in use.
2. Determine available opportunities to compare it with other software to gain competitive advantage.
3. Recommend the university to have a suitable HR information system that is able to address the above concerns.

ACKNOWLEDGMENTS

I would like to acknowledge my graduate students from The University of the South Pacific. Your research work, case studies, class discussions, and research papers were an inspiration to work on this book. Without them, this book would not have gone to publication. My graduate students and I are proud to present the book on *Enterprise Systems and Technological Convergence: Research and Practice*. We would like to thank all the reviewers that peer reviewed all the chapters in this book. We also would like to thank the admin and editorial support staff of Information Age Publishing that have ably supported us in getting this issue to press and publication. And finally, we would like to thank all the authors that submitted their chapters to this book. Without your submission, your tireless efforts, and contribution, we would not have this book.

For any new book, it takes a lot of time and effort in getting the editorial team together. Everyone on the editorial team, including the editor-in-chief is a volunteer and holds an honorary position. No one is paid. Getting people with expertise and specialist knowledge to volunteer is difficult, especially when they have their full-time jobs. Every book and publisher has its own chapter acceptance, review, and publishing process. The editor-in-chief then does his own review and selects reviewers based on their area of expertise and the research topic of the article. After one round of peer review by more than three reviewers, a number of revisions and reviews, a chapter and subsequently all the chapters are ready to be typeset and published.

I hope everyone will enjoy reading the chapters in this book. I hope it will inspire and encourage readers to start their own research on Enterprise Systems and Technological Convergence: Research and Practice. Once again, I congratulate everyone involved in the writing, reviewing, editing, and publication of this book.

Any comments or questions can be emailed to sam.goundar@gmail.com

REFERENCES

Adams, T. L., Taricani, E., & Pitasi, A. (2018). The technological convergence innovation. *International Review of Sociology, 28*(3), 403–418.

Ahmad, N., & Mehmood, R. (2020). Enterprise systems for networked smart cities. In R. Mehmood, C. W. S. See, I. Katib, & I. Chlamtac (Eds.), *Smart infrastructure and applications* (pp. 1–33). Springer.

Da Xu, L. (2011). Enterprise systems: state-of-the-art and future trends. *IEEE Transactions on Industrial Informatics, 7*(4), 630–640.

Dreischmeier, R., Close, K., & Trichet, P. (2015, March 2). The digital imperative. *BCG Perspectives.* https://www.bcg.com/publications/2015/digital-imperative

Ebert, C., & Dubey, A. (2019). Convergence of enterprise IT and embedded systems. *IEEE Software, 36*(3), 92–97.

Magalhães, R., & Proper, H. A. (2017). Model-enabled design and engineering of organisations and their enterprises. *Organizational Design and Enterprise Engineering, 1,* 1–12.

Moon, M. (2016, August 1). 'Pokémon Go' hits 100 million downloads. *Engadget.* https://www.engadget.com/2016/08/01/pokemon-go-100-million-downloads/

Motiwalla, L. F., & Thompson, J. (2012). *Enterprise systems for management* (p. 245). Pearson.

Oghazi, P., Rad, F. F., Karlsson, S., & Haftor, D. (2018). RFID and ERP systems in supply chain management. *European Journal of Management and Business Economics, 27*(2), 171–182.

Papadakis, S. (2007). Technological convergence: Opportunities and challenges. *Ensayos de la Unión Internacional de Telecomunicaciones.* Retrieved from http://www.itu.int/osg/spu/youngminds/2007/essays/PapadakisSteliosYM2007. pdf

Pei Breivold, H. (2020). Towards factories of the future: Migration of industrial legacy automation systems in the cloud computing and Internet-of-things context. *Enterprise Information Systems, 14*(4), 542–562.

Perona, M., Saccani, N., & Bacchetti, A. (2017). Research vs. practice on manufacturing firms' servitization strategies: A gap analysis and research agenda. *Systems, 5*(1), 19.

Secundo, G., Del Vecchio, P., Simeone, L., & Schiuma, G. (2019). Creativity and stakeholders' engagement in open innovation: Design for knowledge translation in technology-intensive enterprises. *Journal of Business Research.* https://doi.org/10.1016/j.jbusres.2019.02.072

Tsiatsis, V., Karnouskos, S., Höller, J., Boyle, D., & Mulligan, C. (2018). *Internet of things: Technologies and applications for a new age of intelligence.* Academic Press.

Usman, S., Mehmood, R., & Katib, I. (2020). Big data and HPC convergence for smart infrastructures: A review and proposed architecture. In R. Mehmood, C. W. S. See, I. Katib, & I. Chlamtac (Eds.), *Smart infrastructure and applications* (pp. 561–586). Springer.

Vom Brocke, J., Maaß, W., Buxmann, P., Maedche, A., Leimeister, J. M., & Pecht, G. (2018). Future work and enterprise systems. *Business & Information Systems Engineering, 60*(4), 357–366.

Walther, S., Sedera, D., Urbach, N., Eymann, T., Otto, B., & Sarker, S. (2018). Should we stay, or should we go? Analyzing continuance of cloud enterprise systems. *Journal of Information Technology Theory and Application, 19*(2), 57–88.

CHAPTER 2

AN ERP IMPLEMENTATION FRAMEWORK FOR REGIONAL ENTERPRISES

Sam Goundar
The University of the South Pacific

Tevita Kengike
The University of the South Pacific

Hosea Vao
The University of the South Pacific

Samaluta Nunaia
The University of the South Pacific

Lewis Alexander
The University of the South Pacific

Tabakea Tareti
The University of the South Pacific

Enterprise Systems and Technological Convergence, pages 23–43
Copyright © 2021 by Information Age Publishing

ABSTRACT

This chapter investigates the best practices for implementing an ERP system by reviewing several related literatures and identifies the critical success factors. Not only that but literature review for existing ERP system implementation framework is also carried out. In addition to these literature reviews, this chapter considers several influencing factors (attributes/aspects) of some of the Pacific countries (Fiji, Tonga, Vanuatu, and Kiribati) enterprises such as their size, budget, business culture, infrastructures, connectivity (network), expertise, type of business, information system, and structure. An ERP system life cycle which is considered an essential topic is covered and was made the basis of this study. With all the information acquired from literature reviews and data collected from the different Pacific Islands enterprises, a relevant framework for an ERP system implementation in the context of the Pacific is developed.

The use of information technology (IT) nowadays has been increasing and still increasing rapidly that it has become a crucial component of every organization in performing their day to day operations. In conjunction with the use of enterprise systems like an ERP system, organizations started to learn the great benefits that an ERP offers.

With an ERP system, all the functions of the organization are unified and enable the sharing of data among them, making access to data instant which results in fast customer service, on time delivery, accurate data, and cost saving which in turn increase the company's profit tremendously. Realizing the great benefits that an ERP can offer, enterprises worldwide have turned to this to gain competitive edge in the business environment. Not only that but an ERP system has numerous best practices business processes built in its logic making it the most reliable enterprise systems.

Despite the fact that an ERP system offers an abundance in benefits, implementation of an ERP system in a workplace is very risky and has a high failure rate of 50%–75% (Al-Mashari & Al-Mudimigh, 2003); however, most of the cases like the famous Hershey's case and others succeeded in their second attempt. These companies experienced a huge loss in their businesses (always in millions and even billions in other cases).

What about the enterprises in the Pacific Islands?

In the Pacific, using an ERP system is unknown as there is no reported evidence of such. This is where several questions can arise such as, "What could be the reasons why enterprises in the Pacific do not use an ERP system?" Is it to due to their size? Or maybe they are too far behind in the technology? Or are they lacking IT experts in ERP systems? Or maybe their organizational culture is not compatible with an ERP system? And many more.

According to a report from the World Bank, the Pacific Islands has a combined population of about 2.3 million with limited natural resources, too remote from major markets, and has a high degree of volatility in their economy. Another report indicated that the Pacific Islands have a shortage of skilled people, limited options for development, inadequate infrastructure facilities, and the very small domestic market. In this big picture of our Pacific Islands, it is assumed that the Pacific Islands cannot afford an ERP system. However, most big companies in the Pacific have already adopted the use of an information system in their workplaces. Most of these companies use separate systems (Silos) especially for accounts, operations, customer services, and more which create bottlenecks as each division does data entry and data storage on their own (no shared data available) making it hard to share data which results in data redundancy and incorrect data.

Research Objective

The main objective of this research is to develop an ERP implementation framework for the South Pacific Islands based on the international best practices. The development of this framework will be based on the findings in the literature review which comprises of the critical success factors (CSFs), the available ERP implementation framework, the unique attributes/aspects of the organizations in the South Pacific Islands, and the ERP life cycle approach for implementing an ERP system.

In some papers, they believed that an ERP system implementation strategy is organizational based, that is an ERP system implementation strategy for one organization may not work for another. So, in theory, an ERP system implementation framework in developed countries may not work for developing countries like the South Pacific.

This chapter starts with reviewing 25 literature that are related to this research followed by the research questions and the methodology that were used in the research. Lastly, the results/finding/outcomes were discussed.

LITERATURE REVIEW

Critical Success Factors of ERP System Implementation

Top Management Support

Top management support refers to the commitment of top management into the project in different areas within the ERP implementation. Such as helping with decision-making, providing adequate resources for the project, and also providing recommendations for key tasks during and after the ERP project. This is the top key critical factor that led to a successful implementation of the ERP system.

Several researchers have cited that top management support is a widely key factor in ERP implementation in both small/medium businesses and large businesses in developing and developed countries. A study conducted by Al-Mashari, Ghani, and Al-Rashid (2006), stated that for a successful ERP implementation, the support of top management will be needed in allocating the required and valuable resources needed and solving any conflict between powers during implementation. Finney and Corbett (2007) also mentioned the importance for top management to involve and foresee any problems that will be encountered during the project. The level of commitment from top management is crucial for the success of the implementation. Amini and Safavi (2013) stated that creating well-defined project goals and objectives are the most crucial tasks for top management in the ERP project.

For the project to be successful, it is vital for top management to involve and support the implementation of the ERP system.

Business Process Re-Engineering

Business process re-engineering (BPR) refers to the changes that are made to the current process of an organization in order to align their business process to the function provided with the ERP system. Several researchers suggested the importance and key factors based on BPR that led to a successful ERP implementation, such as the choices of the organization to modify the ERP system, change their business process, or keep "as-is" (Vanilla; Al-Mashari et al., 2006). It has been recommended by most researchers to avoid customization of ERP systems (Esteves-Sousa & Pastor-Collado, 2000). For developing countries, it is important to first consider the type of ERP, and then consider modifying the ERP system. Some reasons are to reduce errors and to also take advantage of updates and upgrades made (Al-Mashari et al., 2006; Amini & Safavi, 2013; Finney & Corbett, 2007). Companies with experience in BPR are more likely to be successful in ERP implementation (Huang & Palvia, 2001).

ERP Training and Support

ERP training refers to the support that is provided during and after the ERP implementation. A study by Al-Mashari et al. (2006) on ABC Company considered that training should be rated as high priority. Such as the process of knowledge transfer, it has been argued as a very important task as compared to the quality of completing the ERP implementation. Also, ongoing training must be able to cover any related issues to the business and must provide a clear target. Means trainer must ensure that it has the commitment from top management, staff, and end-users, to address any gaps and areas in ERP implementation that need to be addressed. Without addressing any issues raised during the implementation for the team and end-users, the new system won't be able to achieve its goal and benefit from it.

Finney and Corbett (2007) also talks about the importance of support and training based on the issues of job redesign or the changes on how end-users do their normal work, such as developing IT skills and building up knowledge of end-users on how to interact with ERP systems.

Amini and Safavi (2013) conducted a study and proved that training and developing knowledge of users with ERP systems are part of a successful and satisfactory ERP implementation. For example, several studies earlier discovered some important factors which proved the effect of training over the project—inadequate training, adequate testing, adequate time for the implementation to complete on time.

A study carried out by Esteves-Sousa and Pastor-Collado (2000) came up with a conclusion that a successful implementation has adequate training. This means either trainers are from within the company or by consultants, at least they take into account the end-users and also the technical team and the staff.

Several researchers stated above have common ideas that training and support are key factors that led to a successful ERP implementation in both developing countries and developed countries.

IT Infrastructure

IT infrastructure refers to the structure and architecture of the IT within an organization. It has been considered that the IT infrastructure of a company affects the possibility of an ERP project to be successful. A conclusion drawn by Finney and Corbett (2007) and Al-Mashari et al. (2006) that organizations must assess their readiness by assessing the skills and architecture. For some reasons, the company needs to handle the growth of its services and upgrades, and updates must be done for their IT infrastructure if necessary. Some researchers agreed that an inadequate IT infrastructure is a top critical factor to be foreseen for the success of the ERP project. A study by Huang and Palvia (2001) proved some major problems to be considered within infrastructure are telecommunications are improved in some developed countries and Internet services are expensive. To reap the benefits of an ERP system, they must consider different areas such as cost regarding telecommunication and Internet services as Huang et al. (2001) mentioned, whether it benefits the organization or not.

Effective and Better Communication

Effective Communication refers to all the communication processes during and after an ERP implementation. Amini and Safavi (2013) and Esteves-Sousa and Pastor-Callado (2000) define communication in ERP implementation as communication between end-users and all management and phases that are selected for the project. Some researchers believed that another crucial factor to successfully implementing an ERP system. A study made by Al-Mashari et al. (2006) on XYZ Company and ABC Company proved that effective communication between the development team, top management, and end-users allowed sharing of knowledge with each member which led to the success of their system implementation. Additionally, organizations must ensure that their clients are aware of their project to avoid any misconceptions (Finney & Corbett, 2007).

ERP Team Composition

ERP team composition refers to the creating and selection of a project team for an ERP project based on their skills, experience, and other criteria the organization uses for selecting a team. The structure of the team, their skills, and experiences have a high impact on the ERP implementation (Esteves-Sousa & Pastor-Callado, 2000). A study conducted by Amini and Safavi (2013) proved the importance of having an experienced consultant. This means it is important to select an experienced consultant that has the skills required. Some researchers repeatedly conveyed the importance of having a strong and solid team that have a proven reputation (Finney & Corbett, 2007). A conclusion drawn from a study conducted by Al-Mashari et al. (2006) says that in addition to team composition, the organization should involve and work together with the team. This means the organization should increase the payment, bonus, and make offers which will create a creativity team that is willingly to participate actively in the project.

A study by Chaushi, et al. (2016) identified nine CSFs for successful implementations, 12 CSFs for selecting an ERP system, and 11 CSFs for steps in ERP implementation. The first nine CSFs which were identified by Umble, Haft, and Umble (2003), comprised of understanding the organization's strategic goals, the commitment of top management, project management, change management, the team members that are selected, the quality of data, training of all end-users of the organization, measuring of the performance, and the implementation approach for handling multisite issues. The next 11 includes the constitution of the project team that will work on an ERP implementation, change management, the support of management, well defined plan and vision for implementation, customization needed for an ERP system which should be minimal, project management, communication, performance indicators, software preservation and the management of business, and lastly the importance of understanding the IT legacy systems as identified by Nah et al. (no date). The last 11 CSFs as identified by Holland and Light (Holland, Light, & Gibson, 1999) includes the legacy system understanding, ERP implementation strategy, organizational goals and vision, the support from top management, clear project plan and schedules, the importance of hiring a consultant, team members of the ERP implementation, BPR, configurations of the software, the acceptance of the software selected, end-users feedback and on-going support, communication, and troubleshooting of the software.

Motiwalla and Thompson (2012) also identified the CSFs in their book and consider the following as most crucial in successfully implementing an ERP.

Decision-making process. In an ERP implementation, decision-making is crucial to avoid or minimize any implementation issues related to scope, efficiency, and productivity.

Project scope. A well-defined scope is required so that the implementation project is within budget and time.

Teamwork. It is crucial that teams from an organization, external consultants, and maybe new hires if required, work together towards the project goals.

Change management. Because an ERP system may require business process changes, it is crucial for a project manager to communicate these changes well with the users in the organization from top to bottom so that all is aware. This is critical to an ERP system implementation to avoid issues of possible conflicts in the project.

Project Team and Executive management team support. The team should include members from an IT team from within the organization, a consulting team from an external organization and ERP package vendors, and managers from an organization. This will ensure that the ERP project has numerous members with skills and most importantly the need to have top management support.

Existing ERP Implementation Framework

As a result, prove the most ERP framework use for a development organization (Tilahun & Cerna, 2017) has shared the grounded ERP framework based upon service oriented architecture (SAO) which is (Huang, 2011) a software development model that contains the implementation and design of an ERP software for a school environment. The result of this study has been adopted by some of the topmost ERP vendors in the global market, which include SAP/R3, Oracle, and Microsoft Dynamic, have work based on three-tier architecture as follows:

Web Tier (access through web-browser)
Application Tier (end-user interact with the system)
Data Tier (structure of the database and its relationship)

The authors are proposing the new ERP module technique to create a new ERP Framework for the school environment. (Tilahun & Cerna, 2017) review two types of module techniques, which is Message Broker (MB), and Web Service Remote Façade. Additionally, they recommended using Web Service as an ERP module technique. As a result, MB is only based on centralizing manners for communication between modules and it leads to a single point failure (broke) and the causing of the entire system to stop communication (work). Finally, web-based assisting ERP module technique, which is based on an open standard and provides integration between ERP modules; also a platform neutralizes on top of XML protocol based with different methods such as SOAP, WSDL, and HTTP. Figure 2.1 shows the proposed design as a web-based technology.

A theoretical framework for ERP implementation was disclosed with a combination case study conducted (Ibrahim, Sharp, & Syntetos, 2008), and a collection of theories and models from the literature. The soft factor, for instance, a link factor of three different aspects of critical success factor

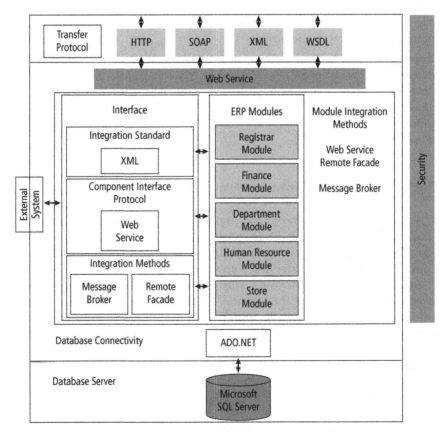

Figure 2.1   Propose ERP implementation framework design.

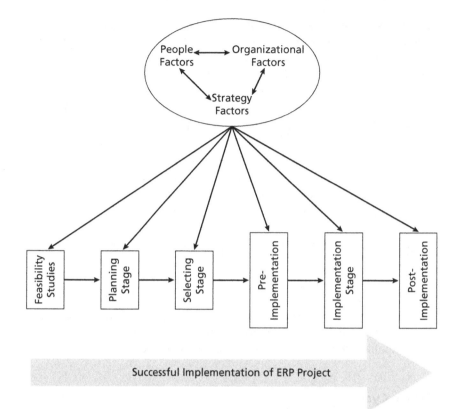

Figure 2.2 Theoretical framework.

(CSF) as Rockhart (1779) has clarified few areas of activities that can receive constant and wisely get the attention of management that form this theoretical framework as shown in Figure 2.2.

Three phases of CSF (theoretical framework)

Strategy related factor. Strategy factor focuses on top management commitment toward ERP implementation with a clear goal focus and scope for the project. Documentation and data analysis of Legacy System required before the new primary ERP system is installed.

People related factor. Making sure the appropriate project team for the job is critical for the success objective of the project. Also knowing the user involvement and employee attitude can be screened by the project team to avoid misunderstanding in the future. Finally providing a training and hand-over documentation of knowledge to IT staff.

Organization related factor. Change management strategy to forecast the management process during the project, which can lead to sufficient work based on decent management throughout the timeline of the project.

According to Pellerin and Hadaya (2008) research, they introduced an ERP framework by adopting the theoretical concept of business process engineering (BPR) with the combination of the existing BPR framework and a selected methodology used in ERP implementation called Accelerated Sap (ASAP) and came up with a framework of implementing an ERP system.

For instance, Sahran et al. (2010) established a new ERP implementation framework that is suitable for a small, and medium sized enterprise organization. They develop a general framework with the integration of three critical components that were needed to be considered within an ERP system implementation, which include ERP implementation methodology, CSF, and ERP implementation activities. The interconnection of these three critical components forms up an ideal framework for ERP system implementation in small and also applicable for medium enterprises.

Goni et al. (2012) developed a framework for the implementation of ERP system, which includes four important capabilities that maintain to form an ERP implementation as shown in Figure 2.3 of the cycle of these critical capabilities that form the proposed framework.

ERP Life Cycle

According to Motiwalla and Thompson (2012), implementation of an ERP system should follow some well-defined steps so that the implementation is done one step at a time (that is you cannot proceed further until the steps are completed well). By using the well-known system development life

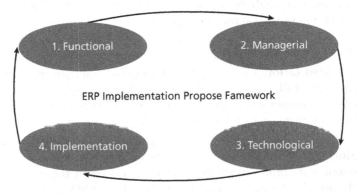

Figure 2.3   Goni et al. (2012) propose ERP implementation framework.

Figure 2.4   ERP life cycle.

cycle methodology, Motiwalla et al. developed an ERP life cycle as shown in the diagram found in Figure 2.4.

In an ERP life cycle, the writers believed that failures occur if change management is not included right from the beginning stages. Change management should be used from the beginning, revised, monitored, and constantly used throughout the duration of an ERP implementation. Subject matter experts, together with the internal users, should work together to implement activities of change management.

The details of an ERP life cycle stages are as follows.

Stage 1: Scope and Commitment

At this stage, the feasibility study is carried out in addition to a scope development of an ERP implementation. All ERP implementation related components and characteristics are also defined at this stage. It is at this stage also that top management commitment is required to the long-term vision and short-term implementation plan that are also prepared. The last important process at this stage is the selection of the vendor which requires the study of existing vendors and their ERP system products. In this selection of vendors the process includes RFB (request for bid) which can take a considerable amount of time but it is crucial to enable the proper selection of a vendor.

Stage 2: Analysis and Design

At this stage, a crucial decision is made with regards to the ERP software together with the selection of consultants and SMEs that are going to be part of the implementation. It is also at this stage that the gap analysis is carried out which involves the comparison of the "as-is" current system and the "to-be" selected ERP system. The design of user interfaces, change management, and reports are also processed at this stage. Not only that but the data conversion from the old system and training of users also form part of this stage.

Stage 3: Acquisition and Development

At this stage, the licensing of the software is made, and the production version of the system is prepared for the users. The activities and tasks with regards to the gap analysis in the previous stage is carried out. It is also at this stage that the change management team work closely with the end users to implement the changes that are required. The data migration which was prepared earlier is done also. The last crucial process at this stage is the configuration of the security required.

Stage 4: Implementation (or Go Live)

At this stage, the final product is released to the users to start using the system. It is at this stage that the selection of the implementation process is crucial, that is whether the final product needs to be implemented and run in parallel with the old system, or piloted (the users are using the system slowly until such time that the old system should be discarded), or phased in which the users use the system in phases until the complete system is in place, or a big bang where the users start to use the new system and the old system is completely discarded. At this stage, the feedback from the users are crucial and they are usually documented and form part of the post implementation in which they are addressed.

Stage 5: Operations

At this stage, on-going support, training, and updates to the system is carried out, which also involves the knowledge transfer and handing over of the system.

RESEARCH QUESTIONS

The following questions are crucial to assist in directing the research towards its main objective:

1. What are the best practices in an ERP system implementation?

2. Identify the influencing factors (organization size, budget, expertise, infrastructure, connectivity, information system, organizational structure, and probably more from different enterprises in the South Pacific?

3. Are there any existing implementation frameworks for an ERP system?

The answers for these three questions will enable us to put together the required components of the proposed ERP implementation framework.

METHODOLOGY

With a focus on the main objective of this study, the following methodology were used:

1. Identify the CSFs
   - The best practices for implementing an ERP were identified by reviewing 10 related papers on CSF. These CSFs were identified by reviewing 10 related papers. These CSFs from the review were listed with their importance and relevance and how suitable they are to the formulation of the framework in the study. The frequently used CSF from the 10 reviews were used in the framework.
2. Study existing ERP implementation framework
   - The existing ERP implementation frameworks were identified by studying and reviewing 10 related papers.
   - The existing ERP implementation frameworks were compared with regards to their contents (components) and their relevance to the target framework in this study. Some parts of these existing frameworks were omitted and some were included in the target framework. The most common components from the reviews were seen to be very crucial and considered to be part of the framework.
3. Providing the Pacific enterprises' data on their organization's attributes including, budgets, connectivity, infrastructure (IT), structure, size, and culture
   - These data were collected via questionnaires that were sent out to 25 enterprises in Tonga, Vanuatu, and Kiribati. The questionnaire was developed comprising the following: organization name, divisions and number of staff in each, number of servers, number of computers (PCs, laptops, or thin client), OS, DBMS, other system applications, latest budget, ISP, Internet connection, and the bandwidth capacity.
   - The data were analyzed and form part of the framework in the study.

4. ERP life cycle
   – The ERP system life cycle as conveyed by Motiwalla and Thompson was also studied in this chapter to give a broader view on this approach and to use it in the development of the framework.

RESULTS AND FINDINGS

Critical Success Factors on ERP System Implementation

After reviewing the literature with regard to the best practices in particular, the CSFs are listed in Table 2.1 showing all the CSFs identified by the authors.

TABLE 2.1   Critical Success Factors Identified by the Authors
Understanding of the organization's vision and goals
Commitment from the top management
Project management disciplines
Change management disciplines
The formation of a team to be involved in the implementation
The quality of data to be used in the new system
Training end-users in the organization
Measuring the performance of the system
The Implementation methods for handling multi-site issues
Team constitution that will work on an ERP implementation
Clear plan and vision for implementation
Minimum customization
Communication
Performance indicators
Software preservation
Managing business
Understanding of the legacy system
ERP strategy
Business vision
The significance of consultation
Personnel, BPR (business process reengineering)
Software configuration
Acceptance
Monitoring and feedback
Troubleshooting
IT infrastructure

Pacific Enterprises Organizational Attributes/Aspects

The data from the questionnaire sent to several Pacific Islands organizations is summarized in Table 2.2.

The data above shows that most of the enterprises in the study are considered small in size and their budget as well. Most of the organizations have good IT infrastructure and connectivity in place which are capable of running an ERP system. The main idea to include the aspects of the organization in the framework is because it is believed that these aspects have influences on the implementation of an ERP system especially in the context of the pacific from which these data were collected.

The main analysis in this study to be used is basically to investigate the most important facts and most importantly the concepts that the authors write as depicted in the literature review. It is assumed that the previous researches are valid and that by using them to develop a framework in this study would greatly contribute to the knowledge in this discipline. To analyze the findings of the authors in the literature review, we identify their findings on CSFs and compare them with what the other authors found and use the most crucial ones accordingly. The same was done with the literature review on the existing framework. The last two components to consider in this investigation analysis are the pacific enterprises' organizational attributes as laid out in the Table 2.2 and last but not least the most important component in this study which is the ERP life cycle that was presented by Motiwalla and Thompson (2012). This ERP life cycle was used in this study as the basis for developing the framework. So, by investigating the CSFs, the components of the existing framework, the organizational attributes and the ERP system life cycle, the following ERP implementation framework is developed.

Proposed ERP Implementation Framework for the South Pacific

By investigating the findings in the literature review in this study, it was found that most of the CSFs identified by different authors are already formed parts of an ERP life cycle. Not only that but one of the frameworks in the literature review uses some components of the ERP life cycle in some way. The close connections of the CSFs and the mentioned framework in the review with the ERP life cycle provided strong evidence that an ERP life cycle should be used as a basis in developing the framework in this study. Not only that but SDLC has been one of the most successful frameworks used in developing a system widely used. So, in developing an ERP implementation framework, it is crucial to use an ERP life cycle as a basis and extend its components by adding the Pacific enterprises' organizational

TABLE 2.2 Summary of Data From the Questionnaires

Enterprise	Branch	Division	Servers	Computers	Budget	System	Internet	Bandwidth
					Tonga			
FIA	2	Account Divisions 4 Staff	1	15	$5,000.00 AUD	Windows Linux Servers (1)	Yes	
MAFF	11	5 Main Divisions Total 146 staff	1	87	$175,000.00 AUD	Windows, FreeBSD (Server) Others: FreeBSD ISP: UCall Internet Con: Fiber Servers (1)	Yes	
PSC	1	7 Divisions in the Office of the PSC and 40 number of staffs	4	32 PC, 10 Laptops, 3 surface Pro	$175000.00 AUD	Windows 4 Servers ISP-USP DBMS–MYSQL	Yes	
TTI	1	Support = 30 Teaching = 36	10	350	$10,000.00 AUD	Windows, Linux MacOS, DBMS–MySQL	Yes	

(continued)

TABLE 2.2 Summary of Data From the Questionnaires (Continued)

Enterprise	Branch	Division	Servers	Computers	Budget	System	Internet	Bandwidth
Kiribati								
MFMRD	4	9	3–physical 10–Virtual	Laptop: 45, Desktop: 70, Thin Client: 10	$122,200.00 AUD	OS: Windows, Mac, Linux DBMS-MSQL, Postgress ISP-ATHKL, Oceanlink, Speed cast	Satellite Connection, IPVPN	1mbps/512kbsp –Satellite 4mbs/1mpbs– IPVPN
MICTTD	4	13	2	90	$8,000.00 AUD	Windows, Linux, Mac	ISP-AHKL Internet Con-Lite	4mbps/512kbps
MHMS	3	Admin/IT 2 staff	4	50 PC, 20 laptops, 30 thin clients	$16,000 AUD	Windows 10 Pro, Window10, Server 2016, Ubuntu Server MSQL, Access	ISP-ATHKL	6 Mbps
Vanuatu								
QBE	1	4	10	13	$280,000.00 AUD	Win 7 Enterprise M-SQL	Digicel	4mbps
RBV	1	5 100 staffs	30	100	$300,000.00 AUD	Windows, Linux OOP/ Relational DB	TVL & Digicel Connect–Fiber	15mbps
VQA	1	15	5	5- PC, 10- Laptop	$500,000 AUD	Windows/MySQL Server	Digicel Gov Broadband	

attribute. To extend an ERP life cycle we need to put all the organizational attributes in the early stages of the life cycle in particular we should include them in the scope and commitment stage because this is where the system scope is prepared. So, in preparing the system scope, the organizational attributes as shown in the findings should be included to ensure for example that the business size and budget is known (as these will determine the selection of the ERP and vendor in a later stage when acquisition is processed as most ERP systems are expensive). It is also important to know the organization infrastructure and connectivity earlier in the life cycle as ERP system requires expensive servers and fast internet connections, this will assist in knowing the readiness of an organization. Not only that but knowing if an organization has an information system in place to ensure what ERP implementation type to use whether a chocolate or a vanilla implementation. So, it is crucial that the organizational attributes should form part of the first stage when the feasibility study is carried out because these attributes will be useful in the later stages of the life cycle. With all that being said the proposed ERP implementation should look as shown in Figure 2.5.

To implement an ERP, the above framework should be followed right from the start to the end keeping in mind the change management which should be considered throughout the life cycle of a project.

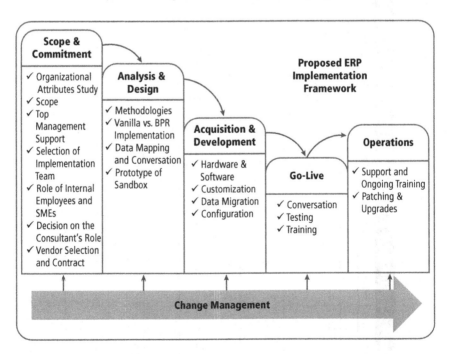

Figure 2.5 Proposed ERP implementation framework.

DISCUSSION

According to this study, selecting a framework from an existing ERP implementation framework in the literature review is not easy. The reviewed frameworks are hard to understand compared to the ERP life cycle which is well laid out in steps which are well defined, so life cycle was recommended as the most suitable framework to use in this study and was used as the foundation of this research.

There have been several studies trying to develop an ERP implementation but none of them were from the Pacific. This study is the first attempt to do one for the Pacific. The proposed framework in this study can also be used by other organizations but the main concern in the pacific is the cost of an ERP system which is too much for enterprises in the Pacific. So assuming that the enterprise in the pacific can afford an ERP system, the framework should work for them either as the framework acquisition stage includes selecting and purchasing of an ERP system which are becoming cheaper nowadays.

To use the framework in the Pacific, it is the responsibility of the organization to determine if it really needs to implement an ERP system prior to the start of the project. It is crucial that the top management is well aware of an ERP system, the costs, the functionalities and the benefits that an ERP system will bring to the company. With all this information in place, an organization can then decide on whether to buy an ERP or not. The decision to purchase an ERP system is crucial in the first place so if the company is ready to buy one, the framework can be used in order to implement an ERP system successfully.

Because of the high failure rate in an ERP implementation, it is crucial to follow best practices approaches and one of them is to use a famous SDLC like approach known as an ERP life cycle. With well defined steps that incorporate best practice CSFs in particular the project management and change management, it is useful for any organization to adopt this framework when implementing an ERP system.

CONCLUSION

Developing an ERP implementation for the Pacific based on the international best practices considered four main elements including the CSFs, the existing framework, the Pacific enterprise attributes and the most important elements which is an ERP life cycle. An ERP life cycle is considered in this research as a basis in developing a target framework because most of the CSFs and an existing framework are already part of the life cycle. So, it is proper to adopt an ERP life cycle and extend it so that it includes all the organizational attributes.

The extended ERP life cycle will incorporate the organizational attributes at the scope and commitment stage making it a framework for an ERP implementation.

This framework may not be so specific to the Pacific but can also be used by any organization that is implementing an ERP system.

This research needs further research on the Pacific to enable future research to be more accurate, relevant, and proper.

RECOMMENDATIONS AND FUTURE RESEARCH

In this research, it is tempting in the first place to develop the framework for an ERP system instead of developing the framework for an ERP implementation (the main objective of this research) because it is not known if enterprises in the Pacific have already implemented an ERP system. With this limitation, this research was carried out with the assumption that enterprises in the Pacific have already adopted an ERP system in their workplaces.

Prior to this research, a research on an implementation of an ERP system in the Pacific enterprises should be carried out so that implementing a more relevant framework for employing an ERP system in the Pacific would make more sense and specific and be based on more accurate information.

The proposed ERP implementation for the Pacific is not too specific for the Pacific but can also be used by all organizations that decide to implement an ERP system in their workplace.

Since this is the first research in ERP in the Pacific, future research should extend this research so that the anticipated ERP implementation framework is more unique to the Pacific. It is also crucial to do more research in this discipline in the Pacific on the use of ERP and the development of an ERP framework. Not only that but research is also needed in the ERP architecture which will enable the inclusion of Pacific related modules into an ERP and probably more.

REFERENCES

Amini, M., & Safavi, N. (2013). Review paper: Critical success factors for ERP implementation. *International Journal of Information Technology & Information System*, 5(16), 1–23. http://dx.doi.org/10.2139/ssrn.2256382

Al-Mashari, M., & Al-Mudimigh, A. (2003). *ERP implementation: lessons from a case study*. Information Technology & People.

Al-Mashari, M., & Ghani, S., & Al-Rashid, W. (2006). A study of the critical success factors of ERP implementation in developing countries.

Business Process Management Journal, 4(1), 276–284. https://doi.org/10.1504/ IJIEM.2006.008866

Chaushi, B., Chaushi, A., & Dika, Z. (2016). Critical success factors in ERP implementation. *Academic Journal of Business, Administration, Law and Social Sciences, 2*(3), 19–30. https://www.researchgate.net/publication/310775844_Critical _success_factors_in_ERP_implementation

Esteves-Sousa, J., & Pastor-Collado, J. (2000). *Towards the unification of critical success factors for ERP implementation.* https://www.semanticscholar.org/paper/ Towards-the-Unification-of-Critical-Success-Factors-Esteves-Pastor/d69f8ce7a 480c53a5b0d7fa3aeb90c80f8a7b7e9#paper-header

Finney, S., & Corbett, M. (2007). ERP implementation: A compilation and analysis of critical success factors. *Business Process Management Journal, 13*(3), 329–347. https://doi.org/10.1108/14637150710752272

Goni F. A., Chofreh A. G., Mukhtar, M., Sahran, S., & Shukor, S. A. (2012). Segments and elements influenced on ERP system implementation. *Australian Journal of Basic and Applied Sciences, 6*(10), 209–221.

Holland, C. P., Light, B., & Gibson, N. (1999). A critical success factors model for enterprise resource planning implementation. In *Proceedings of the 7th European conference on information systems* (Vol. 1, pp. 273–287).

Huang, Z. P. (2011). ERP implementation issues in advanced and developing countries. *Journal of Business Process Management, 7*(3), 221–276.

Huang, Z., & Palvia, P. (2001). ERP implementation issues in advanced and developing countries. *Business Process Management Journal.*

Ibrahim, A. M., Sharp, J. M., & Syntetos, A. A. (2008, May). *A framework for the implementation of ERP to improve business performance: Case study.* Presentation at the European and Mediterranean Conference on Information System 2008, Dubai.

Motiwalla, L. F., & Thomson, J. (2012). *Enterprise systems for management* (2nd ed.). Prentice Hall.

Pellerin R., & Hadaya P. (2008). Proposing a new framework and an innovative approach to teaching reengineering and ERP implementation concepts. *Journal of Information Systems Education, 19*(1), 65–74

Rockhart, J. F. (1979). Chief Executives define their own data needs: a new systems approach, based on the identification of 'critical success factors,' supports attainment of organizational goals. *Harvard Business Review, March,* 81–93. https://hbr.org/1979/03/chief-executives-define-their-own-data-needs

Sahran, S., Goni, F. A., & Mukhtar. M. (2010). ERP implementation challenges in small and medium enterprise: A framework and case study. *Advanced Materials Research, 139–141*(2010), 1636–1639.

Tilahun, K., & Cerna, P. (2017). An enterprise resource planning (ERP) framework for polytechnique colleges in Ethiopia. *Advances in Wireless Communications and Networks, 3*(5), 67.

Umble, E. J., Haft, R. R., & Umble, M. M. (2003). Enterprise resource planning: Implementation procedures and critical success factors. *European Journal of Operational Research, 146*(2), 241–257.

CHAPTER 3

ERP IMPLEMENTATION CHALLENGES AND CRITICAL SUCCESS FACTORS

Sam Goundar
The University of the South Pacific

Roshni Gounder
The University of the South Pacific

Avneel Kumar
The University of the South Pacific

Lalesh Chand
The University of the South Pacific

Ravin Singh
The University of the South Pacific

Oscar Whiteside
The University of the South Pacific

Isaac Ali
The University of the South Pacific

Enterprise Systems and Technological Convergence, pages 45–61
Copyright © 2021 by Information Age Publishing
45

ABSTRACT

One of the most important tools in any organization today is the management information system which aims to provide reliable, complete, accessible, and understandable information in a timely manner to the users of the system. The management information system (MIS) plays a similar role compared to the role of heart in the body; information is the blood and MIS is the heart. The system ensures that appropriate data is collected from the various sources, processed, and sent further to all the needy destinations. The system is expected to address the information needs of an individual, a group of individuals, and the management functionaries: the middle managers and executive level management.

The objective of this chapter is to present a case study of an enterprise resource planning (ERP) implementation by a beverage company in the manufacturing industry that produces and distributes its products both locally and overseas. ERP software has become a critical tool for businesses to ensure that information is managed in a more centralized and efficient manner, since it is an enterprise-wide application software package that integrates all necessary business functions into a single system with a common database. The implementing team needs to create a learning atmosphere that is open to ideas and innovation.

This case study describes three of the major issues that affects successful implementation of ERP, which includes:

1. Consultancy Service (technical support—time zone difference)
2. Employee knowledge, skill, and capability
3. MIS integration (change management) & organization culture

The results of our findings were derived from previous research papers, interviews of organizations staff who were the subject matter experts (SMEs), members of executive management, and the end users. SWOT analysis of survey questionnaires were also done. The case study attempts to highlight the eight-phase framework of ERP implementation within the organization of study and takes an in-depth look at the issues behind the implementation process, by focusing on business and technical as well as cultural issues at the heart of the organization.

Finally, based on the analysis carried out and using the available model and framework the chapter provides recommendations to the organization on how they can reduce the value leakage of its ERP system and ensure future success of the organization through adopting a suitable framework.

OVERVIEW OF THE CASE STUDY ORGANIZATION

In the year of its 60th anniversary, the case study organization cemented its position as the region's leading alcohol beverage company in Fiji. In

2018, together with its parent company more than AUD$1m dollars were invested in implementation of "Microsoft Dynamics AX" an ERP system that will replace three key legacy systems of the organization; BASIS, AC-CPAC, and MISYs.

Being listed on stock exchange the organization has more than 250 permanent employees across the region doing an average yearly net contribution of FJD$36m. With a vision to become a premier place to work, this million-dollar investment was much needed to future proof system environment and avoid substantial risk associated with the failure of legacy systems. With the group's IT roadmap and the rationalized approach in relation to business wide ERPs; Microsoft Dynamics AX was the groups preferred solution for "simpler/smaller" developing markets and got approved by the group IT steering committee.

The diverse operations pose big challenges to the demands on consolidation and reporting. Microsoft Dynamics will remove much of the need to do manual integration and consolidations—providing efficiencies, accuracy, and timelines. Giving a rise to business performance this implementation was more known as "a single source of truth."

One system with tighter integration the company has remotely located sites and diverse manufacturing stretching from the Western Fiji to East Fiji where the head office is situated, and across to Samoa. Increased productivity via business information (BI), Microsoft Dynamics captures a wealth of data in OLAP building our capability in business intelligence. Having a single solution and real time business information facilitates key aspects of the business strategy such as; increased manufacturing efficiencies, improved S&OP processes (including tighter control on inventory and more accurate forecasting), streamlined core financial processes, and empowerment of sales force by providing decision-making information and tools.

If organizations are to succeed in implementing information technology solutions in a complex ever-changing organizational environment, they need to account for problems that could be encountered post implementation. Using a problem-oriented approach this chapter aims to investigate and highlight on the problems and issues currently seen as a drawback on the success on the recently implemented ERP.

METHODOLOGY

The study was based on both qualitative and quantitative analysis. Systematic investigation has been carried out in gathering quantifiable data by performing statistical and mathematical techniques. Descriptive statistics such as percentages and averages were also used to set the confidence levels of respondents.

- Both primary and secondary sources were utilized.
- The case study focused on all levels of the organization hierarchy—executive managers, decisional managers, and the end users.
- A SWOT analysis of the ERP implementation was done (Appendix D).
- Group IT manager, a member of the executive team, three members of the implementation team, and five end users of the system were interviewed.
- A set of 35 survey questions were distributed to 35 people, with 85% response rate (Appendix E).
- 27 research papers were further used to get an in-depth study of the existing context and existing framework would be utilized to provide the best recommendation to the organization.

LITERATURE REVIEW

Management information system (MIS), is defined as a system which provides information support for decision-making within an organization. It integrates systems of man and machine for providing information to support the operations, the management, and the decision-making function within the organization to deliver on its strategic objectives and goals (Aktharsha, & Kalaivani, 2015).

For organizations to have an effective MIS, it requires an integrated information system. The enterprise resource planning (ERP) system is a set of business applications or modules which links various business units of an organization into a tightly integrated single system with a common platform for flow of information across the entire business (Baxter, 2010). This integrated enterprise-wide system will automate the main business functions such as manufacturing, human resource, finance, as well as supply chain management and eventually enable companies to streamline their operations and processes (Zulkifli, Hashim, & Ahmad, 2012).

ERP systems are already well documented in the information systems literature as being difficult to implement within budget, within anticipated time frames and with functionality which is satisfactory to end users (Garg & Garg, 2013).

ERP systems are huge and complex, involve substantial investments of time and money, and bring about considerable organizational change, thus, warrants careful planning and execution for successful implementation (O'Leary, 2004).

Execution of ERP frameworks could be an exceedingly complex project to handle, which is affected not only by technical, but moreover by numerous other components (Ishikawa, 1985). One of the key challenges facing businesses after ERP systems implementation is discerning how to realize pre-implementation benefits (Nwankpa, 2019). We find ourselves in the situation where we have to bear unnecessary costs, redundant data and information, and high operational risks due to the simultaneous updating of various information (Stancu & Drăguţ, 2018).

There have been many obstacles seen in implementing ERP successfully. According to Standish Group's report, around 75% of the ERP projects are classified as failures (Garg & Garg, 2013). Due to high failure rates of ERP implementation, it is of great importance that businesses establish an IT governance framework to assist in the implementation process of ERP to ensure its success. IT governance is one of the most important factors that allow companies to generate business value from IT investments such as ERP (Garg & Garg, 2013).

Vayyavur (2015) has listed the top ten risks that cause ERP implementation failures:

- lack of management commitment,
- insufficient training with users,
- ineffective communication with users,
- inadequate support from the executive,
- lack of effective project management methodology,
- conflicts between department users,
- attempt to build bridges to legacy application,
- composition of the implementing project team members,
- failure to redesign business processes, and
- misunderstanding of change requirements.

In addition, the purpose of IT governance is to ensure IT alignment with organizational goals; that IT ensures competitive advantage; that resources are used responsibly and that IT-related risks are properly managed with adequate visibility, and transparency, providing a forum to which to escalate changes to project costs, timelines, and so on (Fitz-Gerald & Carroll, 2003).

Hooper and Page (1997) describes information systems as the "sum of all tools, techniques, and procedures used by the business to process data."

Information systems deal with the usage of computer equipment, databases, software, analysis models, procedures, and decision-making administrative processes (Turban, Pollard, & Wood, 2018).

In today's competitive and globalized world, the importance of information system has increased rapidly, as the business environment has grown more dynamic and the ability to collect, assess, and disseminate information have become a valuable strategic resource (Gabriel & Ogbuigwe, 2016). Information systems has benefits that include, improved profitability, improved organizational performance and effective and efficient business processes, or working routines on an individual level (Gable, Sedera,

& Chan, 2008). In other words, information systems allow organizations to achieve their strategic goals, increase productivity, and create competitive advantage by means of relevant tools (Al-Aali & Teece, 2014).

Many organizations today adopt outsourcing as part of their business models such as accounting, legal, purchasing, information technology (IT) or administrative support, and other specialized services in order to gain competitive advantage. They showed that through outsourcing organizations had access to larger technology pools, providing the ability to develop products which couldn't have been developed internally. This shortened cycle times and reduced development costs, so that companies could gain a competitive advantage (Fjermestad & Saitta, 2005).

With these things in mind and considering that well over half of all ERP usage endeavors concludes in disappointment, great planning, consolidating worker association, and great communication ought to be at the beat of any organization's list, when considering an ERP implementation process (Barker & Frolick, 2003).

DISCUSSION AND FINDINGS

Given that there is growth in ERP implementations, business and organizations still face several challenges and numerous scholars have explored and identified reasons how such massive intensive capital investments tend not to provide intended results. Most of the not-desired results are not caused by the ERP software but due to the massive changes required and the complexity of human related issues including organizational culture, business processes, back-up technical support, and resistance to change.

Consultancy Service (Technical Support— Time Zone Difference)

During the research it was identified for technical back-up support of the ERP software the organization is reliant on consultants based overseas (in India) which has a time zone difference and affects business productivity and efficiency.

Time-Zone Framework for Efficiency

The consultancy service time difference is a key issue however, Erran Carmel (Carmel, Espinosa, & Dubinsky, 2010) the clock framework of time zone solutions has 10 solutions which are divided into three groups: 24-hour culture, liaison (which encompasses process and culture), and process and technology. For different organizations, this framework will work depending on the industry that the organization is in, for example, finance, human resources, manufacturing, and so on. The most relevant practices for this framework that will solve the problem of time zone for our case study is:

Creating 24-hour culture

- Time flexibility—vendors employees based off-shore will adjust and adapt to the needs of the customer.
- The employees are available at all hours with laptops and mobile phones.
- Employees are expected to respond to issues even after hours (on-call).

Liaisons

- Regardless of time differences, the liaison relies heavily on real-time channels, mostly voice.
- The most effective liaison is often an expatriate linking the organization back to his home country.

Process and Technology

- Escalation protocols. These are guidelines for taking action on problems and questions. Clear protocols minimize the likelihood of a message bouncing around the world in search of the right person.
- Technology choice: whether to use e-mail, a call to the office, or a call to the mobile device.

Awareness technologies. These technologies permit awareness of someone's availability, their current work, their location, and so on. They can include individual calendars, current time zone calendars, holiday schedules, or even desktop video cameras.

Deokar and Sarnikar (2016) identified a clockwork framework that addresses the issues of time- zone differences. One section is liaisons, which are usually the on-site coordinators or middle manager who becomes the human bridge between distant geographic locations and relies heavily on real-time channels (mostly voice; Carmel et al., 2010). Alternatively, a local champion from each department can be identified that can advocate for re-engineering processes and its benefits and advantages to stakeholders and employees (Deokar & Sarnikar, 2016).

Not all of the framework's solutions are equally important, nor are they used with equal intensity at global firms (refer to Appendix A).

Employee Knowledge, Skill, and Capability

Employee skillset and knowledge, capability is a challenge for 100% functionality of the system. In general, good people skills are defined as the ability to listen, to communicate, and to relate to others on a personal or professional level. Good people skills also extend to include problem-solving abilities, empathy for others, and a willingness to work together.

Employee Education and Awareness

A good training evaluation should be able to prove that the program offered: Effective knowledge transfer, cost effective knowledge transfer, training coupled with corporate strategy and business objectives, competitive advantage, organizational change acceptance, and organizational benefits (Dorobat & Nastase, 2012).

Employee Training. In addition, trainees need to feel that the training course is relevant to their jobs. Therefore, it is important at the beginning of the ERP training program to explain to users: What are the objectives and benefits of training providing management and employees with the logic and overall concepts of ERP system. In an organization ERP training must be delivered for several groups: the managerial personnel, key-users, end-users, and the trainers (Dorobat & Nastase, 2012).

ERP Training System Framework. Alternatively, we have identified an ERP training system framework that provides training needs which change during the implementation processes and is diversified. The key reason for an education and training program is to ensure the users are comfortable with the system, and increase their expertise and knowledge. ERP concepts, system features, and hands-on training are vital aspects of ERP implementation. The training needs not only to cover how to use the new system, but also the new processes and understanding the integration of those processes within the system. Therefore, using only one training method may be ineffective (Vayyavur, 2015).

Management Support and Capacity Building. Management support is critical for achieving successful adoption of changed and re-engineered processes and realizing the objectives of process change (Deokar & Sarnikar, 2016). The mindset of the top-level management team should be ready to accept the changes first so that the same can cascaded easily to other subordinates in the organization. With the continuous support, communication and engagement from the management team, the learning and improvement phase will run smoothly (Mott & Ford, 2007). Cultural readiness addresses the issues between organizations in two different regions, such as time zones, work ethic, communications, and the vendor country's political environment (Fjermestad & Saitta, 2005)

Ishikawa (1985) had developed a technique in the 1960s to assist the understanding of the influential factors of ERP implementation. The technique known as the cause-and-effect diagram is a tool that can be used to represent the relationship between some effect that could be measured and the set of possible causes that produce the effect (Berenson & Levine, 1996).

Eight Major Conceptual processes that drive ERP implementation are

- consultant team/vendor,
- team plan,
- announcement,
- involvement of employees,
- business process mapping,
- implementation,
- tracking, and
- evaluation.

For these eight phases to be successful the following approaches are critical:

- *Selection of an ERP software that matches the organizations "to be"* processes (not necessarily the processes the business is using today). It is essential for organizations to keep an eye on the future state of how the business will be run so that it might avail itself for all the incredible benefits an integrated solution can bring (Garg, 2010).
- *Ensure ERP vendors demonstrate their products against the organization's specific and unique needs.* If the vendor is unable to clearly show a road map of the organization ERP requirements and desires, the organization can risk choosing a software based on canned demos and industry "best practices" as opposed to finding a software that truly suits the organization's need (Garg, 2010).
- *Foster alignment of purpose within the executive team.* An ERP project that does not have a unified support system will quickly fail (Garg, 2010).
- *Don't forget your people.* ERP implementation is not the time to clam up on one sided communication only. Top executives need to be honest, transparent, and team oriented in their discussions and request regular feedback to achieve ERP success, "plain and simple" (Aladwani, 2001).

MIS Integration (Change Management) and Organization Culture

Change management is a challenge, changing user mindset to get a buy in from them. Frequent process breakdown seems to be a daily business issue. Change management is a systematic approach to dealing with the transition or transformation of an organization's goals, processes, or technologies. The purpose of change management is to implement strategies for effecting change, controlling change, and helping people to adapt to change.

Alternatively, change management and organizational culture will require certain factors of implementation to facilitate success. These factors include effective management of human resources, adaptive and flexible structure, and familiarity with technology, knowledge transfer, and stronger communication skills. Successful implementation of ERP in most organizations is affected by the organizational culture (Vayyavur, 2015).

Consultant Team

According to our findings it was established that the organization created a complex team structure for its designing and planning of the new ERP system, which made the process difficult to manage. The team was only formed by IT leads and no operation heads involved. Justification for a simple team structure allows, ease of communication, adaptability, ease of coordination, and reduces bureaucracy.

Team Plan

In the implementation methodology, through end user interviews and survey results it was identified that "train **and** test" was not 100% effective. The train and test phase includes developing and delivering end-user training and performing functional user acceptance and parallel testing. The goal is to finalize the applications and ensure end-user readiness for deployment. This gives users the opportunity to experience the real process, practice real tasks, and ask real questions about their own data during training, thus preparing them to perform successfully on their own when the system goes live.

Announcement

During our research it was established that a formal announcement process took place to deploy a new ERP system. As part of the ERP rollout plan, organizations should conduct educational sessions with staff to remind them of the benefits they will gain with the new system. In addition, company-wide announcements should be made from time to time to report on the project's progression and milestones achieved.

Involvement

Employee involvement for the organization. It was revealed that the final selection of team members for the project was not done properly and a few members had quit the project due to skill and capability and had put pressure on other team members.

Change Management

ERP systems are designed to cater to the best practice for any organization and with ERP implementations there is a change in the way organizations do business, and the way employees work. Employees' role or job designs automatically change as some jobs are no longer required while new jobs get created. With information integration and automation, the way in which the organization functions will change improving the planning, forecasting, and decision-making capabilities.

It was revealed that the organization did not have a change manager until 3 months into the project phase, which again took us back to management commitment and this currently affects the productivity and expected efficiencies to be generated from the new ERP system. The organizations facing a lot of challenges in terms of process ownership and individual roles are currently being redefined to ensure 100% benefit utilization for the ERP system. Managing these changes is complex and if not done properly can lead to ERP failure. Dahl (2010) identified three key aspects important for building organizational change management. First, the organization needs to recognize the inseparability of project management and change management. Secondly, the organization needs to create change management awareness and competence. Finally, the organization should integrate activities to turn employee competence into organizational change management potential.

Organizational Culture

Successful implementation of ERP in most organizations is affected by the organizational culture. Organization culture causes approximately half of ERP failures because managers underestimate the efforts necessary to manage the wide range of changes involved in the implementation of ERP effectively.

Zaglago, Apulu, Chapman, and Shah (2013) explored the impact of culture in the implementation of ERP. According to the study, the environment in which ERP systems are developed, selected, and implemented constitutes a cultural or social context. The social context includes different stakeholders, vendors, project teams, and the users of the system. Each of these parties involved in the implementation process have different cultural values and assumptions toward ERP implementation.

Organization culture is a pattern of shared assumptions that the group learns as it evolves and solves its external problems and internal integration. Organization culture is fundamental during the implementation process and the successful adoption of ERP. Organization culture plays a critical role in enforcing rules, values, processes, and practices with the organization at both individual and organization level.

IT Governance Framework

This framework prescribes a set of 37 different IT processes and the means of managing these processes through identifying the inputs and outputs along with key process activities, performance measures, and process objectives to ensure that the IT systems are indeed delivering business value.

The key reasons why organizations use the IT frameworks are to ensure that they use the IT systems in an efficient and effective manner. Further, risk mitigation and performance management are key business imperatives, which the organization must follow so that there are no surprises for its operations and that the business objectives are being met.

Finally, for any business considering a move to ERP, a structured framework needs to be implemented. These frameworks will work as a guide in ensuring that the company's strategic goals are consistently met.

RECOMMENDATION

Many organizations think they are incredibly unique, but the reality is that their product or service offering is unique, but the way they process transactions is the same as millions ofvother companies. It is recommended to seek a solution that has organizations in the same industry as satisfied clients. However, this should not be the sole decision criteria.

As recommended for consultancy services, this will simply give access to a 24-hour service for the organization's issues. Furthermore, the organization will benefit from low costs due to wage differentials and timely response to issues faced. It indirectly increases competitive advantage.

However, there will be some drawbacks to the above suggestion in terms of0cultural differences when collaborating on issues. Another shortfall that may arise can be miscommunication in a hand-off0of a shift and an entire day's worth of work can be delayed.

When businesses are choosing an ERP solution it has to determine whether they are willing to update and or change their internal processes to take advantage of standard functionality. Many organizations find that they haven't updated processes in years and take advantage of0the opportunity to review and improve business processes.

An ERP solution is a great transactional level tool and reporting solution, but the organization needs to see where a customer relationship management solution fits into the picture. The organization needs to decide if it will be part of the ERP solution or if it will use a different solution and integrate it to the ERP solution. One big benefit to an ERP implementation is the removal of spreadsheets and redundant systems. However, the ERP system will not remove every system in the company. Other key pieces of software (not random spreadsheets) may remain in place and those systems usually need to connect to the ERP solution. Regardless of the solution being chosen, the ERP solution must work with some solutions the business uses today. Even something as simple as integration and interaction with office productivity tools like e-mail and spreadsheets is important. For other solutions a common database (SQL, Oracle) or platform (Windows, Linux) are important.

Many people think of ERP as simply a back-office solution. In the case study organization, some users need access to the solution from outside the office like the sales and marketing departments who organize orders remotely or need information on the products and services they sell that are housed in the ERP solution.

Another suggestion for the case study organization is to make use of cloud, but how the solution will be deployed is critical and the organization needs to weigh their options correctly. Some companies only want cloud solutions and others have no interest in the cloud. In the event if the case study organization does deploy to the cloud, it needs to have good communication infrastructure to make it work. With this solution in mind, it is often found that companies have busy or slow seasons to consider. Everyone will want to drive the project to a quick completion, but you need to consider the time required of each department and their ability to participate and complete their tasks on time. One fact is that companies usually need and use less historical data than they think. The key is to find the right balance to migrate enough data to make the system useful and this can have a huge impact on the success of your implementation.

We all understand the core pieces of an ERP system, but not about the additional "systems" in Excel, Access, and so on. A specific tool that is needed to do business with a key customer like large retailers will be able to replace those systems or will allow the business to integrate to them. The organization may need to use a phased approach so as not to introduce too much change at once.

Oftentimes, companies find a consulting firm to assist them with an implementation, but regardless of their approach it is recommended for the case study organization to have an internal project manager that continues to oversee the success of the project post implementation. The case study organization will need to select a person who is respected in the organization and who is willing to embrace the change that comes with the new system and beyond. They will need to be objective and understand the concerns of many different departments.

No matter how well everyone works together, there will be disputes. Oftentimes different departments want what is best for them regardless of the downstream effect. When disputes arise, the organization needs to have a designated person who will make the final call. These designated personnel will take the issues all the way to an executive board or owner. It can be the project manager or a change manager that can make the decision. Having clear guidelines will alleviate a lot of problems down the road. The team has also recommended for MIS integration and organization culture (change management). The benefits will be employee involvement that will promote employee motivation and proper tracking of implementation from the employee and organizations' view. However, it is also important to note that if senior management is not supportive, implementation can fail.

Every ERP system allows you to enter information, some easier than others. However, the big bang for the buck is in producing reports and gathering information. We often find too much of a focus on entering data and not enough thought is given to reporting. Define the outputs you need from the system as part of requirements gathering. People fear change, it is a constant, and an ERP implementation is no different. Once you are live there will be changes needed to the system, and ongoing training will be important to continue to maximize the value from the system. So, you have to define who in your organization will change once you are live. It could be the same project manager or maybe each department head.

Training is obviously an important part for the organization for before and after implementation of the ERP system. The biggest question is whether you will lead the training and develop your own subject matter experts or whether an outside firm will lead the training. Generally, we all recommend train-the-trainer programs. We believe it creates buy-in and an internal team of experts for post implementation support. In order to address employee skill and capabilities, the team has recommended that well trained staff with support of senior management through knowledge transfer. This assists in having access to business process maps and process guidelines. However, there could be some shortfalls that the case study organization needs to consider as well in terms of the employer tends to lose out if trained employees leave the organization or the organization becomes a training ground if there is a high turnover of skilled and trained staff to the market.

CONCLUSION

Nowadays ERP systems are being adopted by various organizations as part ofctheir business growth strategies. However, one must realize that implementation of an ERP system is not a goal but a journey towards the goal. Even after successful implementation, the goal is not achieved until the system is completely used. The satisfaction of the users and the overall performance must be measured periodically to evaluate the success of the implementation and the overall object of having the enterprise level of system. Due to this research, we were clearly able to identify the problem area and offer recommendations to the organization for better performance of the ERP. This approach allows us to clearly identify the key performance indicators as well as their role in the total success of the ERP system.

It is interesting to discover why companies implement ERP systems. For studied cases of this project, there were a number of reasons like the need for a common IT platform, need for cross functional integration, and need for standardizing business processes. In almost all the ERP implementations studied, one common objective is cross functional integration. This is common for both the public and private sector. Cross functional integration essentially delivers some degree of process improvements. However, 1in certain cases the need for standardizing and improving business processes have been identified as a separate and core project objective.

Analysis of the eight phases suggests that business process reengineering (BPR) is considered the main objective and provides a better overview for the process improvements. The process mapping helps business in selecting a suitable and workable ERP system. Improved business processes through the adoption of ERP systems, have allowed organizations to gain competitive advantage in the market through improved performance and quality. Therefore, ERP systems must be regarded as a strategic business tool where failure to implement could result in loss of market share and eventual closure of the business.

An ERP system must be adopted as an ultimate objective of any commercial organization and whilst this will require large investment the returns will more than adequately fund the cost.

In conclusion, our case study project highlights clearly why some ERP implementation projects are successful while others are not. While there are many reasons, human factors in particular were noted as the most significant contributor to the success or failure of the project and this was supported by the literature reviewed by the Dream Team.

The number of ERP solutions is immense, and each has their own unique approach, methodology, and offerings. You must determine if their offerings fit the needs of the organization and not let them dictate to you based on their approach. An ERP solution is really a tool to assist in streamlining business processes. You need to understand and categorize your business processes to identify if you have straight-forward processes and are willing to change and update your processes based on the solution you choose. It is also important to note if you have complex processes that require a highly configured solution. Whatever the case, you will need a solution that fits appropriately.

The typical ERP selection cycle is long and will see many demonstrations and hear from many salespeople. It is key to keep the end in mind. The organization will have to always refer back to their goals and objectives. If it is not sure which solution is right for the company, the business needs to go back to their key requirements and see which solution meets those the best. Our case study organization has finished the ERP implementation in October 2018 and it was a great success. The teams are getting used to the new system.

REFERENCES

Aktharsha, U. S., & Kalaivani, K. (2015). ERP as a functional area of business: An empirical study. *Journal Impact Factor, 6*(1), 200–212.

Al-Aali, A., & Teece, D. J. (2014). International entrepreneurship and the theory of the (Long–Lived) international firm: A capabilities perspective. *Entrepreneurship Theory and Practice, 38*(1), 95–116.

Aladwani, A. M. (2001). Change management strategies for successful ERP implementation. *Business Process Management Journal.*

Barker, T., & Frolick, M. N. (2003). ERP implementation failure: A case study. *Information Systems Management, 20*(4), 43–49.

Baxter, G. (2010). White paper: Key issues in ERP system implementation. Large Scale Complex IT Systems, 3–9.

Berenson, M. L., & Levine, D. M. (1996). *Basic business statistics. Concepts and applications,* 6th ed., Prentice Hall.

Carmel, E., Espinosa, J. A., & Dubinsky, Y. (2010). " Follow the Sun" workflow in global software development. *Journal of Management Information Systems, 27*(1), 17–38.

Dahl, M. (2010). *Rituals of inquisition: European Commission monitring of accessions processes.*

Deokar, A. V., & Sarnikar, S. (2016). Understanding process change management in electronic health record implementations. *Information Systems and e-Business Management, 14*(4), 733–766.

Dorobat, I., & Nastase, F. (2012). Training issues in ERP Implementations. *Accounting and Management Information Systems, 11*(4), 621.

Fitz-Gerald, L., & Carroll, J. (2003). The role of governance in ERP system implementation. In *Proceedings of the 14th Australasian conference on information systems.*

Fjermestad, J., & Saitta, J. A. (2005). A strategic management framework for IT outsourcing: A review of the literature and the development of a success factors model. *Journal of Information Technology Case and Application Research, 7*(3), 42–60.

Gable, G. G., Sedera, D., & Chan, T. (2008). Re-conceptualizing information system success: The IS-impact measurement model. *Journal of the Association for Information Systems, 9*(7), 18.

Gabriel, J. M. O., & Ogbuigwe, T. D. (2016). An empirical examination of the nexus between information systems and organizational performance behaviors of quick-service restaurants in Port Harcourt. *International Journal of Management & Information Systems, 20*(3), 59–72.

Garg, P. (2010). Critical failure factors for enterprise resource planning implementations in Indian retail organizations: An exploratory study. *Journal of Information Technology Impact, 10*(1), 35–44.

Garg, P., & Garg, A. (2013). An empirical study on critical failure factors for enterprise resource planning implementation in Indian retail sector. *Business Process Management Journal.*

Hooper, P., & Page, J. (1997). Organizing information and data flows in business systems. *National Public Accountant, 42*(9), 9–14.

Ishikawa, K. (1985). *What is total quality control? The Japanese way.* Prentice Hall.

Mott, R. K., & Ford, J. D. (2007). The convergence of technical communication and information architecture: Managing single-source objects for contemporary media. *Technical Communication, 54*(1), 27–45.

Nwankpa, J. K. (2019). ERP systems benefit realization and the role of ERP-enabled application integration. In *Advanced methodologies and technologies in business operations and management* (pp. 802–815). IGI Global.

O'Leary, D. E. (2004). Enterprise resource planning (ERP) systems: An empirical analysis of benefits. *Journal of Emerging Technologies in Accounting, 1*(1), 63–72.

Stancu, A. M. R., & Drăguț, B. M. (2018). ERP systems—Past, present and future. *Knowledge Horizons. Economics, 10*(4), 33–44.

Turban, E., Pollard, C., & Wood, G. (2018). *Information technology for management: On-demand strategies for performance, growth and sustainability.* John Wiley.

Vayyavur, R. (2015). ERP implementation challenges & critical organizational success factors. *International Journal of Current Engineering and Technology, 5*(4), 2347–5161.

Zaglago, L., Apulu, I., Chapman, C., & Shah, H. (2013). The impact of culture in enterprise resource planning system implementation. In *Proceedings of the World Congress on Engineering* (Vol. 1, No. 2013, p. 2).

Zulkifli, N., Hashim, R. G., & Ahmad, J. (2012, September). Information mining capabilities in Malaysian SMEs: Specific use of enterprise resource planning system. In *2012 IEEE Symposium on business, engineering and industrial applications* (pp. 431–436). IEEE.

CHAPTER 4

LOCAL ERP IMPLEMENTATION PROCESSES AND STANDARD METHODOLOGIES

Sam Goundar
The University of the South Pacific

Shavindar Singh
The University of the South Pacific

Ayesha Lata
The University of the South Pacific

Mandeep Singh
The University of the South Pacific

Shivanesh Lal
The University of the South Pacific

Enterprise Systems and Technological Convergence, pages 63–83
Copyright © 2021 by Information Age Publishing

ABSTRACT

Local companies in Fiji have implemented and have been trying to implement ERP systems for decades. While a few have been successful with their implementation, many have seen frequent failures. This chapter will compare the implementation practices used by Fijian companies with the standard methodologies. Regardless of companies achieving a success or failure, the purpose of this research will be to bridge the gap between the practices currently used by Fijian companies with that of the standard methods. This chapter will be one of its first to provide insight to future local companies who are planning to implement ERP, hence its contribution towards the global ERP implementors into designing the best strategy will be vital. Analytical hierarchy process will be used to compare the local practices against those of the standard methods and determine the best for companies projecting to implement ERP in future.

With technology emerging day by day, businesses are trying to keep up with the latest innovations. As such, ERP systems have been a subject of keen interest. Enterprise resource planning (ERP) system is an integrated information system that is used to support business processes and resource management within an organization (Hasibuan & Dantes, 2012). While many companies plan and implement ERP systems, the rate of success in local companies in Fiji is significantly low. According to Hasibuan and Dantes (2012), "An ERP implementation success is the score of success in its implementation in an organization." This clearly indicates that the implementation practices, processes, and strategies are what derives an ERP success or failure. Not many companies in Fiji have done an ERP of which, most of them have been successful while others have declared failure. To develop a bottomless understanding of these varying ERP implementation outcomes in Fiji, the research question addressed in this chapter is: How is the implementation process in Fiji different from the best practices used globally?

This chapter explores the similarities and differences of the key success factors, that is, the implementation execution plan and compares with the best practices used globally and recommends the best suites ERP implementation approach for local companies as well as global ERP implementors. With the use of empirical data from 10 different local companies of six different business sectors, the chapter contributes to a deeper understanding of the significance of a well planned and well executed ERP implementation process which has empowered these companies to perceive success. ERP implementation process in the context of this chapter refers to the processes involved during the implementation of ERP in these companies. According to "The Most Popular Software Development Methodologies Overview" (2018), the top five popular choices for ERP implementation include the Agile methodology, Scrum, Kanban, waterfall, and the Lean methodology, with every single one of them having their very own favorable circumstances, drawbacks, and highlights. The Agile procedure has proven to be the most generally utilized methodologies with regards to ERP execution. This chapter therefore uses Agile methodology as the benchmark for those eight local companies and intends to compare their execution plans using the analytic hierarchy process model.

The analytic hierarchy process (AHP) is a structured technique for organizing and analyzing complex decisions. The AHP helps decision makers find one that best suits their goal and their understanding of the problem. It provides a comprehensive and rational framework for structuring a decision problem, for representing and quantifying its elements, for relating those elements to overall goals, and for evaluating alternative solutions. (Analytic Hierarchy Process, 2019)

AHP utilizes an order to structure a decision problem, which deconstructs the problem into its component elements, groups the elements into homogeneous sets and arranges them hierarchically. The general approach of AHP is to decompose the total problem into smaller subproblems in such a way that each subproblem can be analyzed and appropriately handled with practical perspectives in terms of data and information. This is inclusive of the following merits:

- It has the ability to mix qualitative and quantitative criteria in the same decision framework.
- It has the ability to integrate with techniques like goal programming.
- It is possible to incorporate risk factors in the AHP.
- It is very easy to incorporate sensitivity analysis in the AHP. (Parthasarathy & Anbashagan, 2007).

We will use the above merits and approaches to make paired comparisons between the processes involved by local companies in their ERP implementation with that of the three best ERP methodologies, that is, waterfall model, Agile development, and rapid application development. We have broken down the processes into subsets considering the challenges involved in each step. Each of these subsets has been analyzed and compared with these three methodologies to prove which methodology is the best suited for companies implementing ERP. The outcome of this chapter is the identification of the different ERP execution plans used by local companies in comparison with the Agile methodology which is considered as one of the most robust and successful methods. This study is meant to help other upcoming companies in Fiji as well as globally who intend to implement ERP systems as it will provide them with feasible ERP execution options.

This chapter also discusses the limitations where the reader may find the chapter debatable since all results gathered from these local companies have reported successful ERP implementation. Should the data gathered include ERP failures then the conclusion derived on the best ERP practice may have been the other way around. Therefore, a future research study on multiple organizations varying in business processes and sizes could validate the challenge of this research outcome.

BACKGROUND

As technology is gradually increasing its impact in the business environment, more and more businesses are in the process of re-aligning and improving their systems to keep in pace with the ever-increasing technology. With that, one of the important key technological aspects of the business sector is the implementation of ERP systems. Muinde et al. (2016) stated in their work that "Many organizations today are looking for ways in which they can improve their businesses in response to the growing global competition. One approach that has been used in this regard is the implementation of information systems such as Enterprise Resource Planning (ERP) systems." Hassabelnaby and Vonderembse (2011) expressed similar sentiments affirming that information systems are used by firms to maintain their competitiveness by using information systems such as the EPR system.

The research idea and objectives were derived from the growing deployment of ERP systems by local companies in Fiji. However, the rate of success in local companies in Fiji is significantly low. While many have implemented ERP systems in their companies, only a few have been able to successfully complete the implementation and have the system operating. The successful implementations may be in operation; however, they may still be lacking the complete requirements of success. On the other hand, the failures might be due to a number of reasons. Hawking et al. (2007), in his work identified "IT solution selection" as one of the major challenges which this chapter aims to address. Selection is also identified as a major challenge in terms of the scope of the system and the implementation process as stated by Osintsev (2016).

ERP systems are difficult and complex to implement. Rajan and Baral (2015) states in their work that technological complexity is the extent where new technology is more complicated and difficult to adapt to compared to the existing system in use. Since systems are already complex to implement, the methodologies chosen should be proven and suit the needs and objectives of the organization. Hasibuan and Dantes (2012) give importance to technology selection including "ERP software and application, database and hardware used to support ERP system, ERP consultant selection and choosing of ERP implementation strategy and methodology" in the implementation process. This chapter is important as it will outline the differences in the methods used by local companies with that of the standard methodologies.

Therefore, this chapter will present an intuition on the best practices and methodology to use for a successful ERP implementation. This research will identify the methods used by local companies in Fiji in contrast with the standard methodologies and ascertain the best method to be used when implementing ERP systems. Future local implementers will have a guide in selecting an appropriate methodology and can avoid the chances of failures with their implementation. Although there are no common criteria for the best methodology selection, the needs, requirements, and the business objectives derive the method of ERP implementation.

LITERATURE REVIEW

ERP system enables an organization to integrate its business process and enhance efficiency and maintain a competitive position in the market. As stated by Hasibuan and Dantes (2012), "Enterprise Resource Planning (ERP) system is an integrated information system that is used to support business processes and resource management within an organization." These systems integrate between one business unit with other business units. To achieve a successful ERP implementation for an organization, it is a critical mission since ERP systems require large amounts of capital investment, staff engagement, training, process re-engraining, and stakeholders' expectations for successful outcome so the targets are achieved on time. Consequently, it is essential to adapt the best practices of the ERP implementation process for a successful ERP implementation. However, in certain situations some of the procedures of a standard ERP implementation do not align with the implementation for some organizations or countries depending on the requirements. As different organizations have different objectives and business processes, their implementation process differs.

As such, Finney and Corbett (2007) has stated in their work the critical success factors of ERP implementation which include "top management commitment and support, vision and planning, build a business case, implementation strategy and timeframe, vanilla ERP, project management, change management, and managing cultural change" as few of the strategic critical success factors. Similarly, in another piece of work, Dezdar and Sulaiman (2011) stated, "project management, team composition and competence, and business process reengineering" as the factors for a successful ERP implementation. They also have indicated that project management has a positive relationship to ERP implementation success. Sentiments along the same line were also expressed by Dezdar and Sulaiman (2011) in their work where they have identified a "good project scope management, adequate project team composition, comprehensive business process reengineering, adequate project champion role, user involvement and participation, and trust between partners" as some of the critical success factors (Esteves-Sousa & Pastor-Collado, 2000). They have also stated the need for a unified model of critical success factors which can be put in practice to support project management in the process of a successful ERP implementation.

Further to this, organizations use various methods of implementing ERP systems depending on the organization and its needs. The product line, business strategies, and the projected growth of the business determine the need of an ERP implementation and the methodology used in the ERP implementation process. However, choosing the best methodology is quite a complex and multifaceted exercise. "Selecting an appropriate ERP implementation strategy is not something that should come up to without a great deal of planning and proper execution. In choosing a new ERP software, implementation is as important as finding the right program" (Khanna & Arnja, 2012). Lutovac and Manojlov (2012) outlined that it is important for organizations to use a proven methodology in order to condense the risks of implementation and allow for a quicker and efficient enterprise resource planning deployment process. Having an accurate implementation methodology will also ensure that the implementation process is well aligned with the organization's business goals and objectives.

For a successful ERP implementation, a proven methodology needs to be utilized. According to "The Most Popular Software Development Methodologies Overview" (2018), the top five popular choices for ERP implementation include the Agile methodology, Scrum, Kanban, waterfall and the Lean methodology, with each one of them having their own advantages, disadvantages, and features. The Agile methodology is one of the most widely used approaches when it comes to ERP implementation. "Agile is based on the simplicity, to move fast and to deliver operating functionality of the software as fast as possible, starting with the components that are most important for your business" (Fetouh et al., 2011). In another piece of work, Sowan and Tahboud (2015) stated that the Agile methodology can have the ERP implementation the shortest time and with the fastest implementation methods, having the flexibility with requirements change with ease of management. However, there are also certain disadvantages of the Agile methodology. One of the main disadvantages "is the need for a huge amount of interfaces that will lead to high cost and the second is that the implementation may take a long time" (Fetouh, 2011).

One of the other methods frequently used is the waterfall model. Waterfall model is a step by step model where the steps are followed in a sequence. "The waterfall model is the oldest and the most well-known SDLC Model" (Alshamrani & Bahattab, 2015). Waterfall model is most frequently used in cases where eminence is given more importance than the price or schedule or when the existing version of a product needs upgrading to a new version. The waterfall model can be broken down into steps such as the requirement phase, a high-level design phase, the coding, testing, and the maintenance phase. The advantages of the waterfall model are stated as a clear identification of the requirements with easy implementation and minimal resources utilized. However, few disadvantages are also given which is stated as "the problems with one phase are never solved completely during that phase and in fact many problems regarding a particular phase arise after the phase is signed off, this result in badly structured system" (Balaji & Murugaiyan, 2012).

Correspondingly, rapid application development (RAD) is another frequent methodology used in the ERP implementation process. RAD is used if "requirements are well understood and project scope is constrained" (Mishra & Dubey, 2013). The cost of RAD is relatively low with a significantly low level of risk involvement. There is an easy way of change flexibility, completion on a short duration of time with ease of maintenance. A research scholar, Radhika D. Amlani, had identified the advantages of rapid application development as "working software is available much earlier than any conventional method. RAD also produces systems more quickly and to a business focus, this approach tends to produce systems at a lower cost" (Amlani, 2012).

In certain cases, companies have used the hybrid methodology. This is due to the complexity of the selection of the methodologies. As stated by Kilica et al. (2014),

> Since there is a wide range of tangible and intangible criteria to be considered, it is often defined as a multi-criteria decision-making problem. To overcome the challenges imposed by the multifaceted nature of the problem, a three-stage hybrid methodology is proposed. Hence, it entirely depends on the business needs of the particular organization to select the best approach to ERP implementation.

Choices may vary as "different industries may install the same ERP software in totally different processes, while on the other hand, the same industry may implement different software in the same approach" (Khanna & Arneja, 2012, p. 479).

Moreover, the standard methodologies of ERP implementation will be compared against the practices used by the Fijian companies using the AHP. AHP is an efficient decision-making tool used when dealing with complex decisions, enabling decision makers to prioritize their goals and get the best outcome (Saaty, 1980). As stipulated by Saaty (1980), AHP "reduces complex decisions to a series of pairwise comparisons, and then synthesizes the results capturing both the subjective and objective aspect of a decision" (p. 6). AHP works in a comparison manner. A set of evaluation criteria is considered with a set of alternate options from which the best decision needs to be made. AHP is considered to be an important and flexible tool as the final decision is obtained from a pairwise comparison from the evaluation criteria as well as the options provided by the user.

Discussions in the sections above give us a brief impression that selection of an ERP system is quite complex and needs thorough planning, involving multiple criteria. To deal with multiple-criteria problems, a number of techniques are used and one of the most widely used techniques is the AHP. As mentioned by Perera and Costa (2008), "Analytical Hierarchy Process (AHP) is a widely used and well tested method to solve multi-attribute decision making process and has been well received by all concerned" (p. 4). A common set of selection criteria is difficult to establish for ERP software selection and hence AHP can be used to formulate models for selection and decision-making process.

In similar work by Alanbay (2005), AHP has been the focus when selecting an ERP system.

> Choosing which ERP to use is a complex decision that has significant economic consequences; thus, it requires a multi-criterion approach. Analytic hierarchy process (AHP) is a method widely used for this kind of complex decision-making problems. In this paper, a multi-attribute ERP selection decision model is introduced, based on the AHP methodology. (p. 2)

The author has used AHP to do a pairwise comparison of the alternative methodologies against a set of evaluation criteria, grouping them into technology related, user related, and vendor related. The pairwise comparison included comparison of objectives and the sub objectives, with a calculation of weights of each objective and sub-objective according to the AHP methodology.

Thus, as more companies and organizations steer towards re-engineering their business process to keep up with the advancing technology, ERP systems are at the helm of the information backbone. While ERP implementation may bring competitive advantage to a business, the selection of an appropriate ERP system and the correct implementation process seems to be a multifaceted and tedious task. Some of the common standard methodologies are inclusive of the Agile methodology, the waterfall method and the rapid application method. Nonetheless, the choice made to implement an ERP should at the end of the day be able to fully address the organization's business needs and objectives.

METHODOLOGY

The key objective of this chapter is to study the various ERP implementation strategies or practices adopted by the local companies in Fiji. It is known that the result of any ERP is measured by the implementation steps. The indicators used to measure the best implementation practices include tactical, informative, qualitative impacts.

To best suit our chapter's objectives, questionnaires were considered the most appropriate method of gathering data and information. Due to the limitations on the number of companies having implemented or are implementing ERP systems in Fiji, a total of 15 questionnaires were distributed. However, the response only came from 10 companies which represented 6 different business sectors. The respondents were staff at the management level, subject matter experts (SME's), head of IT technical, end users involved in day to day transactions, as well as during development stages.

Other than the questionnaires, since two of the authors of this chapter were from IT companies having implemented ERP systems over a year, implementation documents were also gathered, and observations were made to support the research data. Interviews were also conducted with various consultants, technical leads, and SME's. These interviews were both structured and unstructured. The questions mainly focused on implementation plans, difficulty levels, ways to overcome those challengers, and implementation completion status.

With the use of AHP, we have done pairwise comparisons of the results gathered by questionnaires, observations, and interviews in a tabulated form and matrices have been formed to derive conclusions of most favorable practices for each subset used in the implementation process. The results have been presented considering the below merits as outlined in the introduction:

- It can mix qualitative and quantitative criteria in the same decision framework.
- It can integrate with techniques like goal programming.
- It is possible to incorporate risk factors in the AHP.
- It is very easy to incorporate sensitivity analysis in the AHP.

Table 4.1 provides an overview of the business sectors.

TABLE 4.1 Questionnaires and Responses		
Sector	Number of Questionnaires Issued	Number of Responses
Manufacturing	4	3
Retail and Wholesaling	2	1
ISP and Customer Services	2	1
Educational Institution	4	2
Finance Sector	2	2
Tourism and Customer Service	2	1

RESULTS AND FINDINGS

Getting onboard with an ERP for an organization is a massive chore, which comes with an enormous amount of risks, challenges, and opportunities therefore it is important to have proper planning and management from its selection to successful implementation process. It is known that without proper planning, commitment, and management support there can be massive amounts of losses which organizations can go through.

Taking this into consideration it becomes a huge challenge for ERP vendors while developing ERP systems and delivering a successful implementation by being the best while competing with other vendors around the globe, therefore in this chapter we will discuss the best practices of ERP implementation.

Analytic Hierarchy Process

According to the responses from our survey we have evaluated that the implementation approach should meet the five criteria mentioned above and was common amongst the responses of the survey. We have used the AHP to determine what will be the best implementation approach to meet the selected five criteria.

ERP systems are developed just like any other software applications are developed but there is a major difference between an ERP and a normal software application. However, the approach or method used can be the same in both. We have looked at the three most common system development methodologies in ERP implementation and access using the AHP to determine the best ERP implementation methods.

Step 1: Define the Objective to Determine the Best ERP Implementation Method

1. Waterfall Model
2. Agile development Method
3. Rapid Application Development

Step 2: Proposed Criteria for ERP Development
In deciding the criteria, we have based it on most common challengers faced by locally selected organizations from our survey feedback findings.

Structure elements in criteria.

Adaptive system modules: According to the feedback we got form the survey and which was also common among the organizations was users adapting the system, therefore is it impotent to ensure that when modules of ERP are built, the designers should take into consideration about the layout, usability, and how easily users can adapt to the system and navigate throughout

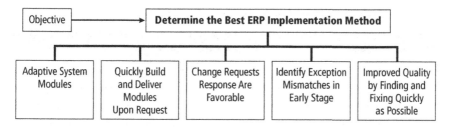

Figure 4.1 Selection evaluation criteria.

the system. The main players of the system are our users and they should not have any difficulty on the usability of the system.

Quickly build and deliver modules or new features upon requests: The approach should have the ability to get system modules or new features ready upon request from the client without taking much time. How fast and the quality of the system matters.

Change request responses are favorable: With ERP implementations, it is a plus point if the system is flexible. This flexibility will enable extra features to e added to the system. Writing extension codes to upgrade the system should not be complex. The developers can only work with the extension codes and manage feature upgrades. They do not have to deal with the core codes of the system. For organisations that are not willing to undergo business process reengineering, then it is important that the system is flexible and can be cus-tomised to meet the client's needs.

Identify expectation mismatches in an early stage: Developing and testing on the go and being well informed if the outcome will meet the client's expec-tation or not. This will also avoid any mismatches or if there is, it can be identified on the early stage.

Improved quality by finding and fixing faults quickly as possible: It matters how quickly faults are fixed and reverted to clients for further tests and comments. Taking too long to respond to clients regarding faults puts up a bad image of the vendor on the organization and market, also clients expect prompt respons-es to stay on track and it also helps when it comes to signing off any modules.

Step 3: Pair Wise Comparison of Elements Against the Five Criteria

TABLE 4.2 Pairwise Comparison Structure		
Criteria	Weight	Rank
Adaptive system modules	25%	1
Quickly build and deliver modules upon requests	18%	4
Change request responses are favorable	15%	5
Identify expectation mismatches in an early stage	20%	3
Improved quality by finding and fixing faults quickly as possible	22%	2

Step 4: Calculation of Weighting and Consistency Ratio

TABLE 4.3 Weightings Calculations

	Adaptive System Modules	
Alternatives	25%	
Waterfall Model	50%	13%
Agile Method	30%	8%
Rapid Application Development	20%	5%
	Quickly Build and Deliver Modules Upon Requests	
Alternatives	18%	
Waterfall Model	20%	4%
Agile Method	50%	7%
Rapid Application Development	40%	7%
	Change Request Responses Are Favorable	
Alternatives	15%	
Waterfall Model	10%	2%
Agile Method	60%	9%
Rapid Application Development	30%	5%
	Identify Expectation Mismatches in an Early Stage	
Alternatives	20%	
Waterfall Model	20%	4%
Agile Method	50%	10%
Rapid Application Development	30%	6%
	Improved Quality by Finding and Fixing Faults as Quickly as Possible	
Alternatives	22%	
Waterfall Model	20%	4%
Agile Method	50%	11%
Rapid Application Development	30%	7%

Step 5: Evaluated the Alternatives According Weighting

However, while agile is the best methodology for ERP implementation according to our finding, this does not mean that other system development methodologies like waterfall and RAD cannot be used within the implementation process. This entirely depends on the type of ERP being deployed with the aim's objectives and requirements of the organizations or

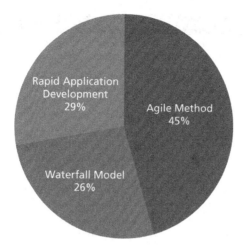

Figure 4.2 Analysis of best methodology.

it can also be hybrid methodology used which is the combination of waterfall and agile which is known as agile waterfall hybrid model.

DISCUSSION

The purpose of this research was to discover if and how the ERP system implementation process in Fiji is different from the best practices used globally. It also intends to discover if there is any favorable method regarding ERP's implementation for organizations in Fiji compared to the traditional software implementations methodologies such as Agile, waterfall, and RAD.

How results were obtained and computed using the AHP. First, we noted the most common challenges from the survey responses as the assessment criteria.

Then weighted the five common challenges faced from most to least challenging to archive during ERP implementation with ranking from highest to lowest (1–5) by comparing each against each other (See Table 4.4).

Together with the criteria we decided to compare the criteria of most common system development methods and weighted amongst each alternative methodology (See Table 4.5).

Then we compared the constancy ratio of each criteria against the three alternative methods exploring that agile development method came up with the highest points which was 45% against the other two alternatives.

TABLE 4.4 Five Common Challenges
Adaptive system modules: The most common and impotent criteria which allows users to adept and adopt to systems easily without constrains and it is at most important therefore we weighted most uppermost criteria (25%).
Quickly build and deliver modules upon requests: The end users expect system modules to be built as soon as possible without knowing the hitches developers face however it is important to deliver asap there for agile and RAD methodologies are best in these scenarios rank 4th on the list (18%).
Change request responses are favorable: changes requests are also as important as others however the change requests go through a change management process for assessments therefore it was ranked 5th on the list (15%).
Identify expectation mismatches in an early stage: It is essential to identify bugs at an early stage to save time and rebuilding the system therefore we have ranked to 3rd place (20%).
Improved quality by finding and fixing faults as quickly as possible: whereas user acceptance is a must the quality of the product delivered paly a very critical part therefore we have ranked to 2nd place (22%).

Success Factors

Three critical success factors were clearly similar in all companies. First, top management support was important in both companies throughout all stages, though its importance varied from stage to stage. In the early stages of the ERP implementation projects, top management support was clearly critical. Top management support is necessary for initiation and ongoing resourcing of such large, expensive, and critical projects. Second, the need for a balanced project team was identified as a critical success factor for all. Balanced project teams contribute to project success by providing a mix of IT people with ERP knowledge and end-users with a good understanding of organizational processes. Thirdly, user acceptance and training is also important in determining the success of an ERP implementation. Most local implementations took a few months to a few years. One of the things which was common among these local companies in relations to the ERP implantation was that it initiated some BPR (business process re-engineering) as denoted in Table 4.8. Other common factors include how willing the users were in adapting to the new system, and how adaptive the system was with inclusion of new modules. Another similarity that was gathered in our research was the company's ability to identifying fault and quickly fixing it.

Digging deep into our main area of research which was to validate the ERP implementation process of these eight companies with that of the best global practices, the results of our findings has proved that Agile methodology is the best and most preferred methodology for ERP implementations within the local companies in Fiji as it is considered as one of the most robust and successful methods. Agile is more focused on user needs hence

TABLE 4.5	Comparison of Three Methods Using the Evaluated Criteria				
	Adaptive system modules	Quickly Build and Deliver Modules Upon Requests	Change Request Responses Are Favorable	Identify Expectation Mismatches in an Early Stage	Improved Quality by Finding and Fixing Faults as Quickly as Possible
Waterfall Model	Most accurate and complete system method to adopt however, it takes more time to build but if managed properly can produce great results therefore we have given highest points.	Waterfall model needs to go through each stage in order to deliver the entire modules, therefore a quick build won't be possible using this model.	Waterfall model must go through its complete iteration therefore it becomes time consuming.	System modules are tested after the SDLC iteration is complete on the testing phase; mismatches can be discovered not in the early stage.	Waterfall model does deliver quality depending on how it is being managed; however, it takes up its time and its complete iteration to deliver.
Agile Development Method	Agile method is fast therefore it may compromise on the appearance and can be complex to usability.	Functional modules can be quickly built and delivered upon requests.	Using agile methodology change requests can be adopted on the go and easily modified.	Mismatches and exception can be easily identified because agile development and testing is done on the go.	This is the best method to use to find bugs quickly and resolve on the since development and testing are done on the go with agile development.
Rapid Application Development	Is fast and easy but is not a complete module; it does not have backend logic.	Can be quickly built but will not have any business logic to compute or process.	Change requests are favorable but it's only a prototype; not a full functional system.	Difficult to gauge since the system module developed using RAD will not have a fully functional module or system.	The process can be tested but cannot be validated.

ensuring the users are comfortable with the system. Agile methodology is also an iterative, team-based approach to development. This approach emphasizes the rapid delivery of an application in complete functional components. This method not only predicts early issues but also allows opportunity to constantly refine and reprioritize the system modules. However, as according to our research, Agile is the most sort of implementation methodology, this doesn't mean any other methodology cannot ensure successful implementation of an ERP. This entirely depends on a business objective.

Our findings of this research can be debated as was that none of our research interest had the failed ERP implementations thus, we cannot generalize that the best local ERP implementation is Agile, however further research can be undertaken to verify this pattern.

Tables 4.6–4.8 show some of the raw data gathered from the questionnaires.

TABLE 4.6 Raw Data Summarized From Questionnaires	
Company:	**List Down the Implementation Plan**
1	The implementation happened in 3 phases: Design, Build, & Implementation
	Design: Consultations were done with key stakeholders during the design phase to see how the existing ERP solution would fit the business needs. Project teams were given the software to get hands-on and test existing business processes before finalizing the customizations or business process re-engineering required. All processes/customizations were outlined and signed off before Phase 2 began.
	Build: During the build phase, the consultants built the system as per business requirements and the project teams tested all scenarios in 2 sets of phases. All issues were noted down in Phase 1 of tests and fixed and re-tested in Phase 2 of tests. All end-to-end business transactions were tested during the build phase. All infrastructure for the system was also out in place during this phase.
	Implementation: This required comprehensive documentation and end user training starting 1 month before going live. All trained users were assessed and provided further trainings if they failed to prepare them before go-live. A UAT environment was provided to all users to train themselves as comprehensively as they could. A month of hyper care period was also included in the implementation phase to fix any urgent issues that arose and to allow the system to stabilize.
2	• Step 1: Planning and organization, System selection • Step 2: Installation—data conversion and loading • Step 3: User training and procedure development • Step 4: Testing and validation • Step 5: Cut-over and go live • Step 6: Follow through and project completion

(continued)

TABLE 4.6	Raw Data Summarized From Questionnaires (Continued)
Company:	List Down the Implementation Plan
3	• Hardware + software purchase • Server installation + backup redundancy configuration • User training on modules • Data transfer from old ERP to New ERP • Data verification on both ERP • Parallel run of both ERP for a month • UAT approved before cut-over and change of ERP to NEW ERP
4	• Gap analysis (old system) • Pre-selection process • Solution evaluation • Gap analysis (new system) • Adoption decision • Project planning • Data gathering/templating • Configuration • Data migration—test environment • Implementation team training • Key user training (KUT) • User acceptance training/testing (UAT) • Integrations • Developments/customizations • Data migration—live • ERP rollout • Ongoing support
5	• Step 1: Requirements gathering/Discussion with stakeholders • Step 2: Analysis/Documentation/Project Plan • Step 3: Implementation • Step 4: Testing/Tanning • Step 5: Go Live
6	• Step 1: Package identification • Step 2: User acceptance testing (UAT) • Step 3: Rectification of UAT feedback • Step 4: Implementation • Step 5: Live area roll-out • Step 6: Maintenance

After completion of the result analysis and findings, we discovered that Agile methodology is the best possible approach to be used in an ERP implementation process

It has been proven that agile methodology is innovative and is used for articulating a well-organized project management procedure allowing for recurrent alterations, in the five criterias we have discussed, Agile is the best method in order to archive or obtain a successful ERP implementation goal.

TABLE 4.7	Most Challenging Steps of ERP Implementation
Company	Define Each Step From Least—Most Challenging
1	a. Design b. User Training c. Testing
2	a. Top Management Support b. User Training c. Data verification d. Post Implementation
3	a. Key User Training (KUT) b. User Acceptance Training/Testing (UAT) c. Integrations
4	a. Business process re-engineering b. User Training
5	a. User Training b. Post Implementation c. Selection/Planning
6	a. Installation - Data conversion and loading b. Cut over and go live c. Testing and validation d. User training and procedure development e. Planning, organization and system selection.

TABLE 4.8	Did ERP Implementation Initiate any BPR?
Company	Did the ERP implementation initiate any business process re-engineering (BPR)? If yes, please outline how it was beneficial and what were the challenges faced.
1	Yes. Change management was the most important aspect of this implementation.
2	Yes. Workloads were reduced, efficiency of reporting, reporting style.
3	Yes. We have adopted to industry standard practices which has provided new insight in all aspects of operations.
4	Especially; workflow improvements.
5	No.
6	Yes. Beneficial and best practices.

CONCLUSION

This chapter has explored the preferred best practices undertaken by the local organizations to ensure that their ERP implementation is a success. Results were obtained and computed using the AHP. These results then were weighted against the five common challenges faced from most to least challenging to achieve during ERP implementation with ranking from highest to lowest (1–5) by comparing each against each other. Together with the criteria we decided to compare the criteria of most common system development methods and weighted amongst each alternative methodology. Results were compared the constancy ratio of each criteria against the three alternative methods exploring that agile development method came up with the highest points which was 45% against the other two alternatives.

The picture that emerges from the study proved that Agile methodology is the best and most preferred methodology for ERP implementations within the local companies in Fiji as it is considered as one of the most robust and successful methods. However, while agile is the best methodology for ERP implementation according to our finding this does not mean that other system development methodologies like waterfall and RAD cannot be used within the implementation process. This entirely depends on the type of ERP being deployed with the aim's objectives and requirements of the organizations or it can also be hybrid methodology used which is the combination of waterfall and agile which is known as agile waterfall hybrid model.

The findings in this study should be of assistance to any local organisations intending to or are in process of implementing ERP.

Recommendations and Future Research

The strategy, methodology and practice engendered by any company implementing ERP is the major factor affecting the amount of challenges and implementation status. Further to our analysis of the adopted practices by local companies in Fiji to that of the best practices used globally, we recommend that Agile methodology is best suited for companies who intend to implement ERP systems. The ability to breakdown individual issues, tackling down the challenges, and ensuring that each arising issue is resolved first before moving to the next step is what makes this Agile methodology the best suited for ERP implementors.

There is a lot of research work done on ERP's addressing the managerial issues, success factors, or challenges whereas our research goes beyond these and validates the best suited methods for implementing ERP systems. Our research has considered implementation steps, challenges, and ways to overcome these challenges and have used AHP which is proven to be one of the best comparison models globally to prove which methodology should be adopted by ERP implementors.

While our research has managed to prove why Agile methodology is best suited, readers will still find it debatable due to the number of responses we received from Fiji which is a very small field of ERP implementations when compared globally. This chapter gives future researchers an insight on what they need to work on more to validate our findings, results, and recommendations.

In order to overturn the conclusions derived from our research, future researchers can dig deep into companies who have had ERP failures and compare their implementation methodologies against the results of the successful implementations which we have used in this chapter.

Since AHP is considered as one of the best when it comes to comparisons, future research studies can use the same framework to validate the results and findings.

REFERENCES

Alanbay, O. (2005). *ERP selection using expert choice software*. https://www.semantic scholar.org/paper/ERP-SELECTION-USING-EXPERT-CHOICE-SOFTWARE -Alanbay/254f53a9d84152ba8345e9a205b1c735c00a98c4

Alshamrani, A., & Bahattab, A. (2015). A comparison between three SDLC models waterfall model, spiral model, and incremental/iterative model. *International Journal of Computer Science Issues, 12*(1), 106–111.

Amlani, R. D. (2012). Advantages and limitations of different SDLC models. *International Journal of Computer Applications & Information Technology, 1*(3), 6–11.

Analytic Hierarchy Process. (n.d.). In *Wikipedia*. https://en.wikipedia.org/wiki/ Analytic_hierarchy_process

Balaji, S., & Murugaiyan, D. (2012). Wateerfallvs v-model vs agile: A comparative study on SDLC. *International Journal of Information Technology and Business Management, 2*(1), 26–30.

Dezdar, S., & Sulaiman, A. (2011). Examining ERP implementation success from a project environment perspective. *Business Process Management Journal, 17*(6), 919–939.

Esteves-Sousa, J., & Pastor-Collado, J. (2000, November). *Towards the unification of critical success factors for ERP implementations*. Paper presentation at the 10th Annual Business Information Technology Conference, Manchester.

Fetouh, A. A., el Abassy, A., & Moawad, R. (2011). Applying agile approach in ERP implementation . *International Journal of Computer Science and Network Security, 11*(8), 173–178.

Finney, S., & Corbett, M. (2007). ERP implementation: A compilation and analysis of critical success factors. *Business Process Management Journal, 13*(3), 329–347.

Hasibuan, Z. A., & Dantes, G. R. (2012). Priority of key success factors (KSFS) on enterprise resource planning (ERP) system implementation life cycle *Journal of Enterprise Resource Planning Studies, 2012*, Article 122672. https://pdfs .semanticscholar.org/57eb/344caf9961631c9402a88a256f7bd07f5223.pdf

Hassabelnaby, H. R., & Vonderembse, M. A. (2011). The impact of ERP implementation on organizational capabilities and firm performance. *Benchmarking: An International Journal, 19*(4/5), 1–17.

Hawking, P., Stein, A., & Foster, S. (2007). The challenges facing global ERP Systems implementations. In J. Cardoso & J. Filipe (Eds.), *Proceedings of the ninth international conference on Enterprise Information Systems* (pp. 415–422).

Khanna, K., & Arneja, G. P. (2012). Choosing an Appropriate ERP Implementation Strategy. *Journal of Engineering, 2*(3), 478–483.

Kilica, H. S., Zaim, S., & Delen, D. (2014). Development of a hybrid methodology for ERP system selection: The case of Turkish Airlines. *Decision Support Systems, 66*, 82–92.

Lutovac, M., & Manojlov, D. (2012). The successful methodology for enterprise resource planning (ERP) implementation. *Journal of Modern Accounting and Auditing, 8*(12), 1838–1847.

Mishra, A., & Dubey, D. (2013). A comparative study of different software development life cycle models in different scenarios. *International Journal of Advance Research in Computer Science and Management Studies, 1*(5), 64–69.

Muinde, C., Lewa, P., & Kamau, J. (2016). The influence of top management support on knowledge sharing during the implementation of ERP systems in Kenya . *The International Journal of Business & Management, 4*(7), 121–129.

Osintsev, A. (2016, April 1). The 5 biggest challenges when implementing ERP for the first time. *Technology Evaluation Centers.*

Parthasarathy, S., & Anbashagan, N. (2007). Evaluating ERP implementation choices using AHP. *International Journal of Enterprise Information Systems, 3*(3), 52–65.

Perera, H. S. C., & Costa, W. K. R. (2008). Analytic hierarchy process for selection of ERP software for manufacturing companies. *The Journal of Business Perspective, 12*(4), 1–11.

Rajan, C. A., & Baral, R. (2015). Adoption of ERP System: An empirical study of factors influencing the usage of ERP and its impact on end user. *IIBM Management Review, 27*(2), 105–117.

Saaty, T. L. (1980). *The analytic hierarchy process.* McGraw-Hill.

Sowan, I. K., & Tahboud, R. (2015). ERP systems critical success factors. *International Journal of Advanced Computer Science and Applications, 6*(6), 191–196.

The Most Popular Software Development Methodologies Overview. (2018, February 7). *Livity.* https://lvivity.com/software-development-methodologies

CHAPTER 5

HOW ARTIFICIAL INTELLIGENCE IS TRANSFORMING THE ERP SYSTEMS?

Sam Goundar
The University of the South Pacific

Anand Nayyar
Duy Tan University, Da Nang

Moniker Maharaj
The University of the South Pacific

Karunesh Ratnam
The University of the South Pacific

Shalvin Prasad
The University of the South Pacific

Enterprise Systems and Technological Convergence, pages 85–98
Copyright © 2021 by Information Age Publishing

ABSTRACT

Enterprise resource planning (ERP) systems have become a crucial part of every business organization. The need for ERP systems have drastically increased over the past decade and it is a key factor in bringing success to any organization. Keeping in mind the impact of ERPS, another notable factor to consider in this time and age is the impact of artificial intelligence (AI). The world is currently digitizing every minute and the involvement of AI in that is quite extraordinary. "Artificial intelligence as an integrated part of the ERP system will affect the very essence of daily operations. AI solutions will most likely take over routine tasks currently performed by humans. Therefore, the development of the new technology is also driven by an increasing need to reduce business operating costs by supporting employees' workflows, thus enhancing the efficiency of the organization's operations as a whole. The development of artificial intelligence is, in other words, a development the companies must follow if they want to stay efficient and competitive.[...] Artificial intelligence has just begun to appear in ERP applications and the addition of the new technology is still a relatively new phenomenon, but the possibilities artificial intelligence adds to the ERP systems must be said to be unlimited" (Gadallah & Elmaraghy, 1993, p. 6). The AI enabled ERP solution has become the soul of everyday tasks. It is transforming the way business works and it can completely change the core of the company's tasks by eradicating the chances of human errors.

During this time and age, the business market is very competitive and every company faces many challenges such as; the high demand of quality products and services, being par with customer satisfaction, and delivering the products on time. Keeping all this in mind, implementing an ERP system brings about many advantages and provides solutions to the above-mentioned challenges. The adoption of ERP systems by businesses has been on the rise in the past 10 years and has become an integral part of every organization. "In those years, industrial markets have undergone important changes, which have transformed the way in which companies must act and perform to maintain competitiveness; changes in management, process technology, customer expectations, supplier attitudes, competitive behavior and many other aspects" (Gadallah & Elmaraghy, 1993, p. 6).

The ERP system has become a crucial part of every organization but with the world digitalizing every minute, there comes a need to update the use of ERP which brings about the topic of integrating ERP with AI. Artificial Intelligence has been one of the key talking points in this technology driven world and every aspect is being done to integrate AI with various services. More than 60 years after AI was first launched, it is finally being used to streamline and boost business efficiency and productivity. "Today, the building blocks are in place for AI to deliver results. Sensors track products at every stop of their life cycle from the shop floor to customer sites.

Cloud solutions enable the collection of millions of data points to create the foundation for machine learning. Personal assistants are readily available to simplify and accelerate information retrieval for more informed decision making" (Lin, et al., 2017, p. 4).

Artificial Intelligence will undoubtedly change and influence the future of ERP systems and will undoubtedly have a decisive impact on the business of the future, regardless of size or industry, but in order to gain value from the new technological advances the companies need to revise their current technology strategies and be prepared to change and adapt to the developments (Metaxiotis, Psarras, & Ergazakis, 2003). Artificial intelligence as an integrated part of the ERP system will affect the very essence of daily operations. AI solutions will most likely take over routine tasks currently performed by humans. Therefore, the development of the new technology is also driven by an increasing need to reduce business operating costs by supporting employees' workflows, thus enhancing the efficiency of the organization's operations as a whole. The development of AI is, in other words, a development the companies must follow if they want to stay efficient and competitive.

In this chapter, the group will be looking at how AI is transforming the ERP systems, the changes it has brought from when ERP systems were first being used without AI, and the new impacts of implementing AI. Also, the group aims to find out if the ERP world is ready to implement AI and study the cases where AI and ERP are already in use. In addition, the group aims to highlight and identify the advantages and disadvantages of using AI in ERP systems.

LITERATURE REVIEW

During the 1990s era, a newfound software emerged into the production and supply chain industry which was known as the enterprise resources planning systems (Hong & Kim, 2002). ERP systems were unlike the traditional IT systems that were implemented and used in organizations at that instance. As per Sudhaman and Thangavel, ERP systems were devised to be able to integrate all or most of the core organizational functions of typical businesses regardless of the type of industry the business was in (Sudhaman & Thangavel, 2015). In short, the ERP systems were a complete package that contained modules which targeted many organizational departments such as finance, human resources, warehouse, and stock procurements as well as retail and distribution, to be all integrated together so that the organization would become one complete organism in a way (Beynon-Davies, 2013). ERP helped widen the keyhole which the businesses could look through and actually be able to know what was being done, or what everyone else was doing in their respective departments at any point in time of their choosing (Lujić, Šimunović, Šarić, & Majdandžić, 2005). This helped the decision-making bodies of the business to be able to better utilize the resources that an organization had in its disposal. Resources when used in the right and optimal manner helped businesses attain their goals, increased profitability whilst helping reducing costs of being in operation (Jagoda & Samaranayake, 2017).

Not all businesses are the same, and of course because of this not all businesses operate in the same manner or have the same workflow. The beauty of the ERP systems is that this packaged software is as mentioned above modular, hence to suit the different business needs across its departments, the modules are flexible and could be customized (Rashid, Hossain, & Patrick, 2002). By default, each module is built in relation to the best practices that an organization can conform to in terms of operation, however to not destroy existing business workflows, these logistics can be changed to suit and serve the business better. The goal is to integrate not the departments but the enterprise (Lujic, Simunovic, Saric, & Majdandzic, n.d.). The independent modules work real time and as such are able to provide updates on the respective departments (Gargeya & Brady, 2005). ERP systems do give businesses the competitive edge as it allows them to utilize their resources in a very efficient manner, however the implementation of ERP systems is very costly and time consuming. Also, the maintenance and further upgrades to the software as well as its conforming hardware are not cheap. However, as time passes, the competition increases and so does the customer expectations, hence ERP systems must always be as updated and fine-tuned as possible to help organizations adapt to the ever-changing business environment (Zughoul, Al-Refai, & El-Omari, 2016). Vendors are therefore continuously working on evolving the ERP systems to be able to help enterprises be able to adapt faster and work more efficiently.

Traditional ERP systems alone are a sensible enough tool to implement and use because of its ability to provide comprehensive reporting. However, in this era, with the vast amount of data being collected via the ERP systems, decision-making bodies within the organizations require a more business intelligence proficient software or tool to help analyze the data and get information that is more precise for improved decision making (Lin, Lin, & Yang, 2017). This is where AI comes in. AI is basically any form of intelligence that is depicted by a software of machine, it can range from simple automation works to that of complex and sophisticated ability of systems making predictions from data analyzed (Oana et al., 2017). AI is the go-to technology that is used so to be able to make a software or machine be able to understand, learn from data collected and to make decisions based on patterns that the computer is able to conceive which could be a tad bit too drastic for humans to be able to see or compute themselves in a short period of time (Sharma & Srivastava, 2017).

AI is used to derive information, relations, and patterns from data sets that would not be feasible to compute in a short period of time by humans, and that too with minimal errors. AI can aid in the extraction of information that may not be able to have been produced via standard analysis procedures (Nemati, Steiger, Iyer, & Herschel, 2002). Liebowitz states that the union of AI and decision support systems with IT systems can actually better the knowledge management as well as organizational decision-making process (Liebowitz, 2001).

One of the ERP system's main functions is to help businesses improve and streamline their workflow and to make better decisions about everything from production to strategy (Subramoniam, Tounsi, & Krishnankutty, 2009). Yazgan, Boran, and Goztepe state in their article, that the utilization of AI in ERP systems can improve the modular functionalities by analyzing larger datasets than it was previously possible. Hence assisting with the evolution of the packaged software (Yazgan, Boran, & Goztepe, 2009). Whilst the traditional ERP systems provided a real time overview of how the resources of the organization was being utilized, to get information from historical data required reports to be run and analyzed by humans in order to be able to pick out patterns to make an informed guess or prediction, however incorporation of AI in ERP systems helps the software to be able to train itself and learn from the historical data captured via the system to provide patterns and predictions in a much shorter time and in a more accurate manner. This will in turn boost organizational performance since information like such can be made available faster and it allows the utilization of human resources to change from doing low-value work such as these forms of analysis to a more high-value sort of work such as making judgements (Plastino & Purdy, 2018).

Moreover, AI in ERP systems can also bring about the automation in heavy workload tasks such as data entry. Manual data entry into the ERP systems is for several organizations a heavy workload which costs many person-hours (Rouhani & Zare Ravasan, 2012). Not only are tasks such as this costly to the organizations, but it also brings about the possibility of the existence of dirty data which can be a result of a human errors (Themistocleous et al., 2001). AI combined with ERP as mentioned above would be able to learn and in turn help create a better workflow so to reduce the effort and time it takes to perform tasks such as data entry, reporting, market analysis as well as stock demand predictions (Chen & Tai, 2005). Metaxiotis, Psarras, and Ergazakis state that the combination of AI and ERP can also improve the business processes. By analyzing historical data, the systems will be able to suggest the most effective internal work processes. For example, by reading an already established workflow, AI will be able to perform the next task and continuously provide the necessary information needed to complete that task (Metaxiotis, Psarras, & Ergazakis, 2003). Keenoy also, had at a point in time stated how there was a need for a smarter way or automations to be applied on the accounting workflows within an organization. So, to fill the gap which required a more analytical and accurate depiction of the information to be derived from data for sales, stock inventory, market requirements as well as manufacturing and stock distribution costs (Keenoy, 1958). AI does not get fatigued, stressed out, or in need of rest. Its only constraints are the hardware on which it runs and the data that it has in its disposal to learn from, hence Ayoub and Payne say that this makes it possible for AI to be used all three, tactical, operational, as well as strategic levels since the system can work overtime without the need to exhaust human resources and be able to provide necessary information for quality human decision-making (Ayoub & Payne, 2015). A smart system is likely to yield smarter solutions.

Going back to the financial and inventory modules of an ERP systems related workflow, these modules are paramount to the organization especially when it comes to either physical stock or financial auditing. Just like Plastino and Purdy, Kokina and Davenport also state that AI is better able to detect required information in a structured manner via automation of repetitive tasks which the auditors are usually burdened with (Kokina & Davenport, 2017). AI is able to recognize required information from documents and making it presentable to the human faction, the auditors who can now waste less time and add more value to their task by doing what they are theoretically supposed to, forecast financial standings, make human decisions and report to upper management faster in terms of organization financial standings (Kolbjørnsrud, Amico, & Thomas, 2016). Administration work is supposed to be making informed decisions, AI integrated ERP systems tend to shift the dynamics of making it possible for administration to do this, make decisions machines cannot, whilst the intelligence embedded in the system takes care of data entry and analysis sides of things.

Artificial intelligence has just recently begun to emerge in ERP applications and the inclusion of this new technology is still a relatively new phenomenon, however the possibilities AI adds to ERP systems can be said to be unlimited. For instance, at the moment AI is being used to automate data entry and streamline workflows, however it is evident that the inclusion of AI into ERP systems is one that will help organizations that take their time to understand it, a competitive advantage on other companies (Martínez-López & Casillas, 2013).

RESEARCH QUESTIONS

Enterprise resource planning system has been dated back from 1990 but its roots date back to the 1960s (Hong & Kim, 2002). Over the last decades, ERP solutions have been evolving with organizations gaining wealth of structured and unstructured data. However, organizations have been struggling to transform those data into meaningful information, which in turn will be able to assist in their decision-making process and further improve customer service. This is where AI comes into play to

- automate and improve complex analytical tasks,
- evaluate data in real-time,
- adjust its behavior with minimal need for supervision,
- optimize asset management,
- improve operational performance,
- decrease downtime,
- increase efficiency, and
- increase accuracy.

In this chapter, we are identifying the issues that are present in the ERP system and how AI will transform the ERP system. After searching through many literatures, we found that most of the literatures were about ERP issues that were present and not how AI involvement can assist in solving those problems faced, such as, sales automation, improved decision-making process, automation of data input and business process improvements. Our chapter will assist organizations and individuals in understating how integration of AI can solve some of the problems faced by ERP systems alone. Research questions that the chapter will be based upon are as follows:

- What are the problems present in the ERP systems?
- How would AI solve those problems?
- Is the ERP world ready for AI?
- Are there any ERP system that has AI?

METHODOLOGY

Research was conducted using the seven-step model for our literature review and is using the methodology of the literature review (Onwuegbuzie & Frels, 2016) book as a guide. Due to the limited timeframe, we had to base this chapter on qualitative analysis only. As such, it is limited to limitations of using qualitative data only. Bjørner (2015) has noted that qualitative methods lack the statistical validity and reliability that quantitative research contributes.

Figure 5.1 and Figure 5.2 represents the seven-step model for a comprehensive literature review that we are using in our research chapter. In Step 1, we identified the main concepts/keywords and stated it as a question. By identifying main keywords in the previous step, we searched (Science Direct, Web of Science, IEEE Xplore, and ACM Digital Library) and read literature to understand its context and to note any relevant literature in the reference section in our second step. To find the relevant information, we needed to use the main keywords, which were, enterprise resource planning, artificial intelligence, machine learning, neural networks, deep learning, and intelligent ERP. In Step 3, we cataloged all the relevant literature and in Step 4, we selected and deselected information that we were going to analyze. In our next step, which is five, we expanded our search by using Google and Google Scholar and used Step 3 and Step 4 again to find similar literature for our analysis. Then, in Step 6, we analyzed literature from step three with its, intended audience, objective reasoning, and coverage. In our final step, citing all the sources used in our research chapter was done.

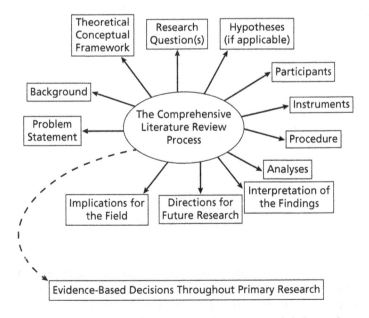

Figure 5.1 The comprehensive literature review process as it informs the various components of a primary research report (Onwuegbuzie & Frels, 2016).

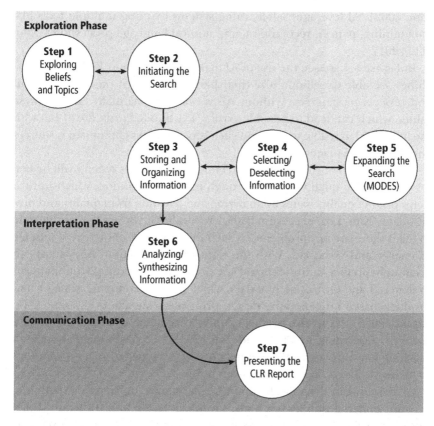

Figure 5.2   The seven-step model for a comprehensive literature review (Onwueg-buzie & Frels, 2016).

RESULTS/FINDINGS

Enterprise Resource Planning system has its roots from the 1960s, which in the last decades has evolved, which is represented in Figure 5.3 (Hong &

2000s	Extended ERP
1990s	Enterprise Resource Planning (ERP)
1980s	Manufacturing Resources Planning (MRP II)
1970s	Material Requirement Planning (MRP)
1960s	Inventory Control (IC) Packages

Figure 5.3   The evolution of ERP Systems: An historical perspective (Patrick, Hossain, & Rashid, 2019).

Kim, 2002). AI leverages self-learning systems by using multiple tools like data mining, pattern recognition, and natural language processing (Oana et al., 2017).

In Figure 5.4, we see the use of AI makes an intelligent ERP system. Machines are able to self-optimize their parameters based on material input and process parameters. Without AI, we have to manually change these values, which can lead to possible errors (Plastino & Purdy, 2018) but with the help of AI, it is able to perform such repetitive tasks in human resources and financial management.

With the help of AI in the manufacturing industry its systems will be better at detecting quality defects through image recognition, which in turn helps predict quality issues by analyzing and learning from quality and process data (Kim, Lee, & Gosain, 2005). Without AI, systems will not be able to tell if there are any problems, as such there is a risk of increased wastage of energy and resources. With the right implementation, AI systems can accurately predict future demand for products by learning from patterns in demand and environmental data, which allows developing same or new products based on generative design principles (Metaxiotis, Psarras, & Ergazakis, 2003). It can also predict maintenance needs by identifying failure patterns. According to Chen and Tsai (2005), we have noted the use of machine learning with ERP systems can assist systems to suggest solutions to incidents based on earlier failure reports.

AI systems can dynamically optimize warehouse utilization, taking into account material outflows, inflows, inventory levels, and turn rates (Martínez & Casillas, 2003). Which in its current state will help improve warehouse management, as it has been noted by Martinez and Casillas (2003) that without AI it can take more than a month and with it can be around 24 hours. It has been a noted case for Walmart, which was able to cut the taking of physical inventory from one month to 24 hours with the help of AI (Staff, 2019) even BMW did similarly.

The use of virtual agents verbally provides operators with information from IT systems upon request even real-time information can be provided with proper implementations. These, in turn, improves customer services, by reducing workload from real agents to virtual agents, which already has a set of common questions or requests that it will be able to serve real-time without the wait of connecting to a real agent.

With our research, we were able to find the list of issues that AI can help, with the multitude of services that are performed by organizations that use ERP system(s). It will help organizations to be able to use this research to better understand the issues that they are facing or would face in the near future and what solutions are available.

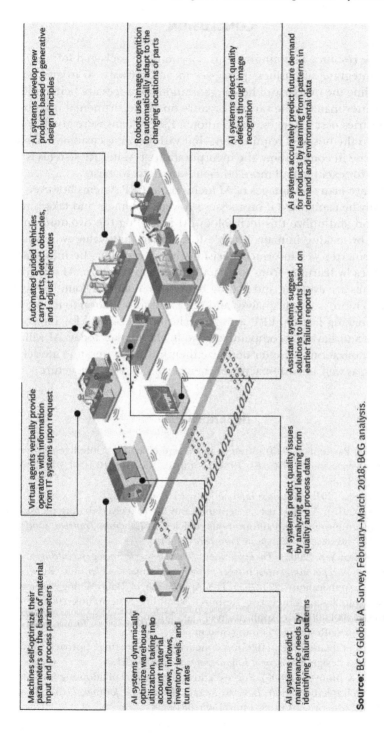

Machines self-optimize their parameters on the basis of material input and process parameters

AI systems dynamically optimize warehouse utilization, taking into account material outflows, inflows, inventory levels, and turn rates

AI systems predict maintenance needs by identifying failure patterns

Virtual agents verbally provide operators with information from IT systems upon request

AI systems predict quality issues by analyzing and learning from quality and process data

AI systems develop new products based on generative design principles

Automated guided vehicles carry parts, detect obstacles, and adjust their routes

Assistant systems suggest solutions to incidents based on earlier failure reports

Robots use image recognition to automatically adapt to the changing locations of parts

AI systems detect quality defects through image recognition

AI systems accurately predict future demand for products by learning from patterns in demand and environmental data

Source: BCG Global AI Survey, February–March 2018; BCG analysis.

Figure 5.4 Mind the (AI) gap: Leadership makes the difference (Duranton, Erlebach & Pauly, 2018).

CONCLUSION

Enterprise resource planning systems is a complete packaged software that aims to integrate all business processes in one software so to give at any point in time the overview of how organization resources are being utilized and to better manage the various organizational departmental tasks using the industries best practices. Conventional ERP systems were good in conforming to the business requirements but with growing customer expectation and rise in competition, the incorporation of AI in ERP systems is paving paths for exciting and more efficient workflows to exist.

There are many advantages of AI inclusion in ERP systems however, and it can only be capitalized if businesses show an openness and take time to understand and utilize this technology. AI is shifting the dynamics in the workflow by making humans be able to perform high value work, that is to make smarter well-informed decisions based on what the information AI provides by learning from the data ERP systems capture. AI integrated ERP systems are evolving and getting better day in and day out, hence giving rise to more accurate analysis and release of information to the human decision-making faction. ERP with AI inclusion is essential for improving efficiency and having a competitive edge in the market today. AI will empower organizations to better optimize their business operating model, applications, as well as supremacy over their technology infrastructure.

REFERENCES

Ayoub, K., & Payne, K. (2015). Strategy in the age of artificial intelligence. *Journal Of Strategic Studies, 39*(5/6), 793–819. https://doi.org/10.1080/01402390.2015.1088838

Beynon-Davies. (2013). *Business information systems*. Macmillan.

Bjørner, T. (2015). A priori user acceptance and the perceived driving pleasure in semi-autonomous and autonomous vehicles. In *European Transport Conference 2015 Association for European Transport* (AET).

Chen, R., & Tsai, Y.-S. (2005). *The application of data mining technology for intelligent enterprise resource planning system*. https://www.researchgate.net/profile/Ruey_shun_Chen/publication/229027335_The_Application_of_Data_Mining_Technology_for_Intelligent_Enterprise_Resource_Planning_System/links/0fcfd50c9d6158bcf4000000/The-Application-of-Data-Mining-Technology-for-Intelligent-Enterprise-Resource-Planning-System.pdf

Gadallah, M., Elmaraghy, H. (1993). A concurrent engineering approach to robust product design. *Concurrent Engineering, 1*(4), 237–251.

Gargeya, V., & Brady, C. (2005). Success and failure factors of adopting SAP in ERP system implementation. *Business Process Management Journal, 11*(5), 501–516. https://doi.org/10.1108/14637150510619858

Hong, K., & Kim, Y. (2002). The critical success factors for ERP implementation: An organizational fit perspective. *Information & Management, 40*(1), 25–40. https://doi.org/10.1016/s0378-7206(01)00134-3

Hossain, L., Patrick, J., & Rashid, M. (2002). *Enterprise resource planning.* Idea Group.

Jagoda, K., & Samaranayake, P. (2017). An integrated framework for ERP system implementation. *International Journal of Accounting & Information Management, 25*(1), 91–109. https://doi.org/10.1108/ijaim-04-2016-0038

Keenoy, C. L. (1958). The impact of automation on the field of accounting. *The Accounting Review, 33*(2), 230–236. http://www.jstor.org/stable/241233

Kokina, J., & Davenport, T. (2017). The emergence of artificial intelligence: How automation is changing auditing. *Journal of Emerging Technologies In Accounting, 14*(1), 115–122. https://doi.org/10.2308/jeta-51730

Kolbjørnsrud, V., Amico, R., & Thomas, R. (2016). *How artificial intelligence will redefine management.* Harvard Business School.

Liebowitz, J. (2001). Knowledge management and its link to artificial intelligence. *Expert Systems With Applications, 20*(1), 1–6. https://doi.org/10.1016/s0957-4174(00)00044-0

Lin, W., Lin, S., & Yang, T. (2017). Integrated business prestige and artificial intelligence for corporate decision making in dynamic environments. *Cybernetics And Systems, 48*(4), 303–324. https://doi.org/10.1080/01969722.2017.1284533

Lujić, R., Šimunović, G., Šarić, T., & Majdandžić, N. (2005, June). Applying of Artificial Intelligence to the Scheduling Problem in the ERP System. In *27th International Conference on Information Technology Interfaces (ITI 2005): proceedings* (p. 149).

Martínez-López, F., & Casillas, J. (2013). Artificial intelligence-based systems applied in industrial marketing: An historical overview, current and future insights. *Industrial Marketing Management, 42*(4), 489–495.

Metaxiotis, K., Psarras, J., & Ergazakis, K. (2003). Production scheduling in ERP systems. *Business Process Management Journal, 9*(2), 221–247.

Nemati, H., Steiger, D., Iyer, L., & Herschel, R. (2002). Knowledge warehouse: An architectural integration of knowledge management, decision support, artificial intelligence and data warehousing. *Decision Support Systems, 33*(2), 143–161. https://doi.org/10.1016/s0167-9236(01)00141-5

Oana, O., Cosmin, T., & Valentin, N. C. (2017). Artificial intelligence: A new field of computer science which any business should consider. *Ovidius University Annals, Economic Sciences Series, XVII*(1), 356–360.

Onwuegbuzie, A. J., & Frels, R. (2016). *Seven steps to a comprehensive literature review: A multimodal and cultural approach.* SAGE.

Plastino, E., & Purdy, M. (2018). Game changing value from Artificial Intelligence: Eight strategies. *Strategy & Leadership, 46*(1), 16–22. https://doi.org/10.1108/sl-11-2017-0106

Rashid, M., Hossain, L., & Patrick, J. (2019). *The evolution of ERP Systems: A historical perspective.* https://faculty.biu.ac.il/~shnaidh/zooloo/nihul/evolution.pdf

Rouhani, S. and Zare Ravasan, A. (2012). ERP success prediction: An artificial neural network approach. *Scientia Iranica, 20*(3), 992–1001.

Sharma, L., & Srivastava, V. (2017). performance enhancement of information retrieval via Artificial Intelligence. *International Journal of Scientific Research in Science Engineering and Technology, 3*(1), 187–192.

Staff, 24/7. (2016, June 3). Walmart testing warehouse drones to catalog and manage inventory. *Supply Chain 24/7.* Retrieved from https://www.supplychain247 .com/article/walmart_testing_warehouse_drones_to_manage_inventory

Subramoniam, S., Tounsi, M., & Krishnankutty, K. (2009). The role of BPR in the implementation of ERP systems. *Business Process Management Journal, 15*(5), 653–668.

Sudhaman, P., & Thangavel, C. (2015). Efficiency analysis of ERP projects: Software quality perspective. *International Journal Of Project Management, 33*(4), 961–970. https://doi.org/10.1016/j.ijproman.2014.10.011

Themistocleous, M., Irani, Z., O'Keefe, R., & Paul, R. (2001). ERP problems and application integration issues: An empirical survey. In *Proceedings of the 34th Annual Hawaii International Conference on System Sciences* (Vol. 9; p. 9045). IEEE Computer Society.

Yazgan, H., Boran, S., & Goztepe, K. (2009). An ERP software selection process with using artificial neural network based on analytic network process approach. *Expert Systems with Applications, 36*(5), 9214–9222.

Zughoul, B., Al-Refai, M., & El-Omari, N. (2016). Evolution characteristics of ERP systems that distinct from traditional SDLCs. *International Journal of Advanced Research in Computer and Communication Engineering, 5*(7), 87–91. https://doi. org/10.17148/ijarcce.2016.5718

CHAPTER 6

USING BUSINESS INTELLIGENCE IN ORGANIZATIONS

Benefits and Challenges

Sam Goundar
The University of the South Pacific

Kennedy Okafor
Federal University of Technology Owerri

Aloesi Cagica
The University of the South Pacific

Praveer Chand
The University of the South Pacific

Shanish Singh
The University of the South Pacific

Enterprise Systems and Technological Convergence, pages 99–144
Copyright © 2021 by Information Age Publishing
All rights of reproduction in any form reserved.

ABSTRACT

Big data, big data analytics, and business intelligence is the buzzword in today's business arena. With the advent of the Internet and in particular the Internet of things, the opportunity that it presents may be too good to pass up. The chance to be able to get to know not just your customers but more so their behavior can help you, in a way, to serve them better. Also, it presents the opportunity to be able to know your competitors and how they are doing in the market given that everything is now connected.

Due to the above fact, the team is inspired to find out whether the realization of the opportunity that big data, big data analytics and therefore business intelligence presents has reached Fiji or not and if some SME have realized it and successfully made the change to incorporate them into their daily business. It would also be interesting to note whether the challenges and benefits that local SME go through are similar to those their overseas counterparts encounter or whether there are differences.

The first part of this chapter focuses on a literature review to further discuss, "What is big data? What is big data analytics?" and also their contribution to business intelligence (BI). The second part of this chapter is also a literature review on benefits and challenges faced by companies overseas who have already achieved some sort of BI. It also discusses past similar research on benefits and challenges. Focus is on the benefits and challenges they faced. The final part of this chapter will be focused on the analysis of the survey that was sent out to IT staff in the different organizations in Fiji. The responses will be analyzed using the decision tree algorithm to validate the findings and also the hypothesis that those who are able to implement BI have a competitive edge than those who have not. We will also be using the Gartner BI Maturity Model to gauge the maturity of BI for the local organizations here in Fiji.

This chapter will be useful to those who are embarking on the journey to achieving BI in Fiji. It will help them understand the benefits and challenges that they may face on their journey and in knowing that will greatly assist them to prepare for what lies ahead on their way to integrating BI in their daily operations.

Any initiative that looks to make a change within the organization will face its own challenges. Be it a technology change, leadership change, business process change or whatever it maybe. Even more so with projects to achieve business intelligence (BI) since the change needed to take place is usually organization wide.

There is no set definition for BI and it can be described as a state of achieving intelligence in the workplace and it can also be used to describe the processes of working towards achieving a state of intelligence. Today's market is more complex and competitive than ever before. With the advent of the personal computers which virtually placed a computer in every home and also the Internet, it has also developed a breed of intelligent users who know what they want and are fully aware of how they want it and also to the point of also knowing your competitor who can provide them the service in a more affordable or timely manner. This is also evident within developing countries where mobile computing has allowed almost every citizen to be in possession of a mobile computer. According to a report back in 2016 by Internet World Stats, there were 380,125 users as of November of 2015 which was around 41.8% of the population and that stat is continuously growing exponentially (see Table 6.1).

Gone are the days where customers come to businesses with an issue and wait to hear a suggested solution. Now the customers are aware of the market and are able to test the waters first before making an investment. With the sudden rise of intelligent customers, businesses need to go a step further and try to gauge how the customers will behave. This is the main contributor of BI where the businesses try to provide up-to-date information to their decision makers. The information is the result of applying analytics on data that is gathered across customers, competitors, market, technology, and the environment. With the decrease in the cost of storage and running high end servers, the opportunity is also now there for the developing countries such as Fiji to take advantage of the usage of BI within their organizations.

There has been a lot of research done in the past to understand BI and how it has changed over the years with the advent of the Internet and the Internet of things. Also with the introduction of cloud computing which greatly assists SME who cannot afford to do BI on their own infrastructure. There has been very little research done on the adoption and use of BI in organizations. According to Gartner, BI adoption is lingering at 30% in most enterprises. In this day and age, it takes more than a VP or C-level executive to champion the adoption of BI. What is needed is a more coordinated approach across organizational processes and technological areas of a company's BI implementation roadmap strategy. Thus increasing the probability of the success of BI adoption (Columbus, 2019).

TABLE 6.1 Fiji Internet Users Statistics (Internet World Stats)

Year	Users	Population	% Pop.	GDP p.c.*	Usage Source
2000	7,500	832,777	0.9%	US $2,861	ITU
2012	181,880	883,125	20.6%	US $3,610	IWS
2015	380,125	909,389	41.8%	US $4,540	IWS

Note: Per Capita GDP in U.S. dollars. *Source:* United Nations Department of Economic and Social Affairs.

This chapter looks to find out whether the implementation of BI is also happening in a developing country like Fiji or not? Also to find out whether the adoption of BI in the organizations is indeed across the organization and finally to find out the benefits and challenges faced during the process of the implementation of BI.

LITERATURE REVIEW

This is the era of big data (BD). "Big data" is generating tremendous attention worldwide (See Figure 6.1). The results of a Google search on the topic rose from about 252,000 hits in November 2011 to almost 1.39 billion hits on April 4, 2012 (Flory, 2012), and then reached the impressive number of 1.69 billion hits in December 2013. This phenomenon is mainly driven by the widespread diffusion and adoption of mobile devices, social media platforms including YouTube, Facebook, Twitter, and the Internet of things related concepts (e.g., RFID technology; Fosso Wamba et al., 2015). Big data analytics services have also created big market opportunities. For example, the researcher of International Data Corporation (IDC) forecasts that BD and analytics-related services marketing in Asia/Pacific (excluding Japan) region will grow from US$3.8 billion in 2016 to US$7.0 billion in 2019 at a 16.3% CAGR (compound annual growth rate; Sun, Sun, & Strang, 2018).

Big data analytics and BI is now an emerging topic of research in the IT field. IT, over the years, has moved from a supporting role to an enabler for most businesses and organizations by creating many improvement opportunities. With the growing need to store business data, most businesses and organizations, regardless of their size, that is, whether small, medium, or large have to store data, both structured and unstructured. This data can grow extremely large that it can be termed as BD. The use of social media platforms by most organizations for certain business objectives can also generate enormous amounts of data. Big data is defined by google as "extremely large data sets that may be analyzed computationally to reveal patterns, trends, and associations, especially relating to human behaviour and interactions" (Chen, Mao, & Liu, 2014, p. 171). Big data analytics is defined as the process in which extremely large data sets are analyzed to uncover hidden patterns, unknown correlations, market trends, customer preferences, and other useful information that can help organizations make more informed business decisions (Labbe et al., 2012).

Large organizations also use BI by analyzing their operational data with analytical tools to present complex and competitive information to planners and decision makers in order for them to make informed decisions in a timely manner. This includes financial institutions, healthcare, and banks which have enormous amounts of data that can be analyzed and presented.

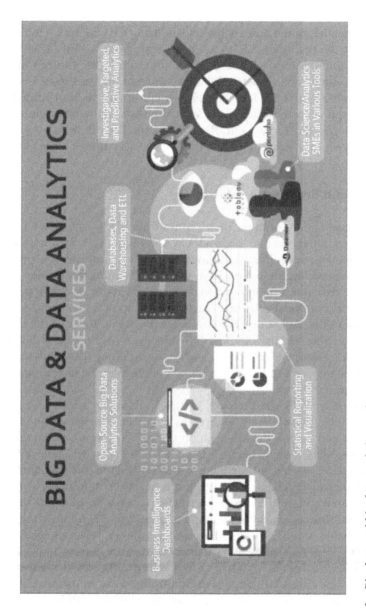

Figure 6.1 Big data and big data analytics services.

The recent development of the Internet of things will also result in an enormous amount of data generated by devices that will be connected to the internet. Such devices include mobile phones, vehicles, refrigeration, air-conditioning units, and so forth. Data generated by these physical devices can then be mined and analyzed by utilizing data analytical tools that can present the recorded data in an intelligent manner. With these tools, the fear of the unknown can be greatly minimized in the future with the existence of such ways to better look into current and past trends which can then help predict the future. This is useful in any field of study be it banking and finance, education, or the health sector. How an organization is able to successfully implement BD analytics and BIe will become a major deciding factor in organizations surviving in the near future if not already.

Big Data and Big Data Analytics

There have been a number of definitions for BD. Gartner IT Glossary defines BD as, "high-volume, high-velocity and high-variety information assets that demand cost-effective, innovative forms of information processing for enhanced insight and decision making" (Gandomi & Haider, 2015, p. 138). Big data is a term applied to datasets whose size or type is beyond the ability of traditional relational databases to capture, manage, and process the data with low-latency. In addition, it has one or more of the following characteristics—high volume, high velocity, or high variety. Big data comes from sensors, devices, video/audio, networks, log files, transactional applications, web, and social media—much of it generated in real time and on a very large scale.

Big data is typically characterized by three important attributes, namely volume, variety, and velocity. The three Vs signify massive data volume, data type variety, and diverse data generation velocity. In terms of data volume, for example, Nielsen can generate around 300,000 rows of real time data per second from live viewing and yield more than one billion records per month to do BD analysis (Prescott, 2014). In terms of data variety, BD analytics of both structured and unstructured data can help companies generate insights from various sources, including consumer transactions, inventory monitoring, store-based video, advertisement and consumer relations, consumer preferences, sales management, and financial data (Schomm, Stahl, & Vossen, 2013; Kambatla et al., 2014). For data velocity, BD analytics can enable real time access and information sharing through local to national governments for improved decision-making (Fosso Wamba et al., 2015).

The three Vs have been expanded to five with the addition of veracity and value (see Figure 6.2). Data veracity is the degree to which data is accurate, precise, and trusted. Data is often viewed as certain and reliable.

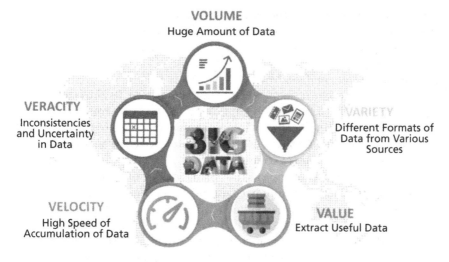

Figure 6.2   5-V criteria of big data.

The reality of problem spaces, data sets and operational environments is that data is often uncertain, imprecise and difficult to trust. After discussing volume, velocity, variety, and veracity, there is another V that should be taken into account when looking at BD, that is, value. It is all well and good to have access to BD but unless we can turn it into value it is useless. By turning it into value I mean, is it adding to the benefits of the organizations who are analyzing BD? Is the organization working on BD achieving a high return on investment (ROC)? Unless it adds to their profits by working on BD, it is useless.

Big data analytics is the process of examining large amounts of data to uncover hidden patterns, correlations, and other insights. With today's technology, it is possible to analyze your data and get answers from it almost immediately—an effort that is slower and less efficient with more traditional BI solutions. Big data analytics can assist organizations/companies to better exploit BD for improving customer satisfaction, managing risks, generating competitive intelligence, and providing real time insights. The growing need to use IT in the business world has led to the developments of large and complex data sets for various organizational functions (Bayrak, 2015).

For the various public and private sectors, organizations and companies capture and maintain huge amounts of data on their customers, products, and various services provided. To leverage this technical data stored and maintained in various digital platforms such as databases and data warehouses, and to translate it into actionable insights a new field called business analytics (BA) also known as Business Intelligence (BI) or big data (BD) has emerged in recent years. BA has evolved and become a part of every major business decision-making process, and it has the potential to transform businesses as it empowers decision makers with data and supports them to make strategic, operational, and tactical decisions (Bayrak, 2015).

Benefits of Big Data and Analytics

In every business be it small, medium, and enterprise, its aim is to be able to analyze how the business is operating, what success margins they have and if they are making profits or losses. These questions are usually raised by senior management. Data is essential for these kinds of analysis and it is very important to business executives.

Big data analytics can improve the management of supply chain from various aspects, including supply chain efficiency, supply chain planning, inventory control and risk management, market intelligence, and real time personalized service (Vera-Baquero, Palacios, Stantchev, & Molloy 2015; Wang & Alexander, 2015). Big data analytics can also assist in the decision-making processes by effectively using BD that is available to be analyzed. While BD can be used to support in the decision making process through BD analytics, it can also be used to innovate new product and service development ideas and understand how diverse sub-firms can collaborate to optimize the operation process in a cost effective way.

In general, there are five prime benefits of BD analytics:

- Increases visibility by making related data more accessible.
- Facilitates performance improvements and variability exposure by collecting accurate performance data.
- Helps in better meeting the actual need of customers by segmenting the population.
- Complements the decision making with automated algorithms by revealing valuable insights.
- Yields new business models, principal, products, and services.

One of the most important applications of BD analytics is knowledge creation, new management principles cultivation, and the economy based on this.

Challenges in Big Data and Analytics

Although BD can help organizations to achieve competitive advantage over its competitors through many aspects, BD analytics still faces a variety of challenges (Assunção et al., 2015). The main challenges of BD analytics includes lack of intelligent BD sources, lack of scalable real time analytics capabilities, the availability of sufficient network resources for running applications, the demand in necessary expansion for peer-to-peer networks, the concerns about data privacy and information security regulations, the problems with data integration and fragmented data and lack of availability of cost effective storage subsystem of high performance (Ahmad & Quadri, 2015; Wang & Alexander, 2015). Also, the requirements of expensive software and huge computational infrastructure to do the analysis cause issues in the implementation of BD analytics for BI (Assunção et al., 2015). Figure 6.3 provides a conceptual classification of BD challenges.

Data privacy and security remains a top challenge in BD and BD analytics. The storage of high volume of data from a wide variety of sources becomes a target for hackers hence the compliance to regulatory requirements, especially laws that governs and protects data becomes an important issue. Since BD analytics is still in its infancy, there are no clear regulations for safeguarding and protecting privacy, and which may harm the public trust on BD storage and its analytics. With BD analytics, the challenge is establishing regulations to set contractual restrictions on the exposing of data to unauthorized people, revealing of the data, restricting the copy of the data, establishing personnel background checks for those who are able to access the data, and setting contractual restriction of the use of specific projects data. The establishment of privacy regulations is the most crucial area for developments in BD for the next 5 years (Leonard, 2014).

While data security and privacy remains a challenge for BD analytics, infrastructure technology (i.e., hardware technology) that supports BD analytics also poses its own challenges in terms of computation, networking, and storage technology. Since BD comes from a variety of sources, the technology is not able to provide a single computing configuration to apply for both real time and scalable analysis. Available network technology to support high bandwidth utilization by BD limits its capability to support real-time applications for BD analytics. There is no well-established rule to predict the growth in storage capacity of magnetic drives (Ahmad & Quadri, 2015; See Figure 6.4).

The storing of BD is only a part of BD analytics. Special techniques are required to analyze BD and this requires special software and specialized technical data analysts who consolidate BD from different sources to be processed and analyzed by softwares that uses algorithms for analyzing the data. Because of the complexity of BD sets, it requires highly skilled data analysts who are highly paid people. In most cases because of the lack of skilled data analysts within the organization, most businesses invest in BD analytics as a service that is offered by cloud service providers.

Business Intelligence

From the beginning of civilization, 1865 to be more precise was when the term business intelligence first surfaced. Businesses, organizations and people in leadership positions have found ways to assist them in making

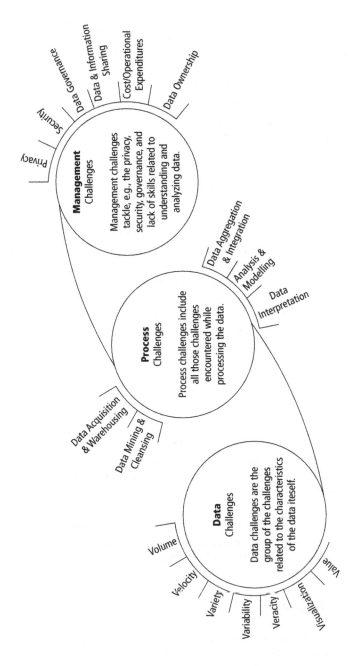

Figure 6.3 Conceptual classification of BD challenges (Sivarajah et al., 2017).

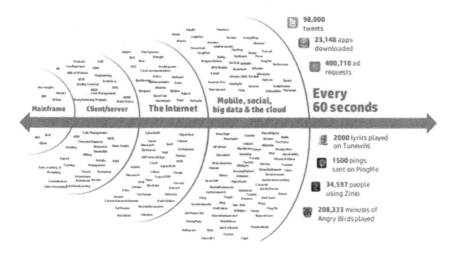

98,000 tweets

23,148 apps downloaded

400,710 ad requests

Every 60 seconds

2000 lyrics played on Tunewiki

1500 pings sent on PingMe

34,597 people using Zinio

208,333 minutes of Angry Birds played

Figure 6.4   Explosion in size of data.

intelligent decisions for their organizations. As the technology world evolved so has been the reliance of businesses on IT as the enabler. With every change in technology it has become more affordable for SMEs to make use of technologies that would otherwise be too expensive to acquire. This is particularly true with the introduction of cloud technologies.

BI is a technology-driven process for analyzing data and presenting actionable information to help executives, managers, and other corporate end users make informed business decisions. The BI objective is to provide high quality information for managerial decision-making (Negash, 2003).

BI requires analysts to deal with both structured and semi-structured data. Figure 6.5 shows the variety of information inputs available to provide the intelligence needed in decision-making.

From Figure 6.5, where OLAP = On-Line Analytic Processing, DW = Data Warehouse, DM = Data Mining, EIS = Executive Information Systems, and ERP = Enterprise Requirement Planning.

With BI, business success is realized through rapid, easy access to actionable information. This access, in turn, is best achieved through timely and accurate insight into business conditions and customers, finances and markets. Successful BI brings greater profitability, the true indicator of business success. And success is never an accident; companies achieve it when they do the following:

- make better decisions with greater speed and confidence;
- streamline operations;
- shorten their product development cycles;

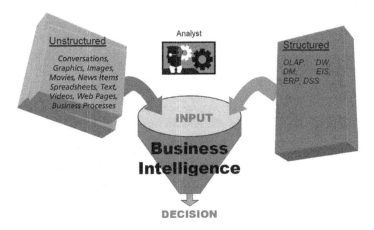

Figure 6.5 BI, input, and output process.

- maximize value from existing product lines and anticipate new opportunities; and
- create better, more focused marketing as well as improved relationships with customers and suppliers alike.

Big Data Analytics and Business Intelligence

Business Intelligence to put it in the simplest terms is making data driven decisions. It includes the generation, aggregation, analysis, and visualization of data to inform and facilitate business management and strategizing. BI goes beyond the data to include what business leaders actually do with the insights they glean from it. BI therefore is not strictly technological; it involves the processes and procedures that support data collection, sharing, and reporting, all in the service of making better decisions.

Data analytics helps make predictions that will help you in the future. It focuses on algorithms to determine relationships between data offering insights and also predictive capability. Analytics breaks down the data, assesses the trends over time, and compares one measurement to another in the process to provide insights and predictive capability. Therefore, if BI is described as the decision-making time then data analytics is the investigative period leading up to the final decision. Analytics helps the business to ask the questions they did not know they had to ask before. This is especially in dealing with unstructured data. This is usually a result of having quite a substantial amount of data. Data analytics therefore uncovers trends, customer preferences, hidden patterns, and correlations which is critical in transforming businesses.

Big Data Analytics & Business Intelligence

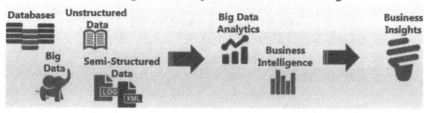

Figure 6.6 Big data analytics and business intelligence.

A combination of data analytics with BI can offer valuable insights from a wide range of data sources to provide a comprehensive view of the business and the market (see Figure 6.6).

Benefits and Challenges

There are many reasons why organizations adopt BI and analytics tools, and many ways these solutions are put to work to benefit the organization. All projects, however, have the common goal to use BI software to turn data into insights and action. As the primary competitive advantage, BI should deliver an increase in the understanding of the forces shaping markets and businesses, and help companies to act on that knowledge. Ultimately, the hope is to be able to outsmart and out-deliver competitors, while proactively addressing customer needs.

Listed below are a list of challenges and benefits that others have come up with after conducting their own research on the challenges and benefits for BI. The data is extracted from BI-Survey.com who carry out comparisons on BI tools, and also does research on BI implementation benefits, challenges, and its adoption.

The team will also be basing their findings from the survey to confirm whether the lists below is also valid for developing countries like Fiji or not.

Benefits of BI. From a survey that was carried out by BI-Survey.com on 2600 BI users. The 10 benefits listed were presented to the BI users to provide insight on the reality of how businesses deal with BI on the ground.

1. Faster reporting, analysis or planning
2. More accurate reporting, analysis or planning
3. Better business decisions
4. Improved data quality
5. Improved employee satisfaction
6. Improved operational efficiency
7. Improved customer satisfaction

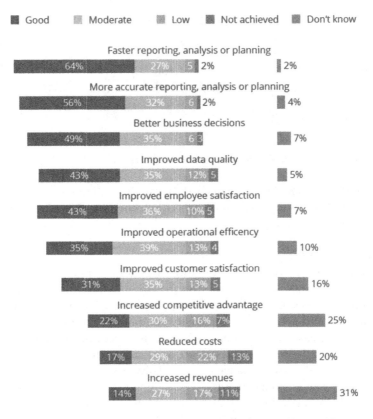

To what level have you achieved the following benefits with BI? (n = 2,618)

Figure 6.7 Top 10 BI benefits.

8. Increased competitive advantage
9. Reduced costs
10. Increased revenues

Of the above 10 benefits, Figure 6.7 shows the result in percentages.

Challenges in BI.   There is great value in well-deployed BI solutions, and they require significant effort to realize this value. Deriving information that can drive action to affect change on organizational performance is an ongoing challenge, as well as enabling that action. That, on top of the fact that 70%–80% of BI projects fail (according to Gartner), is encouraging organizations to look for a better way.

In order to succeed in a BI initiative, organizations should focus on these challenges listed:

1. *Stakeholders:* BI enhances decision-making for the whole organization. By understanding the needs of a wide range of stakeholders, addressing stakeholder needs, skills, and goals is key to implementing BI successfully.
2. *Organizational Culture:* Your culture must support fact-based decision-making, otherwise BI adoption will be difficult. All organizations are unique. You need to leverage your culture to support BI.
3. *Technologies:* Individual departments should not be run like separate businesses, otherwise each will pursue its own technology policy leading to a mixture of standards in the organization. Mixed tools and poorly integrated technology infrastructure leads to a high total cost of ownership (TCO).
4. *Strategy:* BI initiatives should support business strategy but different stakeholders with different BI needs sometimes start independent, tactical BI projects. You must align all stakeholders under one strategy then execute it!
5. *Data:* The difficulty of accurate data collection is frequently underestimated. You need time, resources, and effort to identify and map data. More effort is needed to ensure data is used consistently across the organization.
6. *Processes:* Clear and agreed-upon rules and processes ensure effective adoption of BI. Processes should be changeable and measurable. To be repeatable and adaptable. The only business not changing is one that has closed. The key to successful processes is managing people.

Past Research

There has been past research done on critical success factors (CSF) of BI. Olszak and Ziemba (2012) who divided the CSF into the three main categories and conclude that these factors were critical in the successful implementation of a BI initiative:

1. *Organization:* clear business vision and plan, support from senior management, and competent BI project manager (leadership)
2. *Process:* change management, well defined a business problem, and processes
3. *Technology:* data quality and BI flexibility and responsiveness on users' requirements

Scholz et al. (2010) also performed research on benefits and challenges of BI adoption for SMEs. And their conclusion from the study is that improvements in data support, decision support, and savings (e.g., costs, personnel) were identified as general BI benefit factors and the BI challenges are related to usage, solution and data quality, and interfaces.

Hočevar and Jaklič (2010) looked at business intelligent systems as an investment and highlighted the fact that when evaluating investments in information technology, the effects are not seen directly in higher sales figures, profits, and so on. And therefore as a result, the justification of investments in information technology in general and which is especially the case in BI is still a complicated topic. Hence when evaluating investment in BI, the specifics must be taken into account such as the fact that BI aides in decision-making and management. It is due to this that the investment in BI is often very complex and difficult to measure. The specifics may range from faster and easier access to information for decision-making to improved public relations and a better reputation for the company in the eyes of the business partners which is a dimension which is largely very difficult to evaluate. In this study it was also concluded that for BI it is critical that the investment help the company achieve its strategic objectives. And when the "criteria regarding the complexity of use" is met, that is, the user's education and training and the time needed for executing individual tasks are fulfilled, the users are mostly satisfied with the ease of use of the BI solution and how intuitive the user interface is.

Finally, Schlesinger and Rahman (2016) also concluded on the five challenges below for BI in the context of organizational, process and technology dimension. Defining business goals and limited funding under organizational, lack of expertise and training and user acceptance under process and data management under technology.

STATEMENT OF THE PROBLEM

The focus of our research is to identify local organizations that are using BD analytics/data analytics for BI purposes for their businesses and identify the challenges that they face.

Although BD analytics/data analytics is still new to the local organizations, some may have already implemented some sort of process for data analytics to assist in planning and decision-making. It is assumed that the majority of the large businesses in Fiji already have an enormous amount of data they may have analyzed with BI tools for reporting and business planning purposes.

We will be sending out questionnaires to local organizations to determine these basic questions:

- Have they realized the importance of business intelligence in making informed business decisions?

- What triggered them to reach the decision to look into data analytics and business intelligence?
- Do some organizations also face the challenges of having BD and having to do BD analytics?
- Was the decision to implement business intelligence pushed from management?
- Is business intelligence across the organization?
- If not, how far have they gone with the process of implementation?
- What was their most challenging phase?

Research Questions/Hypothesis

For the purpose of this research, we will be looking to answer the following research questions:

- Are the local organizations utilizing some forms of data analytics and business intelligence for their information management for making business decisions?
- What are the main challenges faced by the local organizations with regards to BD analytics for information management and business intelligence?
- Are the challenges faced by the local organizations of different fields similar or different during the course of implementing BD analytics for their information management and business intelligence?

On reading articles on data analytics and BI, and doing the research it was noted that there has been a lot of research done on what data analytics is and the technologies surrounding it but there is hardly any research on the adoption and use of BD and analytics in developing countries like Fiji where one of the major things to take into consideration is budgetary restrictions.

This chapter will prove useful to organizations in developing countries like Fiji who are still in the initial stages of BI to get an insight on things that can prove challenging during the process and for them to focus on it more.

RESEARCH METHODOLOGY

The team will be doing research on local organizations in Fiji to gauge the realization, adoption, and use of BI in the Pacific and for a developing country. We will also try to compare and contrast the benefits and challenges that the organizations face during the implementation of BI with the benefits and challenges that other countries face which was evident in the research by BI-Survey.com.

The team has initially written a literature review on BD, BD analytics and BI to allow the reader to understand the relationship between the three technologies. This is followed by a literature review of benefits and challenges faced by organizations in other countries and finally a literature review on similar past research in the area of the benefits and challenges of BI as well the CSF for BI initiatives.

The team has prepared a set of 30 questions and has sent it out to a number of IT employees in local organizations. The results of this survey will be analyzed using the decision tree algorithm to validate the findings and we will also be using Gartner's BI maturity model to gauge how mature the adoption and usage of BI is in Fiji. Figure 6.8 shows a model that will be used in this research.

From the responses to the survey and using the Gartner's BI model above, it is clear that most of the organizations in Fiji fall under the "Level 3: Standards" category where the initiative is championed top–down and the organizations already have teams spread across the organization for their BI initiatives and strategy.

The research is a qualitative research based on internet information as well as the responses from the survey questions. The team used WEKA to analyze the answers and gain insights from them. WEKA was also used to construct decision trees from the survey answers.

Level 1: Unaware	Level 2: Opportunistic	Level 3: Standards	Level 4: Enterprise	Level 5: Transformative
Spreadsheet and information anarchy One-off report requests Appoint governance sponsor	Inconsistent data and stovepiped systems Limited users Document-hidden cost of silos	Business executives become BI champions Technology standards start to emerge Projects cross business processes BICC started	Sophisticated program management Deploy an enterprise metrics framework Proactively research new methods, technologies BICC evolves to ACE	Business-strategy-driven performance culture Outside-in perspective CAO/CDO roles well-established Driving enterprise and industry transformation

Figure 6.8   Gartner's BI maturity model.

RESULTS/FINDINGS

The survey was filled by 20 IT staff in different local organizations. The analysis of the survey was done in three parts. The survey was made up of a total of 30 questions and it contained a mix of

- *multiple choice questions (21 questions)*—where the responses were restricted to a limited choices;
- *multiple answer questions (8 questions)*—where the respondents could choose a number of suggested answers; and
- *one text question*—where the respondents were asked to give their advice for anyone who is currently facing challenges or is intending to embark on their journey towards a BI organization.

The team also made use of the WEKA software for analysis purposes to try and create a decision tree from the data. All the questions with restricted options were able to input into WEKA unfortunately two questions which had multiple levels of answering were not input into the WEKA software simply due to our not being able to find a way to enter all the data into WEKA without errors. This was mainly due to the fact that WEKA is pretty new to the team.

The analysis below will be divided into two main parts where the first section is the analysis of the individual survey question responses and the second section is the analysis with regards to the input done on WEKA and the results and rules that were provided by the data mining software.

Analysis of Individual Questions

Question 1: 20 Respondents
Which of the following best describes your current job level?

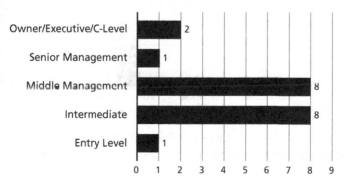

The majority of the respondents to our survey were in intermediate to mid-level management. This showed that they were more likely to be aware of the organizational changes happening within their respective organizations.

Question 2: 20 Respondents

How do you rate your individual proficiency with BI and analytics?

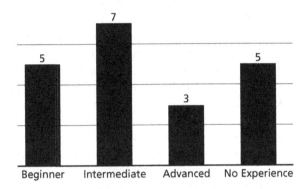

In the second question majority of the respondents rated themselves as having intermediate expertise level in BI and analytics. This also clearly showed that BI & analytics is also starting to make waves in a developing country like Fiji hence organizations are spending time to research and study about it.

Question 3: 20 Respondents

What is your understanding of the term business intelligence?

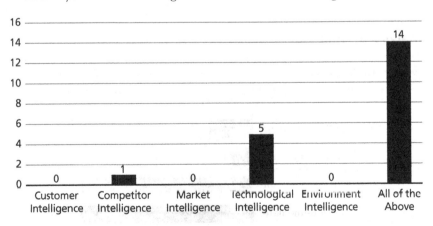

From the responses for Question 3 it was also evident that the driving team for the BI initiative was IT. This is also seen as a challenge since BI and analytics is supposed to be a top–down driven initiative and also implemented organization-wide in order for the benefits of it to be fully realized.

Question 4: 14 Respondents

According to you, what is the overall maturity level of your organization's efforts with BI and analytics initiatives?

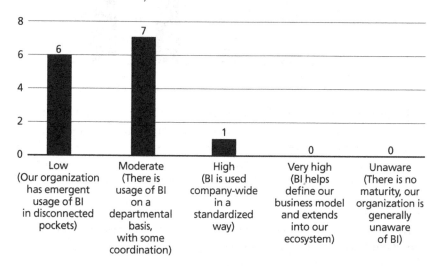

Note that from Question 4 onwards the responses have dropped below the 20 initial number. This may be because those who chose not to answer are not aware of the progress of the BI initiative in their organizations. This could also have been due to an oversight on the research team's part which is to place an abbreviation or an explanation of some words used within the survey. It was interesting to note however that a respondent considered his/her organization to have a "high," that is, company-wide BI initiative. From the responses to this question, it is also evident that even though the realization may be there for the benefits of BI & analytics, there are very few who have implemented information management solutions that have fully removed silos within the local organizations. In developing countries like Fiji, this could be due to cost. This is also a question posed to the respondents later on within the survey.

Question 5: 19 respondents

How would you rate the importance of improving your BD analytics capabilities for your organization?

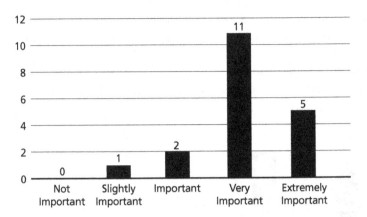

The responses to Question 5 evidently shows that in most organizations, BD/data analytics capabilities are ranked very important. It is also interesting to note that even though some organizations, that is, five respondents consider a BI initiative extremely important or even critical to the survival of the business, the majority didn't think it was that critical.

Question 6: 14 Respondents

Which of the following best describes the purpose of your organization's business intelligence initiative? (Select all that apply)

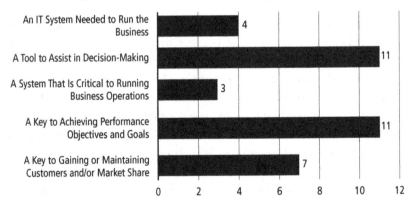

From the responses to Question 6, it was evident most organizations still do not understand the BI initiative in its entirety. The responses showed that the BI initiative is still seen as just an IT system. The realization of the magnitude of the change that needs to be met for the BI initiative to be considered successful and for the satisfaction of all the BI purposes above is still not realized in Fiji. It is to be noted that BI is a continuous process that should aim to achieve all of the purposes listed.

Again for this question, only 14 responses were made on the survey and the reasons could still be similar to the reasons stated in the questions above.

Question 7: 14 Respondents

What are the objectives of business intelligence initiatives in your organization? (Select all that apply)

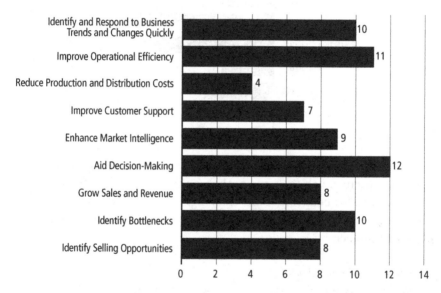

Objectives can be seen as the tasks to be taken to achieve a goal in working towards a BI purpose as seen in Question 6. The responses to this particular question shows that in the least, the organizations in Fiji know what they want to achieve from their BI initiatives. The top choices prove this.

Question 8: 14 Respondents

Which of the following are included in your business intelligence landscape and strategy for next year? (Select all that apply)

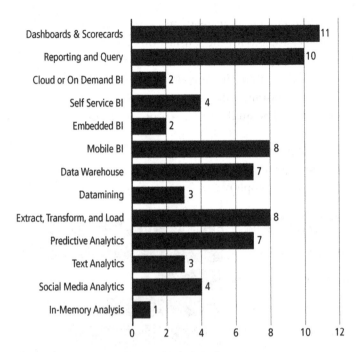

From the responses to Question 8, it is also clear that the local organizations want pretty much the same as their overseas counterparts from their BI initiative. This could be more challenging for the local organizations however due to the budgetary requirements for the implementation of a proper BI project.

Question 9: 14 Respondents

Does your organization have a group of business, IT, and information analysts working together to define BI strategy and requirements [e.g., a business intelligence competency center (BICC) or center of excellence (CoE)]?

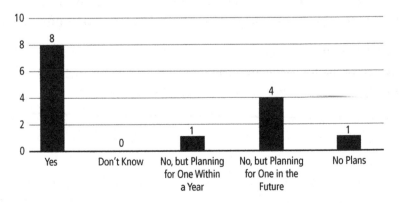

The responses to Question 9 shows that the local organization is indeed taking the BI initiative seriously. The fact that there is a team present within the organization to drive the BI strategy shows that the local organizations are working towards an organization wide BI implementation which is how it should be.

Question 10: 19 Respondents
How satisfied are you with your data management processes?

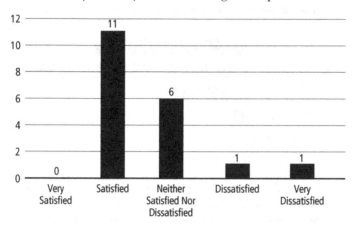

From the responses to Question 10, most of them are satisfied with the current data management processes. It seems evident that organizations in Fiji still haven't taken into account the processing and analysis of unstructured data. This is also evident in the other questions covered later on.

Also, there were some respondents who were neither satisfied nor dissatisfied with their current data management processes within their organizations.

Question 11: 19 respondents
Does your IT department currently have a formal strategy for dealing with data analytics and business intelligence?

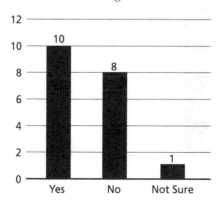

It was also pleasing to note that the local organizations already have formal strategies for their analytics and BI initiatives. Even though the number of those that do not have it followed closely behind but they may still be in the initial stages of implementing their BI initiatives.

Question 12: 19 Respondents

In terms of your core business, what data sources are you tasked to analyze for business intelligence? Choose all that apply

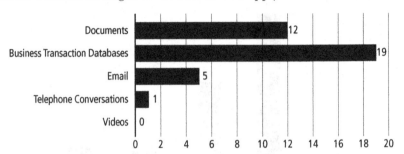

It should be noted from the responses from Question 12 that local organizations are still very new to processing and analyzing unstructured data such as email, telephone conversations, and videos. They are still used to the traditional analysis and processing of structured data from databases and documents.

From the previous responses with regards to the objectives of the BI initiatives, this will definitely change in the near future.

Question 13: 14 Respondents

What percentage of users in your organization have the tools and know-how to analyze data in a self-service BI environment, without close IT involvement?

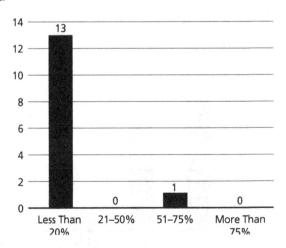

From the responses to this question, there still is a lot of work to be carried out in the organizations to create awareness to non-IT users on BI and its benefit to everyone. There will also need to be a look at tools that may be complicated to set up but simple for end-users to use for BI so that there is not a heavy requirement on training for the BI solution post implementation. Usually these tools follow a similar look and feel to everyday applications that users are already familiar with such as social media applications, mobile application, and so forth.

Question 14: 18 Respondents

For the data sources you are asked to analyze, please rank them in order of the top sources of data for your organization—"1" being the top most and "n/a" for not applicable.

Rank	Choice	Distribution	Score	Times Ranked
1.	Business Transaction Database		78	18
2.	Documents		66	17
3.	Email		49	16
4.	Telephone conversations		34	16
5.	Videos		19	17
		Lowest ▬▬▬▬▬▬▬ Highest		

From the responses to Question 14 it is evident that local organizations are only currently processing and analyzing structured data mostly. From the responses, about 72% of the respondents ranked business transaction database as the most likely source of data for data processing and analysis and 69% ranked documents second. Email came in a close third at a ranking of 75% for the third most likely source of data for data processing and analytics. The least source of data is video which was ranked last 82% of the time. From the distribution of the data using standard deviation and mean, again, databases scored 78 and followed closely by documents. The least score was videos.

This will most likely not change in the near future locally as organizations are still in the process of implementing their digital strategy with BI.

Question 15: 18 Respondents

Are you currently processing and analyzing unstructured data sources to get new insights?

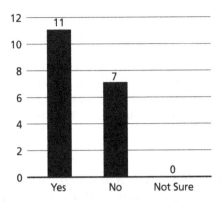

The responses to Question 15 reflects the fact that local organizations are already beginning to analyze unstructured data to get new insights and still a significant percentage of the dataset still don't.

Question 16: 18 Respondents

Will you be tasked to process and analyze unstructured data sources in the next 12 to 18 months?

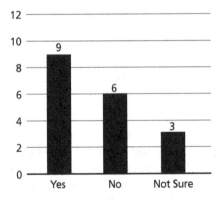

It is interesting to note that even though local organizations have mentioned analyzing data such as email, videos, and phone conversations, still quite a significant percentage of the dataset do not believe they will be analyzing unstructured data in the next 12 to 18 months. This may be due to the lack of understanding the difference between structured and unstructured data. Again this could have been avoided if the survey had a table of abbreviations and definitions.

Question 17: 16 Respondents

What percentage of your organization's current data analytics is done in real time, and what percentage is done in batch processing?

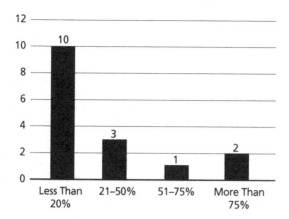

From the responses to Question 17, it is clear that most of the current analytics done in local organizations are still done manually with 10 respondents placing their level of automation at <20%. Also from the responses, two organizations have more than 75% automation being used currently within their organization.

Question 18: 15 Respondents

What percentage do you predict will be your organization's percentage of real time vs. batch data analytics in 2020?

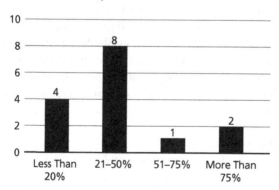

From the responses from Question 18 it can be seen that even though the local organizations are moving it slowly, the majority have a projection of achieving 21%–50% automation of analytics to be achieved by the year 2020.

Question 19: 12 Respondents

Which business intelligence tool(s) have you used or heard of? (Select all that apply)

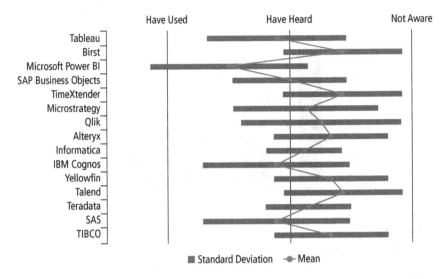

NB. A local organization also uses STATA which is a software for statistics and data science.

From the above results it is noticed that local users tend to be favorable towards Microsoft Power BI. 58% of the respondents said they have used it already while 25% have heard of the software and 17% are not aware of its existence. Organization should not let themselves be dictated into using a certain tool for BI. The BI tool should be a fit for the organization as a whole and not just a section of it. Also from the feedback, there is just a small level of familiarity with the tools available out there. Since developing countries have budgetary issues and given that BI projects, in order for them to be implemented properly, it would be recommended that organizations take the time to research on the appropriate tools for BI that suit their business needs.

Question 20: 11 Respondents

Please provide the frequency of your tool(s) usage.

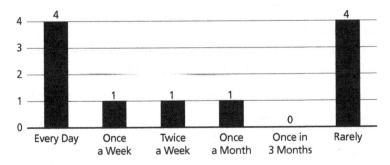

From the above stats of the responses to Question 20, it is clear that local organizations still do not have BI instilled within their daily operations. It can be that local organizations are still on their way to realising the full potential of BI. It is also to be taken into account that BI implementation is an expensive investment that may take some time to realise its return.

Question 21: 11 Respondents
Do you import data from multiple systems and create a separate database or warehouse for analysis?

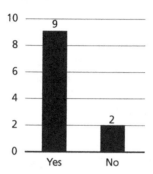

From the responses to Question 21 it is also evident that organizations are also using the idea of data marts to separately store and analyze data from different systems.

Question 22: 15 Respondents
From the BD challenges listed below, please rank the first three in order of significance to you, first being the most significant.

Rank	Choice	Distribution	Score	Times Ranked
1.	Data Governance / Policy		81	13
2.	Data Infrastructure		71	14
3.	Data Integration		68	15
4.	Data Compliance / Regulation		66	13
5.	Data Visualization		56	14
6.	Data Growth		54	14
7.	Data Variety		47	14
8.	Data Velocity		37	13

Lowest ▮▮▮▮▮▮ Highest

From the list of BD challenges, 33% of the respondents rated "data governance/policy" as the top most significant challenge that they face and a score of 81 from the data distribution. Coming in at a close second is "data visualization" which has 33% of the respondents voting it second most significant challenge with a score of 56 from the data distribution. It is interesting to see data governance topping the list as this is also a challenge to organizations in other parts of the world. This also highlights the lack of a governing body locally which plays a significant role in organizations being able to follow accepted standards and proper governing when it comes to their data.

Question 23: 15 Respondents
From the obstacles listed below, please rank the first three in order of priority to you, first with the highest priority.

Rank	Choice	Distribution	Score	Times Ranked
1.	Shortage of skilled Data Analyst professionals		98	15
2.	Security Concerns		93	15
3.	Data Replication capabilites		72	15
4.	Capital / Operational Expenses		68	15
5.	Unmanageable Data Rate		66	15
6.	Increased Network Bottleneck		56	15
7.	Insufficient CPU power		44	15
8.	Greater Network Latency		43	15

Lowest ▬▬▬▬▬▬▬ Highest

From the responses to the BI obstacles listed in Question 23, 47% of the respondents ranked "shortage of skilled data analyst professionals" as the top obstacle with a score of 98 taking into account the standard deviation and mean. Ranking behind that at 40% is "security concerns" and a score of 93 from the data distribution. This is also in par with the list of obstacles that other countries face. Due to the fact that the cost of storage and compute is getting really affordable, the demand for data scientists will only increase as organizations realize the criticality of knowing about their data.

Question 24: 15 Respondents
How clearly do you understand the scope of BD demands from your organization users and data analytics experts?

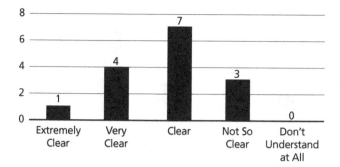

From the responses to Question 24, local organizations seem to understand clearly the scope of the requirements that will be needed when dealing with BD demands from users and data scientists.

Question 25: 15 Respondents

How interested would you be in learning more about infrastructure and software that is built for BD analytics, and how to deploy and optimize the infrastructure for performance and cost?

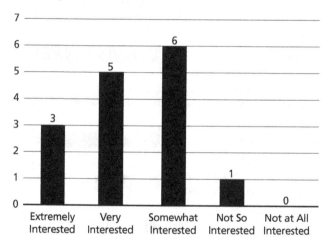

From the responses to Question 25 it is evident that local organizations are very interested in learning about the ideal environment, that is, infrastructure and software BD analytics. This will need to be taken into considerations when local organizations look to also process and analyze unstructured data and also with the advent of the Internet of things, it will be advisable to keep BD at the back of your mind when implementing analytics.

Question 26: 15 Respondents

How interested is your organization in using a third party cloud service provider (such as Amazon's Elastic MapReduce) to analyze your data sets?

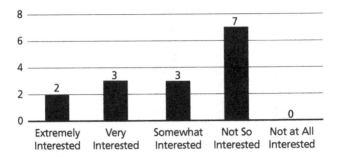

It is very interesting to note the response to Question 26 on cloud providers for BI. Seven out of the 15 respondents chose "not so interested." This can be due to the data governance issue that was highlighted in a previous question. This should be addressed so that organizations find it easier to follow guidelines and are also protected by laws if they choose to host their data with third party solutions providers.

Question 27: 15 Respondents

What are the biggest concerns and/or roadblocks in moving your data to a third party provider for processing, analytics and storage? Choose all that apply.

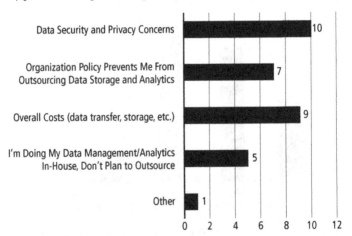

From the responses to Question 27, it is again obvious that most organizations are more concerned with the privacy of their data and its security when it comes to using the cloud solutions. This should be addressed by the local government of the day to set up a governance body to create standards, and so on, that can be followed and enacted into law in Fiji. This may also be an issue in other development countries but will be confirmed if a study is done of a comparison of a few developing country strategies towards BI and the cloud.

Question 28: 10 Responses

How do you rate your organization's current business intelligence tool(s) in the following characteristics?

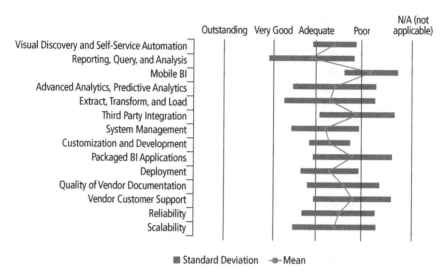

Standard Deviation ●Mean

From the responses to Question 28, it is also clear that most of the organizations think that their current BI tools are "adequate." There was an obvious lack of recognition given to "Mobile BI" along with "advanced and predictive analytics." This will need to change in the future if organizations are to get the most out of social-media and mobile platforms. Also in future the need to also analyze and process semi-structured and unstructured data will grow.

Question 29: 14 Responses

What standard for BD analytics are you most interested in having the industry address? Choose all that apply.

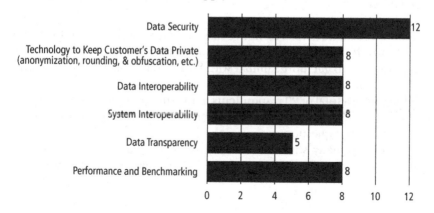

Again as shown from previous responses to previous questions, the most significant concern to local organizations is "data security." The other standards ranked a close second however with all of them getting a response of 8 except for "data transparency" which was selected by 5 respondents as also concerning.

Question 30: 8 Responses

In your experience evaluating, planning and/or implementing data analytics and business intelligence projects in your IT environment, what is the single most important piece of advice you could offer to another IT manager just starting the process?

- Set realistic goals based on current capabilities.
- Need to standardize data with a good governance first. To have a good data strategic plan for the future.
- Proper/detailed project planning and requirements gathering.
- Understand the real needs for your organization.
- Understand the different components, bridge gap with non-technical stakeholders, manage expectations.
- Explore and identify solution that meets business process and requirement. Streamline business process if need be. Prepare proposal for board of directors endorsement and recommendation inclusive of planning and implementation phase.
- First understand the nature of the organization and its need then create your data strategy to either consolidate and streamline data repositories and review the data needs of your current reporting. Establish data stewards or champions to create awareness of the data security and to ascertain the usefulness of the data to that particular department. Have process improvement reviews with the business so that everyone is on the same understanding as well as continuously conduct research for data insights to assist in decision-making or monitoring.
- In my opinion, the most critical factor is proper requirement gathering and analysis in consultations with the key stakeholders.

Data Analysis Using WEKA and the Decision Tree (J48) Construct

Out of the 30 questions from the survey, six questions were not entered into WEKA. If this research were to be worked on in the future, a requirement would be to get more familiar with WEKA to be able to enter any kind of dataset into the software.

There were a total of 20 respondents to the survey but for the WEKA data we used only 15 of the responses and removed five which had more than 50% unanswered questions.

One of the many shortfalls for the research team is the formulating and distribution of the surveys *before* deciding how the responses will be analyzed. Due to this, we were not able to get an accurate decision tree using WEKA based on all the data that was input.

Decision Tree With Only Questions With Set Answers

However, we were able to construct the decision tree below which is from the dataset of questions with a static set of answers. This is from 15 respondents and 24 questions of the survey.

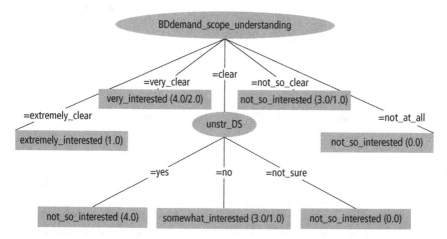

From the above decision tree it can be concluded that when the respondent had a clear understanding of the scope of BD demands, there was more of a chance that they will be processing and analyzing unstructured data sources and were therefore not so interested to learn more about the infrastructure and software for BD.

However, also when the respondent has a good understanding of the scope of BD but they are not analyzing and processing unstructured data, they are somewhat interested in learning more about the infrastructure and software for BD.

And lastly, when the respondent has a good understanding of the scope of BD but they are not sure whether they are currently analyzing and processing unstructured data, they are not so interested in learning more about the infrastructure and software for BD.

Decision Tree After Adding 3 Dynamic Questions Into the Dataset

After adding the data for purpose, objectives, and strategies of BI, below is the decision tree.

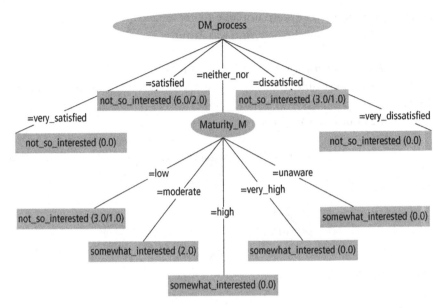

From the above decision tree, it can be concluded that when the respondent is neither satisfied nor dissatisfied with their organization's data management process, and the organization's BI maturity level is low, he is more likely to be not so interested in learning about the infrastructure and software for BD.

However, if he is neither satisfied nor dissatisfied with the data management process and the organization's BI maturity level is moderate, they are somewhat interested in learning more about the infrastructure and software for BD.

Decision Tree After Adding All the Answers From Survey Except the Answer for Advice i.e., Q30

The decision tree's accuracy (Figure 6.9) was 50% and since we only considered 14 out of the 20 respondents, the final decision tree was for only seven results. This is also due to the fact that the team failed to tailor make the survey questionnaires according to how we planned to analyze it.

From the decision tree (Figure 6.9), it is to be noted that "purpose" is a dynamic attribute that has the possibility of having the 5 answers below. The respondents could have selected 1 of the 5 or all of the 5 according to the BI purpose that was fit for their business:

1. IT system needed to run the business
2. Tool to assist in decision-making
3. System critical to running business operations

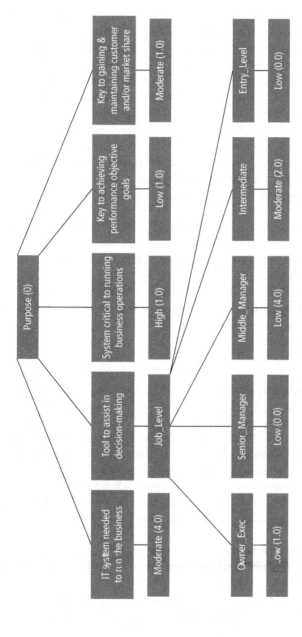

Figure 6.9 Decision tree after adding all the answers from survey except the answer for advice.

4. Key to achieving performance objective goals
5. Key to gaining and maintaining customer and/or market share

Therefore, it can be concluded that for respondents that regarded their organization's BI maturity level at moderate, most of them regarded their BI purpose as not just an "IT system needed to run the business" but also a "key to gaining and maintaining customer and/or market share."

From the decision tree it can also be noted that all of the respondents viewed one of their BI purpose as an "IT system needed to run the business" and of all these respondents, four of them were middle managers and regarded their organization maturity level as a "low" and two which were intermediate level staff regarded their organization maturity level as "moderate" while the one who was at the owner/executive level, regarded his/her organization's maturity level also at a "low."

Note the descriptions of the different maturity levels:

- *Low:* Our organization has emergent usage of BI in disconnected pockets.
- *Moderate:* There is usage of BI on a departmental basis, with some coordination.
- *High:* BI is used company-wide in a standardized way.
- *Very high:* BI helps define our business model and extends into our ecosystem.
- *Unaware:* There is no maturity, our organization is generally unaware of BI.

Also something to note on the ratings that the respondents placed on the organizations they represent is that it may not truly reflect the current BI status within their organization. Hence, it is more advisable to rate the BI maturity level for the organizations based on the overall survey answers and not just based on the particular rating that they placed for the single survey question on what they think their organization's BI maturity level is. It is to be also noted that this was the approach taken by the research team in concluding that most of the organizations in Fiji were at Level 3 of BI maturity according to the Gartner maturity model.

Research Questions and Answers

- Are the local organizations utilizing some forms of data analytics and business intelligence for their information management for making business decisions?

  From the survey carried out, it was clear that all the respondents are currently already in the process of analyzing their data in some form or the other and they have already realized the importance of being able to interpret your data. Even though most data sources are still just from structured sources, however, the use of analytics is already present in Fiji.

- What are the main challenges faced by the local organizations with regards to BD analytics for information management and business intelligence?

  From the survey the three primary challenges faced by local organizations is data governance, security, and the shortage of data scientist professionals.

- Are the challenges faced by the local organizations of different fields similar or different during the course of implementing BD analytics for their information management and business intelligence?

  Most of the challenges faced by local organizations are similar across the board regardless of the field that the organization is associated with.

- Are the challenges similar or different to their counterparts in other countries?

  Most of the challenges faced by local organizations are indeed similar to their counterparts in developed countries with one challenge really standing out for local organizations which is data governance. This puts out a challenge to government to setup a governing body for IT standards in Fiji.

DISCUSSIONS

For this research, we are expecting to have a better understanding of BD analytics with BI and the role that it plays in not only managerial and executive decision making but also other aspects of information technology such as monitoring and trending.

There may be some differences in the benefits and challenges made due to the lower revenues earned by organizations in developing countries. There may also be times when the move towards BI is not favorable as this will remove all manual processing thus will also remove corruption.

Post Research

From the analysis of the survey and also using Gartner's BI maturity model, most of the organizations in Fiji seem to fall in the third level of maturity as shown in Figure 6.10.

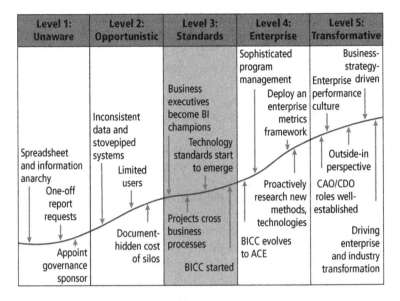

Figure 6.10 Maturity level for FIJI.

It can also be seen from the results of the survey that most local organizations are still not aware of the full capability of BI if it is implemented correctly within the organization. Most organizations still only analyze and process data from structured data sources but it will quickly change in the future in order for them to have a competitive edge.

Most organizations are still wary of the cloud option with regards to security and privacy and where their data will reside. Also there is a high concern for the lack of skilled data scientists who are able to interpret the data and map them to business processes. It is also interesting to note that most of the organizations have minimal level of automation embedded into their BI implementation.

It can also be seen from this research that most local organizations are lingering on the third level of their BI initiative as per the Gartner model. There can be some research done into the details of why the organizations are not moving forward with their BI adoption. It may well be because of the cost that it would take to truly invest in a BI solution that will provide real time updates for effective decision making, ease of use for end-users so the organization wide initiative is also reflected on the BI implementation where the solution needs minimal supervision from IT to use as well as a solution that will enable the organization to also analyze and process data from unstructured data-sources such as emails, web-site activities, phone calls, videos, and so on. Due to the fact that most of the organizations are stagnant on their BI adoption it can be seen that most of them have also not fully realized the benefits of BI such as automation and real time processing and analysis for decision-making.

This research chapter aimed to answer the below questions:

Q1: *Has the realization of the importance of BI reached Fiji and are there implementations of some sort of BI taking place?*

From the answers to the survey, BI is being carried out in local organizations in some form to assist in better understanding data but it is currently mostly on the analysis of structured data.

Q2: *Is the adoption of BI in the organizations across the organization or is it seen more as an IT project?*

From the answers to the survey it is clear that most of the organizations have committees for BI that is setup with staff members from across the organization which means that yes, BI is across the organization.

Q3: *Are the benefits and challenges faced similar as compared to their international counterparts in the same field?*

From the responses from the survey, it is evident that local organizations and therefore organizations within a developing country and in the Pacific have similar benefits and challenges that their international colleagues face.

CONCLUSION

This research was mainly to find out whether BI is also prevalent in a developing country like Fiji considering the fact that an investment in a BI solution can prove very costly and time consuming and also very difficult to gauge its success. It was also done to find out the challenges that local organizations that are currently utilizing analytics for some sort of BI are facing currently as well as the challenges they face in moving forward with their BI adoption.

It is to be noted that most of the local organizations still have not fully realized the benefits of BI. From the responses from the survey, most of the respondents responded with "poor" or "adequate" when asked about the current capabilities of the BI solution. Some of the respondents still viewed BI as an IT project instead of an organization wide one but in this space it was interesting and pleasing to note that most of the responses realized that BI was more than just an IT project and also had teams within the organization from the different sections who were championing the BI initiative.

It can also be highlighted in the results that there isn't a governing body in Fiji to implement standards for IT that will allow organizations to incorporate things legally—things such as a cloud solution. Most organizations were not interested in a third party solution which could also be due to the lack of a governing body in Fiji. The discussion about data sovereignty and ownership of the data if it were to be hosted outside of Fiji came into question as a concern as well.

Finally the findings for this research can also be tied back to the challenges that were covered by the researches highlighted in the literature review for similar work. The findings also highlighted the fact that for a BI initiative to succeed, that is, be realized within an organization it has to

- have the support of the management,
- be an investment that will be measured by improved decision-making and ease-of-use instead,
- need to have the appropriate skill and people to be able to use the tool effectively,
- be able to meet the user expectations for ease-of-use and effective turn-around time, and
- be a continuous process.

RECOMMENDATIONS AND FURTHER RESEARCH OPPORTUNITIES

This research contributes to the research community in the Pacific in helping them understand the challenges that local organizations face. This is likely similar to other Pacific Islands as well as other developing countries but this in itself can be cause for further research on the adoption and usage of BI in developing countries.

Flaws in Our Research

- The questionnaires were sent out to organizations before we had the chance to decide on how we were going to analyze the data.
- Due to the first point, we tried to fit the data into the chosen analysis option, that is, decision tree.
- The survey was possibly too long and some of the respondents were too bored to answer all the questions. Shorten the survey to only the required questions.
- Not all the questions were mandatory. Once the survey is of an agreeable length and with only the required questions to achieve what is required of the survey, make all the questions mandatory.

- Have a broader dataset. The survey was sent to 20 respondents but it had two or three who worked at the same place.
- Have a control variable such as the respondent has to be in management to allow for better assumptions to be made for other organizations based on the research.
- Have a table on abbreviations as well as a glossary so respondents are able to understand the technical jargons used within the survey.

Further Research Opportunities

- If the team does get to have another chance to re-do this research, we would tailor it to make the survey questions so that it can be in more correlation with the proposed analysis for the decision tree. This will allow for more room to be able to interpret the data and apply it more generally to other research papers based on rules that the decision tree will identify.
- There is also an opportunity to conduct a longitudinal study on a single organization within a developing country from the time when they are in the planning stages right up to when the BI initiative is implemented according to the organization requirements. This will assist in understanding the benefits and challenges that the organization, staff, and management faced before, during, and post-implementation.
- This research was more qualitative and was mainly based on Internet research and analysis of the survey questionnaires; it would also be interesting to gauge exactly how an organization decides that their BI initiative was a successful one.

REFERENCES

Ahmad Bhat, W., & Quadri, S. M. K. (2015). Big Data promises value: Is hardware technology taken onboard? *Industrial Management & Data Systems, 15*(9), 1577–1595. https://doi.org/10.1108/IMDS-04-2015-0160

Assuncao, M., Calheiros, R., Bianchi, S., Netto, M., & Buyya, R. (2015). Big Data computing and clouds: Trends and future directions. *Journal of Parallel and Distributed Computing, 79–80*(2015), 3–15. https://doi.org/10.1016/j.jpdc.2014.08.003

Bayrak, T. (2015). A review of business analytics: A business enabler or another passing fad. *Procedia–Social and Behavioral Sciences, 195,* 230–239. https://doi.org/10.1016/j.sbspro.2015.06.354

Chen, M., Mao, S., & Liu, Y. (2014). Big data: A survey. *Mobile Networks and Applications, 19*(2), 171–209.

Columbus, L. (2019). *BI adoption and implementation strategies in 2019* [Web blog post]. https://selecthub.com/business-intelligence/5-strategies-increasing-bi-adoption/

Flory, M. M. (2012). THE BIG KAHUNA. *Marketing Research, 24*(2), 3–3.

Fosso Wamba, S., Akter, S., Edwards, A., Chopin, G., & Gnanzou, D. (2015). How 'big data' can make big impact: Findings from a systematic review and a longitudinal case study. *International Journal of Production Economics, 165*, 234–246. https://doi.org/10.1016/j.ijpe.2014.12.031

Gandomi, A., & Haider, M. (2015). Beyond the hype: Big data concepts, methods, and analytics. *International Journal of Information Management, 35*(2), 137–144. https://doi.org/10.1016/j.ijinfomgt.2014.10.007

Hocevar, B., & Jaklic, J. (2010). Assessing benefits of business intelligence systems: A case study. *Management, 15*(1), 87–119

Kambatla, K., Kollias, G., Kumar, V., & Grama, A. (2014). Trends in big data analytics. *Journal of Parallel and Distributed Computing, 74*(7), 2561–2573. https://doi.org/10.1016/j.jpdc.2014.01.003

Labbe, M., Martinek, L., & Stedman, C. (2012). *Big data analytics.* https://search businessanalytics.techtarget.com/definition/big-data-analytics

Leonard, P. (2014). Customer data analytics: privacy settings for "Big Data" business. *International Data Privacy Law, 4*(2014), 53–68.

Negash, S. (2004). Business intelligence. *Communications of the Association for Information Systems, 13*(13), 177–195. https://doi.org/10.17705/1CAIS.01315

Olszak, C. M., & Ziemba, E. (2012). Critical success factors for implementing business intelligence systems in small and medium enterprises on the example of Upper Silesia, Poland. *Interdisciplinary Journal of Information, Knowledge, and Management, 7*(2012), 129–150. http://www.ijikm.org/Volume7/IJIKMv7p129-150Olszak634.pdf

Prescott, M. E. (2014). Big data and competitive advantage at Nielsen. *Management Decision, 52*(3), 573–601. https://doi.org/10.1108/MD-09-2013-0437

Schlesinger, P. A., & Rahman, N. (2016). Self-service business intelligence resulting in disruptive technology. *Journal of Computer Information Systems, 56*(1), 11–21.

Schomm, F., Stahl, F., & Vossen, G. (2013). Marketplaces for data: An initial survey. *SIGMOD Record, 42*(1), 15–26. https://doi.org/10.1145/2481528.2481532

Sivarajah, U., Kamal, M. M., Irani, Z., & Weerakkody, V. (2017). Critical analysis of Big Data challenges and analytical methods. *Journal of Business Research, 70*, 263–286.

Sun, Z., Sun, L., & Strang, K. (2018). Big data analytics services for enhancing business intelligence. *Journal of Computer Information Systems, 58*(2), 162–169.

Vera-Baquero, A., Palacios, R. C., Stantchev, V., & Molloy, O. (2015). *Leveraging bigdata for business process analytics.* The Learning Organization.

Wang, L., & Alexander, C.A. (2015). Big data in design and manufacturing engineering. *American journal of Engineering and Applied Sciences, 8*(2), 223–232. https://doi.org/10.3844/ajeassp.2015.223.232

CHAPTER 7

E-COMMERCE AND E-BUSINESS INNOVATIONS WITH ERP SYSTEMS

Sam Goundar
The University of the South Pacific

Irfaz Mohammed
The University of the South Pacific

Jyotika Devi
The University of the South Pacific

Jashneel Lal
The University of the South Pacific

ABSTRACT

The continuous advancements in technologies and higher accessibility to new and improved technologies are becoming the enabler and leading to digital transformations in the entire business industry and for the national economy of any country. It opens up opportunities to improve business practices and processes and offers ways to do business in a more dynamic, better, smarter,

Enterprise Systems and Technological Convergence, pages 145–156
Copyright © 2021 by Information Age Publishing
145

faster, transparent, and accountable way. It also enables businesses to explore ways to move from cash payment collection systems to cashless; electronic and digital payment systems. The reason for introducing electronic payment collection solutions is not to remove cash collection systems but to use it as a more transparent and far better option than cash. Digital or e-payment solutions (going cashless) are a very important part of e-commerce and ebusiness innovations. This chapter aims to study the literature available for electronic payment solutions with the objective to highlight the scope of Fiji's envisioned journey towards a "cashless society." This research is in alignment with the Fijian government's vision and moves towards a cashless society. Our research aims to study the current condition and situation, identify gap areas and list down all the action items on how the cashless mechanisms can be implemented at the different industry levels within the Fijian economy and what will be the major driver in Fiji's journey towards cashless. The research will be based on survey and follow-up interviews with mobile network operators as solution providers, stakeholders of the relevant industries, and most importantly with groups of people from the general public who will be impacted the most by these cashless initiative implementations.

E-commerce came into existence in the 1960s after the very first disruptive innovation of the Internet. E-commerce platforms allow electronic payment collections as an alternative to cash payment systems (Kabir et al., 2015). Since its introduction e-commerce has transformed and changed the manner in which people buy and sell goods and services and has totally changed the dynamics and structure of the entire local and global business industry. Electronic payment options for the sale of goods and services became extremely popular and an essential part of everyone's life. It brought globalization and opened doors for trade at a global level with more options for the consumers to choose from and gave access to people to the rest of the world (Choudhry, 2015).

Cashless society is achieved through the use of smart-devices and smartphones with near-field communication (NFC) capabilities which will be used to execute the transactions electronically, thus becoming a popular tool to address the negative impacts on cash usage on the national economy. A cashless society replaces notes/coins with smart and innovative digital payment systems and solutions (Worthington, 2006). Electronic payment solutions in e-commerce bring numerous benefits for both sellers and consumers in the form of tracking transactions better, saves time, saves cost, increases in trust between sellers and buyers, and payouts are done faster (Antwi et al., 2015). For example, the Fijian government was able to effectively distribute eTransport care, home care, farm care funds on the M-PAi-SA cards within a click of a button to assist all the people who were affected during the events of Tropical Cyclone Josie and Keni in April 2018.

Electronic payments which are common in Fiji are ATM transactions, use of debit/credit/master cards, through online and mobile banking and mobile money, eTransport payments, and M-PAiSA payments. In the context of Fiji, a developing nation state, cashless society implementations will bring greater benefits for economic survival and sustainability. Cashless payment mechanisms are essential at different levels of the industry for example, supermarket channels, construction, hardware channels, transportation industry including bus, shipping, taxi, licensed carrier, licensed mini buses, licensed hire, sporting events, and so on. In order, to get a better understanding and insight, understanding the current situation is extremely important as this will help in examining the gaps, and develop action plans and priorities for the future. This research therefore, will examine the readiness indicator of a cashless society in Fiji and will also look at current digital financial services particularly those provided through a mobile money platform in any urban or rural area with the help of mobile network operators. This research will also focus on alternative ways to fast track and speedup the journey towards cashless Fiji, for example, the role of government in development and implementation of new electronic payment mechanisms and solutions.

LITERATURE REVIEW

Electronic Payment System—Definition

Electronic payments are transfers of electronic value in the form of payment from the payer to the recipient through an electronic payment mechanism. The electronic payment services allows customers to access, manage their bank accounts or mobile wallet accounts and transactions (Hidayanto et al., 2015). In other words, electronic payment refers to online e-commerce transactions conducted over the Internet (Junadi, 2015).

Cashless Society Definition

Cashless society means transforming from cash to cashless or non-cash instruments and transactions (Thomas et al., 2013). Furthermore, a cashless society could be defined as one characterized by less notes/coins in circulation issued by central banks of the country (Olusola et al., 2013). Based on previously done research, a cashless society refers to the initiative to change from cash to cashless economic transactions.

Indicators of a Cashless Society

M-PESA, is a disruptive innovation which enables people to do transactions without having a bank account by just using their mobile phones.

Hughes and Lonie found within the first month, M-PESA had been recorded over 20,000 accounts in the case of Kenya, clears signs that M-PESA fills gaps in the market (Lonie, 2007).

Mobile Money Adoption in the Developing World

Mobile money ecosystems create the platform for mobile transactions and these ecosystems use a currency known as mobile money or m-money; mobile money allows consumers to store electronic value in a mobile wallet on their mobile phone. Mobile phone companies tend to be "young and fast moving," unlike the traditional banks, who are old, conservative, and slow moving (Lonie, 2007). Mobile money ecosystems now facilitate the purchase of bus tickets, groceries, prepaid airtime, and micro-insurance (Jenkins, 2008). In many countries, mobile subscribers can use mobile money for a wide range of transactions, including bill payments, domestic and international remittances, loan receipts and repayments, and payroll deposits. The identified factors that enhance or impede the adoption of mobile money are as follows. Consumers will welcome and freely use mobile money services and platforms once they start trusting the mobile money ecosystem, have been exposed to mobile phones from a young age, and encounter positive experiences with mobile money agents.

Mobile Money Payment System in Fiji

In Fiji the number of people owning mobile phones far exceeds the ones with a bank account (Cave, 2012). The mobile money platforms and services are primarily facilitated by three mobile network operators (MNO); Vodafone, Digicel, and Inkk, which collectively reach an estimated 95% of Fiji's population (Rika et al., 2015). Banks are leveraging MNOs' reach to improve their services to the rural communities and areas. The largest MNO in Fiji is Vodafone, with a share of the mobile network estimated at 88%. Vodafone's nearest competitor is Digicel, and the third mobile operator named Inkk-mobile, the lowest cost network provider that uses Vodafone Fiji's network infrastructure. In 2010, Vodafone launched Fiji's first mobile money service, known as M-PAiSA. Based on the M-PESA product in Kenya, M-PAiSA in Fiji was launched to facilitate disbursement of loans and for microfinance institutions such as SPBD to receive repayments from customers in rural and remote areas, but later evolved to include utility bill payments. M-PAiSA enables rural dwellers to receive loans (Sathye, 2014), welfare allowances (Leonard, 2011), and salary payments. Vodafone also facilitates foreign remittances in collaboration with World Remit, Home-Send, and Ria.

PROS AND CONS OF CASHLESS SOCIETY IMPLEMENTATION IN FIJI

It is important to understand the scope of cashless society in Fiji and measure the advantages and disadvantages to see whether the implementation will be beneficial and impact will be more positive than negative for Fiji.

Advantages—Positive Implications

The implementation of cashless payment systems will bring various qualitative and quantitative benefits for Fiji. Some of the benefits which the cashless society will bring for Fiji are as follows:

Quantitative Benefits

Benefits for Government

1. Cost savings in following areas:
   a. reduces incidence of theft and pilferage;
   b. manpower—going cashless will free up headcount associated with cash handling which could be redeployed; and
   c. paperless—stationary savings.
2. Time saving and greater efficiency in delivery of service
3. Quick and secure reconciliation of payments
4. Reduction in warehousing and data storage related costs

Benefits for Citizens

5. Lesser number of visits for basic services like social welfare, utility payments, and so on (cost and time savings)
6. Easier and better access (near home/village)
7. Convenience and greater access to services especially for people in the remote, rural, and island areas

Qualitative Benefits

Benefits for Government

1. Corruption and black money prevention—corruption kills the growth of any country thus implementation of cashless systems will help decrease corruption related activities and prevent systemic loopholes and leakages.
2. Transparency and accountability through digital payment and audit trails, easy and fast access to future retrieval of transactional records—better tax revenue management and monitoring.
3. Help achieve economic stability.

4. Better staff productivity—Government staff can devote their time to higher productive causes of policy and designing benefits for the people since the e-payments would save time and hassle of handling funds and accounting for them on a daily basis.
5. Innovation and modernization of the payment mechanisms.

Benefits for Citizens

1. Empowerment: Citizens would be empowered to access services in a time and manner of their choosing rather than being dependent on particular office hours and the resultant delays.
2. Wider reach: With the electronic platforms and means of e-payment citizens will have a wider and easy reach for the government services and its delivery.
3. Improve welfare especially for those in the rural remote and island areas and promotes financial inclusion.

Benefits for Relevant Industry Stakeholders

1. Reduce the risk of high cash-handling volumes which exposes them to the risk of thefts, robberies, and many other cash related other crimes.
2. Reduce the cost of banking services and safe deposits of money—funds are automatically remitted to the bank account by the cashless systems solution provider.

Disadvantages—Negative Implications

The first and foremost subject and issue regarding cashless systems that leads to resistance from affected stakeholders is privacy issues. Implementation of cashless or electronic payment systems means each and every transaction will have a digital record and government and revenue and customs departments will have full access to the consumer transactions and reports. Access to this highly confidential information gives the governments, revenue and customers departments, and relevant banks substantial power and as a result leads to privacy issues. In the context of Fiji, privacy issues are not a huge indicator to determine whether people would want to use cashless services or not.

Furthermore, cashless payment mechanism has a lot of financial risks that can take place at the time of processing the transaction. Some of these issues include:

1. Security and authenticity of payments—customer/seller authentication, proof-of-transaction authorization.
2. Transactional data security—security issues surrounding hackers, and so on.

To mitigate this risk, government plays a major role in ensuring the tender for such projects are given to a solution provider who are proven to be credible, highly reliable and are a licensed solution provider with the country's Central Bank that is the Reserve Bank of Fiji. In addition to this, government also plays a major role to ensure relevant acts and regulations are passed to ensure full compliance by the solution providers at all times.

Benefit and Risk Analysis

After analyzing the positive and negative aspects, we can say that the gains and benefits from the cashless system implementations will outweigh the associated risks and negative implications. The implementation of the cashless society mechanisms in Fiji could bring by far greater benefits for the Fijian economy and for the entire population of Fiji.

RESEARCH METHODOLOGY: PROGRESS AND READINESS INDICATOR OF CASHLESS SOCIETY

We have used various research methods to study the current condition and situation and to identify the most important readiness indicators of the cashless journey for Fiji. We have used the findings of this research to identify the gap areas and list down all the action items on how the cashless mechanisms can be implemented at the different industry levels within the Fijian economy and what will be the major driver in Fiji's journey towards cashless.

The research methods include survey, desktop research, follow-up interviews with mobile network operators as solution providers, stakeholders of the relevant industries, and most importantly with groups of people from the general public who will be impacted the most by these cashless initiative implementations.

Research and findings are based on the following key items.

Accessibility to Digital Financial Services

Today almost everyone has smartphones and instant access to the Internet. The combination of this brings powerful capabilities and immense potentials. Services are getting closer to people than ever before and now available on the fingertips as a result of continuous increase in smartphone penetrations, instant access to the Internet and access to more different applications and global platforms. Continuous advancements and new developments in technology are the major enablers which is entirely transforming how people look at things and actually do things; in other words all of this is being made possible through disruptive innovation.

Mobile phones in particular smartphones in our palms are becoming the major enabler and driver of our behavior, the way we communicate, the way we seek knowledge, satisfaction and happiness, and this driving the manner in which the world is going forward.

Taking this in mind, we have interviewed the telecommunications giant who control 95% of the telecommunications market share in Fiji, which is Vodafone Fiji to understand their market position and roadmap in terms of enabling digital financial services in Fiji.

The findings of the interview with Vodafone Fiji are as follows:

Vodafone Fiji has robust capabilities to execute electronic payment transactions. A few examples to substantiate its expertise and capabilities in this domain are as below:

- Fiji's population—880K, total number of subscribers on Vodafone's network 1.2 million, total number of smartphone users over 500K, total number of active social media users 480K.
- M-PAiSA mobile money: Vodafone Fiji has been operating the M-PAiSA mobile money solution since 2010 now. The total number of M-PAiSA system handles an average of 350,000 transactions per month with values exceeding an average of 10 million FJD per month
- The Vodafone Fiji M-PAiSA in 2011 jointly with Vodafone global won the GSMA award for best Mobile Money for the Unbanked Award in Barcelona. http://www.biztechafrica.com/article/another-global-award-m-pesa/462/

The data gathered through interviewing Vodafone Fiji shows strong growth in the number of M-PAiSA users and M-PAiSA transaction volumes which indicates people have started to know the advantages of digital financial platforms and services (see Figure 7.1). People have gained trust on the system and have started to actively transact using the digital platforms.

Technology and Infrastructure—Use Case

In October 2017, the Fijian government regulated the bus industry and made it mandatory for the entire bus industry to go 100% cashless. This gave birth to the eTransport Air Fare Ticketing system, Vodafone Fiji is the sole provider of eTransport system on public buses around the country—arguably the most heavily used electronic payment platform currently in Fiji.

Under this project more than 1 million e-transport cards have been issued. Today, approximately 120 million transactions in the form of bus fare

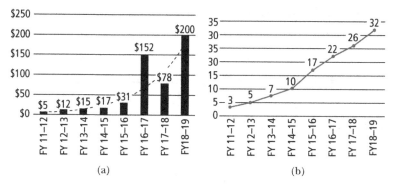

Figure 7.1 Two graphs that show the total M-PAiSA industry value and the number of M-PAiSA users that have grown over the last few years. (a) M-PAiSA Industry Value ($); (b) Average Users Per Month.

payments are done using the e-transport payment system annually which runs on the foundation of Vodafone Fiji's M-PAiSA mobile money system. On average, approximately 9mil electronic fare transactions of a total value of $10m are processed each month through the M-PAiSA system with all the 61 individual bus operators receiving their daily fare collection settlements electronically in their bank accounts the next day. The M-PAiSA/e-transport project maintains a network of 1200+ e-transport top-up agents, many of whom also double up as M-PAISA agents. This also means that Vodafone has already deployed 1200+ smart POS, which is the more than total number of PoS all the banks in Fiji combined have deployed in the market. The two graphics in Figure 7.2 show the total volume of transactions and the number of customers who have used the cashless bus fare ticketing

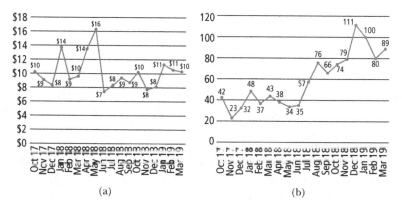

Figure 7.2 Two graphs that show the total volume of transactions and the number of customers who have used the cashless bus fare ticketing system: (a) Total Value of Card Top Up; (b) Unique Cx Transaction.

system. This, again, strongly indicates that technology and infrastructure is available to move in the cashless direction.

SPEED UP THE JOURNEY THROUGH DIFFERENT TECHNIQUE

Government Leadership

Government plays a major role in being the enabler and enforcer of the cashless society. Government also plays a major role to fast track the entire transformation and transition process by passing the mandatory implementations acts and regulations. Such has also been noted from success stories of other countries like China being the successful role model.

Innovative Payment Solutions

M-PESA in Kenya, has been a disruptive innovation which enabled people to do transactions without having a bank account by just using their mobile phones. Hughes and Lonie found within the first month, M-PESA had been recorded over 20,000 accounts in the case of Kenya, clears signs that M-PESA fills gaps in the market (Lonie, 2007). In the context of Fiji, Vodafone Fiji has the M-PAiSA platform and integration with the banking giants in Fiji with the likes of BSP and ANZ will allow free flow of money from bank accounts to mobile wallets and promote digital payments and transactions more conveniently.

CONCLUSION

From the findings of our research we conclude that the advantages of a cashless society in Fiji outweighs the negative aspects and disadvantages. Moreover, understanding progress and readiness indicators of a cashless society will help in getting future ready and developing the scopes for future developments and transitions. Our research, therefore indicates the infrastructure and platforms are already available and the growth in the number of users on the digital platforms indicate that people have started to trust the digital payment ecosystem, thus indicating that Fiji is on the right track in terms of getting ready to transform into a cashless society. Government's leadership will be a major enabler of this transition through enforcement of policies and a strong digital Fiji roadmap will lead the way to cashless Fiji.

RECOMMENDATION

Based on our findings from this research chapter, our recommendation is a cashless society in Fiji should be built on the foundation of the mobile payment platforms enabled by the big telecommunications providers like Vodafone Fiji. They have far greater reach to the rural, remote, and island population and have the capacity to take services on the fingertips of people. Mobile payment platforms like M-PAiSA enabled by solution provider Vodafone Fiji have proven to be reliable, trusted, and have been proven to have the driving force and competitive advantage for this cashless society transformation for Fiji.

RESEARCH QUESTIONS

Q1: *What does the government perceive as the main benefits of achieving a cashless society for the Fijian economy?*

Q2: *What do the consumers (as a whole) and also rural users perceive as the main deterrents to using cashless payment systems delivered either through a mobile platform or card payment mechanisms?*

Q3: *What does the relevant stakeholders in the supermarket, transportation, construction, and hardware industry perceive as the main deterrents to using cashless payment systems?*

Q4: *What are some of the advantages and disadvantages of going cashless in the context of Fiji?*

Q5: *What are some of the readiness indicators in terms of progress towards a cashless society?*

Q6: *What are some of the challenges that the consumers of Fiji and the solution providers may face in terms of providing the digital wallet top-up services and the distribution electronic values especially in the rural areas?*

Q7: *How can Fijian government's leadership and innovative plans help in progress towards a cashless society?*

REFERENCES

Antwi, S. K., Hamza, K., & Bavoh, S. W. (2015). Examining the effectiveness of electronic payment system in Ghana: The case of e-ZWICH in the Tamale metropolis. *Research Journal of Finance and Accounting, 6*(2), 163–177.

Cave, D. (2012). *Digital islands: How the Pacific's ICT revolution is transforming the region.* https://www.lowyinstitute.org/publications/digital-islands-how-pacific-ict-revolution-transforming-region

Choudhry, A. (2015). Future of payments: ePayments. *International Journal of Emerging Technology and Advanced Engineering, 5*(1), 110–115.

Hidayanto, A. N., Hidayat, L. S., Sandhyaduhita, P. I., & Handayani, P. W. (2015). Examining the relationship of payment system characteristics and behavioural intention in e-payment adoption: A case of Indonesia. *International Journal of Business Information Systems, 19*(1), 58–86.

Jenkins, B. (2008). *Developing mobile money ecosystems.* International Finance Corporation.

Junadi, S. (2015). A model of factors influencing consumer's intention to use e-payment system in Indonesia. *Procedia Computer Science, 59*, 214–220.

Kabir, M. A., Saidin, S. Z., & Ahmi, A. (2015). *Adoption of e-payment systems: A review of literature.* https://aidi-ahmi.com/download/publication/2015_ICoEC_kabir_saidin_ahmi.pdf

Leonard, M. (2011). *G2P: Expanding financial inclusion in the Pacific report.* https://www.findevgateway.org/paper/2011/01/g2p-expanding-financial-inclusion-pacific-fijis-transfer-social-welfare-recipients

Lonie, N. H. (2007). M-PESA: Mobile money for the 'unbanked.' *Innovations, 2*(1), 63–81.

Olusola, M., Oludele, A., Chibueze, O., & Samuel, O. (2013). Cashless society: Drive's and challenges in Nigeria. *International Journal of Information Sciences and Techniques, 3*(2), 1–11.

Rika, N. J., Finau, G., & Samuwai, J. (2015). *Mobile money services in rural Fiji: Perceptions, challenges and opportunities.* Fiji Institute of Accountants.

Sathye, M. P. (2014, June). *Mobile value added services for inclusive growth: A study of women micro-entrepreneurs in Fiji.* Paper presented at the Pacific Asia Conference on Information Systems, Chengdu, China.

Thomas, H., Jain, A., & Angus, M. (2013). *MasterCard advisor's cashless journey: The global journey from cash to cashless.* https://newsroom.mastercard.com/wp-content/uploads/2013/09/Cashless-Journey_WhitePaper_FINAL.pdf

Worthington, S. (2006). The cashless society. International Journal of Retail Distribution Management, *23*(7), 31–40.

CHAPTER 8

IMPACT OF ERP SYSTEMS AND ERP CAPABILITIES FOR ORGANIZATIONAL SUCCESS

Sam Goundar
The University of the South Pacific

Rukshar Khan
The University of the South Pacific

Ravinesh Singh
The University of the South Pacific

Shivanesh Lal
The University of the South Pacific

Geol Lal
The University of the South Pacific

Siddarth Singh
The University of the South Pacific

Enterprise Systems and Technological Convergence, pages 157–175
Copyright © 2021 by Information Age Publishing
157

ABSTRACT

ERP systems are crucial for organizations in order to manage and automate its business effortlessly to possess a competitive advantage. This research was conducted with the purpose to understand the relationship between ERP systems, ERP capabilities will contribute towards achieving a competitive advantage. The chapter also examines the impact of ERP capabilities on decision-making efficiencies. The research is based on telecommunication companies in Fiji who have adopted ERP systems for their daily business process. Organization Fit Perspective and Porter's model will be the key drivers for this research in order to understand the relationship between independent and dependent variables. Lastly, the aim of this chapter is to investigate the impact of ERP capabilities on differentiation and low cost advantage of competitive advantage.

Competition across business environments has increased enormously due to the acceleration of technology evolution. Intense competition among rivalries has made each organization to enhance their competitive advantage in order to survive and compete in the market.

According to Quinn and Hilmer (1994), the best way to achieve success is through integration of information systems. An improved and efficient system is capable of leading to more efficient management of business processes, thus increasing customer satisfaction and improving competitiveness.

As stated by Elgohary (2019), a competitive advantage is achieved when an organization can process and function any one thing more effectively and efficiently than others in that same industry segment or across the entire industry. However, Frimpon (2012), states through the strategic role of information systems, which is to develop products, services, and competencies, helps to provide business to gain advantages over competitors.

O'Leary (2000) states that companies adopt an enterprise resource planning system, as the system is considered as a business management software which allows companies to integrate its business transactions into one single system. This module-based application provides a centralized database, which allows all the business functions to have access to.

ERP systems play a vital role in increasing the effectiveness of management functions by providing information needed for planning and monitoring process. The implementation of ERP is both an investment and a backbone for the company to improve efficiency and performance as well as to develop the business.

Gargeya and Brady (2005), states that implementing an ERP system often constitutes an organization's largest information systems (IS) investment. On the other hand, Ram, Corkindale, and Ming-Lu (2015) suggests that during the implementation of the ERP system it tends to affect the company's performance and forces it to reengineer its internal environment in order to meet the demand of the information flow. Nemati and Mangaladurai (2014) claim that ERP systems can offer high value to any organization in maintaining a solid competitive edge and achieving long-term profitability.

Furthermore, many organizations invest enormous amounts of resources in ERP solutions without understanding or analyzing the linkage to achieving a competitive edge. Implementation of information systems such as ERP is associated with the ability to offer innovative products and services to the organization to resource effectively, in order to increase the barriers to entry for new competitors and to increase the bargaining power with customers and suppliers. As stated by O'Leary (2012), ERP system is a tactical decision support tool that helps an organization to gain advantage competitively by optimizing the available resources in the business and integrating business processes.

Likewise, some researchers agree that an ERP system's capabilities is linked to an organization's competitiveness in their respective market. The debate about the relationship between ERP systems and competitive advantage is based on the unique collection and dynamic management of the firms' resources and capabilities (Beard & Sumner, 2004).

Thus, in this chapter the researchers will discuss the linkage and adoption of ERP solutions in an organization and towards achieving a competitive edge. The chapter will also explore the significance of ERP capabilities towards decision-making.

The rest of the chapter is structured as follows. The background describes the ERP evolution and its contributions towards competitive advantage. The problem statement discusses the current problems faced by organizations on implementing ERP systems and on achieving competitive advantage. The research objective will set out the objective of this chapter clearly thus guiding the research forward.

The literature review section will analyze the current paradigms and frameworks used to justify the use of ERP systems and how organizations have achieved competitive advantages. Research methodology highlights the use of organization perspective fit and Porter's forces towards driving this research. In addition, the results validate the research hypothesis and questions using descriptive, correlation, and relatability coefficient mechanisms.

Lastly, the set of propositions are concluded and future direction on research about competitive advantage and ERP are discussed.

Background

In order to replace the legacy silo systems, ERP systems emerged as ERP systems provide an integrated and unified solution for organization's information processing needs (Lengnick-Hall, Lengnick-Hall, & Abdin-nour-Helm, 2004).

The major aim of ERP systems is to support the process-oriented view of the organization, as well as standardization of business processes across business functions within the organization. ERP's most important characteristics is its ability to automate, unify, and integrate an enterprise's data and business processes across the entire organization, in almost a real-time environment.

Moreover, Mata, Fuerst, and Barney (1995) state that a firm has a competitive advantage when it implements a value creating strategy which has not been implemented by the potential or current competitors. Porter (1980) describes competitive advantages as the positional superiority based on a combination of differentiation and cost superiority.

Hence, many businesses have their own custom processes set in place; however, several of these organizations reengineer their non-standard processes to accommodate the ERP in order to take advantage of updates in the future, benefit from the standardized best-practice processes, and avoid irretrievable errors which could be very costly (Krusemark, Kiehl, & Newman, 2016). Therefore, this could intensely decrease the system customization costs.

Problem Statement

Organizations are facing tremendous challenges as they endeavour to improve their competitive position and performance while adjusting to the rapid changes in the market environment, especially with the fierce international competition. In order to survive in the high technology subtle market, organizations have to keep in pace with the evolution of technology to enhance their competitiveness. Through adopting and upgrading the technology, it gives opportunity to the organization to achieve competitive edge from its rivals.

Thus, organizations need to automate their business processes by adopting the right technology. A successful implementation of ERP can allow the organization to simulate and improve process and profitability. It also gives the opportunity for organizations to outperform its rivals and to achieve a competitive advantage using ERP (Elgohary, 2019).

ERP system allows all organizations to integrate inter and inter organizational functions, it also helps to simplify access which is related to information. ERP system also helps organizations to improve performance and allows organizations to make better decisions efficiently. ERP systems helps businesses to create value, which helps organizations to achieve a competitive advantage.

However, researchers have no consensus whether the ERP system itself leads to a competitive advantage or does it require additional input. In addition, there is a lack of studies in ERP, which conveys that ERP is a competitive advantage creator.

Furthermore, many businesses consider the ERP system output as a set of information transactions and ignore the benefit of this information in managing business more efficiently (Ross, 1999).

Thus, studying ERP systems and its productivities is significant in order to optimize its utilization and improve businesses. The relationship between achieving a competitive advantage and implementing a successful ERP system is vital, as any organization has to possess competitive advantage to be able to survive and compete in highly dynamic markets.

Lastly, this chapter contributes to the field of ERP and competitive advantages as it focuses on the main capabilities of ERP. The chapter will provide in depth analyses on the effect of each capabilities group in creating competitive advantages for enhancing decision-making efficiently.

Research Objective

1. To understand the linkage and adoption of ERP solutions in an organization and towards achieving a competitive edge.
2. To investigate whether organizations fit depend on successful implementation of ERP.
3. To determine whether ERP capabilities depend on each other or can achieve competitive advantage independently.

LITERATURE REVIEW

In a competitive global, each organization must have a sustainable competitive advantage in order to be able to differentiate itself and outdo its rivals to survive in the market competition. As stated by Bakri (2017), competitive advantage is the organization's ability to attract customers through its prestige products and increase customer perception and satisfaction.

Porter (1998) states that organizations can achieve competitive advantage through the demonstration of low cost advantage and differentiation advantage. Low cost advantage can be achieved by an organization if the costs of the value producing activities are less than other competitors. On the other hand, a differentiation advantage allows organizations to distinguish itself from its rivals by offering a unique product. Through differentiation, companies can benefit by allowing the company to charge a premium price and allow the company to grow overall demand and to capture the markets from its competitors.

McGrath, Tsai, Venkataraman, and MacMillan (1996) states that there are three successive stages in the rise and fall of competitive advantage such as the building advantage, the lull period, and the collapse. However, a firm can only sustain a competitive advantage when it is implementing a value strategy which has not been implemented by potential competitors. In order to avoid degeneration and achieve sustainability, organizations must constantly reinvest into factors, which create ambiguity and barriers to imitation.

Thus, a number of various frameworks have been developed in order to source out competitive advantage; among them is Porter's competitive forces. Through its approach, it helps organizations to find its position in an industry in order to defend itself against the competitive forces.

Moreover, a successful project planning, implementation, process alignment, and utilization of ERP systems would be a source of competitive advantage. Addo-Tenkorang and Helo (2011) states that there is a consensus between researchers that the ERP system itself cannot contribute towards competitive advantage. It has to be implemented successfully and integrated with business resources. In support Moe, Fosser, Leister, and Newman (2007) states that ERP systems do not offer competitive advantage alone as it needs to be coupled with intellectual and social capital. The benefit of implementation lies in the quality of integrated business process and organization information flow.

On the contrary, other researchers have urged that ERP can be part of making a competitive advantage. An ERP system has the potential of eliminating competitive advantages that organizations possess even before implementation due to a common system approach, failure in implementation can lead to extensive switching cost.

Furthermore, without the optimal use of available resources an organization cannot implement a successful ERP system. Addo-Tenkorang and Helo (2011) states that ERP systems through its capabilities can create opportunities and tangible and intangible benefits. Kalling's (2003) research focused on how ERP systems and strategic management processes can lead to a competitive advantage. In his research in order to improve understanding and the process to achieve competitive advantage, he used the concept of bricolage.

Barney (1991) used a resource based view approach, which represents a potential source of competitive advantage when it is rare, valuable, and non-substitutable. Thus, in his paper he suggested that an organization could achieve competitive advantage by optimizing the available resources. Somers and Nelson (2004), proposed three major business drivers for adoption of ERPs in their paper which are improving productivity, satisfying customer demands, and providing competitive advantage.

Becker (2005) states that for organizations to create a competitive advantage it must build its capabilities to implement an ERP system successfully and to outperform its rivals. Capabilities are considered the major factor that influences, organization performance, and competitive advantage.

In addition, these capabilities are from technical and management skills. Management skills have the ability to conceive and exploit IT applications to support and enhance business functions. Wade and Hulland (2004) state that IT resources cannot lead to competitive advantage dependently as they need to be complemented by organizations resources.

According to Quinn and Hilmer (1994), businesses can increase the competitive advantage by focusing on resources, which provide unique value for their consumers. Beard and Sumner (2004) argue that through a reduction of cost or by increasing revenue of an organization, ERPs may not provide competitive advantage to an organization. However, they do suggest that it can add value by increasing information, accurate and faster processing of transactions, and better decision-making.

Whether a business has competitive gain or not from an ERP system can, to a splendid extent, be said to be dependent on how we outline competitive advantage. There are many distinct definitions of competitive advantage; however, a basic definition is that the agency achieves (as before described) above ordinary financial performance. If this scenario is maintained, the competitive benefit is deemed to be sustained.

If the organization is a first mover in the experience that it is the first business enterprise that makes use of this type of aid in a precise way, it can pretty without difficulty acquire competitive advantage; however it will probably be quick lived. The length of time that the competitive gain lasts is a question of how hard it is for others to imitate the usage of that resource.

The potential that the query of how assets are exploited by the organization is the principal thing when it comes to whether the competitive benefit turns into sustainable or not. When it comes to development of ERPs, the conclusion is that exploitation via establishments must be viewed in terms of how sources are organized and how governance and/or management over ERP development, implementation, and utilization are effective.

Barney (1991) states that the concept of competitive advantage needs to be understood from the perspective of sustainability. A major area for sustained competitive advantage is through strategic management approach by using SWOT framework. On the other hand Alomari, Amir, Aziz, and Auzar (2018) led a research to explore the relationship between ERP systems and management control (MC), represented by technocratic and socio-ideological, enhancing an organization's competitive advantage. They found that both technocratic and socio-ideological associated positively with competitive advantage.

Additionally, the study revealed that only technocratic forms of MC mediated the relationship between ERPs and competitive advantage. Not much research has been conducted on the relationship between ERP and competitive advantage nor on ERP capabilities. More research has been done on the implementation and benefits on ERP systems.

However, there are a few studies that focused on the mature system and achieving competitive advantage, but there is a lack of clarity whether there is a relationship between ERP and competitive advantages. Thus, in order to structure our research, we adopted the framework based on organization fit perspective. By using this framework, it will help in finding out the factors that lead into achieving a competitive advantage and how an ERP system fits into organizations. There have been some researchers who have used this framework and contributed that implementation of an ERP is an important factor in regards to organization fit.

In addition, Porter's 5 forces will be used to understand the bargaining power, new entrants and rivalry among telecommunication companies in Fiji. This will also help to identify who is the leader and is there any potential for new entrants or the market is too intense for new entry. The model will also give insight into how ERP allows organizations to achieve competitive edge though if they are using the same system.

Lastly, the research aims to contribute and fill in those gaps that have not been researched on ERP and competitive advantage. It is also aiming to give an insight on whether ERP is the catalyst that drives towards achieving a competitive advantage for an organization.

RESEARCH QUESTIONS

1. What is the linkage between ERP solutions towards achieving a competitive advantage?
2. What are the ERP capabilities that contribute towards competitive advantage?
3. How to measure success of an ERP system into an organization?
4. What are the competitive advantages with ERP systems for an organization?

RESEARCH METHODOLOGY

This research framework has the premise that ERP capabilities have an impact on competitive advantage for an organization. Based on the literature support researchers suggest the importance of capabilities such as to build on the ERP capabilities, which are IT capabilities represented in integration, information access, IT skills and agility, organizational capabilities represented in qualified human resources and top management support, as well as enhance decision-making efficiency.

Hypothesis Development

Hence, ERP implementation and ERP capabilities are discussed and hypotheses related to these variables are developed.

H1: *Organization Fit of ERP is positively related to ERP implementation success.*

H2: *ERP system has a positive effect on competitive advantage.*

H3: *ERP capabilities have a significant effect on decision-making efficiency.*

Measures and Sampling

Thus, in order to verify the hypothesis and conduct the research qualitative and quantitative approach was adopted to formulate the questionnaire and interview.

Firstly, by using the qualitative approach a semi-formal interview was conducted with Vodafone and Digicel staff. The main purpose of the interview was to find out the type of ERP used by the organization, the components of ERP adoption and how the ERP system contributes towards better decision-making as well as whether it contributes to competitive advantage.

Secondly, with a quantitative approach a rate scale questionnaire was constructed to identify the components used by both the organizations. The aim of the questionnaire was to identify the ERP capabilities and contribution towards competitive advantage and to identify the relationship between independent and dependent variables.

To measure the capabilities the questionnaire was designed into four segments, which were IT capabilities, organization capabilities, competitive advantage using low cost advantage, competitive advantage using differentiation advantage, and decision-making efficiencies.

The first phase IT capabilities deals with system integration, IT skills, information access and agility. The second phase deals with organization capabilities such as HR and top management system. The third phase demonstrates the two categories of competitive advantages. The measurement of differentiation advantage can be measured by measuring the customer's responses and quality of the product whereas the low cost advantage can be measured by efficiency. The last phase deals with decision-making efficiency, which reflects the relationship between the dependent and independent variables. Ten questionnaires were given out—five were given out to Digicel and the other five to Vodafone.

Moreover, in order to understand the competitive advantage of an organization with ERP systems the organization fit perspective and Porter's forces model will be used to understand the relationship between ERP system and competitive advantage. In order to measure the organization fit of ERP the research will focus on the degree of alignment between ERP model and organization needs in terms of process, data and user interface. The organization fit is the independent variable of this research.

Lastly, for analysis statistical methods such as descriptive statistics, correlation analysis and moderated regression analysis has been used.

RESULTS

The implemented ERP modules at the telecommunication organization in Fiji are presented in Table 8.1, which shows that the common module used is financial followed by CRM and SCM.

Vodafone Fiji Limited uses Sage 300 Accpac ERP system for mostly finance and tracking inventory jobs and general ledger. The ERP system provides ease of use for customer service training as well as has custom reports to fit the business need for an organization. On the other hand, Digicel uses Microsoft Dynamics GP ERP system. Unlike Vodafone, Digicel focuses on the Finance module of ERP to keep track of its finances.

From the interviews and literature review it is clear that though most organizations use the same ERP or similar ERP it depends on the organization and how they are using the application for decision-making. A system that can produce information, which can help in decision-making, gives the organization a step ahead of its competitors. Likewise, both Vodafone and Digicel use the system based on their business model to compete in the market and both of them are doing well in their areas of products and services.

In the Fiji market for telecommunication, Vodafone Fiji has a huge customer base compared to Digicel.

Descriptive Analysis

Descriptive statistics, correlations between variables and reliability coefficients are summarized in Table 8.2. From the descriptive statistics, it shows that the mean for the research variables are greater than two, hence indicating that the perception of ERP capabilities and its impact on competitive advantages and decision-making is valid.

In addition, the reliability coefficient is greater than 70, while the poor coefficient is below 0.60 as endorsed by Rizkallah (2002). In this research, the weaker variables in terms of ERP capabilities are information access and human resources. Likewise, the research scale for reliability coefficients are between 0.6 and 0.89, thus indicating good internal consistency.

TABLE 8.1 ERP Implementation Modules at Digicel and Vodafone

ERP Modules	Financial	Customer Relationship	Supply Chain Management	Business Intelligence	Supplier Relationship Management	Quality Management
Frequencies	2	1	1	1	1	1
%	00	50	50	50	50	50

TABLE 8.2 Descriptive Analysis for ERP Capabilities

		IT Capabilities				Organization Capabilities		
Variables		Information Access	IT Skills	Integration	Agility	Human Resource	Top Management Support	Decision-Making Efficient
Means	Items	3.4	3.06	2.95	2.8	2.1	2.10	4.8
Reliability		0.68	0.77	0.75	0.83	0.6	0.89	0.8
Correlations	Low Cost	0.6	0.56	0.6	0.6	0.6	0.6	0.64
	Differentiation	0.58	0.7	0.6	0.7	0.7	0.65	0.6
	Decision-Making	0.75	0.7	0.75	0.86	0.7	0.7	0.99

The relationship between independent and dependent variables are demonstrated by the correlations in Table 8.2. From the results it can be inferred that information access, integration and agility, which are independent variables, have a stronger positive correlation, which are between 0.75 and 0.86 for efficient decision-making being the dependent variable.

On the other hand, the remaining independent variables are moderately correlated with decision-making efficiency. Likewise, all the independent variables also have a moderate positive correlation with low cost advantage, which is also the same for differentiation advantage (see Table 8.3 and Figure 8.1).

Industry Rivalry

Currently, the market has three top competitors such as Telecommunication Fiji Limited (TFL), Vodafone Fiji, and Digicel. The competition between the three is always fierce. Since, Fiji has a smaller population compared to other countries having three competitors is feasible for the market. Each of these companies offer the same services with something additional and new to offer. There is a high healthy competitor among the organization by offering new and better products and services from each other.

TABLE 8.3   Benefits of ERP Implementation

Operational Benefits	Managerial Benefits	Strategic Benefits	IT Infrastructure Benefits	Organizational Benefits
Cost reduction	Improved decision- making and planning	Business growth and partnership	Business flexibility for changes	Change work patterns
Enable to process changes and automate business processes	Improved performance in different operating divisions	Business development innovations	IT costs reduction	Improve working patterns
Cycle times reduction	Better resource management	Cost leadership and external links	Improvement in the capacity of IT infrastructure	Build common vision
Productivity improvement		Generate product differentiation		Facilitates organization learning
Quality improvement				Empower workers
Customer service improvement				

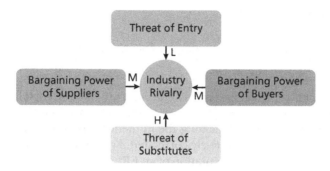

Figure 8.1 Porter's 5 forces for telecommunication companies in Fiji.

Bargaining Power of Buyers

Since, there are three competitors, the bargaining power for customers is medium as they can take advantage of products and services being offered from the organizations. However, Vodafone has a huge customer base compared to the others.

Bargaining Power of Suppliers

The bargaining power is medium since all of them offer similar products hence, the suppliers have the edge to bargain in order to stay put in the competition. For instance, Vodafone and Digicel both sell iPhone and Samsung; hence, the price variation attracts customers.

Threat of Entry

Due to being a small market the threat of entry is low, as the key players already have taken the market and have huge customer bases. For a new entry to survive will be difficult thus the entry is low. For example, Ink was a major competitor for Vodafone a few years ago; however, Vodafone Fiji Limited bought the organization and knows Ink is part of Vodafone.

Threat of Substitution

The threat of substitution is high since all the competitors want to step ahead of each other whether through its products or services. Currently, TFL is the only organization that provides optic fiber for the internet hence, they have an edge in competition. On the other hand, Vodafone has progressed a lot with its Mpasai. Mpasai is a mobile wallet for transactions. Just a few days ago they launched a QR payment through the application which will surely give them the competitive edge. Vodafone also is the leader for e-transport hence, they have achieved a lot of customer base as well as market range with its various products.

Testing Hypothesis

H1: *Organization fit of ERP is positively related to ERP implementation success.*

Verification result: Support

From the correlation analysis it can be inferred that the correlation coefficient or organization fit and ERP implementation success is lower that the conspicuous level. Thus, indicating the implementation success of an ERP and organization fit are positively correlated. From the result it can be said that upon successful implementation of an ERP in an organization can help the organization to fit properly in an organization. Failure in implementation will lead to increase in cost and can lead to no competitive advantage (Table 8.4).

Hence, this result imitates the organization fit of ERP and its ERP implementation success resulted as suggested by Hong and Kim (2002). The result indicates that when organizational fit of ERP increases, eventually the ERP implementation success will be positively influenced. Therefore, for an organization to achieve a competition advantage it must do the implementation of an ERP successfully.

H2: *ERP system has a positive effect on competitive advantage.*

Based on the hypotheses test it results that ERP systems are positively related to competitive advantage as the scores are between $\beta = .70$ and $p > .50$. Thus, ERP systems can replace complex and manual interfaces between various systems with cross functional transaction automation and standardisation. As stated by Heizer and Render (2011), order cycle times can be reduced and results can be improved for throughput, delivery speed and customer response times.

H3: *ERP capabilities have a significant effect on decision-making efficiency.*

Low Cost Advantage

From the test results, it clearly indicates that ERP capabilities collectively have a significant effect on low cost advantage. This contributes to 45% of

TABLE 8.4 Reliability of the Measurements	
Measure	Cronbach's alpha
Organization Fit of ERP	0.96
Implementation Success	0.80
ERP Capabilities	0.99
Organization Resistance	0.92

changes in low cost advantage whereas the other 55% changes are reflected by other factors. Likewise, the *t*-test reveals that IT capabilities have a significant impact on low cost advantages while organization capabilities do not have any significant effect on low cost advantages. Thus, low cost advantage is reflected through IT capabilities instead of organizational capabilities.

Differentiation Advantage

From the test results, it clearly illustrates that there is a significant effect of ERP capabilities collectively on differentiation advantage. There is a contribution of 60% of changes in differentiation advantage whereas the other 40% are affected by other factors. The *t*-test indicates that both IT and organizational capabilities have significant effect on differentiation advantage while compared to low cost advantage.

Decision-Making Efficiency

Based on the test results it is illustrated that there is a significant effect on ERP capabilities collectively on decision-making efficiency. The ERP capabilities collectively contribute 65% of changes towards decision-making while the other 35% is affected by other factors.

Hence, from the *t*-test the IT capabilities have a significant effect on decision-making efficiency whereas the organizational capabilities do not have any significance. Therefore, the hypothesis is accepted in terms that ERP capabilities contribute towards decision-making efficiency but not in terms of organizational capabilities.

Discussion

Based on the results, it is clear that ERP IT capabilities do not independently affect the competitive advantage but can affect decision-making efficiency. Information access and agility have a significant effect on low cost advantage but does not have any significance on differentiation advantage.

Moreover, all the IT capabilities affect the decision-making efficiency except for IT skills. ERP organizational capabilities however, can affect the competitive advantage and decision-making independently. From this result it shows that qualified human resources officers affect differentiation advantage and decision making efficiency but does not affect low cost.

In addition, ERP capabilities all collectively affect differentiation advantage significantly, whereas low advantage and decision-making efficiency are only affected by IT capabilities. Decision-making efficiency has a significant effect on both low cost advantage and differentiation advantage as shown in the structured model (Figure 8.2).

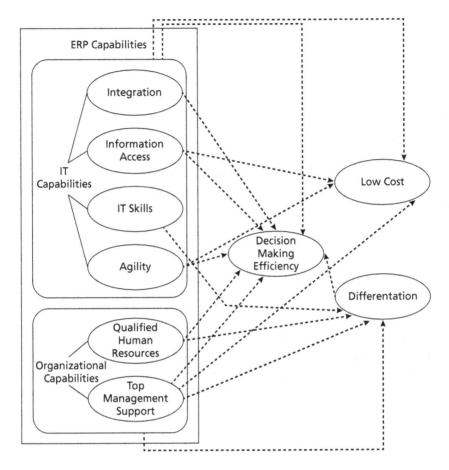

Figure 8.2 ERP capabilities structured model.

CONCLUSION

ERP systems are crucial to seamless and accelerate business transactions and processes. It also provides several benefits for organizations to enable them to increase customer satisfaction and increase business process. The research main aim was to measure and identify the link between ERP system ERP capabilities that lead towards competitive advantage.

The ERP capabilities focused in this research are IT capabilities and organization capabilities on decision making efficient and competitive advantages in terms of low lost and differentiation advantage.

In conclusion, after reviewing various related literature and design and conducted data from two major telecommunication companies in Fiji, the data was analyzed and the hypotheses were tested. From the analyses, it can be inferred that the frequencies of ERP modules and success implementation leads into organization fit for the ERP system. A successful implementation also contributes to achieving competition advantage at the initial stages and later depending on the organization business model.

The descriptive statistics illustrates that all the items reflect their contribution towards efficient decision-making and competitive advantages. The reliability values also indicate that all the items are consistent and valid except for low cost as it is not valid to be used due to poor reliability and consistency. In addition, the correlation demonstrates that all independent values have a moderate positive relationship with low cost and differentiation advantage except for IT skills and agility as it has a strong positive relationship with differentiation advantage.

Furthermore, from the hypothesis testing it can be concluded that there is no indirect relationship between competitive advantages and IT capabilities. Whereas, ERP organization capabilities and decision-making have a direct relationship with competitive advantages.

Thus, having ERP systems can help organizations to achieve one or more competitive advantage and improve performance. ERP systems minimize the error on process and lower cost production to gain competitive advantage in cost leadership and increase the firm's performance. Therefore, ERP implementation is believed to be complex and must be carefully managed to reap the benefits of it.

REFERENCES

Addo-Tenkorang, R., & Helo, A. T. (2011). Enterprise resource planning (ERP): A review literature report. In S. I. Ao, C. Douglas, W. S. Grundfest, & J. Burgstone (Eds.), *Proceedings of the world congress on engineering and computer science* (Vol. 2; pp. 20–35). Newswood Limited.

Alomari, I. A., Amir, A. M., Aziz, K. A., & Auzair, S. M. (2018). Effect of enterprise resource planning systems and forms of management control on firm's competitive advanatges. *Asian Journal of Accounting and Governance, 9,* 87–98.

Bakri, A. A. A. (2017). The impact of social media adoption on competitive advantage in the small and medium enterprises. *International Journal of Business Innovation and Research, 13*(2), 255–269.

Barney. (1991). Firm resources and sustained competitive advantage. *Journal of Management, 117I*(1), 99–120.

Beard, J., & Summer, M. (2004). Seeking strategic advantage in the post-net era: Viewing ERP systems from the resource-based perspective. *The Journal of Strategic Information Systems, 13*(2), 29–50.

Becker, M. (2005). A framework for applying organizational routines in empirical research: Linking antecedents, characteristics and performance. *Journal of Industrial and Corporate Change, 14*(5), 817–846.

Elgohary, E. (2019). The role of ERP capabilities in achieving competitive advantages: An empirical study on Dakahlia governorate companies Egypt. *The Electronic Journal of Information Systems in Developing Countries, 85*(9), e12085.

Frimpon, M. (2012). A restructuring of the enterprise resource planning implementation process. *International Journal of Business and Social Science, 3*(1), 23–243.

Gargeya, V. B., & Brady, C. (2005). Success and failure factors of adopting SAP in ERP system implementation. *Business Process Management Journal.*

Heizer J., & Render, B. (2011). *Competitive advantage from operations.* Pearson Learning Solution.

Hong, K. K., & Kim, Y. G. (2002). The CSFs for ERP implementation: An organizational fit perspective. *Information and Management 40,* 25–40.

Kalling, T. (2003). ERP systems and the strategic management processes that lead to competitive advantage. *Information Resources Management Journal, 16*(4), 46–67.

Krusemark, E. A., Kiehl, K. A., & Newman, J. P. (2016). Endogenous attention modulates early selective attention in psychopathy: An ERP investigation. *Cognitive, Affective, & Behavioral Neuroscience, 16*(5), 779–788.

Lengnick-Hall, C. A., Lengnick-Hall, M. L., & Abdinnour-Helm, S. (2004). The role of social and intellectual capital in achieving competitive advantage. *Journal of Engineering and Technology Management, 21*(4), 307–330.

Mata, F. J., Fuerst, W. L., & Barney, J. B. (1995). Information technology and sustained competitive advantage: A resource-based analysis. *MIS Quarterly, 487–505.*

McGrath, R. G., Tsai, M. H., Venkataraman, S., & MacMillan, I. C. (1996). Innovation, competitive advantage and rent: A model and test. *Management Science, 42*(3), 389–403.

Moe, C. E., Fosser, E., Leister, O. H., & Newman, M. (2007). How Can organizations achieve competitive advantages using ERP systems through managerial processes? In G. Magyar, G. Knapp, W. Wojtkowski, W. G. Wojtkowski, & J. Zupančič (Eds.), *Advances in information systems development* (pp. 37–46). Springer.

Nemati, S. A., & Mangaladurai, D. (2014). *Impact of enterprise resource planning in supply chain management.* Retrieved from http://www.diva-portal.org/smash/get/diva2:1309425/FULLTEXT01.pdf

O'Leary, D. E. (2000). *Enterprise resource planning systems: Systems, life cycle, electronic commerce, and risk.* Cambridge University Press.

Porter, M. E. (1980). Industry structure and competitive strategy: Keys to profitability. *Financial Analysts Journal, 36*(4), 30–41.

Porter, M. E. (1998). Clusters and the new economics of competition. *Harvard Business Review, 76*(6), 77–90.

Quinn, J. B., & Hilmer, F. G. (1994). Strategic outsourcing. *Sloan Management Review, 35*(4), 43–55.

Ram, J., Corkindale, D., & Ming-Lu, W. (2015). Enterprise resource planning adoption: Structural equation modeling analysis of antecedents. *Journal of Computer Information Systems, 54*(1), 53–65.

Rizkallah, A. N. (2002). *Researchers evidence in statistical analysis: Testing and interpretation.* Cairo: Cleopatra for Printing and Computer.

Ross, J. (1999). Dow Corning Corporation: Business processes and information technology. *Journal of Information Technology, 14*(3), 253–266.

Somers, T. M., & Nelson, K. G. (2004). A taxonomy of players and activities across the ERP project life cycle. *Information & Management, 41*(3), 257–278.

Wade, M., & Hulland, J. (2004). The resource-based view and information systems research: Review, extension, and suggestions for future research. *MIS Quarterly, 28*(1), 107–142.

CHAPTER 9

EXTENDING EDUCATIONAL ERP SYSTEM'S FUNCTIONALITY TO USERS ON THE EDGE

Sam Goundar
The University of the South Pacific

Jeshika Solanki
The University of the South Pacific

Jekope Qoro
The University of the South Pacific

Pranil Sadal
The University of the South Pacific

Rigamoto Fonmanu
The University of the South Pacific

Enterprise Systems and Technological Convergence, pages 177–188
Copyright © 2021 by Information Age Publishing

177

ABSTRACT

Enterprise resource planning (ERP) systems provide large organizations with the ability to share information between their cross-functional business units. ERP systems in turn may span over various geographical locations as with the case of multinational organizations. Sharing of information becomes a critical focus for these organizations which may then lead to the implementation of cloud computing services. ERP systems now also have the capability to be hosted on the cloud which enables the information sharing to be available at a central location. However, this gives rise to deficiencies such as availability, speed, and network latency issues especially for developing countries particularly in the south pacific. As an alternate solution, an additional layer between the cloud and the end devices can be introduced to improve service delivery and performance—fog computing layer. The University of the South Pacific is such an organization that can benefit from the amalgamation of its enterprise system with an extension of its student registration process to the Edge per se, using the devices and technologies that students have access to.

Enterprise systems have grown to be the top solution for organizations that are looking to improve their current business situations by provisioning them with the competitive edge over their counterparts. Large organizations that have multiple business units tend to have independent information systems that don't share data with each other. Enterprise systems serves as a solution to this "information barrier" that companies encounter where different business departments aren't able to share timely data and information with each other. Enterprise systems solutions have also further developed their products to be cloud capable. This meant that enterprise systems services were hosted on the cloud and organizations didn't need to worry about space issue requirements nor the need to uphold high maintenance costs that come with large data centers.

Many companies have opted for cloud computing for better performance of enterprise systems but again there are still some unsolved issues such as unreliable latency, lack of mobility support and location—awareness (Yi, Li, & Li, 2015). Due to this reason, fog computing which extends cloud computing has been slowly moving into the general market and thus most companies are now experimenting with this solution. Fog computing brings computational power closer to the edge of the network by enabling edge devices such as network towers and network routers to have processing power. Therefore latency issues are overcome and quality of services is improved. Fog computing is adopted for analyzing timeliness or critical data in the edge nodes to minimize the latency and offload the huge traffic flow. Furthermore, in order to achieve better accuracy, potential information collecting technologies for enterprise information systems have been followed, such as "Internet of things" (IoT), "Internet of people," and the

"Internet of Data" (Chao, Hu, & Chen, 2018). Fog computing is envisioned as the improvement factor for cloud computing, given the many benefits it offers to its users. Latency is one of the main issues that organizations encounter with cloud computing and fog computing counters this with reducing the data load being taken to the cloud. Reducing network costs by saving network bandwidth and processing selected data locally instead of sending them to the cloud for analysis. Fog computing allows the collaboration of different physical environments and multiple devices which promotes flexibility. Scalability is also a major benefit that fog computing brings because the number of edge devices are able to share the processing load from multiple connected devices.

Tertiary institutions have also tapped into the benefits of cloud and fog computing to help manage and provide a better service to their students and staff (Munjal, 2015). As stated in Munjal (2015), higher education institutions have experienced 55% in cost reduction since their deployment of cloud services in their campuses. This reinforces the fact that cloud and fog computing definitely can positively impact and improve services offered at tertiary institutions. The University of the South Pacific (USP) is the leading higher education institution in the South Pacific where it boasts a total of 14 campuses spread across the different island nations. In 2016 alone there was a head count of 27,642 registered students in the university. Each year the student headcount increases which introduces the need for scalability and flexibility which are some of the main benefits that cloud and fog computing have to offer.

LITERATURE REVIEW

Network giant Cisco introduced its IOx framework that enables its customers to develop, manage, and run software on network devices (Stojmenovic, 2014). These devices include IP video cameras, switches, and routers. This framework equips developers with the tools needed to improve their fog network and push computing power as close as possible to the edge (Stojmenovic, 2014). From this we can see the potential benefits that fog computing can bring to the cloud computing world where big data latency issues are constantly encountered. Especially with higher education institutions where scalability of network resources is critical to the future growth of the organization. Distance learning has been a key tool of universities where professors share their ideas through streamed online video. Fog computing can serve as a tool to help manage network bandwidth efficiently and decrease latency to the end users or students.

Industries continually move big data to the cloud for processing and may face issues with computational timing or network bottleneck. One can see how fog computing can be a great solution to this latency issue many networks face daily. Consider the security/surveillance industry, a shopping mall records massive amounts of video data that require processing and storage with the cloud and depending on the network bandwidth this may give rise to computing latency. Fog computing helps with the latency issue because it aims to move the processing closer to the edge. If the IoT were upgraded to enable intelligence on edge devices and coupled with having edge servers close to the edge devices; then this would allow video analysis to be processed locally and remotely (Wang, Pan, & Esposito, 2017). Surveillance and security response times may also be reduced during emergency situations because monitoring, analysis, and detection are all computed locally and data is not sent across to a remote data center. As proposed by Wang et al. (2017) when an emergency situation happens data will be routed to the nearest edge node for processing and will have higher priority for analysis and processing.

Given the many benefits that cloud computing has to offer, it still faces drawbacks with the timely delivery of services to its customers. Large data being generated from end devices go through network bottlenecks and cause high latency within the network. This has led to Cisco introducing the fog computing architecture that is believed to be the solution to many of the issues faced with cloud computing (Dasgupta & Gill, 2017). The aim of fog computing is to place contents and application services as close as possible to consumers or end users. The main difference between fog and cloud computing is the fog location awareness where it extends the clouds architecture to be present in the users location. One can note the potential that fog computing has to offer to the business world not to mention the education sector.

In a rapid changing and highly competitive higher education sector, universities have turned to information technology to be the engine that helps drive its services (Rabaa'I, 2009). The implementation of ERP systems in higher education institutions provides them with a strategic advantage over competitors because they're able to integrate different departmental functions and have a more streamline cost effective approach. The main benefits that the tertiary institutions get from ERP systems are improved information access for all students and staff, improved delivering of services for students and student administration and more importantly increase in income due to the decrease in expenses (Rabaa'I, 2009). Interestingly, there is little research present that addresses the major benefits that fog computing has on ERP systems within the higher education sector.

RESEARCH QUESTIONS AND OBJECTIVES

New USP students each year will almost always feel the strain of adapting to college life. Such factors include the change in environment, the challenge of unit and course terminology and the timely provision of key information that would assist students in career path choices. USP campuses span over a large geographical area which makes navigation for the newly initiated user a nearly insurmountable task. Course handbooks and terminology provide somewhat of a culture shock to most high school students who must either adapt to its rigorous extensive explanations or seek advice from a seasoned university scholar. Course advisors even in the best organized form geared to provide advice to students cannot necessarily reach all students. Although these issues seem to affect new university students, other issues also impact the seasoned university student as it takes several years for students to fully adjust to university life. Finally, as with all universities, many studies have been garnered to improve the learning experience by assimilating whatever information gathered into the extensive university ERP system.

Given the backdrop of Pacific Island technologies and environment, this chapter seeks to unravel what can be done to soften the impact of such student enrollment issues while considering the current and available resources. Since USP's main campus is located in Fiji and the country is still a developing one, the Internet speed will not be as fast as its neighboring countries Australia and New Zealand. It is commonly understood that humans are now in the mobile technology age and as such, the availability of mobile smartphones are ubiquitous to university students. This chapter hopes to theoretically

- introduce the e-Student ERP system module to assist new and continuing university students,
- portray the advantages of the new e-Student ERP module and its applications on how it can enhance the student life experience,
- suggest the adaptability of the new student ERP module by extension to fog computing technologies with the usage of the available smartphone edge devices, and
- propose the possibilities of what the student ERP module can bring to general living.

METHODOLOGY

In order to achieve research objectives above, one must first review the current academic environment the proposal is based on. The University of the South Pacific is one of three main colleges located in the Fiji Islands and as such is the central university for all students in the Pacific Islands. Its main campus is located at Laucala in Suva and welcomes students from the surrounding islands like Tonga, Samoa, Marshall Islands, Kiribati, Solomon Islands, Papua New Guinea, Niue, and many others. Every year, the number of students registering for both the undergraduate and graduate programs generally increases across each school as per annual report statistics released by the university (The University of the South Pacific, 2016). An influx of students each year is evident of population growth and the interest of students to pursue further educational development. One cannot deny the impact of sustainable catering for all new students who are enrolled into the University and the care required to integrate each student seamlessly into their educational streams.

The Student Academic Services (SAS) is USP's assigned department to assist with all student related matters of enrolments. Although the department comprises of at least 20 skilled staff and senior student assistants, it is evident in the long lines each semester of the need to thoroughly assist new and continuing students. Queries and tasks range from the usual enrolment queries to change of programs and to simple matters such as locating certain distinguished professors and buildings. It is simply a definite need of a tool to assist the SAS team and to alleviate the flood of queries the department handles come enrollment periods.

USP's various faculties also provide course counselors who interact with new students to discuss matters of career paths and course units. New students almost always have to navigate the vast gigantic campus by asking for directions from multiple security personnel and staff in order to locate the USP course counselors. In addition to this, students must also queue up in lengthy lines in order to have an appointment as there is currently no availability to schedule such discussions. Furthermore, many new students may also waste hours in order to finally decide to settle into the career of choice. There is a great possibility that if short career videos of the most common career paths were provided, this would definitely assist students on how to navigate and locate the resources that best suit their needs. Reviewing the current approach by the University of the South Pacific, a mind map was constructed on how the current operational details of the enrolment process and also of the integration of the new suggested ERP module, that is, e-Student ERP system module (see Figure 9.1).

The proposed e-Student ERP module would be an additional connectivity point using fog computing technologies as an interface to the university's overall student ERP system. As such, the e-Student ERP module would be engraved into a portable wristband which would act as the connecting medium on the edge of the network. The portable wristband would be used to store the following basic information:

1. student bio-data consisting of blood type, allergies, emergency contacts which can be used in emergency situations;
2. GPRS maps of the university campus detailing the latest information of faculty advisors, faculty tents, and key student geographical

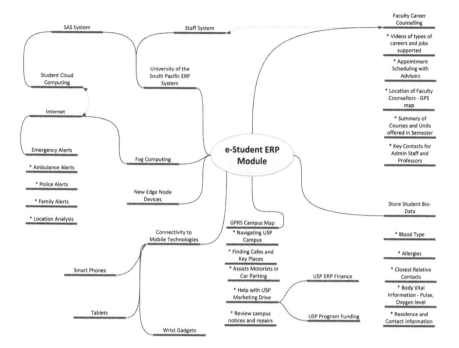

Figure 9.1   Mind map of the proposed e-student ERP module.

information, for example, student academic services office, the library, lecture theaters; and

3. categorized sections of all faculties and career path videos.

All the three major components above would use what is already available and accessible to most students, that is, a mobile smartphone or a tablet. Figure 9.2 shows the suggested networking diagram of the proposed e-Student ERP module.

With this information, a SWOT analysis was developed against the feasibility of the proposed e-Student ERP module and outlined in Table 9.1.

RESULTS

An initial assessment of the University of the South Pacific students was done by analyzing a select subset of available students. The selected subset of ten students were selected at random from both undergraduate and postgraduate students. The summary of their responses to the main queries governing the research objectives is collectively listed in Table 9.2.

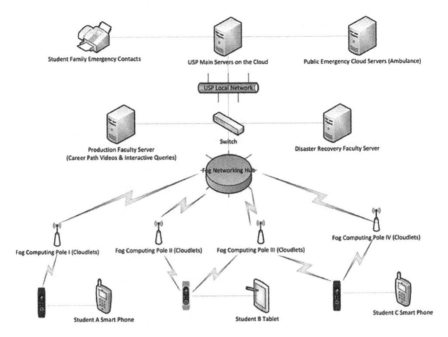

Figure 9.2 Networking diagram depicting the fog computing e-student ERP module communication channel.

Though the survey subset of results may seem insignificant or skewed, it still however poses the opportunity for the university to consider technological advances that not only would assist the generic student body but itself as an educational institute that is adapting to the current trends. The retrieved results tend to indicate the need for the University of the South Pacific to consider advances to using fog computing in conjunction with the university's already existing enterprise system for its staff and students. To stay ahead of the usual status quo of society, concurrent steps into the unknown must be reviewed as possibilities.

There are multiple factors that can be used to further improve this research study into the usage of an e-Student ERP module via an e-Student Wristband with a mobile device. These factors include the possible selection of a better subset of student responses that could better represent new undergraduates and post-graduate students that undergo the enrolment process of the university. In addition, technology specifications on the syncing of e-Student Wristbands with mobile devices and cloudlet nodes would suffice to lay foundational advances into the usage of fog computing to enable technological connectivity. Finally, the context of what would be entailed per student informational data that would be shared in the suggested

TABLE 9.1 SWOT Analysis on Using Mobile Edge Devices

Strengths	Weaknesses
1. Using readily available mobile technologies, e.g., student smart phones and tablets. 2. Low latency of fog computing. 3. Integrates with the current technology bandwidth technologies—no cost to improve networking speed. 4. Less Queues for USP SAS as students can self-help themselves. 5. Videos detail major career paths and assist students to focus in on planning and learning. 6. Scheduling of student counselling sessions with faculty advisors. 7. e-Student ERP module can interact with university ERP system and other modules, e.g., finance and admin. 8. e-Student ERP module and technologies can be re-used for other university events, e.g., USP open day or foreign dignitary campus navigation. 9. In-house maintenance and customization of e-Student ERP module. 10. Improves USP campus-student experience from student statistical data collection in the cloud. 11. Saves time and cost for university by maximizing productivity of USP staff to provide timely and accurate advice for the students who need it.	1. Purchase of fog computing node devices may be costly. 2. Purchase cost of custom e-Student Wristbands.
Opportunities	**Threats**
1. May even interact with ambulance or police authorities in case of sudden student illness. 2. Provide paramedics with vital student information. 3. Self-contact student's family in case of emergencies.	1. Day to day weathering effects on e-Student wristbands. 2. Hacking and loss of private vital student information.

TABLE 9.2 Survey Responses on Current ERP Systems Functionality

Questions	Tabulated Response
Q2. Enrollment experience in USP	3–Average
Q3a. Navigating USP campus to find correct advisors	3–Average
Q3b. Advice given by faculty advisors to help you map your career path	3–Average
Q3c. Availability of resources (maps, videos, contact info)	2–Poor
Q3d. Availability of faculty advisors and appointment scheduling	3–Average
Q3e. Overall time to finally make a decision	3–Average
Q4. Do you own a mobile smart phone or a tablet?	100%
Q5. Probability to use an e-Student Wristband	100%
Q6. Probability to store personal health information	100%

new e-Student ERP system would prove the possibility of using fog computing with ERP systems.

CONCLUSION

A theoretical review of the possibilities of uniting both the ERP systems with fog computing has been affirmed by this chapter. This marrying of technologies can be made possible by extending an educational systems ERP system to the Edge. In fact, by the introduction of a theoretical e-Student ERP system module that specifically utilizes the connectivity between a custom specialized e-Student wristband and a student's smartphone/tablet, this would virtually open possibilities of the usages both foundational technologies provide. The advantages and possibilities that come from the creation of the new e-Student ERP module far outweighs the threats and weaknesses of such a technology. In addition, the adaptability and usage of the new student ERP module can prove useful not only to the university's already existing ERP system, but may be extended to vital public emergency services. In essence, by proposal of the new e-Student ERP module technology, the possibilities open a whole world of wonder created by the conjoining of the majestic ERP systems and the effective fog computing technology.

APPENDIX: INTERVIEW QUESTIONS

1. Please indicate your personal details and level of Study:
   a. Name:
   b. Student ID:
   c. Undergraduate/Post Graduate:
   d. Length of Study in USP:
   e. What are you are studying in USP:

2. Rate your enrollment experience from 1–5 in USP
   (where 1 is *Poor*, 3 is *Average*, and 5 is *Great*) on your:
   a. First Year/Foundation: _____
   b. Second Year: _____
   c. Later Years: _____

3. Indicate from 1–5 during your first Enrollment process
   where 1 is *Terrible*, 2 is *Difficult*, 3 is *Average*, 4 is *Good*, and 5 is *Great*.
   a. Navigating USP campus to find correct advisors: _____
   b. Advice given by faculty advisors to help you map your career
      path: _____
   c. Availability of resources (maps, videos, contact info): _____
   d. Availability of faculty advisors and appointment schedul-
      ing: _____
   e. Overall time to finally make a decision: _____

4. Do you own a mobile smart phone or a tablet?
   a. Yes
   b. No

5. If there would be an option to provide an e-Student Wristband to
   assist you with your enrollment experience by connecting to your
   mobile smart phone/tablet, would you use it?
   a. Yes
   b. No

6. Would you consider storing personal health information about
   yourself in the e-Student Wristband (e.g., blood type, allergies,
   emergency contact information, body vitals information, e.g., pulse
   and oxygen saturation) in case of an emergency on you—all to assist paramedics and emergency officers to better assist you?
   a. Yes
   b. No

7. The introduction of the e-Student Wristband would assist which groups mostly?

   a. new undergraduate students
   b. university students from neighboring Pacific Islands and rural communities
   c. university students from the major Fiji cities and towns
   d. all students

8. If you have any comments on how USP can improve the student's enrollment process *or* any comments on the introduction of a new e-Student Wristband to ERP module, please state below:

REFERENCES

Chao, H.-C., Hu, B., & Chen, C.-Y. (2018). Fog Computing and internet of everything for emerging enterprise information systems. *Enterprise Information Systems, 12*(4), 371–372. https://doi.org/10.1080/17517575.2017.1405076

Dasgupta, A., & Gill, A. (2017). *Fog computing challenges: A systematic review.* https://pdfs.semanticscholar.org/464e/1b60b1bec898840dccd5c27b543a9c353ba2.pdf

Munjal, M. (2015). *Cloud computing in higher education: Opportunities, challenges, and counter measures.* https://www.researchgate.net/profile/Meenaakshi_Munjal/publication/276416898_CLOUD_COMPUTING_IN_HIGHER_EDUCATION_OPPORTUNITIES_CHALLENGES_AND_COUNTER_MEASURES/links/555987f308ae6943a876c1ec.pdf

Rabaa'i, A. (2009). Identifying critical success factors of ERP systems at the higher education sector. In K. Batiha (Ed.), *Proceedings of the third international symposium on innovation in information and communication technology* (pp. 133–147). British Computer Society. https://eprints.qut.edu.au/29841/1/29841.pdf

Stojmenovic, I. (2014). *Fog computing: A cloud to the ground support for smart things and machine-to-machine networks.* http://ksuweb.kennesaw.edu/~she4/2015Summer/cs7860/Reading/91FogComputing.pdf

The University of the South Pacific. (2016). *2016 annual report.* https://www.usp.ac.fj/fileadmin/files/dvcltss/Facts_Stats/USP_Annual_Report_2016_Extract.pdf

Wang, J., Pan, J., & Esposito, F. (2017). *Elastic urban video surveillance system using edge computing.* https://dl.acm.org/citation.cfm?doid=3132479.3132490

Yi, S., Li, C., & Li, Q. (2015). *A survey of fog computing: concepts, applications and issues.* http://www.cs.wm.edu/~liqun/paper/mobidata15-fog.pdf

CHAPTER 10

CUSTOMER RELATIONSHIP MANAGEMENT ISSUES AND ANALYSIS

Sam Goundar
The University of the South Pacific

Sandra Kaitu'u
The University of the South Pacific

Ledua Turaganivalu
The University of the South Pacific

Sireli Nakasava
The University of the South Pacific

Robert Vuidreketi
The University of the South Pacific

Tauala Katea
The University of the South Pacific

Jone Vodo
The University of the South Pacific

Enterprise Systems and Technological Convergence, pages 189–207
Copyright © 2021 by Information Age Publishing

ABSTRACT

Customer relationship management (CRM) is used to manage and analyze customer interactions within an organization. The aim of the research is to identify and analyze CRM problems in a public entity in order to increase value from the CRM functions. The research will run through the information system Success model consisting of three influential factors namely: (a) system characteristics, (b) utility characteristics, and (c) performance. The proposed holistic approach is based on a review of factors and essential elements in order to have a clear understanding on the problems, and develop specific evaluation criteria of the three areas of CRM systems. It will then have the survey analysis to be validated and to have a comprehensive indulgent of the feasibility of the model.

The management of customer relationships has become a priority factor for many organizations (Becker, Greve, & Albers 2009). But the factors behind CRM success and also what constitutes CRM is an issue of considerable debate (Eid, 2009; Krasnikov, Jayachandran, & Kumar 2009). The research will investigate and identify the problems of CRM at a public entity. Our research is based on a CRM system that was introduced at a public entity in 2016 to automate the selection and allocation of residential vacant lots to customers. Before the introduction of the CRM, the main problems faced was the huge number of customer complaints in the underlying principle of awarding the nominal number of available residential vacant lots from the substantial applications received. But there is limited knowledge about the effect of CRM applications on a firm's customer knowledge. Likewise, Xu and Walton (2005) argued that very few studies have been established to address customer knowledge acquisition in the context of CRM implementation. This is necessary but not sufficient. Any organization committed to CRM must take into account the importance of its relationship with its customers, because this is one of the key competitive advantages within an organization nowadays.

In achieving CRM success, evidence suggests that strategic, organizational, and technological issues are all important (Roberts et al., 2005). A clear understanding of what factors lead to CRM success is the significant starting point for effective CRM implementation and deployments (Roh, Ahn, & Han, 2005).

The research will be focused on the three specific areas of an information system success model as follows:

1. the system characteristics area (system quality, information quality, and service quality),
2. the user area (perceived usefulness and user satisfaction), and
3. the performance area (personal performance and organizational performance).

This will be guided by the operational definitions of each variable used in the study model. While there is an improvement in the system characteristics area of the system, there are still limitations to the user area and performance area of the newly introduced CRM system. The approach will fully understand the restrictions and verify the viability and efficacy of the survey analysis outcome.

The interaction between employee and customer helps the customer make an informed decision and foster customer satisfaction and loyalty (García-Murillo & Annabi, 2002). Similarly, customer referral value plays an important role in maximizing profitability (Kumar, Aksoy, Donkers, Venkatesan, Wisel, & Tillmanns, 2010) to achieve CRM success.

LITERATURE REVIEW

CRM is a customer focused strategy that integrates sales, marketing, and customer care service in order to create, add value for the company and customers (Chalmeta, 2006). Many organizations are implementing CRM but at the same time faced internal and external issues which led them to fail. One of the main reasons is the intuition and way in approaching CRM that are not at all adequate. Different methodology being practiced can be also a factor that contributes to failure and changes the demand for CRM solutions which is not satisfactorily integrated and complemented the technological aspects of CRM.

This research investigates the process of a CRM system that considers the relationship of a customer and employee in utilizing the system introduced into the organization. Similarly Sharma (2014) provides interpretations of performance management measures introduced to reveal if the indicators are appropriate to serve the strategies of the organization. A recent study showing the benefit and relationship of using CRM and knowledge management that was carried out in 2003. This study shows that integrating both the approaches in knowledge reduces the risk of failure in CRM (Gebert et al., 2003). In the context of multi-product financial services firms, drawing the customer closer to the service production and delivery process can lead to deeper relationships through increased mutual understanding, building of relationship switching costs, and increased opportunities for cross-selling (Eisingerich & Bell, 2006).

CRM is the outcome of the ongoing development and combination of marketing ideas and new obtainable data, technologies, and organizational approaches. Customer needs and wants keep changing day by day. The customer is the life blood of any organization to be successful and generate profits. Customer creation cost is higher than customer retention cost, thus the need to adopt CRM techniques for maintaining life relationship and ensure customer loyalty and retention (Rayen & Sreeranganachiyar, 2017). To assess the current situation, a questionnaire was used, then its validity and reliability were verified (Najafi et al., 2017).

For organizations that now manage its customers as its principal industry, CRM is its core proficiency, and also most likely its competitive advantage (Liew, 2008). The demands on software enterprise responding to competitive markets become higher and higher, so how to elevate the CRM level of software enterprises and establish «customer-focus» development strategy are the problems that software enterprises are confronting (Reinartz & Kumar, 2003).

STATEMENT OF THE PROBLEMS

The System Characteristics

Ideally, CRM users capture data from customers' forms, and enter it into the system. In reality customers' information in the system are not verified based on embedded system checks to meet the accuracy rate of information quality. The consequences will be inaccuracy of customer's information (data) which may lead to incorrect decision-making when accessing customers application and incorrect allocation of housing development lots.

A review should be conducted on the current information system based on the analysis provided—whether the system is to be updated/upgraded and/or a whole new information system needs to be installed that includes a validation and editing process feature. This will not only improve the accuracy rating but also improve the timeliness of the application process and decision-making.

The Utility Characteristics

The area of CRM systems namely the "user area (perceived usefulness and user satisfaction)." According to the technical acceptance model (TAM), users' adoption of information technology is determined by "perceived usefulness" (PU) and "perceived ease of use" (PEOU) and thus assumed to determine a person's attitude towards using the technology. To test the perceived usefulness and perceived ease of use, survey questionnaires were formulated. The questionnaire was prepared to gauge the usefulness of the CRM used by the organization which was distributed to the staff of the organization as the users of the system.

Some of the common problems from the user area are noted below:

1. Lack of efficiency that resulted in more time spent on administrative work, and also duplication of work processes from one department to another.
2. Conflict of interest in terms of system generated reports where two departments are using different types of information systems.
3. Missing Data—data was not fully captured into the system that resulted in an incorrect report.
4. Lack of communication between users that affects customer services.

The Performance Characteristics

CRM is gradually significant to many organizations and identified as one of the key factors to increase their returns through a longer-term relationship and loyalty. Many organizations have adopted and invested deeply in information technology (IT) assets. This will create and manage better their interactions with their customers (Bohling et al., 2006). It tracks that the bigger the knowledge about how organizations successfully build and combine their technical and administrative capabilities, the better will be our understanding of how CRM impacts performance.

One of the key problems being identified throughout this research study is the confidence level of employees within the organization in utilizing the SMS platform.

A CRM can improve organizational performance by improving sales efficiency, increase net profit, reduce customer management cost, and reduce business process cost. A major problem identified in this research is that CRM does not have any direct impact on the improved organizational performance. But there are technical operational factors that do affect these areas.

RESEARCH QUESTIONS

Our research will be a descriptive approach under the quantitative method. We have identified the three areas of CRM systems as listed below to identify the problems within these areas, and evaluate and draw solutions to address these issues.

1. the system characteristics area (system quality, information quality, and service quality),

2. the user area (perceived usefulness and user satisfaction), and
3. the performance area (personal performance and organizational performance).

We will conduct face to face interviews, distribute written questionnaires, collect responses from most users (employees), and conduct the analysis to interpret the results in addressing key problems and their solutions respectively.

METHODOLOGY

The research will be guided by the customer relationship management success model that consists of three influential factors:

1. system characteristics,
2. utility characteristics, and
3. performance.

Furthermore, the specific evaluation of the three areas of CRM systems includes:

1. the system characteristics area (system quality, information quality, and service quality),
2. the user area (perceived usefulness and user satisfaction), and
3. the performance area (personal performance and organizational performance).

The detailed evaluation criteria of the three areas will be developed, and its validity will be verified by a survey administered to CRM system users and customers. The survey will be analyzed through the quantitative method, and the results were used to confirm the feasibility of the model.

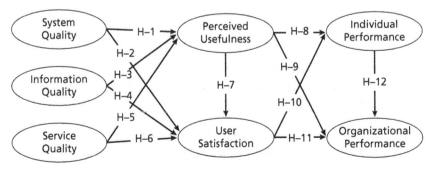

Figure 10.1 Hypothesis tested for relationship between different evaluation criteria. *Source:* Choi, Rho, Park, Kim, Kwon, & Choi 2013)

TABLE 10.1	Operational Definitions of Variables Used in the Study Model		
Construct	Operational Definition	Item	Reference
System quality	Performance and functionality of information systems	Ease of Use, Affinity, Ease of Learning, Ease of Navigation, Skillful Use, Convenience	[11,16]
Information quality	The degree to which information obtained from the system meets the requirements and expectations of the user	Accuracy, Timeliness, Ease of Understanding, Relevance, Reliability of Information	[11,18]
Service quality	The improvement of convenience and reliability of service and business process using information system	Reliability of System, Stability, Rapid Recovery, Security, Rapidity	[11,16]
Perceived usefulness	The degree to which a user believes the system is helpful to perform a task	Prompt Proceeding, Improvement Performance, Efficiency	[16,19,20]
User satisfaction	The degree to which an overall system features provides satisfaction to users	System Satisfaction, Information Satisfaction, Overall Satisfaction	[12–15]
Individual performance	Positive or negative influence to perform individual job using information systems	Ease of Work, Inconvenient in the Absence, Rapid Job Performance, Helpful to Job Performance, Stress in the Absence	[12–15]
Organizational performance	Improved financial profit and organizational efficiency using information systems	Increase in Net Profit, Increase in Sales, Increase in New Customer Sales, Cost Reduce in Cusomer Management, Cost Reduce in Business Processes	[21]

Source: Choi, Rho, Park, Kim, Kwon, & Choi 2013

The operational definitions of the variables used in the study model are shown in Table 10.1.

RESEARCH AND FINDINGS

System Characteristics

Questionnaires were presented to the respondents of the said public entity that is using the CRM system on a daily basis, and also have vast and exceptional experience in performing their individual tasks on the system. Interviews were also conducted to validate their responses to the provided questionnaires. All responses were statistically analyzed using the descriptive analysis method and results tabled with a spreadsheet outlook. The questionnaire was further divided into three areas: system quality, information quality, and service quality. There was a 100% response rate to the questionnaires. The 15 questions designed for the system characteristics constructs received no inconsistent or random error response. The analysis from the data gathered and Figures 10.2 and 10.3 illustrate the outcome of the research summarized in Figure 10.4.

Figure 10.2 illustrates that 78% of users are satisfied with the level of accuracy of the system.

Figure 10.3a illustrates that 70% of users are satisfied with the level of system reliability and 30% are very satisfied. And for navigating through the different components Figure 10.3b illustrates that 67% are satisfied and 33% are very satisfied.

The summary of the results shows average scores for *organization performance 4.74, service quality 4.55, information quality 4.27,* and *system quality 4.60*

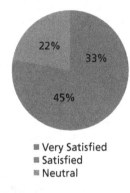

Figure 10.2   Meets requirement and expectation of accuracy.

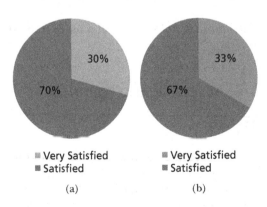

Figure 10.3   (a) System reliability, (b) Navigating through the different components.

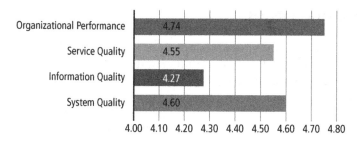

Figure 10.4 Summary of results.

(see Figure 10.4). It shows that there is a higher score on the *very satisfied* comparison with *satisfied* and the other factors. The outcome has given the positive impact on the system characteristics in this survey from its users.

The results further found that within the three constructs were three components from each that scored below 4.5, and these are

- navigating through the different components of the system,
- meets the requirement and expectancy of accuracy, and
- system reliability.

The "accuracy" component received the lowest score out of the three components prompting a consideration into requirement and expectancy of accuracy.

The solutions provided to the problems are as follows:

1. There should be system integrations which allow multiple computer systems to talk to one another, optimizing performance and reducing the need to handle the same data over multiple systems.
2. Proper system training of key employees who are daily users to ensure accurate data is input to the system.
3. Upgrading and updating your computer systems ensures faults, bugs, and inefficiencies identified over time are repaired or avoided altogether. Reduce inefficiencies, remove faults, and increase performance and reliability.
4. The accuracy of entering data should be verified and linked with the respective organizations. For example banks, FNPF, FRCA, and so on. The systemic and holistic approach states that CRM should be the core of organization that are customer oriented. This can be achieved by customizing business processes and integrating them into CRM systems. It also helps the organization to coordinate and maintain the growth of different customer contract points for future communications channel.

Utility Characteristics

Respondents of the questionnaires were from the marketing, work assessment, customer relation, and valuation department who are the users of the system from the entity. A questionnaire survey was used to gather research data. Measurement of the constructs were adapted from previous literature to ensure survey content validity. A five-point has been chosen, from 1 *strongly disagree* to 5 *strongly agree*. The measures for both effort expectancy and social influence were derived from previous studies (Venkatesh, Morris, Davis, & Davis, 2003).

Listed below are some of the solutions to the problems:

1. Delegation of work task, asking for help or passing the task to be done by another staff member who is available is very crucial. In delegation the management should well inform the staff member on what needs to be done and with a set deadline, clear communication with the staff involved to avoid mistakes.
2. The management needs to review the system process to find solutions as to which system should be followed, or rather upgrade both systems so that they give the same result.
3. The solution for missing data, this is during the point where data entry process takes place. A supervisor or team leader should check the records in the file and sign it off to confirm that all data is correctly input into the system.
4. As for lack of communication, one of the solutions is to address key critical areas. This will certainly allow organizations to target the most critical areas and find linkages among them effectively.

The summary of the findings as presented above shows user satisfaction: 4.46 of average score, prompt proceeding: 3.8, improved performance: 3.71, and efficiency: 3.64 (see Figure 10.5). Summary shows that there is a higher score on "user satisfaction" in comparison with "efficiency" and other factors.

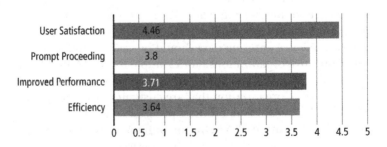

Figure 10.5 Summary of findings.

The expectation is that the percentage of the "efficiency" would be higher as the "user satisfaction" and "improved performance" scores is high. The CRM systems problems encountered by the "users" like "lack of communications" could have an impact on the results shown on the graph.

The research finds that although the "user satisfaction" scores are high, the "efficiency" scores are lower. This factor could be attributed to other organizational aspects like lack of communications and conflict of interests of the users of the system. Past researchers find that there are other reasons for using technology such as; user friendly interfaces with regards to organizing information, effortless navigation, and retrieving information retrieval for the customer needs. Information technical and investors of technology need feedback from the customers on their technology for strategic decision-making (Bolar, Tesfamariam, & Sadiq, 2017).

A recommended solution to this is to consider the socio technical perspective of the implementation system of the customer management system and to ensure there is a best fit of the system and other aspects of the organization. A research using the conceptual model and partially based on DeLone and McLean's (1992) taxonomy of information system success was carried out in an electric utility company. The model considers the relationship between other aspects of the organization comprising the information system and the organization service excellence. The results have shown that system quality, information quality, and employee IT characteristics influence employee IT performance, which in turn influences the service quality at the organizational level. Technical support directly impacts service quality (Bharati, 1998).

A holistic approach of the organization is to be considered due to the interrelatedness of the functions and processes within the organization and other external factors that can have an effect on the performance to be considered.

Performance

There was a qualitative research carried out on the individual performance construct under the performance area. 27 respondents answered questionnaires from the marketing, customer relations, work assessment, and valuation department of the public entity and the results of the findings indicated that 11% indicated that there was no change in their stress level and 89% indicated that their stress level increased from using the CRM system (see Figure 10.6).

The stress level results of the research highlight a scenario that the users of the crm system do not have technical skills and probably new staff who have no previous training on the use of the CRM.

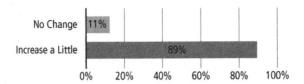

Figure 10.6 User stress level.

Solution to address this increase in stress level is to conduct induction training to the new staff and existing staff and conduct 6 monthly or annual refresher training to empower them and give them the confidence to effectively use the CRM system which will directly reduce their stress level and increase productivity. This recommended refresher training will give staff the much needed insight into the functional utility of the CRM system.

The research is answered in a significant way from the findings in highlighting critical significant characteristics of the three functional areas of CRM that need to be integrated with the operational tasks to maximize the usefulness of the system. The findings summarizes valuable knowledge for consideration which is a significant role in the development of the organization's productivity and knowledge. Another important contribution is the organization's ability to effectively use CRM to become customer-oriented. CRM implementations allow management and manipulation of huge customer databases with minimal effort, in organizing data acquired from various sources into a centralized location to improve customer services and products provided by offering data in real-time to help in the decision-making process.

DISCUSSIONS

System Characteristics

Based on the results and findings, the respondents are not relying on the accuracy of the CRM system and how the data captured were not accurately verified nor were any quality control embedded into the system to provide quality checks and validity of the data stored. The other two components that received below 4.5% scores are "navigating through the CRM system" and "system reliability."

Given the period of the implementation of the system, it seems that there was no proper review done to check the effectiveness and efficiency of the CRM system. From the three constructs of system characteristics which is "system quality," "information quality," "service quality." System quality had the lowest rating of 4.27%, scored above 4.5% are organizational performance, service quality, and system quality.

The research found that the respondents were in the higher score of satisfied to very satisfied in relation to the CRM system. However on average, none of the respondents with regards to system characteristics were consistent with the highest score. CRM systems received positive responses but within these positive responses were indicators found for further improvements.

The management would need to consider investing more on their current CRM system, where certain alternatives need to take precedence. However, Sudirman, Govindaraju, and Pratiri (2014) states that the benefits from information system (IS) investments arise when the use of IS provides some positive impact to the organization in terms of business impacts and individual impact. Below are solutions to the problems that would need significant improvement on the back end and positively affect the output which is customer satisfaction.

- Verification process to be programmed into the system for information quality checks.
- System up which includes small or minor improvements around the focused area.
- System/software upgrade which is a complete new version of the CRM system.

The primary focus of this research was to investigate the use of the CRM system and its problems. The limitations was that we could have included the software developers or IT professionals that were responsible for implementing the system, which would have given a greater insight into the back end part of the system itself.

Utility Characteristics

Based on the findings, we have identified that the user is satisfied with the information system in place. It has shown in the diagram that even when the system is user friendly, it still does not improve the user performance. In our findings we also found that the users are not confused when using the customer relationship information system. Users find it easy to get the SMS to do what they want to do. As for efficiency in terms of the usage of information systems, the rate for efficiency is the lowest to compare it with other findings of the research.

In this research we found that the users are satisfied with the information system. In terms of efficiency the rate has dropped, this is due to the fact that not all the important data is captured into the system. Other areas such as user satisfaction, prompt proceedings, and the improved performance findings, all have shown that the users are happy and are satisfied with the information system. Lack of management support for the information system in the organization could be another factor affecting the results of the survey.

From the users perspective they are happy and satisfied with the use of information systems. When it comes to efficiency the findings have shown that there's a drop in percentage. There is still more time spent on administration, more staff are hired to work on the application, and to meet the number of demands. I would recommend a system online for customers to apply online to avoid all this manual input and handing over manual applications. With the online system it will assist the team to just check on all applications and make a decision.

From the findings we have through the questionnaire and face to face interview with the users, we found that the use of information systems is up to the expectation of the user. This is basically in terms of inputting data and accessing data for report. When it comes to efficiency the drop in percentage has indicated that there is still some room for improvement in terms of the work process of the organization.

Implementation of data collection method, since we're doing research on one of the government subsidiary organizations, there's some information withheld and not released to us such as the profit and loss statement for us to identify the organization growth in terms of development.

The Performance Area

Findings from the study highlighted that CRM has a significant impact on individual performance while it does not have a major impact on the organizational performance. It was validated from the research that lack basic technical skills and understanding the functional capabilities utility of CRM greatly contributes to effective individual performance. The study also identified that CRM has little impact on the organization performance in particular to the improved financial profit and organizational efficiency of using information systems. This is because the organizational performance also depends on other operational functions of the organizations. Major limitations of the research is the availability and accuracy of the data relevant to the areas of this study.

CONCLUSION

System Characteristics

The satisfaction level of the research question has given greater insights as to how effective the CRM system is, and the impact it has on system/

technology on the organization. The findings have supported the need to review its current CRM system.

Choi et al. (2013) indicate that achieving competitiveness is crucial from the design phase of the CRM system to the system characteristic area. There were limitations identified after concluding with our findings as we only look at the average satisfactory criterion rather than the individual user and performance and personal experience of using the CRM system.

Grover, Cheon, and Teng (1996) assume that system quality is completely linked with information quality and administrative impact, and information quality is certainly connected with administrative impact. The organization has the capabilities to also introduce new CRM systems to capture the full potential of its customer base.

Solution—Online Access and Offline Access

Online access control systems often feature things like remote management that allow users to log into a specific online portal from any smartphone, tablet, or other device they may have to view analytical data about usage. They can see the current update of their registration and what is the progress, all without ever setting foot in the building in the first place. It also reduces manpower in the organization for data input, reports can perform by a minimum number of staff.

> When it comes to making the right decision to meet your needs, it is important to note that the "one size fits all" approach will not work. Both online and offline systems have advantages that the other does not, which is why a healthy mixture of both, employed strategically, will be the best fit to help you meet your unique challenges. (Kollmann, Kuckertz, & Kayser, 2012)

As we can see founded on the outcome of discoveries we have in relation to the utility characteristics, we can say that even if we have a good or better information system in place, it will be of no use if we don't have the right person to use it. We look at it from the performance side, where users need to perform as well in order to meet the organization goals.

The Performance Area

It is important to understand the operational process and identify the major functional factors for the development of the CRM system to have maximum effectiveness to the performance of an organization. CRM is based on relationship marketing theory that is the main areas of modern marketing development generating a variety of topics for researchers and customer relationship initiation is the identification of customers' needs integrated into the development of the system to best fit into the organizational operational function to maximize performance. CRM is widely used globally as a tool to improve and enhance organizational performance. Significant is the result which will be used to confirm or reject the underpinning problems of the study.

RECOMMENDATIONS FOR THE FUTURE

System Characteristics

The system characteristics on this research was mainly focused on the usability and functions of the CRM system and how it impacts the organization as a whole. The IT professional was not included in the research as they are responsible for the implementation of the system. It would have added value and back end insight into the whole research. More related research papers on previous studies would have broadened our understanding on the particular topic in relation to the CRM system and its impacts on its users. Also increase the number of samples that would include an organization that is using the similar CRM system. Overcoming the limitations on this research by looking at the overall structure of the organization and its performance and how the CRM system affects the individual structure of the business.

Utility Characteristics

Getting CRM software to fit with your existing workflow and databases isn't easy. A lot depends on the people setting up the system (Campbell, 2000). You can pay big money for an outstanding system but if the people setting it up don't understand your core business, you get garbage. The CRM software surveyed is a system set up to collate the information of the applicants or customers. The information is manually provided through the filling of a form and then data entry clerks input the data on to the system. If information is provided wrongly by the customer on the form or if the data entry clerk entered the information incorrectly this will definitely affect the applicant's chances of receiving the product or service and can impact the organizations image in a negative way. The results of the survey shows that the users of the system are competent with its use.

Since we're doing research for a government subsidiary organization, one of the drawbacks is the information withheld for the management to our team of research. Improvement can be the tactics used instead of interviews and questionnaires we may need to seek prior management approval to carry out the research.

If we're to extend the research we may need to use a valid measure for the utility to validate the results of the survey.

Limitations can be minimized if management of the organizations support the survey. All areas of improvement can be shared with them for improved system and performance for the future of the organization.

The Performance Area

Human, systematic, or random errors could have affected the results and have major flaws on the study. Adoption of more than one model could improve this study in giving it a broader perspective of the topic. Further extension into this research should focus on the integrated development of CRM into the operational functions of organizations to holistically contribute to the organizational performance. This research can be used to gain new knowledge on the different characteristics of CRM and can extend the areas of study with the use of other models relevant to CRM.

REFERENCES

Becker, J. U., Greve, G., & Albers, S. (2009). The impact of technological and organizational implementation of CRM on customer acquisition, maintenance, and retention. *International Journal of Research in Marketing, 26*(3), 207–215.

Bharati, P. (1998). *Strategic management of information technology for service quality: A study of the electric utility industry* (Order No. 9918373). e-library.ru

Bohling, T., Bowman, D., LaValle, S., Mittal, V., Narayandas, D., Ramani, G., & Varadarajan, R. (2006). CRM implementation: Effectiveness issues and insights. *Journal of Services Research, 9*(2), 184–194.

Bolar, A. A., Tesfamariam, S., & Sadiq, R. (2017). Framework for prioritizing infrastructure user expectations using quality function deployment (QFD). *International Journal of Sustainable Built Environment, 6*(1), 16–29.

Campbell, K. K. (2000). Make every customer your best friend: Customer relationship management software could be your killer sales app, but implementing CRM isn't plug-and-play: The magazine for canadian entrepreneurs. *Profit, 19*, 99–100.

Chalmeta, R. (2006). Methodology for customer relationship management. *Journal of Systems and Software, 79*, 1015–1024.

Choi, W., Rho, M. J., Park, J., Kim, K. J., Kwon, Y. D., & Choi, I. Y. (2013). Information system success model for customer relationship management system in health promotion centers. *Healthcare informatics research, 19*(2), 110–120. https://doi.org/10.4258/hir.2013.19.2.110

DeLone, W. H., & McLean, E. R. (1992). Information systems success: The quest for the dependent variable. *Information Systems Research, 3*(1), 60–95.

Eid, R. (2009). Factors affecting the success of world class manufacturing implementation in less developed countries. *Journal of Manufacturing Technology Management.*

Eisingerich, A. B., & Bell, S. J. (2006). Relationship marketing in the financial services industry: The importance of customer education, participation and problem management for customer loyalty. Journal of Financial Services Marketing, 10(4), 86–97.

García-Murillo, M., & Annabi, H. (2002). Customer knowledge management. *The Journal of the Operational Research Society, 53*(8), 875–884.

Gebert, H., Geib, M., Kolbe, L., & Brenner, W. (2003). Knowledge-enabled customer relationship management: Integrating customer relationship management and knowledge management concepts. Journal of Knowledge Management, 7(5), 107–123.

Grover, V., Cheon, M. J., & Teng, J. T. (1996). The effect of service quality and partnership on the outsourcing of information systems functions. *Journal of Management Information Systems, 12*(4), 89–116.

Kollmann, T., Kuckertz, A., & Kayser, I. (2012). Cannibalization or synergy? Consumers' channel selection in online–offline multichannel systems. *Journal of Retailing and Consumer Services, 19*(2), 186–194.

Krasnikov, A., Jayachandran, S., & Kumar, V. (2009). The impact of customer relationship management implementation on cost and profit efficiencies: Evidence from the U.S. commercial banking industry. *Journal of Marketing, 73*(6), 61–76.

Kumar, V., Aksoy, L., Donkers, B., Venkatesan, R., Wiesel, T., & Tillmanns, S. (2010). Undervalued or overvalued customers: Capturing total customer engagement value. *Journal of Service Research, 13*(3), 297–310.

Liew, C. A. (2008). Strategic integration of knowledge management and customer relationship management. Journal of Knowledge Management, 12(4), 131–146.

Najafi, A., Rezaei, S., & Rodi, A. D. (2017). The effect of electronic customer relationship management on customer relationship quality: Evidence from mellat bank of arak city. Journal of Economic & Management Per*spectives, 11*(3), 539–548.

Rayen, L. P., & Sreeranganachiyar, T. (2017). A study on problems faced by the customer in relation to customer relationship management practices. *Sumedha Journal of Management, 6*(3), 24–38.

Roberts, M. L., Liu, R. R., & Hazard, K. (2005). Strategy, technology and organisational alignment: Key components of CRM success. *The Journal of Database Marketing and Customer Strategy Management, 12*(4), 315–326.

Roh, T. H., Ahn, C. K., & Han, I. (2005). The priority factor model for customer relationship management system success. *Expert Systems with Applications, 28*(4), 641–654.

Sudirman, I., Govindaraju, R., & Pratiwi, A. A. (2014). Information system quality and its impact on individual users' benefit: Analyzing the role of knowledge enablers. *Jurnal Teknik Industri, 16*(2), 65–74.

Sharma, N. N. (2014). Performance management systems in the public housing sector: Dissemination to diffusion. *Australian Accounting Review, 24*(1), 2–20.

Reinartz, W. J., & Kumar, V. (2003). The impact of customer relationship characteristics on profitable lifetime duration. Journal of Marketing, 67(1), 77–99.

Venkatesh, V., Morris, M. G., Davis, G. B., & Davis, F. D. (2003). User acceptance of information technology: Toward a unified view. *MIS Quarterly,* 425–478.

Xu, M., & Walton, J. (2005). Gaining customer knowledge through analytical CRM. *Industrial Management & Data Systems, 105*(7), 955–971.

CHAPTER 11

ANALYZING HUMAN RESOURCE INFORMATION SYSTEM IN ORGANIZATIONS

Sam Goundar
The University of the South Pacific

Vinash Singh
The University of the South Pacific

Dhiraj Kumar
The University of the South Pacific

Akashdeep Bhardwaj
University of Petroleum and Energy Studies

Sunil Kaushik
University of Petroleum and Energy Studies

Enterprise Systems and Technological Convergence, pages 209–219
Copyright © 2021 by Information Age Publishing
209

ABSTRACT

This research was conducted to assess how the use of human resource information system (HRIS) affects HR functions of the organization. HRIS research is very limited in Fiji and the Pacific as a whole therefore there was a need for this study. This chapter uses the DeLone and McLean HRIS success model integrated with some incumbent HRIS factors providing a comprehensive view into vital factors affecting HRIS in the HR department.

A standardized questionnaire was used to collect quantitative data. The results from this research showed there were a total of six different factors that affect the use of HRIS in the HR divisions of government organizations. These factors are: usefulness, a faster decision making process, system quality, ease of use, subjective norms such as social and peer pressures, and system unification. The effect of these factors was measured which showed that system quality, service quality, and the ease of use has a positive impact.

Further to this, the impact of HRIS on the HR division, in relation to performance and productivity was also investigated with the sample population. It was established that HRIS has a positive and significant effect on the productivity as well as the performance of the HR division in government organizations.

"Human resource is considered as the most valuable resource in any organization because other resources make things possible but only human resource makes things happen" (Opatha, 2009, p. 1). On the other hand, information is also considered as the most valuable resource an organization could have to get a global competitive advantage in today's world. The addition of information technology to the human resource industry has revolutionized the contemporary workplace. "HR professionals now have an increased capacity not only to gather information, but also to store and retrieve it in a timely and effective manner" (Usman, 2012, p. 2).

"In terms of Human Resource Information System (HRIS), it has been described as an integrated system to collect, process, store, analyze, retrieve and disseminate critical information, which can provide useful support in HR decision making, coordination, control, analysis and visualization of an organization's HRM activities" (Moussa, 2014, p. 2). HRIS has linked all HR functions to a highly optimized database which has improved the efficiency and effectiveness of HR departments of any organizational body.

Additionally, Dessler (2000) identified that the organizations are opting implementation and usage of HRIS as it is a system that has the likely favorable results: (a) competitive advantage; (b) increase in the efficiency of HR activities and the line management of the organization; (c) elevate the organization to another level, as it generates a mixture of HR-related documents, and (d) capable of assessing HR activities concerning the organization's strategic plans. HRIS has more applications apart from storing and retrieving data such as forecasting HR needs, generating reports, performance appraisals, employee training and development, policy, and practice reviewing (Bohlander & Snell, 2004).

Furthermore, private and public sectors have their own reasons in the implementation and adoption of an HRIS. Public sector organizations' (for example health and education) core tangible goals are different from those of private sector organizations, which are mostly driven by the economic sustainability elements. "Due to budget timing restrictions, public sector organizations may be subject to constraints of budgeting cycles which may be dictated by political influences or periodic changes in political priorities" (Virginia, Maria, & Ana, 2007, p. 3).

However, this chapter uses the DeLone and McLean HRIS success model integrated with some incumbent HRIS factors providing a comprehensive view into vital factors affecting HRIS in the HR department. Thus, this study replicates the study carried out by Aletaibi (2016), which reviews the extant literature related to the HRIS success and develops and validates a multidimensional HRIS system success model based on IS success theories such as the technology acceptance model, user satisfaction, and DeLone and McLean information system success model. This integrative model will be used to assess the success of HRIS in a government Ministry and recommend ways to improve on areas which may be lacking.

LITERATURE REVIEW

Human resource is the greatest asset an organization possesses and it has to be looked after and nurtured properly to ensure that the organizations flourishes. "The 21st century saw "changes in the labor demographics, the 'war for talent', skill shortages and several other factors" (Wiblen, Grant, & Dery, 2010, p. 1). This is compelling all organizations to "consider new ways by which they can efficiently manage their human capital" (Wiblen et al., 2010, p. 1). Evident in most organizations today, one way to achieve this is through information systems. "To achieve organizational goals, traditional human resource management (HRM) process has been shifted to strategic HRM through significant contribution of information technology (IT)" (Alam, Kadar, Loo, & Hong, 2016, p. 2).

Most organizations give priority and invest in HRIS "while other organizations have failed to realize its short-term and long-term benefits" (Alam et al., 2016, p. 1). Organizations which realize the importance of HRIS "are becoming more and more dependent and use them for their daily management so as to achieve their goals and take more advantage of HRIS" (Noutsa et al., 2017, p. 1). "HRIS is a platform for the organization to be more competitive through proper communication with other systems. It reduces the boundaries of the system which create hurdles for both vertical and horizontal communication within the organization" (Majid, 2009, p. 3).

In a paper titled "A Resource-Flow Model of the Human Resource Information System" by Raymond and Gerardive (1995), they proposed a resource-flow model of the HRIS, based on system theory, as a framework for organizing and assessing HRIS components. "These model views applications in terms of activities that are performed as personnel flow through a firm" (Raymond & Gerardive, 1995, p. 2). The HRIS is the most recent functionally oriented information system. HRIS is computer-based application software. The term HRIS is used in two different ways. "One use regards it as an organizational unit and other use regards the HRIS as an entire computer based applications that process human resource information" (Raymond & Gerardive, 1995, p. 1).

According to this view, HRIS can be defined as "a computerized tool for the collection, storage, maintenance, and retrieval of information about people and their job" (Raymond & Gerardive, 1995, p. 2). As such, the HRIS is an example of a functional system, similar in organizational positioning to the marketing information system, the manufacturing resource planning system, and the accounting information system."

In another study titled, "Role of Human Resource in Information Technology Alignment in Organizations: A Metric Based Strategic Assessment Framework," the author defined various metrics to evaluate alignment of organizations business activities with HRIS. "Information technology (IT) is increasingly becoming an important factor and fundamental to support business processes in organizations" (Harekrishna, 2006, p. 1). "IT acquisitions are quite productive in supporting transactions and in aiding coordination mechanism provided the organizational resources and business processes are properly aligned with the IT" (Harekrishna, 2006, p. 2).

However, many IT acquisition projects fail due to improper alignment of the business process with IT. "Role of human resource (HR) is quite critical to such alignment process. It is important that acquiring organizations display HR capability to support alignment process especially in the pre-acquisition stage to minimize the post-acquisition shocks" (Tannenbaum, 1990, p. 1). In this chapter the role of HR in IT alignment process is discussed through some metrics during the pre-acquisition stage. A framework is developed and causal relationships among metrics are discussed. This framework is then tested for its fitness and applied to a case for appreciation. "HR involvement is an important aspect in all the stages of IT acquisition process" (Harekrishna, 2006, p. 2).

"In order to ensure a better and effective use of the IT acquired, HR involvement is required the most in the pre-acquisition stage in order to effectively manage subsequent stages" (Harekrishna, 2006, p. 3). Policy, attitude of strategic decision makers, decision-making style in the organization;

perception of users on IT (fear of losing importance and/or anxiety to use technology) also influence end-users in accepting IT. In this chapter they discussed a model that an organization can apply to assess its internal preparedness to manage the IT acquisition process. "Application of the model in the cement company revealed many important reasons behind the current status of IT" (Harekrishna, 2006, p. 3). The model stressed the importance of strategic and tactical level managers to understand the processes in the pre-acquisition stage and then organize a measuring tool to monitor the acquisition process. Studying only the pre-acquisition stage is the limitation of the study and therefore, "in the next stage of the research it is intended to expand the horizon of this model and apply it for the IT acquisition stage and Post acquisition stage" (Harekrishna, 2006, p. 3).

METHODOLOGY

There were a total of 52 employees in the division of which 50 employees were given the questionnaire as two employees were on leave. Forty-one questionnaires were returned of which all were completely filled. This gave a response rate of 82%.

Data Collection, Sampling, and Research Instruments

This portion of the chapter details the sampling of the data collection method employed in this chapter. It also outlines the key operational measures of variables which are also utilized in this chapter.

This research chapter uses quantitative data analysis. "Quantitative methods provide an important survey instrument for a wider coverage of the sample and allow accurate data measurement" (Aletaibi, 2016, p. 4). "Quantitative methods are widely used in IS research for quantifying the impact of factors affecting the adoption rate or use of IS technologies in various backgrounds" (Kaplan & Duchon, 1988, p. 2). Hence, quantitative methods have been employed to investigate between independent and dependent variables.

In order to ensure the validity and reliability of this chapter it became imperative to collect and analyze data which became a resource for this study as it assessed HRIS and its impact on HR employees. The samples for the purpose of this research were the employees in the HR division of a government organization. This chapter uses both primary and secondary research. Primary research was in the form of data collection and secondary research dealt with using information from sources that already existed which were acknowledged appropriately and were applicable.

For primary research (data collection) a pre-tested questionnaire from Aletaibi (2016) was used. In order to enlist the factors impacting the adoption of HRIS in organizations a HRIS adoption model from Aletaibi (2016) also was used which has been tested in organizations in Saudi Arabia. This chapter has also developed hypotheses relating to the impact of the constructs mentioned above based on the HRIS model.

The measurement instrument (questionnaire) used in this research was extracted from a study already carried out in Saudi Arabia titled, "An Analysis of the Adoption and Use of HRIS in Public Universities" (Aletaibi, 2016). This research had used studies on IS success and HRIS adoption from several countries and reviewed it forming the basis for the development of questionnaires in their research. This questionnaire was developed by using instruments proposed by DeLone and McLean (2003) and Urbach, Smolnik, and Riempp (2010), which had already been validated.

The research instrument developed in this study was based on system quality, information quality, use, user satisfaction, service quality, usefulness, and subjective norms. The research used a closed questionnaire type which gave the respondents the option to choose the answer which they think is the best.

The questionnaire consisted of a 5-point likert scale which ranged from *strongly disagree* to *strongly agree*. This type of likert scale has been used by numerous similar researches as it provides researchers with several probable scores and also elevates the statistical breakdown. It was ensured that the majority of the staff in the HR division were part of the survey as they are the daily users of HRIS.

Written ethical approval was obtained from the head of the organization before conducting this research. However, respondents were given five working days to complete the questionnaire after which it was collected. Confidentiality was maintained while carrying out the data collection and no respondents name was asked or filled in the questionnaires given out.

Quantitative Data Analysis

Statistical package for social sciences (SPSS) software was used to analyze the data collected using the questionnaire. This was also used to determine data reliability as well as to perform the principal component analysis (PCA). This was done to determine which items in the constructs loaded very well.

The steps employed to conduct the quantitative analysis in this chapter were derived from a modified approach that was used by Aletaibi (2016). In order to demonstrate the strength of contribution of the said constructs in increasing HRIS usage and the government organizations' HRIS adoption usage (dependent variables) multiple regression analysis was carried out.

These tools showcase the significance of every construct (independent variable) in the model. In addition to this, correlation analysis was also carried out. This was done to establish and understand the relationship between two variables. This entails the strength and direction of the relationship between the variables. The Kendall Tau-b test was used to obtain non-parametric correlation analysis between observed variables and research variables.

The tested hypothesis of the research is given below.

H1: *System quality will positively affect the use of HRIS.*

H2: *System quality will positively affect user satisfaction with HRIS.*

H3: *Information quality will positively affect the use of HRIS.*

H4: *Information quality will positively affect the user satisfaction of HRIS.*

RESULTS

The analysis carried out below gives understanding in regards to the quantitative relationship between the factors involved in the HRIS use model by analyzing the data collected using the questionnaire as described in the methodology section.

From Table 11.1 it can be articulated that all the workers in the HR division used HRIS regularly to perform basic HR functions.

Principal Component Analysis

In order to reduce the high number of usually related items into a variable, factor analysis is carried out. "The different items in a questionnaire may represent a trait" (Aletaibi, 2016, p. 2). "The commonly related items adhere to a trait, thus forming a factor" (Aletaibi, 2016, p. 2). The size of the sample is a major player when it comes to the reliability of factor analysis.

TABLE 11.1 Computer Use

Computer Use		Frequency	Percentage %
Valid	Never	0	0
	Daily	30	73
	Weekly	11	27
	Total	41	100

Correlation

Correlation analysis was done in order to comprehend the relationship between two variables. This would show the strength and relationship between the variables. In this chapter, non-parametric correlation was carried out from Kendall Tau-b test between observed ranked variables and the research variables as shown below.

The correlation test shown in Table 11.2 implies that age has a significant negative correlation with HRIS user satisfaction ($b = -0.231$, $p < 0.01$) along with the impact on the organization ($b = -0.0138$, $p < 0.01$). As the workers who use HRIS age increases, they become less satisfied. The satisfaction with HRIS is higher for the lower age group of the employees compared to the higher age groups. The younger age group is new to HRIS use. Hence, they are more satisfied than those employees who have been using it for several years. Additionally, it can also be observed that age and organizational impact has a negative correlation which lets us conclude that as employees age increases, it has a negative impact on organizational performance.

In government organizations, the older working group may begin to rely heavily on the younger generation hence; self-efficiency and performance may decline as the age increases. However, it should be noted with the increased use of computers, staff satisfaction is greater ($b = 0.124$, $p < 0.05$). Furthermore, it can also be noticed that the role of education is not vital in HRIS user satisfaction. The test in Table 11.3 shows that all the research variables have a positive significant correlation with each other.

Multiple Regression Analysis

The hypothesis of this chapter was tested using multiple regression analysis. This is a very useful method as it analyzes the relationship between dependent and independent variables. These techniques independent variables are weighed to come up with regression variation which is used

TABLE 11.2   Kendall's Tau-b Test: Non-Parametric Correlation

	System Quality	Information Quality	User Satisfaction	Use of HRIS	HRIS Adoption Usage
Age	−.077	−.092	−.231	−.008	−.138
Education	.040	.030	.096[*]	.081	.044
Computer Skill Level	.039	.069	.077	−.011	.054
Use of Computer	.103	.099	.124	.067	.126
Use of Internet	.033	.061	.086	.067	.097

[*] $p < 0.05$, [**] $p < 0.01$

TABLE 11.3 Kendall's Tau-b Test: Non-Parametric Correlation (2)

	System Quality	Information Quality	User Satisfaction	Use of HRIS	HRIS Adoption Usage
System Quality	1.000	0.532**	0.455**	0.286**	0.445**
Information Quality	0.530**	1.000	0.437**	0.339**	0.432**
User Satisfaction	0.489**	0.324**	1.000	0.320**	0.530**
Use of HRIS	0.286**	0.388**	0.330**	1.000	0.498**
HRIS Adoption Usage	0.441**	0.443**	0.510**	0.489**	1.000

* $p < 0.05$, ** $p < 0.01$

to explain its contribution towards the independent variable (Hair et al., 2006). This analysis helps in better understanding the relationship between system quality, information quality, user satisfaction, use of HRIS and HRIS adoption usage which were positively and moderately correlated with HRIS adoption usage. The summary of this analysis is tabulated below.

As per Table 11.4, F-stats gave (F = 32.29 which is also significant at 1 percent (Sig. F = 0:000) which shows the model is fit to be used. The table also shows that there are no multicollinearity problems (the multicollinearity statistics shows that the tolerance indicator for system quality, information quality, user satisfaction, use of HRIS and HRIS adoption usage are greater than 0.1 and variation inflation factors [VIF] are all less than 10). This reinforces that there is a significant relationship between perceived HRIS system quality, information quality, user satisfaction, use of HRIS, and HRIS adoption usage.

The results also indicated that the variables; namely, system quality, information quality, user satisfaction, and use of HRIS are positively associated with HRIS adoption and usage. It can be inferred that these variables are the key to HRIS adoption usage. Moreover, the findings also indicate that the most important variable that explains the variance in HRIS adoption

TABLE 11.4 Multiple Regression Analysis

Independent Variables	HRIS Adoption Usage				Collinearity Statistics	
	Beta	t-value	Sig.	Result	Tolerance	VIF
(constant)		2.39	0.02			
System Quality	0.338	5.145	0.00**	Accept	0.599	1.67
Information Quality	0.161	2.372	0.02*	Accept	0.563	1.776
User Satisfaction	0.039	0.607	0.54	Reject	0.638	1.568
Use of HRIS	0.096	1.312	0.02*	Accept	0.482	2.077

$n = 230$; *Significant at p, 0.05 level (2-tailed); **Significant at p, 0.01 level (2-tailed)

Overall Model: F = 32:29; p, 0.01; R^2 = 0:419; Adjusted R^2 = 0:406; Durbin-Watson test = 1:922.

usage was system quality and were significant at the 1% levels ($p < 0.01$). The results indicate support for the entire hypothesis.

RECOMMENDATIONS

1. Organizations should provide training to their employees on the use of HRIS. Lack of proper and enough training may have a negative impact on the use and success of HRIS. This will also affect the efficiency and effectiveness of HR outputs and affect the entire organizational performance.
2. Service quality is poor at times mainly due the delays with fixing faults to the HRIS system. This has to be addressed in order to increase the efficiency of HRIS and HR functions.
3. Organizations to have a support team internally rather than externally which takes too much time to respond to any requests.
4. Therefore, heads of human resources should divert their attention to improvement of service quality and efficiency.

CONCLUSION

This chapter examined the factors which could possibly boost the acceptance and the use of HRIS in a government organization as well as to see it influences the organizational performance. Therefore, attention was given to the employees of the organizations who use HRIS daily.

The successful implementation of HRIS also depends on improved communication between various departments of the organization. The findings of this study reported that only HR departments of organizations make use of HRIS and these are not linked to other departments. This means that there are unclear communication procedures and channels across various departments of the organization. Therefore, this study recommends that the roles of different departments be analyzed, and that a robust HRIS be implemented in order to link the services of HRIS to other departments. This will improve communication between systems and between personnel, increasing the level of success of HRIS within the organization."

REFERENCES

Alam, G. R., Abdul Kadar, M. M., Loo-See Beh, & Hong, C. S. (2016). Critical factors influencing decision to adopt human resource information system (HRIS) in hospitals. *PLoS One, 11*(8), e0160366. http://dx.doi.org/10.1371/journal.pone.0160366

Aletaibi, R. G. (2016). A*n analysis of the adoption and use of HRIS in the public Universities in Saudi Arabia* (Unpublished PhD Thesis). Coventry University.

Bohlander, G., & Snell, S. (2004). *Managing human resources* (13th ed.). South-Western Thomson.

Delone, W. H., & McLean, E. R. (2003). The DeLone and McLean model of information systems success: a ten-year update. *Journal of Management Information Systems, 19*(4), 9–30.

Dessler, G. (2000). *Human resource management* (8th ed.). Prentice Hall.

Hair, J., Black, W., Babin, B., Rolph, E., & Tatham, R. (2006). *Multivariate data analysis* (6th ed.). Pearson.

Kaplan, B., & Duchon, D. (1988). Combining qualitative and quantitative methods in information systems research: a case study. *MIS Quarterly*, 571–586.

Majid, R. (2009). Measuring the effectiveness of human resource information system in the national Iranian oil company an empirical assessment. *Iranian Journal Of Management Studies, 2*(2), 129–145.

Noutsa, A., & Wamba, S. F., & Robert, J. K. K. (2017, March). *Exploring factors affecting the adoption of HRIS in SMEs in a developing country: Evidence from Cameroon.* Paper presentation at the International Conference for a Better Life and a Better World, Paris.

Opatha , H. D. N. P. (2009). *Human resource management: Personnel.* Department of Human Resources University of Sri Jayewardenepura.

Tannenbaum, S. I. (1990). Human resource information systems: User group implications. *Journal of Systems, 41*, 27–32.

Urbach, N., Smolnik, S., & Riempp, G. (2010). An empirical investigation of employee portal success. *The Journal of Strategic Information Systems, 19*(3), 184–206.

Virginia, B., Maria, P., & Ana, I. J. (2007). Drivers, benefits and challenges of ICT adoption by small and medium sized enterprises: A literature review. *Problems and Perspectives in Management, 5*(1), 103–114.

Wiblen, S., Grant, D., & Dery, K. (2010). Transitioning to a new hris: The reshaping of human resources and information technology talent. *Journal of Electronic Commerce Research, 11*(4), 251–267.

CHAPTER 12

EXPLORING THE COMPETITIVE ADVANTAGE OF ERP IN TELECOMMUNICATIONS

Sam Goundar
The University of the South Pacific

Kunal Lal
The University of the South Pacific

Ashneel Kumar
The University of the South Pacific

Kavish Sen
The University of the South Pacific

Siddarth Singh
The University of the South Pacific

Enterprise Systems and Technological Convergence, pages 221–235
Copyright © 2021 by Information Age Publishing
All rights of reproduction in any form reserved.

ABSTRACT

Over the decades, the growth in the telecommunication and Internet service providers has extended tremendously. The rapid growth has led the telecommunication and Internet service providers to find innovative ways to provide better customer-oriented service to guarantee fast, reliable, efficient, and best customer experience. The South Pacific is no different, the telecommunication industries in the region have invested huge amounts of funds to improve their operational efficiencies to gain competitive advantage over other similar service providers. The key percentage of the funds that each of the service providers spent on is to improve their company profile to upgrade and improve their current business information system to an enterprise resource planning (ERP) system. The value, rarity, imitability, and organization (VRIO) framework and resource-based view (RBV) model has been employed to evaluate if investment into and ERP system was not only to improve operational efficient but was the investment into an ERP software exploited enough to gain maximum benefit for the future of the company. This chapter aims to illustrate the real competitive advantage, if any, an industry in the telecommunication and Internet market would get through ERP upgrades against their competitors. The outcomes of the chapter is to evaluate if there are real system and business benefits in ERP upgrades or are there alternative solutions to better financial investment in the developing ICT world for the Pacific. Through the use of this research the telecommunication and Internet industries in the region would gain an insight to evaluating the existing use of their ERP systems and upgrade strategies for the maximum return on investment.

The push to become the leading brand for Internet and telecommunication service providers in the South Pacific, the ISP companies tend to invest in huge volumes of funds into their company information system (IS) infrastructure. The main aim of the investment is to have better control of internal organizational operations, to improve monitoring of network performance, monitor stock in inventory, have better evaluation of company finances, transparency of department functions, have understanding of the business processes, and to improve organization efficiencies for the growth of the company. One such IS is the ERP, which has now become the key software for the functionality of any well managed ISP company. ERP is a software package, a set of integrated business applications that are utilized to enable information flows within and between processes across the organization (Konthon, Suwan-Natada, & Sompong, 2016). ERP systems are designed to provide, at least in theory, seamless integration of processes across functional areas with improved workflow, standardization of various business practices, and access to real-time up-to-date data (Mabert, Soni, & Venkataramanan, 2003). ERP in many organizations are for operational and transactional processing such as; financials, inventory, purchase, order management, and detail reporting (Helmy, Marie, & Mosaad, 2012).

ERP system upgrades are complex and could take a long duration, from few months to years to be fully implemented to achieve its full functionality. Emerging ICT companies in the rush to set up shop to capitalize on the demand for Internet and telecommunication by the people of the Pacific Islands, often tend to be unaware of the challenges and ERP system upgrade could bring and are also unaware of the time it would take to expect any real return on investment (ROI) from upgrading to an ERP system. Instead of developing IT systems in-house, more and more companies are turning to the new off-the-shelf ERP upgrades solutions to plan IT resources more effectively and manage their legacy systems (Al-Mashari, Al-Mudimigh, & Zairi, 2003). Organizations need to understand the system adaption from the user's perspective to prepare their employees to face new challenges and learn how to make good use of the technology to reap tangible benefits (Chang, Cheung, Cheng, & Yeung, 2008).

PROBLEM STATEMENT

There are many different modules of ERP software packages available in the global market to support different types of information systems for telecommunication and Internet industries. ERP systems can be described as a modularized suite of business software (Forslund, 2010). ERP is extensive software systems that integrate a number of business processes, such as manufacturing, supply chain, sales, finance, human resources, budgeting, and customer service (Weinrich & Ahmad, 2009). To have a complete one-solution software aiming to address the challenges faced in the Internet and telecommunication industry will be to upgrade from existing ERP software to a new version ERP system with added industrial module. Would investing in ERP upgrades provide real ROIt against the invested time and cost? Hence the need to study and assess the purpose of upgrading to an ERP system and its fit for purpose to address efficiencies.

RESEARCH OBJECTIVE

The research team aims to get insight into the types of ERP system being used by the different Internet and telecommunication vendors in the South Pacific. The chapter is to investigate the real need, for the migration towards the ERP upgrades from current ERP software or legacy systems and to weigh out the ROI from the use of the new ERP systems with added functionality. Was the motivation by which telecommunication companies invested in the upgrade of the ERP system achieved in the anticipated duration and cost, or was the investment into the ERP system taken on board following global market trends on its use without knowledge on how to gain any competitive advantage over other similar vendors?

LITERATURE REVIEW

While there are many ERP software solutions available in the market, the vendors who are looking to invest in ERP systems are still unable to segregate the best ERP system to upgrade to, in order to address the challenges of the information systems as per their business model and processes. The companies are unable to grasp the purpose that an ERP software serves and the different forms of ROI an ERP upgrade could offer. A study by Kwasi and Salam on the use of the technology acceptance model (TAM) for the ERP implementation evaluated the impact of shared belief in the benefits of technology and widely recognized technology implementation success factors on the perceived usefulness and perceived ease of use of the ERP system (Amoako-Gyampah & Salam, 2004). The chapter discussed the usefulness of business process reengineering to match the full capabilities of the ERP software. As also discussed in the paper by Staehr, the actions of managers at all levels who have the authority to make decisions regarding the ERP planning, implementation, and its use equates to achieving business benefits from ERP system (Staehr, 2010). The paper also discussed areas of improvement in ERP management practices in order to obtain maximum benefits. To fully capitalize on the use of the ERP, it also depends on the relationship between the information technology staff and the general management. One such study shows that IT staff find general managers lack technological awareness or interest in the ERP system while managers think IT staff produce systems which are over budget, systems are implemented late and often fail to address business needs (Chang, 2006).

Companies fail to gain competitive advantage over the ERP system due to failures in correct implementation of the ERP system. ERP system success depends on the rigor of the project management process; scope creep, poor risk management, inadequate allocation of human resources over time, and lack of management support are common reasons for poor ERP implementation and use (Chen, Law, & Yan, 2009). An ERP system upgrade often requires years of implementation and post implementation support to become part of the business functionality and assist in achieving strategic goals. Another reason why the ERP system fails to provide competitive advantage is the direct consequence of the lack of knowledge on how to successfully utilize the ERP tool by its users. Such as, the amount of time it takes for the company staff and stakeholders to learn on how to use the system, the number of input errors due to lack of understanding of the steps required to complete a business process, unclear instructions, and lack of system helpfulness to ease the operation functionality (Topi, Lucas, & Babaian, 2005).

Upgrading to an ERP system could have an impact on the business model, business processes, staff roles, and the executive decision-making structure. As discussed in the paper by Kanellou and Spathis, the ERP software was incorporated in the organization with a main focus to improve the accounting aspects of the firm. The ERP was used to reap accounting benefits to increase flexibility in information generation, increase integration of accounting applications, to improve quality on report, statement of accounts, and to make decisions based on timely and reliable accounting information (Kanellou & Spathis, 2013). The competitive advantage is often lacking in such ERP upgrades due to lack of analysis on the business needs for the ERP system and the system requirements. There has been many key driving facts highlighted in research papers over the years on reason why firms adopt and carry out ERP upgrades such as globalization of business, business process re-engineering to focus on process standardization, flexibility of emerging client/server infrastructure, and the trends towards collaboration among global software vendors (Moller, 2005).

RESEARCH QUESTIONS

The research team focused on the reasons why Internet and telecommunication companies in the South Pacific region would invest in an upgrade of their ERP systems and if the motive behind the investment was achieved. The research questions tries to capture if the ERP upgrades provided any competitive advantage over rival vendors or was its potential limited. The research questions concentrate on performing an analysis using the VRIO framework from the resource based view (RBV) model to measure if the ERP upgrade provided competitive advantage and if it did, then what these advantages were over other vendors in the country who were providing the same service. The research questions revolved around the company's reason for ERP upgrade; the name of the newly implemented ERP system and the additional functionalities it offered to different departments compared to old ERP; whether the ERP upgrade brings about positive or negative changes; whether the ERP upgrade brings any competitive advantage for the firm looking at the Internet and telecommunication market in their country; or if there were any projected, tangible, or intangible ROI from the ERP upgrade. The survey ends with trying to gather facts from organization staff on their view of the ERP upgrade and if it was fit for purpose as anticipated.

The firms had invested a lot of funds and time into upgrading the information system for a collaborative ERP system for the betterment of the company's inner department functions. Hence the research question is a way to measure if the ERP upgrade venture had had any real impact on the ROI for the firm. The research questions efforts is to gain knowledge on the type of ERP software used by telecommunication industries, the number of years that it has been in use after the upgrade, the department and stakeholders who have access to work with the ERP system, and if the ERP software was patented to the organization to provide a competitive advantage.

METHODOLOGY

The methodology used to support the data collection and analysis for this research chapter was achieved through literature review, a survey questionnaire, and interviews. The research team searched and studied relevant journals published in reference to ERP systems and its competitive advantages from accredited publishing sources. Journal articles which focused on ERP software, ERP system benefits and challenges, ERP implementation and models used to evaluate ERP were selected for review. Relevant literature on the use of VRIO framework on different business models were also selected to investigate the key features that are taken into consideration to agree if an organization had achieved competitive advantage. The research team decided to take a combination of quantitative and qualitative approach for the collection and analysis of data to support the chapter.

An online survey questionnaire was developed to assist in a quantitative approach to gather information about the ERP system that the companies had recently upgraded to. The questionnaire was sent to at least one ISP company in the neighboring fourteen Pacific Island countries and the focus group was the lead IS manager or chief technical officer of the company. The question form was divided into two key sections, the first section was centered on a general company profile such as the name of the upgraded ERP system, the department of the company using the ERP system, how long ago was the ERP system upgraded, the percentage of the companies work process operated by the upgraded ERP, and the Pacific country the industry was based in. The second section of the questionnaire developed to support the VRIO framework with the aim to capture detailed competitive advantage a company got from ERP upgrades. The questionnaire had a mixture of nineteen questions with the majority of the questions requiring a binary yes or no response to keep the survey easy and fast to complete. Some of the questions also provided additional text input where the respondent had an option to enter discussion details so support their binary selection. The questionnaire was sent to companies in each of the 14 countries in the South Pacific of which 7 country firms responded with sufficient information making the response rate of 50%. The chapter by Dillman, points out that surveys addressed to companies would have an average response rate of 40% (Dillman, 2007), thus our study response rate seems to be above average.

The data was also collected through two successful interview sessions with technical officers of two ISP companies in Fiji. The interview meeting was an informal discussion of 30 minutes on the ERP system upgrade that had taken place in the company, the benefits of the new ERP on the company operations and the competitive advantage the ERP system brought, in-terms of added features and department functional modules. Facts of company operations pre ERP upgrade versus post ERP upgrade were noted. The interview also saw the opportunity to discuss the limitation of the ERP system used previously and the key reason to persuade the company executives to agree to ERP upgrade to the latest version or a totally new ERP software. To evaluate the collected data through the quantitative and qualitative approach, the research team agreed on performing the analysis using the VRIO framework from the RBV model.

The RBV model focuses primarily on the internal characteristics of a firm (Beard & Sumner, 2004). RBV is useful in determining whether the Internet and telecommunication company's strategy on ERP upgrade, a valuable resource for the company, has created any impact. In our research the RBV model as shown in Figure 12.1, is used to determine if the company's strategic decision on the ERP system upgrade has gained additional tangible and intangible benefits in contrast to the previous ERP

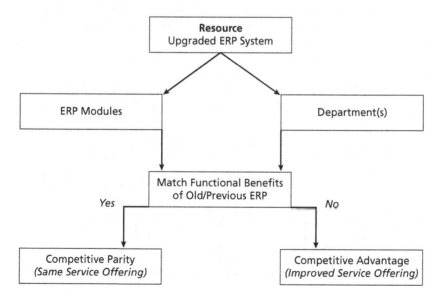

Figure 12.1 Resource based view of ERP upgrade.

software. The positive answer leads to competitive advantage, meaning the upgraded ERP has additional functionalities which the company can exploit to maintain lead over rival vendors. The negative answer leads to competitive parity which in other words means the new ERP functions are not new or unique in comparison to old ERP systems giving the company little to no ROI. RBV informs understanding of linkage between type of IT—ERP system, and the nature of the business process and organization performance (Shang & Wu, 2004).

The VRIO framework is structured with a number of questions about resources and capabilities using four indicators of VRIO (Ariyani, Daryanto, & Sahara, 2018). In the research paper, VRIO analysis tries to answer what distinctive characteristics an upgraded ERP system should have to increase a company's competitiveness (Charana, 2014) as illustrated in Figure 12.2.

Value—whether the upgraded ERP system makes the business process more efficient and can be exploited to provide system and business benefits. Does the ERP upgrade help the business perform its operation tasks and provide customer experience better than its competitors? The ERP system which is a software resource is only valuable if it provides strategic value to the company (Cardeal & Antonio, 2012).

Rarity—is the new ERP system rare in the sense that only your company is able to use this software in the country of operation and cannot be owned by competitors? The newly upgraded ERP system is rarely owned by similar telecommunication and Internet companies. Resources that are possessed by several firms in the marketplace cannot provide competitive advantage as they cannot design and execute a unique business strategy in comparison with rival companies (Madhani, 2010).

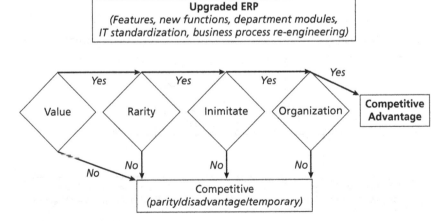

Figure 12.2 VRIO analysis on ERP upgrade.

Inimitability—can the functions of the ERP be imitated by other ERP systems which rival companies could have access to? The upgraded ERP system business process strategies that cannot be easily imitated. Imitation of the ERP system by the competitors should result in financial burden affecting their operations. Is the telecommunication company having the upgraded ERP ownership patent?

Organization—raises the point, if the upgraded ERP is being used to its maximum potential with equal support from company operation staff and higher managers. If all the service offering by the new ERP is fully deployed for the organizational use and benefit. Does the firm align its business process and policies to be able to fully realize the potential of the new upgraded resource (Pesic, Milic, & Stankovic, 2012). The simultaneous execution of the four characteristics of the company's ERP resource and its combination provides realization of a firm's goals (Marichova, 2018).

Hence through the assistance of RBV and VRIO the following hypothesis is proposed:

H1: *If the ERP upgrades improve a current business process through inclusion of a new ERP module with new features, and/or incorporates additional business departments which were previously not part of using the ERP system, then the firm has competitive advantage in the market.*

H2: *An ERP upgrade provides value to the organization in terms of system and business benefits.*

H3: *Patented ERP has competitive advantage over unpatented ERP.*

H4: *Upgrading the ERP system would allow companies to explore possibilities for increased profitability and market expansion.*

RESULTS

The core aim of the research was to capture the motive behind a telecommunication and Internet company investing in ERP system upgrades and if there were real ROI. The research targeted the telecommunication and Internet sector in the South Pacific countries. Through interviews and on-line circulation of questionnaires to at least one company representative in each of the 14 Pacific Island countries, the research team was successful in getting adequate information from seven different country companies hence achieving a 50% positive response rate as illustrated in Figure 12.3.

The responses from each country's telecommunication and Internet was analyzed using the RBV model to record if there were competitive advantages from the ERP upgrade in terms of added features and departmental use. Table 12.1 breaks down the response received from each country

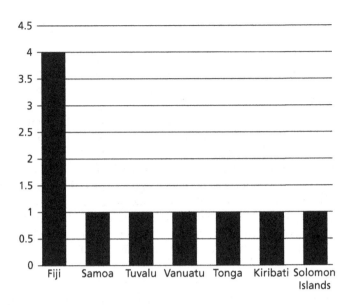

Figure 12.3 South Pacific country response rate.

TABLE 12.1	RBV Analysis on Upgraded ERP				
Country	Company	Similar or New Module	Additional Department	Changes From Old ERP	Competitive Parity or Advantage
Fiji	A	New	Yes	Significant	Competitive Advantage
	B	Similar	No	Moderate	Competitive Parity
	C	Similar	Yes	Moderate	Competitive Parity
	D	New	No	Significant	Competitive Advantage
Samoa	E	New	Yes	Moderate	Competitive Advantage
Tuvalu	F	Similar	Yes	Moderate	Competitive Parity
Vanuatu	G	New	Yes	Significant	Competitive Advantage
Tonga	H	New	Yes	Significant	Competitive Advantage
Kiribati	I	New	Yes	Significant	Competitive Advantage
Solomon Is	J	New	Yes	Significant	Competitive Advantage

context. The research team data was based against the features and functions of the old ERP to the upgraded ERP.

The results highlighted that mostly the telecommunications industries invested in the ERP system to include new modules in a bid for the company to keep up to par with the developing ICT sector. Advances in the e-commerce and cloud computing are some of the reasons an ICT company would invest in their ERP system upgrade to reach global markets and provide a more interactive interface for its clients. Another reason for the ERP upgrade was to provide better transparency for the flow of company stock, finances, and client feedback. Hence the inclusion of department(s) mentioned were finance, warehouse, and helpdesk, which were previously not part of the old ERP but are now using the new ERP accessing the centralized database.

This proves the hypothesis (H1), that ERP upgrades improves business processes and provides firm competitive advantage only if there are significant changes from old ERP systems else the competitive advantage will last only for a short term. It is also noted that a more technology developed Island state such as Fiji, has more competitive parity since it has more market players in the ICT sector in comparison to the smaller Island nations who may be the only company providing the service in a country giving them a more competitive edge in using their ERP system.

Upgraded ERP brings better system and business efficiencies. System efficiencies in the form of improved performance as the upgraded ERP license can handle higher number of subscribers for the firm, which was a limitation of older ERP due to reaching the maximum subscriber threshold. Better system performance in the capability of handling hundreds of simultaneous requests with synchronized record keeping.

The research also investigates the different ERP software upgrade solutions bought by the firms and using the VRIO framework analysis if the software provided competitive advantage for the firms. Table 12.2 and Table 12.3, details some of the ERP software upgrades and was measured against the four VRIO characteristics to show if each was addressed.

TABLE 12.2	VIRO Analysis on Different ERP Upgrades					
Upgraded ERP Software	Years in Use	Value	Rarity	Inimitable	Organization	Competitive Parity or Dis/Advantage
Accpac	10	Yes	No	No	Yes	Competitive Parity
SAP	10	Yes	No	No	Yes	Competitive Parity
Technology One	5	Yes	Yes	No	Yes	Competitive Advantage
Procure	5	Yes	Yes	No	Yes	Competitive Advantage
Microsoft Dynamics	?	Yes	No	No	Yes	Competitive Parity
SunSystems	3	Yes	No	No	No	Competitive Disadvantage
Rodopi	8	Yes	No	No	Yes	Competitive Parity
Ubersmith	3	Yes	No	No	Yes	Competitive Parity

TABLE 12.3 Percentage Measure on VRIO Classes an ERP Upgrade Would Have					
Of the Total 8 Responses	Value %	Rarity %	Inimitable %	Organization %	Competitive Parity or Dis/Advantage
Yes, Upgraded ERP Offered:	100	25	100	87	Competitive Advantage and Parity
No, Upgraded ERP Did Not Offer:	0	75	0	13	Competitive Disadvantage

The tabulated results prove the hypothesis (H2), that ERP upgrades brings system and business benefits. The business benefits are, improved monitoring of business performance indicators, increased transparency in the flow of work and reporting structure, better sharing of information between departments and operating as one entity, and to have accurate accounting of business stock and finances. Organization also saw cost savings in buying support services and renewing licenses of different software across different departments. Overall upgrade of ERP systems provided added value in all organizations to gain some form of competitive advantage.

The rarity and inimitable characteristic of the upgraded ERP did not receive a favorable response if a company would get competitive advantage if the upgraded ERP system was patented to restrict use by competitors and if the business process re-engineering done for effective use of the upgraded ERP could not be imitated. The survey results showed that none of the telecommunication and Internet service providers considered their upgraded ERP to be rare in the sense that other rival vendors would not be able to procure or have access to. This is understandable due to the fact of evolving IS technology at a rapid rate. Comparing two ERP systems, a feature not available in one ERP software against the second ERP software could see it available in the next upgraded version of the second ERP software. For organizations to have complete ownership of upgraded ERP, it would incur additional expensive fees to patent the software over the already expensive ERP upgrade. Similarly, upgraded ERP are also vulnerable to imitation of business processes. The scope of the telecommunication functions and operations is not a complex or hidden knowledge from similar service offering vendors. It is not so different to imitate the business process of upgraded ERP due to competing firms offering the same service products and having similar department functions. Hypothesis (H3) is disproven since upgraded ERPs are not patent as organizations do not see real business benefit. On average patent upgraded ERP would offer competitive parity. Value and rarity are required for temporary competitive advantage, additionally value, rarity, and inimitability is required for sustained long-term competitive advantage (Jugdev, 2019).

The final characteristic used in the VRIO analysis is organization, this discusses if the upgraded ERP system is adapted well in the organization for maximum ROI. In our research case, the majority of the respondents said the organization was organized enough to make the full use of the upgraded ERP. The organization context was in the preparedness of its staff with adequate training to understand ERP function and different modules that are introduced. The demarcation of roles and functions with information sharing and motivation behind business process re-engineering that would be rewarding to business and its staff. The study revealed that telecommunication and Internet companies investing in ERP upgrades have had experience in using the ERP systems and would have operating procedures already in place to assist in quick adaptation to upgraded ERP. The core motive for organizations is to incorporate business expansion reaching into e-commerce and offering better customer experience through CRM modules. Hypothesis H4 is proven to be correct as upgraded ERPs offer better collaboration within an organization department leading to rewarding and profitable business. The management incorporation with system functionality would need to function hand in hand to allow the upgraded ERP system to deliver on its potential.

CONCLUSION

After the analysis of collected data using the RBV model and VRIO framework it can be concluded that ERP upgrades do offer competitive advantage, however can only sustain the competitive advantage till the next new ERP module or ERP package is released. As the competition becomes more and more intense in the business environment, firms are paying more attention on how to achieve and maintain competitive advantages (Kim, Lee, & Shin, 2015). The upgraded ERP can offer many system and business benefits such as; reduced cost of operation, offer quality systems in the advancing computing technology, offer better security, and performance for handling confidential company data with real time data synchronization across all departments, leading to a better productive environment for higher profit margin. ERP upgrades in this era is evolving from incorporating different departmental applications to now incorporating other business ERP's together. Upgrading an ERP system offers better chances of adapting to the latest information technology systems over an ERP which is a decade old. Future research can be done in country specific ERP systems and in ERP as a cloud service. With the advancements of cloud service and software as a service being an attractive solution to reducing cost, ERP systems could be implemented online in the future. Companies would save cost from purchasing the upgrade of ERP software and will have the flexibility to use an on-demand service structure for ERP upgrades.

REFERENCES

Al-Mashari, M., Al-Mudimigh, A., & Zairi, M. (2003). Enterprise resource planning: A taxonomy of critical factors. *European Journal of Operational Research, 146*(2), 352–364.

Amoako-Gyampah, K., & Salam, A. F. (2004). An extension of the Technology acceptance model in an ERP implementation environment. *Information & Management, 41*(6), 731–745.

Ariyani,W., Daryanto, A., & Sahara. (2018). Operationalization of internal analysis using the VRIO framework: Development of scale for resource and capabilities organization (Case study: XYZ company animal feed business unit). *Asian Business Research Journal, 3*(1), 9–14.

Beard, J. W., & Sumner, M. (2004). Seeking strategic advantage in the post-net era – Viewing ERP systems from the resource-based perspective. *Journal of Strategic Information Systems, 13*(2), 129–150.

Cardeal, N., & Antonio, N. (2012). Value, rare, inimitable resource and organization (VRIO) resources or valuable, rare, inimitable resources (VRI) capabilities: What leads to competitive advantage? *African Journal of Business Management, 6*(37), 10159–10170.

Chang, H. (2006). Technical and management perceptions of ERP importance, implementation and benefits. *Info Systems, 16*(3), 263–292.

Chang, M. K., Cheung, W., Cheng, C. H., & Yeung, J. H. Y. (2008). Understanding ERP system adaption from the user's perspective. *International Journal of Production Economics, 113*(2), 928–942.

Charana, D. O. (2014). *Competitive advantage: Resource and capabilities: VRIO and VRIO Frameworks.* https://www.coursehero.com/file/45017640/Competitive-advantage-Resources-and-Capapdf/

Chen, C.C., Law, C. C., & Yan, S. C. (2009). Managing ERP Implementation failure: A project management perspective. *IEEE Transactions on Engineering Management, 56*(1), 157–170.

Dillman, D. A., (2007). *Mail and internet services: The tailored design method.* Wiley.

Forslund, H. (2010). ERP systems' capabilities for supply chain performance management. *Industrial Management & Data Systems, 110*(3), 351–367.

Helmy, Y. M., Marie, M. I., & Mosaad, S. M. (2012). An integrated ERP with web portal. *Advanced Computing: An International Journal, 3*(5), 1–8.

Jugdev, K. (2019). *The VRIO framework of competitive advantage: Preliminary research implications for organizational innovations as dawn from a project management study.* http://citeseerx.ist.psu.edu/viewdoc/summary?doi=10.1.1.336.7010

Kanellou, A., & Spathis, C. (2013). Accounting benefits and satisfaction in an ERP environment. *International Journal of Accounting Information Systems, 14*(3), 209–234.

Kim, S., Lee, J., & Shin, K. (2015). The Impact of project management assets on VRIO characteristics of PM process for competitive advantage. *Productivity and Quality Management, 15*(2), 153–168.

Konthon, K., Suwan-natada, P., Sompong, A. (2016). The investigation of ERP and E_business effects in Thailand: A resource based view. *Journal of Business and Retail Management Research, 11*(1), 116–123.

Mabert, V. A., Soni, A., & Venkataramanan, M. A. (2003). Enterprise resource planning: Managing the implementation process. *European Journal of Operational Research, 146*(2), 302–314.

Madhani, P. M. (2010). Resource based view (RBV) of competitive advantage: An overview. *Indian Management Research Journal, 1*(2). https://www.researchgate.net/publication/45072537_Resource_Based_View_RBV_of_Competitive_Advantages_Importance_Issues_and_Implications

Marichova, A. (2018). Application VRIO framework to evaluate capabilities of the construction firm to create competitive advantages. *International Journal of Engineering Sciences & Research Technology, 7*(8), 362–369.

Moller, C. (2005). ERP II: A conceptual framework for next-generation enterprise systems. *Journal of Enterprise Information Management, 18*(4), 483–497.

Pesic, M. A., Milic, J. V., & Stankovic, J. (2012). *Application of VRIO framework for analyzing human resources role in providing competitive advantage.* https://tmstudies.net/index.php/ectms/article/viewFile/447/725

Shang, S. C., & Wu, T. (2004). *A model for analyzing organizational performance of ERP systems form a resource-based view.* http://www.pacis-net.org/file/2005/334.pdf

Staehr, L. (2010). Understanding the role of managerial agency in achieving business benefits from ERP systems. *Info Systems, 20*(3), 213–238.

Topi, H., Lucas, W., & Babaian, T. (2005, May). *Identifying usability issues with an ERP implementation.* Paper presentation at the 7th annual International Conference on Enterprise Information Systems, Miami, FL.

Weinrich, K. I., & Ahmad, N. (2009). Lessons learned during a decade of ERP Experiences: A case study. *International Journal of Enterprise Information Systems, 5*(1), 55–75.

CHAPTER 13

MEASURING THE SUCCESS OF ERP WITH THE DeLONE AND McLEAN MODEL

Sam Goundar
The University of the South Pacific

Azhar Buksh
The University of the South Pacific

Karpagam Masilamani
The University of the South Pacific

Nickil Rajan
The University of the South Pacific

Khushant Prakash
The University of the South Pacific

Enterprise Systems and Technological Convergence, pages 237–255
Copyright © 2021 by Information Age Publishing
237

ABSTRACT

There's a fast growing use for Enterprise Resource Planning (ERP) systems being done all over by a majority of businesses globally and the measuring of the success of these types of information systems should be done for firms where it is implemented. The firms nowadays invest in a large portion of financial resources towards implementation of these information systems (IS), as assessing the success of such IS doesn't not happen due to a lot of reasons, including lacking in the knowledge level of what is to be assessed for success determining for an IS such as ERP. The DeLone and McLean (D&M) model development has occurred and has been majorly utilized for IS success measuring, therefore the use of this model will be utilized to measure the success of IS. Also there are three main dimensions of D&M model on which more focused discussion will be done in this chapter which are as follows: user satisfaction, system quality, and information quality. The use of qualitative and quantitative data analysis techniques will be used for various research literature review, with structural equation modeling approach being used to examine and summarize the statistical data collected through interviews and questionnaires. In this chapter we will be focusing on retail industries in Fiji in which information systems like ERP are implemented and measure success using the D&M model based on individual and organizational units of analysis.

The level of competitiveness in the business environment rises at a high rate, as the increase in demand for better quality of service daily is making it challenging for businesses to operate efficiently. Computers have become more than just a business advanced technological tool. The implementation of such IT technologies enables the organization to operate effectively and efficiently. Enterprise resource planning (ERP) system is one of the IT tools which businesses implement in order to meet the demands and needs in the current world of business. The implementation of ERP also will allow businesses to have more real time visibility and provide better management of business operations. The implementation is not the simplest task to achieve, as these types of systems can be large and difficult to manage, thus to make sure the implementation is successful it needs to be carefully planned and executed (Gupta, 2000). There are a number of advantages that an ERP implementation brings such as improving the organization's effectiveness and efficiency by adding more value to business in terms of automating and integrating of business processes, data and practices can be shared, and accessing information real-time (Ragowsky, 2005).

Even though the measurement of success of ERP is vital as it involves investment of a lot of human resources and financial expenditures. There has been an attempt made in this chapter to analyze, evaluate and discuss the success of ERP system implementation using the D&M model. The D&M model has been discovered to be very useful as a framework regarding organizing success measurement of IS. Researchers usually preferred using the model to measure and understand IS dimensions. Furthermore, the D&M model consists of six key success variables: system quality, information quality, use, user satisfaction, individual impact, and organizational impact, as Figure 13.1 shows this original IS success model (DeLone & McLean, 1992) and in this chapter to help make it easier to measure the success. Out of the six variables of success measurement, only three will be focused on for this research: system quality, user satisfaction, and information quality (Figure 13.1 shows this original IS success model [DeLone & McLean, 1992]). DeLone and McLean was later modified to introduce an updated version of the DeLone and McLean (2003), where an addition of service quality and the merging of individual impact and organizational impact on net benefits (Figure 13.2 shows this updated IS success model [DeLone & McLean, 2003]).

The updated version of DeLone and McLean (2003) IS success model and relationships was evaluated by making use of both qualitative and quantitative research data analysis. For the quantitative data analysis analytical data was collected through questionnaires and surveys from the retail

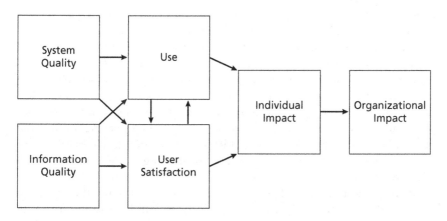

Figure 13.1   IS success model (Delone & McLean, 1992).

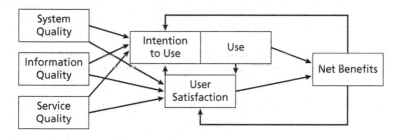

Figure 13.2   Updated success model (DeLone and McLean, 2003).

business in Fiji which have an ERP system implemented. The following next sections will be highlighting various explanations why the D&M model was the choice of model used to measure the success for this literature review. A detailed description of techniques made use of in order to achieve and organize the research, also a more thorough revised summary of all the past related literature papers. The results gained from the literature review and the statistical information which was collected and analyzed using the structural equation modeling (SEM) technique then presented in statistical format for much easier understanding for the readers. The last section of this chapter will highlight the effects of this body of research for researchers interested in assessing IS success.

LITERATURE REVIEW

A Critical Success Factors Model For Enterprise Resource Planning Implementation (Holland & Light, 1999) mainly focuses on the importance of ERP and difficulties of implementing ERP. They have used a critical success factor framework to measure the difficulties with the old legacy system, top management, business vision, business strategy, client consultants, and business process re-engineering. The research considered about the tactical and strategic plan are their main objectives. They have done the case study in eight companies to calculate the critical success factors. They have also mentioned the growth of ERP in the organization. The organization has to consider choosing the vendor, vendor analysis, business policies and procedures, user involvement, business process re-engineering, implementation plan, and design. In this case ERP software is not developed in house by the IT department but they purchased something that was already developed which suits the organization.

At the same time, modifying the ERP software will make the organization benefit, but changing the business process will lead to failure of an organization so it is always better to customize the ERP software according to business requirements. There was a comparison between two companies, Statco and Threadco. They measured the Statco and Threadco companies with strategic and tactical plans. In Threadco where the ERP implementation was done to the whole organization to get fully functional at one time and the other Statsco was done stage by stage fast tracking implementation but they did not run both of the systems in parallel. Statco implemented the SAP ERP with full functionality as quickly as possible, and Threadco implemented it in a safe process. The implementation process became slow and complex, but still they achieved their goals. The lesson learned from this case study is before implementing ERP the organization should be organized, design the goals, architecture, consultants, even software configuration need to be known and understand the old systems nature to avoid the failure in the implementation process.

A study (Ullah, Baharun, Khalil, Siddique, & Sami, 2017) concerned on the performance of users found the impacts of user performance. The authors focused on success and failure of ERP in terms of user performance and the result is to measure whether the users are being benefited using the ERP system or not. They have understood the benefits of ERP and it provides so many advantages but when it comes to implementing it, it has a lot of issues. ERP improves the business process by improving productivity, the customer service and integration between departments, information sharing, and so on. Most of the implementation process has a higher failure rate when compared to the successful implementation of ERP in the organization. Because of technological difficulties both information technology and IS have major challenges. The research done the literature review about the user performance but surprisingly none of the studies have described the purpose of ERP in user performance. Some of the literature reviews have explained about the implementation strategy, post-implementation, pre-implementation. They have also studied various literature to focus on user performance including D&M IS success model, task technology fit, technological acceptance model, and end user computing satisfaction model to evaluate the importance of user performance still there is lack of proper information provided. Further research is needed to focus on efficiency, effectiveness, and the impact of user performance at user level needs to be improved.

The paper, "Managing Risks in Enterprise Systems Implementations," focuses on the implementation of ERP (Scott & Vessey, 2002) which is a case study based on two companies where one was the silicone industry and the other a drug distribution industry. Two companies FoxMeyer and Dow Corning implemented SAP R/3 at same time. But with the different vision and top management issues one company succeeded and the other failed in the implementation stage. The Foxmeyer goal was to get the advantage from the ERP so they installed warehouse automated software. Issues with both companies is that they went bankrupt and lawsuits were filed against them. FoxMeyer has done the quantitative analysis by collecting the information from online resources and then ran the simulation to meet the business requirement but it did not meet requirements the business process changed by customizing the system.

As their focus on organization changed, Scott and Vessey (2002) used a model for risk factor in ES implementation. They had a well defined project plan and Dow Corning collected the information from in-depth interviews. But did the vanilla implementation because it is easy.

The problems were lack of user involvement, lack of management, lack of cost, lack of business vision, no proper consultants, and lack of training for the user. They maintained the business with business processes and information technology to support the re-engineering process in the organization.

The model for risk factor in (Scott & Vessey, 2002) were that Enterprise Systems implementation has tactical, strategic, and organizational level inter-relationship. At last the Dow Corning implementation became a success but the FoxMeyer implementation failed because the senior manager was over confident that the ERP software would manage the business needs without the involvement of employees. So no proper importance and training was given to the employees. Employees are the backbone of an organization to achieve success.

The research measures the ERP implementation, ERP benefits, and ERP critical success factor of ERP. The background of these papers (Al-Mashari, Al-Mudimigh, & Zairi, 2003) mentioned about the MRP I AND MRP II where these were not able to meet the business requirements so to be more advanced and to replace MRP I AND MRP II the tools or software which arrived in the market is called enterprise systems. The enterprise system can benefit the organization by providing productivity, sales, financial statement, decision-making, manufacturing, human resources management by integrating all the processes into a centralized system. ERP's most important feature is integrating the business process and IT infrastructure into one centralized system and it is the first method to combine the IT in the software market.

The two things ERP consists of are tangible and intangible. According to Seddon and Shang, it is divided into five main components: operational, strategic, static, IT, and infrastructure. Critical success factors failure and success are divided into process success, correspondence success, interaction, and expectation success.

According to Seddon and Kiew (1999), they try to replace the D&M IS success model with their new model which is system quality, information quality, user satisfaction, and their use are related to each other. They have debated about use and usefulness; which is to be considered more important? In components of information quality, timeliness, accuracy, and requirement gathering are some of the issues accessed. In components of system quality, system quality defines the error, ease of use, consistency of user interface, feedback rates in active system, documentation, and also checks the quality of the system and maintainability of the source code. In components of usefulness, usefulness measures the job performance of the individual user when they use the system.

This literature review of so many authors are mostly focused on measuring and trying to justify the hypothesis used in the Seddon and Ying model. We have reviewed seven research papers to get the answer to measures the user satisfaction. Each author has used a different model to calculate the results. The data was collected from large numbers of users from the organization. The results were analysed by using methods such as Cronbach alpha and Pearson correlation matrix, ordinary least square, linear regression, and the structural equation model.

First, they have the long and short term which has five factors included: EDP staff and services, information product, vendor support, information product, and knowledge or participation. From this they have justified that the hypothesis has been properly justified. Second, they considered the user satisfaction in their new model research and found it to justify Hypothesis 2. Third, they considered the end user computing satisfaction model which has five factor questions regarding information quality and one question regarding the ease of use. With end user computing satisfaction methodology they have justified the answer for Hypothesis 1 and 2. From measuring the perceived usefulness and ease of use they have found the solution to Hypothesis 3. But Hypothesis 4 has less evidence to be justified. As the result of the research Seddon and Kiew (1999) have concluded that use is not as important but usefulness is very important to measure the success of the system. To justify the hypothesis they had various research because it is very complex to measure whether usefulness is success of a system or user satisfaction is important to measure the success of IS. Some authors mention usefulness is better than user satisfaction. The increase in usefulness will lead to increases in user satisfaction but not the reserve process.

According to Sumner (1999), the enterprise information management projects are necessary to understand the information management to get the competitive advantage. The authors have done a case study in eight different industries with different ERP systems. The main aim is to integrate the business process with different departments in the same centralized process. SAP, Peoplesoft, and Oracle ERP software has been applied to integrate the business process. The findings are project characteristics, critical factors success, project justification, project management, and solution for each industry using the enterprise wide system.

The common problems that evolve in this, according to (Summer, 1999) case study is the lack of user training, lack of top management issues, and large number of consultants. Less business process re-engineering was required, but when the software was modified, it created many technical issues when integrating from one department to another. Some of the issues were integrating module by module. The cost of training has increased substantially than estimated. Having a highly skilled workforce leads to an increase in the budget of an industry. So managing the IS needs experienced knowledge to maintain the project success.

The authors (Topi, Lucas, & Babaian, 2005) focused on analysing the process of usability in ERP systems. The methodology which they have chosen is collaboration. In the collaboration framework there are three main objectives which are: commitment to mutual support, commitment to joint activity, and commitment to mutual responsiveness. The chapter has done research in a Fortune 500 company to understand the problems of users and also get the knowledge about usability problems in large scale enterprise systems. The collaboration framework is supported by a conceptual framework to find the problem of users in the ERP system.

A case study done in Fortune 500 (Topi, Lucas, & Babaian, 2005) using collaborative theory was the first try to find the problem of the user by using the system in large scale ERP implementation. The data was collected from conducting interviews with ten employees from the same organization except for a single employee. The main objective of implementing the ERP is to solve the problem of the post purchase maintenance process.

After implementing ERP (Topi, Lucas, & Babaian, 2005), it has caused a major effect on the user. Even though it does not affect the organization with a major impact it still needs to be considered, as users are real assets to an organization. Users are not able to generate the essential report with the system. They are bugs to fix during the transaction process, new systems have complex words to understand by the user. Even the experienced users were struggling to work with the new ERP system. The manual data retries are needed for most of the transaction process. The system made the users do complex work rather than automating it.

The solution to this should be clearly defined goals, communication between parties, and trainers should explain the terminology in detail to improve the user. With the collaboration theory having concluded the usability of the system, mutual responsiveness and commitment to mutual support causes the difficulties.

The integrated success model (Zaied, 2012) for evaluating IS in public sectors has attempted to propose a new integrated information success model with the replication of two methods which are the technology acceptance model and the D&M IS success model. The data was collected among Egypt to analyze the success of the integrated IS model.

The proposed new integrated information success model has ten elements. They have measured the ten elements (Delone & McLean, 1999): information quality, service quality, system quality, user involvement, perceived ease of use, perceived usefulness, behavior intention, management support, training, and user satisfaction with the correlation coefficient method. There was correlation between some elements in the proposed integrated IS success model. As a result from the analysis done by interviews, surveys found information quality (Zaied, 2012) to be considered as the most important factor in IS success and user involvement has been rated as less important. Even though it is less important, user involvement affects an organization's growth or success.

The four components that are mentioned (Yuen & Chan, 2010) on the effect of retail service quality and product quality on customer loyalty are:

retail service quality, retail product quality, perceived customer loyalty to staff, and customer quality to store. Each component is measured individually. The service quality was measured and most have used SERVQUAL method. To measure the product quality they considered an eight dimension framework but they did research on only three dimensions as it was considered as important to measure the product quality. The three dimensions are aesthetics, product features, and customer perceived quality.

The survey (Yuen & Chan, 2010) was done in the window fashion gallery industry, the questionnaire was sent to current customers to measure the customer loyalty to staff and store range from agree to strongly disagree. The questions were sent to customers from different aspects. After some analysis, they filter the unimportant dimensions which don't support the requirements. Finally, the results they found only support three dimensions that satisfy the customer loyalty to store: problem solving, physical aspects, and reliability support to loyalty stores; whereas, one dimension supports personal interaction to loyalty staff.

Zaied (2012) and Seddon and Kiew (1999) tried to replace the IS success based on D&M. Most of the components were adapted to measure the IS success model. Information quality—relevance, understandability, accuracy, conciseness, completeness, understandability, currency, timeliness, and usability. Service quality is the best and popular method to measure the quality of service quality and system quality is measured as perceived ease of use with technology acceptance model. Technology acceptance model (TAM) can measure the system quality as perceived ease of use. Calculate the user satisfaction the authors do not measure the user satisfaction as alone they include in information quality, system quality, service quality. Calculate the net benefits, measure the organizational benefits, and increase the profit are important aspects to consider in a yearly report than the user of a system.

The four main strengths to consider (Delone & McLean, 2008) IS a success model: measures have already been tested in enterprise systems on validity, eliminating the use as it is difficult to get the independent variables, even user satisfaction is also eliminated because of the complex variables. it measures the multidimensional and complex nature of IS success by constructing the validity.

In this chapter, DeLone and McLean (2008) mainly focused on the individual level or organizational level of measuring and evaluating the various success constructs and relationships. The author did comparision of 15 pairwise of the IS success model. The strength of this model is that the instrument was tested within the context of the enterprise system to ensure its validity. The six components of IS models were compared with three dimensions of system use, user satisfaction, and net benefits. Each component was measured using specific models and techniques. The key dimension of information quality comes under the end user satisfaction and measuring the system quality is based on the technology acceptance model (Seddon & Kiew, 1996; Topi et al., 2005). While measuring the service quality can be based on factor confirmatory analysis which was suggested by some of the authors. Measuring the user satisfaction used two models which are end user computing support and user information satisfaction which not only measure the satisfaction but also related to information quality, service quality, and system quality. There were lots of methods to measure the net benefits, the author has used the perceived ease of use, perceived usefulness and effectiveness to fit the organizational and individual level. Whereas the organizational benefits are received from top management. Some research supported the hypothesis, some does not support it, and some have mixed support of both.

In this chapter, Viehland and Shakir (2005) talk about making sense of the enterprise systems implementation. The authors highlight the process model for ES implementation. The authors also mention the implications of managers, which are, contingency planning, professional advice, user training, and testing. The research paper shows the organization and technological decision processes for ES implementation. The author uses the five conceptual models to examine the strategy of the decision-making process. This chapter is important because it looks at the ES implementations to see the senses it creates and how managers take the decision-making processes.

According to Garg (2010), the main objective of this chapter is to identify and validate the critical success factor for ensuring successful implementation of ERP packages for the retail industry in India. The study has found some solutions to implement ERP implementation in the retail industry. The solutions are by planning the work, design, ERP life cycle, top management, business process, technical process in the first phase of implementation so it can avoid additional charges and time savings in the implementation and it has two functionality which is workflow management and transaction processing function. Some of the critical factors are cross functionality, effective communication, project management, faster successive deliverable, transformational leadership, training, professional development of the IT workforce needs to be considered. The questionnaires are collected from the top management, product selection, project management, team composition, training, and education.

The author's research in the paper, focuses on the factors that are found (Viehland & Shakir, 2005) critical to ERP implementation success, which are change management programs and culture, teamwork and composition, monitoring and evaluation of performances, project management, software development, top management support, and so on. The author uses the Markus and Tanis ERP life cycle model to illustrate the importance of these factors. This research paper is important as it puts emphasis on the critical factors of successful implementations of ERP systems.

The main objective of this research (Wang & Liao, 2006), is to find the relationship between business to citizens in e-government. This chapter has used D&M IS success model which has six fundamental components. The authors have used the IS model and it helps to collect the data. They have created the questionnaire to get the knowledge of users who have already used the e-governance. They proposed and validated the comprehensive, multidimensional model of e-governance system model. They considered the system quality, service quality, and information quality as the system development level and system use, user satisfaction, and perceived benefits belong to the system effectiveness influence level.

The main factor is to measure the success and failure of ERP systems. ERP is to integrate back end operation to the front end operation for their success (Al-Sabaawi, 2015). They have used two new functionality, to integrate their universities administration to get student administration, human resource facilities management, and financial system that have been used by existing systems to systematic and cost effective to gain good advantage. Even though ERP provides lots of benefits, implementation is the difficult process. This paper resembles the eight critical factors for the success which are commitment and support of top management, project management, user training and education, business plan and vision, technological infrastructure, change management, and communication.

According to the research that was done in Taiwan (Tsai et al., 2010), the implementation of purchased ERP systems was the focus of study. The survey done in Taiwan was to compare the IS performance with D&M model. Measuring IS and service quality by ERP system vendor and consultant. The service quality can be measured by many methods but SERVQUAL is the best fit to get an approximate result. The productiveness of the IS is to create the ERP performance.

The author's (Garg, 2013) advantages are to identify the factors that influence the ERP implementation in Indian retail sector. Most of the retailers in India use the automation but not merged with one another. The cause and effect diagram was constructed to know the root cause of a specific problem. The research question what factors influence the ERP implementation can be solved by cause and effect diagram. The questionnaires are prepared by the ERP consultants and data collected are processed through statistical software. There were eight items removed because it did not achieve the high demand as needed for factor analysis. Finally, after the iteration in each level are completed until the ERP consultants are satisfied the total of 21 items are used for the factor influencing ERP implementation.

The aim of this chapter (Delone & McLean, 2008) is to measure the components in different ways and interdependent of IS success. To measure the success of the IS model they have carried out a lot of literature reviews that have implemented, created, and verified the actual model. The author researched on the same path to measure the IS success and update the IS model from 1992. The update model has achieved the vast growth in collision of IS success on organizational and individual impacts. Recommendation has suggested "service quality" plays an additional dimension of IS success given the importance of IS support, especially in the e-commerce environment where customer service is critical.

This research paper measures IS success according to dimensions, and interrelationships. DeLone & McLean (2003) model of IS success looks at six components. These six components are confusing to understand in terms of its relationship with each other. There are further difficulties in analysing the results. The author combined the two phrases into one single model. The IS success clarified are the casual variance and process models, the casual is the measured by qualitative approach and process is measured by qualitative approach has caused trouble to the researchers to understand. Seddon (1997) has taken this as an opportunity to make a model of respecified and extension by considering only the variance.

The main research has been done to measure the components IS uses from the D&M model (2008). First, the author tried to explain that the benefits of using the system should improve the users' work. But many other researchers mentioned it has been the disadvantages to calculate the use of a system. Second, the author mentioned that information quality, system quality, and service quality is included in IS use. IS use is just to understand the characteristics of the user but is not to consider important in any IS success. Third, the use is measured as user satisfaction, individual and organization impact. So the three measures of IS use have mentioned use is not an important variable in the IS success model of the D&M model. However, Seddon has found the new four variables. The measure has some limitations to calculate as many methods such as structural modeling techniques, linear regression, and correlation coefficient.

STATEMENT OF THE PROBLEM

In this chapter we will convey research on the success of ERP in the retail industry, which will be determined by the D&M model. The research is based on the retail industries in Fiji. From this research we are trying to resolve the issues faced by the organizations who wish to seek the importance of having an ERP system. With the D&M model, this shall portray an image or results that will illustrate the success for the use of ERP systems.

RESEARCH QUESTIONS

Through research it is considered that one of the major concerns faced by the executives in IT is the quality of information technology. For effective IT quality improved strategies to be laid down by the information officers, it is important to get the correct and accurate quality of IT for any organization. Hypothesis are made such that the organizations have been impacted by a greater number of information quality and service quality. We convey a survey to test this hypothesis and use the D&M model to highlight the importance of IT service quality for the performances of the organizations that use ERP. We discuss the implications and research for practice. The D&M model performs a great fit for the data that was observed. For both the end-users of ERP, the internal users and external, the critical and important parts of the operation, structure and improvement to the services and products provided by the organization are determined by the success and effectiveness of the implementations and use of the ERP systems.

METHODOLOGY

In order to complete this research chapter, the D&M (1992, 2003, 2008) IS success model was chosen to help in measuring the success of the IS like ERP systems, as the key factors of that is being concentrated in this research are as follows: system quality, user satisfaction, and information quality. The use of both qualitative and quantitative data analysis methods had been used. The qualitative data analysis was done through reading and analysis of past related research literature that was already published by notable researchers.

Most of the studies (Seddon, 1999; Delone & Mclean, 2003, 1993, 2008; Seddon & Kien, 1997; Tsaur & Hsu, 2010) have explained about the D&M IS success model as partial and fully, and have tested each components individual to get the desired results. The six components placed a vital role to measure the IS success. There are so many approaches used to measure the variables, for example, structural equation model, technology acceptance model, linear regression, cronbach method, and LISREL (Wang & Liao, 2006). We tried to measure the success in this chapter in an organization which is a retail industry and they had just the basic Microsoft office to record the transaction process, their asset, accounting information, sales and order details, payroll details, HR information which is very backward in technology. After the issues arose in the retail industry with the old system the management had an idea of ERP to be used for solving the problems. After discussion with the management to make the organization grow big in the market, the project leader made a decision to implement ERP. As they did not have any software before, they decided to buy the ERP software. After the decision they found the consultant, vendor to negotiate about ERP. The consultant helped in preparing from first phase to last phase of implementation planning. Later, they implemented the ERP software.

The majority of this chapter focuses on the idea of measuring the success of ERP systems that are implemented in the local retail industries. However, we will also focus on trying to relate those results gathered from research papers based on the global industries with the local industries implemented ERP systems. The quantitative data analysis involved collecting and analyzing the data from the retail industries which currently have an IS systems such as enterprise resource systems implemented, which was done through the following ways:

1. conducting interviews adapted from Seddon & Kiew (1996) and Topi et al. (2005);
    - main employees in the organization such as chief finance officers, managers, and IT staff were interviewed in helping to gather the information about the organization and the current implemented system.
2. preparing and distribution of questionnaires adapted from Seddon and Kiew (1996) and DeLone and McLean;
3. trying to understand the current business process and the current implemented systems; and
4. online surveys emailed to those employees;
    - There were a total of 40 questions adapted from DeLone and McLean in the survey and respondents in our survey responded to answering the questions by 5 category choices of answers which were available, that were as follows: *very satisfied, satisfied, ok, dissatisfied, very dissatisfied.*

Later, the data collected from the various methods mentioned above was analyzed using structural equation modeling techniques, the LISREL package, which validates the currently used IS model of success, as the results gathered from the study are consistent in terms with IS success factors that explains the success of ERP systems and then it is applied to examine the causality relationship among the presented variables (Pearl, 2000).

FINDINGS

The correspondents from the organization included:

- top level management,
- executive members,
- department managers,
- support staff,
- IT staff, and
- project support staff.

These people were selected based on their involvement in the project from the start until its implementation and post implementation.

EVALUATION MODEL (FIGURE 13.3)

Information Quality

Both users and management are satisfied with the current information output. While few, from both users and management level, are used to the old format of data they are ok with the current one. Some, from both levels of the organization, are really satisfied with the new format of data. Generally, user satisfaction regarding the information received from the new system surpasses expectations from the old system (see Figure 13.4).

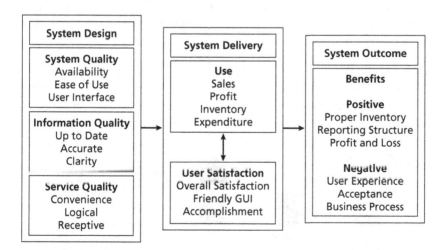

Figure 13.3 Evaluation model.

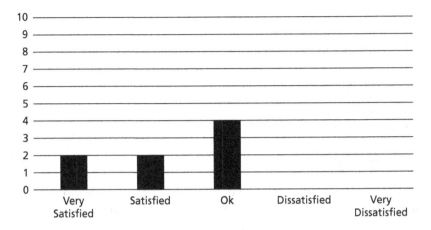

Figure 13.4 Information quality feedback.

Service Quality

The majority of users are happy with the overall satisfaction of the ERP. While a few are still grasping the new system indicating that it has reduced their work speed. This is generally common with long-term users of the old system. Managers have indicated that they have more controlled access and have clear indication of the system and usability (see Figure 13.5).

System Delivery

This has received a mixed reaction from both users and management level. While some are happy but not satisfied with the ERP. Some want

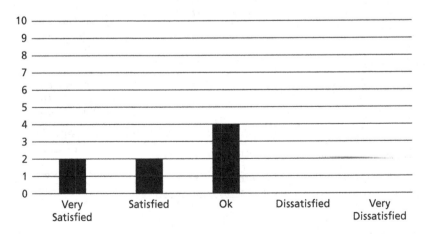

Figure 13.5 Service quality feedback.

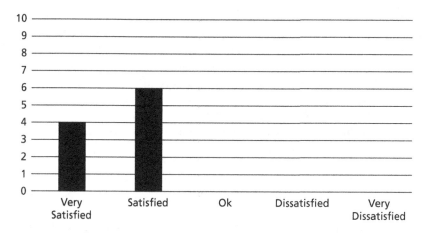

Figure 13.6 System delivery feedback.

further improvement to the ERP while others are still exploring its full capacity (see Figure 13.6).

RECOMMENDATIONS AND FUTURE RESEARCH

While many published research literature recently have shown solid support in terms of the various suggested interrelationships between the D&M model success dimensions, as still there is further research required in order to help explore on relationships between the success variable dimensions in D&M model where not much research has been conducted. Also empirical research is required in order to create a strong interrelationship through the different contextual restrictions that exist. The first step taken in this research is analyzing the results achieved which have been constructed on analysis of individual and organizational units, then it was discovered that there was not enough empirical evidence available to help estimate the majority of current relationships between success variables on an organizational level. Using other IS success models can also be considered to help measure success of IS like ERP and the results gained from use of that success IS model can be compared with results gained from use (D&M model, 2008). Also in future research the use of complex functions, like curvilinear effects, affects the relationships between constructs of IS success variables. There also exists a number of extra condition boundaries which require attention as follows: (a) examination of the type of system, (b) the voluntariness of the system, and (c) success measurement timing (i.e., this refers to the difference among the time when the system is being implemented and the time of it took for measurement). Secondly, there will be need for further research to be done for the relationships that exist amongst the variables of success used in this research information quality, system quality, and user satisfaction in order to clearly present the success rate of an IS such as an ERP. Finally, it was discovered that researchers continue to struggle in making use of system use as a success variable for measurement of (Wang & Liao, 2006) IS success. This will require studies which will be done in the future to evaluate/analyze by making use of comprehensive and much consistent measures so that it provides a much clearer understanding of the effects which use has on the success variables user satisfaction and information quality.

CONCLUSION

To conclude based on our finding and research, no system can be 100% perfect. It is because all minds do not function alike, not that one is superior than the other, but it is because one digests information and data very differently and uniquely than others. Our organization is also facing the same issue. It is not that the ERP is not fulfilling the requirement but the user and the information provided by the new system is still new for users and organizations.

REFERENCES

Al-Mashari, M., Al-Mudimigh, A., & Zairi, M. (2003). Enterprise resource planning: A taxonomy of critical factors. *European Journal of Operational Research, 146,* 352–364.

Al-Sabaawi, M. Y. M. (2015). Critical success factor for ERP implementation success. *International Journal of Advances in Engineering and Technology, 8*(4), 496–506.

Delone, W., & McLean, E. (1992). Information systems success: The quest for the dependent variable. *Information Systems Research, 3*(1), 60–95. https://doi .org/10.1287/isre.3.1.60

Delone, W., & Mclean, E. (2003). The Delone and Mclean model of IS success: A ten-year update. *Journal of Management Information, 19*(4), 9–30.

DeLone, W., & McLean, E. (2008). Measuring IS success: Models, dimensions, measures, and interrelationships. *European Journal of Information Systems, 17*(3), 236–263.

Garg, P. (2010). Critical success factors for enterprise resource planning implementation in indian retail industry: An exploratory study. *International Journal of Computer Science and Information Security, 8*(2). https://arxiv.org/ pdf/1006.5749.pdf

Gupta, A. (2000). Enterprise resources planning: The emerging organizational value systems. *Industrial Management & Data System, 100*(3), 114–118.

Holland, C., & Light, B. (1999). A critical success factors model for ERP implementation. *IEEE Software, 16*(3), 30–36. https://doi.org/10.1109/52.765784

Pearl, J. (2000). The logic of counterfactuals in causal inference. *Journal of American Statistical Association, 95*(450), 428–435.

Ragowsky, A. S. (2005). Assessing the value provided by ERP applications. *Communications of the Association for Information Systems, 16,* 381–406.

Scott, J. E., Vessey, I. (2002). Managing Risks in Enterprise Systems Implementations. *Communications of the ACM, 45*(4), 74–81.

Seddon, P., & Kiew, M. (1996). A partial test and development of Delone and Mclean's model of IS success. *Australasian Journal of Information Systems, 4*(1), 90–109. http://dx.doi.org/10.3127/ajis.v4i1.379

Sumner, M. (1999). Critical success factors in enterprise wide information management systems projects. In J. Prasad (Ed.), *Proceedings of the 1999 ACM SIGCPR conference on computer personnel research* (pp. 297–303). Association for Computing Machinery. https://doi.org/10.1145/299513.299722

Topi, H., Lucas, W., & Babaian, T. (2005). Identifying usability issues with an ERP implementation. In C.-S. Chen, J. Filipe, I. Seruca, & J. Cordeiro (Eds.), *Proceedings of the 7th international conference on enterprise information systems* (pp. 128–133). ICEIS.

Tsai, W.-H., Tsaur, T.-S., Chou, Y.-W., Lui, J.-Y., & Hsu, J.-L. (2010). Evaluating the information system success of ERP implementation in Taiwan's Industries. In *The 2009 Proceedings of the IEEE International Conference on Industrial Engineering and Engineering Management* (pp. 1815–1819). IEEE. http://doi.org/10.1109/IEEM.2009.5373177

Ullah, A., Baharun, R., Khalil, B., Siddique, M., & Sami, A. (2017). Enterprise Resource planning system and user performance. *International Journal of Applied Decision Sciences, XI*(3), 377–390. https://www.researchgate.net/publication/326826780

Viehland, D., & Shakir, M. (2005). *Making sense of enterprise systems implementation. University of Auckland Business Review, 7*(2), 28–36.

Wang, Y.-S., & Liao, Y.-W. (2006). Assessing E-Government system success: A validation of the DeLone and McLean model of information system success. *Government Information Quarterly, 25*(4), 717–733.

Yuen, E. F. T., & Chan, S. S. L. (2010). The effect of retail service quality and product quality on customer loyalty. *Database Marketing & Customer Strategy Management, 17*(3/4), 222–240.

Zaied, A. N. H. (2012). An integrated success model for evaluating information system in public sectors. *Journal of Emerging Trends in Computing and Information Sciences, 3*(6), 812–825.

CHAPTER 14

ANALYSIS OF ETHICAL ISSUES IN HRIS USING THE PAPA MODEL

Sam Goundar
The University of the South Pacific

Subhash Appana
The University of the South Pacific

Uaitelose Fonohema
The University of the South Pacific

Seluvaia Vea
The University of the South Pacific

Mele Fonua
The University of the South Pacific

Enterprise Systems and Technological Convergence, pages 257–276
Copyright © 2021 by Information Age Publishing

ABSTRACT

Information system (IS) is an important aspect of the communication industry. It is a storehouse of vital information for the company as well as for the employees. Many companies in Tonga use the IS to retrieve information about the employees' leave history and other personal data for reference and promotion purposes. It is therefore important that the IS in the telecommunications company in Tonga is accurate and that access is secure given the company's heavy dependence on the human resource information system (HRIS) information for promotion and other related benefits.

In this chapter, we analyze the ethical issues of the HRIS using the PAPA model, in terms of privacy, accessibility, accuracy, and property. To do this, we review the current policies within the telecommunications company and consider if there is a need for development of standards for accessing information in the HR department in view of the PAPA model.

This chapter is important because it serves to inform those who want to access data in the HR of the ethical policies and procedures of the company to protect the employee's information. The HR information is readily available to employees in the employee self service (ESS) portal of the company's website, where employees can access (with a password) their information on payslips and leave accrual at any time from anywhere. Superiors in the company such as divisional managers also have access to the information through a central database and if the information is changed, the employee has a right to know what their rights are and what they can do if such rights are violated.

The contribution to the field of knowledge is not only to assist the company to improve compliance with its ethical policies on their IS, but also to find gaps in the HRIS, find solutions, and present them to the telecommunications management in order to improve the use of the current system. PAPA model will indeed be a useful model to be presented to the executive of the company to be used in HRIS.

It is the intention of this chapter to advise the executives and management of the telecommunications company, its board of directors and the employees at the main offices in Tongatapu on why such a system exists in the organization and how important the safe keeping of their information is.

It is not clear to what extent ethical issues have been viewed by the organization, thus the focus question of this study: Is the HRIS system protected ethically, in view of privacy, accuracy, accessibility, and property rights as per the PAPA model.

INTRODUCTION

Background

In today's information and communication age, there is a constant reference to IS and management of IS. In the digital age data, storage, and retrieval are done through various systems and interfaces. An IS, therefore, can be defined as a set of coordinated networks of components which act together towards producing, distributing, and/or processing information. An important factor of computer-based IS is precision, which may not apply to other types of systems.

This research was conducted at a telecommunications company in Tonga. The telecommunications company was established on February 5, 2001 as a public enterprise. It is 100% government owned and governed by an ICT board of directors with its own board. At present the government of Tonga is the sole shareholder, nevertheless there is a plan to invite prospective shareholders to invest in this telecommunications company as part of the Tonga participant scheme.

The company provides a wide range of local and international voice and data services cooper network via GSM. Its services include but are not limited to local and international telephone services, Internet services, public Internet and facsimile, prepaid phone cards, GSM mobile cellular phone, and directory assistance.

This telecommunications company previously used a manual system where their employees started by recording their attendance in a manual attendance book. Their leave requests are applied using manual forms and recorded manually. The payroll summaries and calculations all depend on the records received by the HR department.

Problem Statement

Nowadays anyone can access information from anywhere with mobile or cell phones, desktops, Internet, and social media hence information is no longer confidential and private. It is therefore important at an operational level that employees are aware of what they are doing with information they can access at work and if their rights have been violated within the HRIS.

As such, this investigation helped to clarify what is ethical and unethical with the company's IS. If the ethical and social issues are not addressed, the company may face a lot of unnecessary cost, poor performance, erosion of quality, and decline in public confidence in the service of the company.

Therefore it is important to pursue this research to ensure that employees have a clear understanding of the company's expectations on ethical and social matters of the company's IS.

RESEARCH OBJECTIVES

This research focussed on finding the linkage and/or gaps between the current used HRIS in the company and the PAPA model introduced by Mason which is the four most crucial ethical issues of the information era in 1986 of PAPA.

The research investigated and analyzed the ethical issues in accessing data at this telecommunications company. The chapter is important as a result of the study highlighting the strength and weaknesses of the current HRIS. Furthermore, it informs decision makers of relevant areas for improvement in terms of policies and procedures and also informs and raises awareness with employees on the important aspects to consider and be aware of the consequences and its costs to them as well as the secondary users. It will also help employees understand the need to protect information they are privy to access due to their being employed at this company. Lastly, it also helps employees to reassess their loyalty to the company and their sense of organization citizenship.

Nowadays anyone can access information from anywhere with phones, desktops, Internet, and so forth while previously the public were only made aware of matters published in the paper or announced on the radio. In today's era with different generations of social media and communication, information is no longer confidential and private. Thus, it is considered important at an operational level that employees are aware of what they are doing. They need to be aware if their rights have been violated within the HRIS.

As such, this investigation is worthwhile as it helped clarify what would be regarded as ethical and unethical by the company's IS. If the ethical issues are not addressed, the company may face a lot of unnecessary costs which may lead to poor performance and erosion of quality, and also a decline in public confidence in the service of this company. Therefore it is important to pursue this research to ensure that employees have a clear understanding of the company's expectations on ethical and social matters of the company's IS.

LITERATURE REVIEW

In the 20th century, the revolution in technology has spawned a new set of ethical and social concerns that were not anticipated by many organizations, many years ago. Many people today lead complex online lives and may not even realize how their personal information is being collected and used. These cause ethical and social issues arising from the use of technology in all areas of our lives and in business, in particular have led to the creation of a new branch of ethics, known as techno-ethics. Even though technology makes businesses more efficient, faster, and easier to complete, there are important issues raised regarding privacy of office emails, cyber peek at what employees do with company assets which have legal implications. Employees also use social media to screen applicants (Luppicinni, 2010). The continuous utilization of the internet and wireless network resources jeopardize the information security system (Guo et al., 2011).

The HRIS is an integrated system mostly used to collect data, govern, record, and to deliver and present data for HR and hence promotes and transforms appropriateness of transforming human resource performance (Hossin, Tomanna, Gerbi, & Zhang, 2018). Many computer operators have become experts in manipulating information available to them which were collected from customers. Some websites send cookies to speed up the searching while storing important information on the searchers.

Mason introduced the PAPA model which consists of four broad categories of information ethical issues namely privacy, accuracy, property, and accessibility (Woodward, 2011). Having accurate information is very important when it comes to legal matters. In the eyes of the law, if any information is accurate in court, it would not be able to provide an effective defence. China has enormous information resources (Zhang, 2011). This shows how very strong and well developed its IS is compared to Tonga. However, the level of education and the habits of use of information were among the ethical issues affecting the security of IS. This means that employees with lower levels of education may be expected to have a lower knowledge of IS or computer skills. They would be more prone to show unethical use of IS by passing information they are privy to access to friends and others without proper authorization. The Tonga Communication Corporation ethical policy was developed to ensure there is clear and simple guide on what employees can do and cannot do which include ethical use of properties, records, and information:

> Establish corporate ethics policies that include information systems issues. And also establish principles of right and wrong so that it can be used by individuals acting as free moral agents to make choices to guide their behavior (Anonymous, 2012)

Laudon et al. (2018) reported his study where one university shared students' personal information with third parties. The university offered a loan scheme for students but in some cases, the date of birth, address, and email address were difficult to acquire. To address the situation, this personal information was put in a national student loan data system for ease of access by loan agencies and guarantors which was inappropriate use of the database. Though the information was valuable for the loan companies, the sharing of information was without the students' knowledge. It is against human justice and unethical to do this behind the scene as it would make students lose confidence in the university's system. Moreover, it would make students reluctant to release their personal information to other companies when they graduate and get employed.

Allen et al. (2015) show that the organization today requires an effective information security policy. This may include the roles and responsibilities of the officer responsible for security of information. Hu et al. (2011) identified that for ensuring the system security, it was not enough nor effective to impose punishment alone but to educate employees on the good values of adhering to company security policies. Employees who had low self-control were more likely to overestimate the benefits of the misconduct whereas employees who had strong moral ethics were less inclined to violate the security of the IS. In recruitment, the HR manager can consider this as a selection criteria for new employees.

Shayo and Lin (2019) noted that the ideal reporting structures of the information security will vary for organizations according to their own mission, maturity culture, resources, capabilities, decision-making, and governance. However, they recommended a chief information security officer as best practices for evolving an effective reporting structure in organizations. Alkahtani (2019) concluded that organizations needed to educate the workforce of the information security policy and develop their necessary understanding of the information security system. This allows the employees to identify and report security threats and risks which helps in the improvement of IS awareness.

With regards to the research model, this research used the model developed by Mason to introduce and map issues within an IS. Woodward (2011) referred to this as the four broad categories of ethical issues of the information age; namely, privacy, accuracy, property, and access—known as the PAPA model. The categorizing of ethical issues would allow management of this telecommunication company to prioritize the most pressing issues to deal with first in the company. However, the disadvantages of this model is that it confines to only four ethical issues and does not cover moral issues in information technology (Parrish, 2010).

RESEARCH QUESTIONS

The research questions were as follows:

1. What are the ethical issues on the use of HRIS at a telecommunication company using the PAPA model?

2. What are the positive and negative ethical issues around the use of HRIS using the PAPA model?

METHODOLOGY

Research Model and Theories Used

This research was conducted by reviewing the telecommunications company's existing HRIS, using the PAPA research model. This research model was used to investigate the ethical issues in terms privacy, accuracy, property, and accessibility using 86 employees, randomly selected from this telecommunication company, a government-owned telecommunication company.

This was taken from 86 employees in the main island only, excluding the employees in the 5 major islands in which this telecommunications company operates.

Quantitative and Qualitative Analysis

In conducting this study, both primary and secondary methods of sourcing data were used in order to obtain more comprehensive information for the issues under investigation. The crucial data for this research was collected mainly from primary data sources including structured closed and open ended questionnaires (Appendix A) on ethical issues with IS based on the PAPA model.

The team used a descriptive type of qualitative methods as we described the opinions of respondents on the advantages, disadvantages of the HRIS as well as challenges encountered and improvements to be made. In addition, the cross-sectional methods (Hossin et al., 2018) were used to collect information on the entire participants because the team contacted the participants once with the survey questionnaire.

The participants for this research were chosen randomly from employees who have been employed for various lengths of time at the telecommunications company. They have been involved in the HRIS for some time. We believed that these participants would be able to provide details of the information relevant for this study. Amongst the participants in the survey were management level staff and supervisors from top and middle level management, as well as general employees from finance, HR, marketing, customer service, and IT departments.

A quantitative analysis of the responses to the closed questionnaires was conducted and recorded in a table of results. The data collected was organized in a table and tally into frequency. The processed data was to draw graphs, interpret results, and analyze any trend or relationships displayed by the variables. The results were processed into graphs and interpreted.

A qualitative analysis of the responses to the open questionnaires was also conducted. The various responses were tabulated and interpreted.

The participants that were targeted for this investigation were the employees of a telecommunications company in Tonga. A letter of intent was sent to the general manager of the company requesting permission to use the employees for the intended survey. A preliminary visit was done to the company's office to identify and randomly select the names of the employees that would be used for the survey. If the response from participants was not forthcoming, participants were contacted via telephone and/or email to maximise the response rate.

Ethical Considerations

The participants were invited by letter to participate in the survey so their involvement was voluntary. There was no potential harm to the project nor would it place participants in positions of danger hence there were no major ethical issues for consideration in this research.

RESULTS/FINDINGS

There were 86 employees (Appendix B) that participated in the research. Most participants were from the IT and technical unit, followed by customer service, HR, and the marketing department. The least number of participants were from finance. An analysis of the results is presented in the findings below.

Figure 14.1 illustrates that of the 86 employees at this telecommunication company who participated in the research, a large proportion of the participants (98%) were aware of the HRIS. This accounted for the high weekly usage by employees of the HRIS shown in Figure 14.2. There were only a few participants (2%) who were not aware of the HRIS. Under such circumstances, the supervisor accessed the HRIS for them and applied leave on their behalf.

Most participants (80%) were also aware that their personal information was kept in the HRIS telecommunication company. More interestingly, most of these participants were also mindful that there were ethical issues associated with keeping their personal information in the HRIS.

Figure 14.2 shows how frequent the participants used the HRIS at the telecommunications company. Most of the participants (54%) used the HRIS weekly, 24% used it monthly, 15% used it daily, and 7% never used the

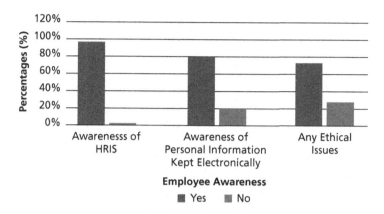

Figure 14.1 Percentage of participants awareness.

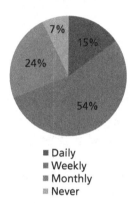

Figure 14.2 Graph showing frequency of HRIS use.

system. The reason identified for the ones that never use it was because the supervisor applied their leave on their behalf, and this explained the 2% that never used the HRIS in Figure 14.1.

However, there is risk associated with this practice because the employee took it for granted that the supervisor was acting with good faith. Figure 14.3 identified some reasons for using the HRIS. The most reasons for employees using the HRIS was to view their leave balance (41%), view payslips and payments (28%), and to print these out (26%). Few of the participants use the HRIS to apply for leave (3%) or update contact information (2%).

In contrast, the reasons for supervisors and managers using the HRIS vary a lot from employees' reasons due to their position in the organization structure and the differences in the level of supervision and authority they have.

Figure 14.4 identified that 19%–24% of managers and supervisors use it to update information on leave and payslips. These updates are important

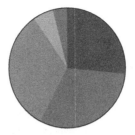

■ View Payslips and Payments 28%
■ Update Contact Information 2%
▨ Apply Leave 3%
■ View Leave Balance 41%
■ Print Payslips and Payments 26%

Figure 14.3 Proportion of various purposes for employees using HRIS .

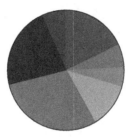

■ Enter Employee Personal Information 11%
■ Assign Business Assets 8%
■ Update Leave Balance 24%
■ Update Payslips and Payments 19%
■ Reporting Purposes 10%
▨ Accessing Personal Records and Recruitment Info 13%
■ Promotional Purposes 7%
▨ Recording Employee Demographic 8%

Figure 14.4 Proportion of managers and supervisors using HRIS.

to employees as reflected in Figure 14.3, most participants use the HRIS to view their leave balance, payslips, and payment details. The HRIS was not used much for promotional purposes (7%) assigning of assets and recording employee demographic (8%). However, some participants used the HRIS to access personal information and recruitment information (13%) and 11% entered employee personal information.

Figure 14.5 highlights the proportion of the ethical issues of the PAPA model used in this research. Most of the participants were concerned with the privacy (39%) of their personal information as Figure 14.1 showed that

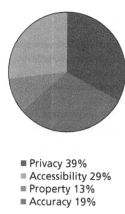

■ Privacy 39%
■ Accessibility 29%
■ Property 13%
■ Accuracy 19%

Figure 14.5 Proportion of ethical issues identified by PAPA model.

most employees were aware that there exists an HRIS at the telecommunications company and their personal information was kept in there.

The ethical issue with accessibility was a concern of participants (29%), followed by accuracy of their personal information (19%), and property (13%) was the lowest concern of the participants.

The main advantage of the HRIS at this telecommunication company was identified in Figure 14.6 as storing information and data such as payroll, payslips, and leave.

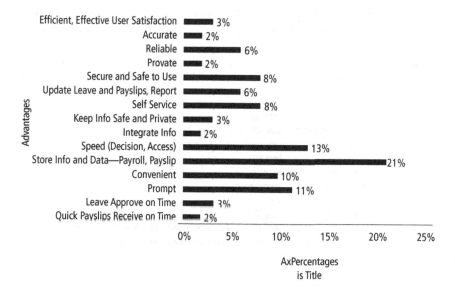

Figure 14.6 Advantages of HRIS.

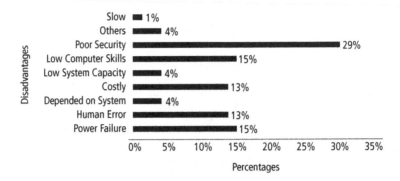

Figure 14.7 Disadvantages of HRIS.

This was followed by quick access to information for decision-making (13%), prompt retrieval of information (12%), and convenient use of the system (10%). Other important advantages included but were opted by few participants included efficiency, safe keeping of information, and timeliness of leave approval (3%). Other participants thought that the HRIS system was secure, reliable, and enjoyed the self-service it provided.

Figure 14.7 identified that the main disadvantage of the HRIS was poor security (29%) followed by low computer skills of users and power failures (15%), human error during input of data as well as cost (13%). There were other thoughts that the slowness (1%) of the system was a disadvantage but it seemed that many enjoyed the self-service as reflected by Figure 14.6 despite any slow service. There were concerns that employees would become dependent on the HRIS system (4%) and the low system capacity (4%) identified by IT employees.

Figure 14.8 identified cost (42%) to be the main challenging factor for the HRIS at the telecommunications company. It seemed that participants

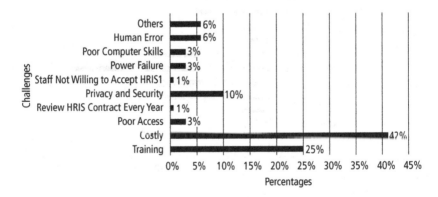

Figure 14.8 Challenges of the HRIS.

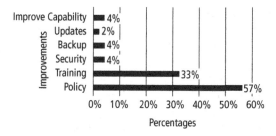

Figure 14.9   Improvements for the HRIS.

were aware that it is very expensive to purchase the software or contract an expert to develop the system. As such, this implied that it is a cost to the company to purchase and maintain the HRIS. Training (25%) was also identified to be a challenge in terms of users needing training due to lack of computer skills or being a new employee hence the elevated need for training. Privacy and security (10%) were also identified to pose challenges as well as other reasons including human errors (6%).

Although the telecommunication company has an existing ethical policy (Anonymous, 2012), Figure 14.9 shows that policy is the most demanded improvement to be made. There needs to be a policy improvement or development for the HRIS to address the ethical issues identified by the PAPA model in order to ensure that the HRIS effectively operates at the telecommunication company.

DISCUSSIONS

The research title "Analysis of Ethical Issues in a Telecommunication Company" carried out identified ethical issues based on the PAPA model. This is a large company and contributed revenue to the government by means of annual dividends hence it is important to identify and explore the ethical issues raised in this study to ensure privacy, accessibility, property, and accuracy of information are addressed for the benefit of the company.

Ethical Issues Using Papa Model

The findings of this research's main ethical issue viewed as important from this research was privacy, followed by accessibility and accuracy, followed by property which is viewed as lowest. This research supported an empirical study of the Mason framework in which the findings validate the PAPA model (Peslak, 2006).

Privacy means the right to be free from secret scrutiny and to determine whether, when, how, and to whom, one's personal or organizational information is to be revealed. Privacy of information implies security of information from access by third parties or unauthorized access. Accuracy is the condition or quality of being true, correct or exact, free from error or defect. Property refers to intellectual property and its right because once it is provided, it is complicated to keep the information as it becomes communicable and more difficult to be reimbursed. Accessibility issues are concerned with who has the permission to access the information, who holds the rights or keys to access it, what data an individual or organizations are privileged to acquire and with which safeguards and under what terms and conditions. It is therefore important that the telecommunication company implement security measures and firewalls to prevent hacking of HRIS. Employees inside the company may act to sustain and improve organizational information security though study on the motivation factor for doing this was limited. (Lowry & Wilson, 2016).

The protection of personal data is a topic entirely relevant and very current. In Europe both the right to respect for his or her private and family life, home, and communications (privacy) and the right to the protection of personal data constitute fundamental rights, as provided for respectively by Articles 71 and 82 of the Charter of Fundamental Rights of the European Union (Fabiano, 2019).

Many employees of this company that participated in the survey in Figure 14.1 who were aware of ethical issues with their personal information being kept electronically showed that the privacy of their personal information maintained by the company was their main concern (39%). One of the important personal information that is culturally sensitive to discuss in one's age and a disability. It is not culturally friendly and polite in Tonga for someone to ask for a person's age but this can be obtained from the HRIS.

The managers and supervisors are mainly the ones that can access employee's personal information weekly other than the employee. This was when they used it for leave approvals and monitoring of employees attendance in their division. It is therefore a matter of self-control for these managers and supervisors to keep the information they are privy to confidential and secure within themselves and the company. Self-control has been identified as a major factor influencing individual behavior in the social science, neuroscience, criminology, and information security literature (Hu et al., 2015).

Unethical use of IT, related to activities such as hacking, software piracy, phishing, and spoofing, has become a major security concern for individuals, organizations, and society in terms of the threat to IS security. Unethical use of IT is a complex phenomenon and multiple interventions at various levels may be required to combat this growing threat to IS security (Chatterjee et al., 2015).

The second ethical issue of the PAPA model that participants were concerned about was accessibility. The reason for their concern was due to power outage which may affect the availability of this service to employees at unpredictable times. Moreover, the lack of computer skills was a limitation to accessing the HRIS.

Though there were lesser concerns about property and accuracy compared to privacy and accessibility, it did not mean that they were any lesser important. Employees have a right to know what is being done with their personal information as it is their intellectual property. Sometimes people are not aware of the possible risks related to the full use of their personal data, especially when they are not informed about the purposes of processing.

Positive and Negative Ethical Issues of HRIS Using Papa Model

The idea of negative ethics, a new conceptual model that emphasizes the role of negative definitions in morality (Guseinov, 2014). The main ethical and social issues raised by IS centers around privacy and security of information. Information is viewed to be stored safely by the HRIS which is an efficient way of record keeping. Moreover, HRIS enables employees to have a quick update of leave, update reports, and enjoy the self-service of the system. Managers and supervisors have information available in HRIS for decision-making.

Although computer systems work to be more efficient in the workplace, they have some negative impacts. The poor network and power failure would affect the effectiveness of the system. For example, computer errors can cause serious harm to individuals if the personal information is inaccurate. If the error is on attendance, it can affect the employee's performance management in terms of effective and efficient time management. The lack of employees' computer skills to operate the HRIS and unwillingness of employees to accept the HRIS are a hindrance to employees.

Some employees have lost their jobs from downsizing some companies when computers replaced employees that used to do the manual filing and record keeping. Such manual record keeping has become unnecessary with the HRIS in place.

Moreover, there were concerns about security of information where supervisors have access to HRIS to update leave balance and payslips. The integrity of the information is entrusted to these supervisors hence their commitment, as insider, and self-control are important positive ethical issues to guide them in this respect.

Advantages and Disadvantages of the HRIS

There were numerous advantages that participants identified with the HRIS. This included the convenience of accessing the system and the self-service. Some participants also indicated that this was a good way of keeping the company's records as it gives the management and supervisors the opportunity for timely decision in matters related to human resource issues since the information was readily available.

There were some indications of repletion in responses where participants favored the HRIS for security purposes. It seemed that they implied that the information was safer in the HRIS than in paper records used before by the company. However, the fact that some of the participants indicated in Figure 14.1 that they were not aware of any ethical issues explains the security purposes that these participants implied.

Challenges

The most common challenges identified from the research is lack of computer skills and being new to use the system. This means that new employees could not use the HRIS but most were willing to be trained to know how to use it.

The cost was another challenging factor because it is expensive to purchase the software, let alone having to contract an expert to develop it for the company. There was also the need for ongoing maintenance of the system to ensure it continued to provide the necessary information effectively and efficiently for users.

Privacy and security were again identified by participants to be challenging factors as well as a disadvantage of the HRIS. They expressed their concern with their right to their personal information kept secure and private in the company. However, security awareness processes are associated with interrelated changes that occur at the organizational, the technological, and the individual level (Fabiano, 2019; Tsohou, Karyda, Kokolakis, & Kiountouzis, 2015).

Areas of Improvement

In the light of the information gathered from participants, there was a strong indication from participants for training on how to use the HRIS for new employees and for technical staff who hardly use it at all but depend on their supervisors to apply leave on their behalf. This would ensure that users would be well versed with the system and enjoy its convenience.

Moreover, there was also a strong indication to review ethical policy on HRIS to secure all access. However, the company had a Code of Ethics Policy (Anonymous, 2012) which may need to be reviewed and circulated to employees from time to time as good practice and to increase its awareness with employees.

CONCLUSIONS

The HRIS at this telecommunication company is an important tool for pooling together of employee's information, especially and was mostly used for viewing payslips and payments. As such, poor security of the HRIS is a problem identified from this study that needs to be addressed. Based on the PAPA model, this research highlighted higher concerns with privacy and accessibility of information compared to accuracy and property ethical issues. Telecommunication companies are challenged by the high cost of the software and maintenance. But with a good policy in place on the use of HRIS and ongoing staff professional training, the ethical issues can be effectively managed.

Having identified these ethical issues, the company and related institutions can implement strong preventive measures to control unauthorized access to the company's HRIS from external sources. The company may continue to upgrade and improve its HRIS in protecting it from unethical practices to protect employees who are the most important assets of an organization.

RECOMMENDATIONS AND FUTURE RESEARCH

The following recommendations are made to the management and governance of this telecommunication company for their prompt consideration to enhance the service of the HRIS in the company:

1. Revise existing ethical policy to strengthen HRIS security.
2. To include in its annual training plan a schedule of in-house training by the HR division to deliver to divisions on ethical issues with the HRIS based on PAPA model.
3. The ICT manager to be responsible for monitoring unethical uses of IS.

Limitations

The study could not cover participants from outer islands due to time limitations hence the finding is confined to the employees in the main

Island offices of this telecommunication company only. This study did not pursue detailed analysis of responses by divisions and did the study set out to test the significance of the findings.

Future Research

This study does provide the basis for future research to explore these ethical issues on a larger scale, by comparing the ethical issues at this telecommunication company as a public enterprise with a government ministry in Tonga.

APPENDIX A—QUESTIONNAIRE

Research Questionnaire
Telecommunication Company

1. How often do you use the HRIS software/system?
   - Daily
   - Few times a week
   - Never
   - Others—please specify _____

2. Please indicate the purpose for which you access or utilize the HRIS software/system.
   - Entering employee personal information
   - Recording customers demographics
   - Information purposes
   - Accessing personal records, including admission details
   - Reporting purposes
   - Apply for leave
   - Approve leave
   - Others—please specify _____

3. In your opinion, what are the advantages (if any) of using HRIS?

4. In your opinion, what are the disadvantages (if any) of using HRIS?

5. What are some of the challenges of using HRIS? Please list.

6. Do you think there are ethical issues with the use of HRIS?
   - Yes (Please go to Question 7)
   - No

7. Identify which of the following issue(s) concerns you:
   - Privacy
   - Accuracy
   - Property
   - Accessibility

8. In your opinion, what are some areas of improvement you would suggest to the HRIS system/software?

APPENDIX B—NUMBER OF PARTICIPANTS BY DIVISION

TABLE 14.1 Number of Participations per Division at the Telecommunications Company

Divisions	Number of Employees
Customer Service	19
Marketing	14
Human Resource	14
Finance	12
Others—Information Technology, Technical	27
Total Employees	86

TABLE 14.2 Number of Employee's Awareness of the Company HRIS System

Employees	Yes	No
Awareness of HRIS	98%	2%
Awareness of personal information kept electronically	80%	20%
Any Ethical issues	72%	28%

REFERENCES

Alkahtani, H. K. (2019). Safeguarding the information systems in an organization through different technologies, policies, and actions. *Computer and Information Science, 12*(2), 117–125. https://doi.org/10.5539/cis.v12n2p117

Allen, J. H., Crabb, G., Curtis, P. D., Fitzpatrick, B., Mehravari, N., & Tobar, D. (2015). Structuring the chief information security officer organization. *Journal of Computer Science and Information Technology, 7*(1), 1–20. http://jcsitnet.com/journals/jcsit/Vol_7_No_1_June_2019/1.pdf

Anonymous. (2012). *Ethical policy.* Tonga Communications Corporation.

Chatterjee, S., Sarker, S., & Valacich, J. S. (2015). The behavioral roots of information systems security: Exploring key factors related to unethical IT use. *Journal of Management Information Systems, 31*(4), 49–87.

Fabiano, N. (2019, April). *Ethics and the protection of personal data.* Paper presentation at the 10th International Multi-Conference on Complexity, Informatics and Cybernetics, Orlando, FL. https://www.researchgate.net/publication/334374184_Ethics_and_the_protection_of_personal_data

Guo, K. H., Yuan, Y., Archer, N. P., & Connelly, C. E. (2011). Understanding non-malicious security violations in the workplace: A composite behavior model. *Journal of management information systems, 28*(2), 203–236.

Guseinov, A. A. (2014). Negative ethics. *Russian Studies in Philosophy, 52*(3), 56–72.

Hossin, M. A., Tomanna, T., Gerbi, D. Y., & Zhang, S. (2018). Impact of information system on transformation of human resource performance: an exploratory study in Oromia radio and television organization. *Journal of Human Resource and Sustainability Studies, 6*(1), 37.

Hu, Q., West, R., & Smarandescu, L. (2015). The role of self-control in information security violations: Insights from a cognitive neuroscience perspective. *Journal of Management Information Systems, 31*(4), 6–48.

Hu, Q., Xu, Z., Dinev, T., & Ling, H. (2011). Does deterrence work in reducing information security policy abuse by employees? *Communications of the ACM, 54*(6), 54–60.

Laudon, J. P., & Laudon, K.C. (2018). *Management information systems: Managing the digital firm* (15th ed.). Pearson. https://www.pearson.com/us/higher-education/product/Laudon-Management-Information-Systems-Managing-the-Digital-Firm-15th-Edition/9780134639710.html

Lowry, P. B., & Wilson, D. (2016). Creating agile organizations through IT: The influence of internal IT service perceptions on IT service quality and IT agility. *The Journal of Strategic Information Systems, 25*(3), 211–226.

Luppicini, R. (2010). *Technoethics and the evolving knowledge society.* Information Science Reference-Harshey.

Parrish, J. (2010). PAPA knows best: Principles for the ethical sharing of information on social networking sites. *Ethics and Information Technology, 12,* 187–193. https://doi.org/10.1007/s10676-010-9219-5

Peslak, A. R. (2006). PAPA revisited: A current empirical study of the mason framework. *Journal of Computer Information Systems, 46*(3), 117–123.

Shayo, C., & Lin, F. (2019). An exploration of the evolving reporting organizational structure for the chief information security officer (CISO) function. *Journal of Computer Science and Information Technology, 7*(1), 1–20. https://doi.org/10.15640/jcsit.v7n1a1

Tsohou, A., Karyda, M., Kokolakis, S., & Kiountouzis, E. (2015). Managing the introduction of information security awareness programmes in organisations. *European Journal of Information Systems, 24*(1), 38–58.

Woodward, B. N. M. (2011). Expansion and validation of the PAPA framework. *Information Systems Education Journal, 9*(3), 28–34. https://isedj.org/2011-9/N3/ISEDJv9n3p28.pdf

CHAPTER 15

AN ANALYSIS OF A UNIVERSITY'S ERP IMPLEMENTATION

A Case Study

Sam Goundar
The University of the South Pacific

Sanjay Singh
The University of the South Pacific

Goel Lal
The University of the South Pacific

Ashish Tiwari
NIT Kurukshetra

ABSTRACT

The main purpose of this case study is to analyze Fiji National University's (FNU) legacy information management systems and its related issues. The

Enterprise Systems and Technological Convergence, pages 277–289
Copyright © 2021 by Information Age Publishing
All rights of reproduction in any form reserved.

chapter will summarize FNU's journey towards identifying its issues, documenting the requirements, selecting the right vendor, and current project progress.

Fiji National University is Fiji's newest university, formed in 2010 after the merger of six major training institutions, which included Fiji Institute of Technology, Fiji School of Medicine, Fiji School of Nursing, Fiji College of Advanced Education, Fiji College of Agriculture, and the Lautoka Teachers College. In 2012, the Fiji Maritime Academy and in 2013, the Training and Productivity Authority of Fiji also became part of FNU.

When the institutions merged, the challenges related to managing student data multiplied and became more complex. Certain institutions came with their own information systems, while others had only manual records. The library inherited the Horizon Library Management System from the school of medicine. The finance and HR departments, and two of the other major divisions inherited Navision and PayGlobal from the Fiji Institute of Technology. In 2013, the software was upgraded. Three of the student management systems were standardized for newly formed colleges. The College of Engineering Science and Technology, College of Humanities and Education and College of Business, Hospitality, and Tourism had similarly adapted to the information system known as "Premium" inherited from Fiji Institute of Technology. Premium was developed in-house and the code was maintained by FNU. It was easier for FNU to modify the application to support the new needs of FNU. The College of Medicine, Nursing, and Health Sciences inherited the application from Fiji School of Medicine. The application was developed externally by a local vendor and there was a valid service level agreement (SLA) contract. The application known as StudentSoft was modified by the vendor for a fee to support the needs of the college. When training and productivity authority became part of FNU, their needs could not be catered by the existing two student management systems. TPAF had an application which was partially developed by an off-shore firm which closed down prior to completing the application. The best option was to take the existing application and extend it where possible until an alternate solution is identified.

This case is analyzed using the problem-oriented approach. The problem-oriented approach is applicable to real life situation cases. This chapter will identify all the problems with the current information systems at FNU. Finally, the recommendation and action plan will be specified.

MAJOR PROBLEMS IDENTIFIED

1. *Unique student identity*
   With multiple systems on hand, students end up with the same ID numbers and some students receive multiple ID numbers when they change colleges that require change in system. This creates

havoc when these same IDs for different student's accounts need to be created in Active Directory, Moodle, or email platform.

2. *Student validity verification*

    Students upon payment of fees receive a sticker which states validity of a student for a particular study period. During examination periods, students who do not pay complete fees, or make last minute payments, or even those who do not get the sticker for validity on their ID cards cause chaos during the examination period. The current system being stand alone does not have an easily accessible student validity checker.

3. *Issues with reporting*

    Having multiple applications, with duplicate IDs and contaminated and missing data create issues while generating reports for external parties such as Fiji Higher Education Commission and the Tertiary Loan Scheme Board. Generating reports from standalone systems such as the financial management system that require some data from other systems also becomes tedious. The government of Fiji is working with the Fiji Higher Education Commission on identifying new ways of distributing government grants and current systems will require much manual data processing to provide the required data to the Fiji Higher Education Commission. The current system will have financial impact on maximizing the amount of grant universities can receive.

4. *Delays in text file reconciliations*

    Since applications are not linked to one another, certain groups of people are required to generate text files at various times. Delays in generation of text files often creates issues with periodic reporting. This then impacts auditing, due diligence process, and timely decision-making.

5. *Limitation on use of Moodle.*

    With lack of integration with Moodle, the course creation and student enrollment are also chaotic for a couple of weeks at the beginning of every study term. The students enroll in a course in Moodle assuming it is also done in the student management system and becomes a problem when a student is denied access to facilities for not being enrolled in student management systems.

6. *Lack of standard process*

    Each of the three student management systems have a different process flow and functionality. This often confuses students and creates difficulty for faculty or staff to provide correct advice to students. This is one of the other challenges for integrating existing applications.

7. *Limited self service functionality*

   Most of the services require students and staff to visit a campus and submit a completed form. There is inefficiency in moving the forms from table to table for actioning. All data from the forms are not entered into the system.

8. *Customization limitations*

   While FNU has source codes for some of the applications, the coding practices and demand for overnight feature releases has led to poor programming results. The databases are poorly non-normalized, lack data validations, and accept quite a large amount of ambitious and dirty data with certain tables having over 100 fields and no one knows what some of the fields are used for. There is no centralized code repository and developers have multiple versions of source codes. There is barely any as-built documentation for any application developed in-house.

9. *Container loads of manual record*

   With the lack of any document management system, most of the manual data are stored in containers. Occasionally, records are needed to be searched and it takes lots of time. The containers have also become a hazard and an eyesore for visitors and need to be relooked at.

10. *Application accessibility*

    While some of the applications can be accessed externally, there are challenges accessing most of the other applications, which are native to certain operating systems only.

11. *Old legacy servers*

    FNU has some of the oldest servers running without support and limited backup capabilities. With increasing value of data and need for reporting and analysis, these servers are underperforming.

12. *Network challenges*

    FNU has campuses across Fiji and it is challenging to connect every campus with enough sustainable bandwidth. The cost of dedicated bandwidth in Fiji is very high ranging from $500 to $1,000 per Mbps per month.

13. *Inefficient disaster recovery service*

    FNU believes to host disaster recovery (DR) in geographically separate cities and hence maintains its DR in the western part of the country. The existing DR was only sufficient to run 10% of the services hosted in primary servers.

14. *Lack of scheduling capabilities*

    Lack of scheduling software requires large groups of faculty and staff to sit together and make timetables for coming study terms. This takes a lot of time and effort. Yet during the beginning of the study period, there are lots of clashes. In some cases where clashes cannot be avoided, the students are unregistered from courses. This impacts students study paths as well as leads to loss in revenue.

The system limitation also has an impact on overall university policy. The policies are written and enforced only to the extent that the system can support.

THE BEGINNING

The journey towards having an ERP system at FNU was rough. The vice chancellors and the councils played a critical role in determining a way forward for an integrated system.

2010–2014

After the merger and formation of FNU, under the leadership of Vice Chancellor Dr. Ganesh Chand and Chancellor Dr. Iqbal Janiff, the university focused on teething issues of the day to day student management system. The management at that time believed that FNU should develop its own student management system. During this period, the university also considered procuring or developing a timetabling solution.

2015–2016

In 2015 and 2016, the change in leadership saw the university being operated directly by the council without the vice chancellor. This is when the management decided to get an external consultant to review the student management system and assist the university in making the right choice. The university also decided to procure the timetabling solution.

The tender was called, and the analysis of the bids were taken to the management. The management then decided, instead of getting the student management system and timetabling system separately, the university must gather all the requirements and look for a solution that solves entire university issues related to IT. Deputy Chancellor Arvind Maharaj emphasized looking at the Asia Pacific market for solutions as we might be able to procure something that is cheaper and better when compared to products from the United States or United Kingdom.

2017–When It All Began

In 2017, the working group was formed by reps from each business unit including power users and management with IT. Prior to writing the tender specification document, FNU invited multiple vendors from India, New Zealand, Pakistan, Africa, and the United States to present their solution to FNU functional members. This enlightened FNU to assess their requirements. A detailed tender specification was prepared.

EVALUATING THE BIDS

Round 1

The tender documents were evaluated for general compliance. Those bids that did not meet basic compliance were eliminated.

Round 2

The shortlisted bidders were invited to do a presentation to the working group. The working group evaluated the functionality of the tender. The tender was evaluated based on the technical and functional components by the working committee.

Round 3

Based on the results of the first post-bid presentation, more bids were eliminated. This left the final three bidders meeting the technical score threshold. FNU knew by then that no bidder could provide a solution that would solve 100% of FNU's problems. The three remaining bidders were then invited to do a thorough presentation and clarify any questions of the working committee. After the final presentations, the bidder scores were finalized. These scores were then compared against the commercial analysis and bidders were ranked in order.

Round 4

The Banner 9 solution from Ellucian was leading the scoreboard. A team of functional and technical experts then visited the university of the South Pacific, Australia Catholic University, Charles Sturt University, and Western Sydney University to gain insights regarding their Banner solution implementation. The visiting team compiled all the gaps identified and the management acknowledged and accepted those gaps. The decision was made to go with Banner 9 by July 2019.

THE NETWORK CHALLENGE

FNU has six primary data centers located in campuses ensuring data is closest to the greatest number of users. With Banner ERP solution in consideration, there was a need to improve network connectivity and reliability. Fiji National University by March 2018 connected to Australia Academic and Research Network (AARNET). The 1 Gbps Internet provided FNU with opportunity as well as challenge. Since FNU had 30 sites connected via multiprotocol label switching (MPLS) network running open shortest path first (OSPF) protocol, there was need to ensure every campus now have enough MPLS bandwidth to support wide area network (WAN) traffic as well as internet traffic travelling through the AARNET network. The entire FNU WAN was collapsed and a new WAN of 30 sites were done by May 2018.

THE SERVER REQUIREMENT

FNU prefers to run the application on its own datacenter for various reasons:

1. Data is available in raw format to FNU.
2. Application can be tweaked based on FNU's requirements.
3. Data is closest to the users.
4. Lower total cost of ownership.

FNU has been running most of its application on legacy servers. The computer and storage requirements for Banner software could not be met by the servers. The tender was called to procure a modern state of the art server that is robust, scalable, reliable, faster, and software defined.

Three of the leading hyper converged technology solutions were bided. This included Nutanix, VMWare's vSAN, and Cisco's Hyperflex both on all flash and hybrid options. Looking at the cost and evaluating the usable capacity as well as the overhead consumption of resources by controller VMs, a decision was reached to procure all flash vSAN technology running on Lenovo Hardware. The total specification of the purchased server included over 200 terabytes of usable storage, 2.4 terabytes of random access memory, and 192 core intel gold processors. Each of the servers are connected through a redundant Mellonox switch running a Cumulus software defined network operating system. Each of the servers is connected to each other over 40 gigabits per second hybrid copper breakout cables. The benefit for this solution is that it is scalable and as and when there is need for more compute or storage, more servers can be added without having to shut down any services.

NEED FOR BACKUP

No matter how new and reliable the servers are, there is always a need to have backups to recover from any unforeseen disaster. FNU required a smart and software-defined backup solution and thus procured 120 TB Rubrik brik running 4 nodes. This Rubrik brik connects to the redundant Mellanox switch by 80 gbps bandwidth and provides much faster backups. The benefit for this solution is that it is scalable and when there is a need for more storage space, more briks can be added without having to shut down any services.

THE DISASTER RECOVERY CHALLENGE

Based on previous experience, FNU knew that the servers in the Disaster Recovery (DR) site cannot be undersized. A true DR solution would ensure that the servers in DR will be an exact replica of the production site. A high performing DR server will assist FNU lower its recovery time objective (RTO) as well as recovery point objective (RPO). Therefore, the servers in the DR site, including switching and the backup appliance, are exactly the same as in the primary data center. To ensure that the MPLS network traffic does not get affected, a separate layer two network connectivity between the primary datacenter in DR datacenter is created to ensure backup and replication does not get affected during peak traffic and that backup and DR traffic does not affect other WAN based traffic.

THE UIMS PROJECT INITIATION

FNU has a vision for highly efficient and integrated information systems. FNU calls its visionary project university information management system (UIMS). The management team from Ellucian visited FNU for a 3-day project overview session in late November 2018. The entire management team with functional and technical experts from FNU participated in a 3-day requirement and scope verification workshop.

SETUP OF THE BANNER ENVIRONMENT

After the new servers were installed in December 2018, FNU began deploying all the pre-production and production Banner instances. From FNU's responsibility perspective, FNU made all the servers available for the actual solution to be installed by the Ellucian's technical team.

However, Ellucian changed the project start date to January 28, 2019 for unspecified reasons. Now, doing that placed tremendous pressure on FNU to now meet the go-live dates in a shorter amount of time. After negotiations, Ellucian began installing the software in January. By the end of February, the training instance was ready for the project to commence.

The project was officially kicked off on January 28, 2019. This is when the consultants came to FNU to spend 2 weeks with the functional teams.

SCOPE CHALLENGES

When the consultants began their requirements gathering sessions, most of our requirements could not be met. A simple response from them was that it is not in the scope. This placed lots of pressure on functional team leads and the project management team to look at best options.

FNU has adopted Western Sydney University's "Adopt and Adapt" approach, where we adopt Banner 9 as it is, and to adapt FNU's processes to the processes that Banner supports. This allows FNU to realign its process to an internationally accepted process. This also ensures that FNU follows best practices to perform any modifications which are not lost during feature upgrades.

THE CREEP CULTURES

FNU has poor commitment to scope. As soon as the project funding and scope was identified, additional software such as DegreeWorks and Ellucian Talent Management were procured. This increased amount of work that FNU must deliver within the same amount of resources, cost, and time.

The project manager advised the steering committee that this needs to stop as "the project teams plate is already full." Any feature improvements will be considered as the second phase of the project. This ensures that focus is maintained on what FNU has committed to so that this can be implemented successfully before moving on to the others.

REVIEW OF FNU'S PROGRESSIVE STATUS

FNU followed the approach as illustrated by Deep, Guttridge, Dani, and Burns (2008) to analyze the ERP solution. By choosing Ellucian Banner, FNU also aligned itself to other major universities in the region (University

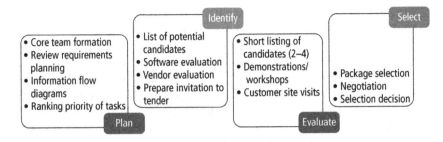

Figure 15.1 ERP system selection process.

of the South Pacific) so that knowledge and resources can be shared between the two universities.

As per Deep et al. (2008), FNU complied with the following steps (see Figure 15.1).

Step 1: Plan

1. Formed the working group.
2. Created current and future state process flow diagrams.

Step 2: Identify

1. FNU identified potential candidates and asked them to demo their application so that a detailed requirements document could be done.

Step 3: Evaluate

1. After the tender was called, FNU shortlisted the candidates and eliminated candidates using a comprehensive process.
2. FNU visited customer reference sites to verify bid claims on compliance.

Step 4: Select

1. The price was further negotiated.
2. The modular components were selected based on FNU's needs.
3. The contract was signed to materialize the strategic alliance and partnership.

ERP CHARACTERISTICS

A good ERP solution must have the following characteristics:

1. *Flexibility*—The system should be able to adapt to the changing organizational needs. Most of the Banner software component is open source with Banner 9. FNU has procured an ethos integration module, which allows Banner 9 to interface with each other using any API based standard protocols.

2. *Modular and open*—The organization should have the flexibility to procure what is required and later on add on or remove components without affecting each other. Having open architecture allows customers to tailor the application as per organizational need as well as to enhance its capabilities without having to rely on the supplier for continuous professional services engagement for any tweaks. The Banner application is Modular. FNU has procured various modules and there are plans to procure more modules to bring in more value for the students.

3. *Comprehensive*—Banner 9 is a comprehensive solution itself, however it has partnered with hundreds of other solution providers that can be used to leverage Banner capabilities. FNU has procured Adirondack Housing Director and Cornerstone Talent Management to leverage Banner 9 capabilities as these solutions are validated and supported by Ellucian.

4. *Systems Integration and Communications*—Banner 9 comes with ethos, which is a solution that allows Banner to interact with any other system within the organization boundaries, external or in cloud to interact with one another. It also leverages the functionality to run certain Banner 9 modules in cloud while the others on premise.

5. *Demonstrate Best Practices*—Banner is widely used in Australia, and the United States with many other universities in all parts of the world. Banner has evolved over the period and uses the best business practices.

6. *Secure*—Banner has role-based access. FNU has procured an ethos identity server that works on WSO2 technology to run Single Sign On services. This will ensure that users are authenticated securely and then they are able to securely move between applications without having to login multiple times. FNU has also procured Barracuda Web Application Firewall to protect all services against web-based attacks, including Denial of Services Attack, SQL injection, cross site scripting (XSS), and more.

7. *Reporting*—FNU has procured Argos Forms and Argos Reporting through an Ellucian partner to provide this functionality. This will

allow users to create or generate their own reports when and wherever required, without having to bother IT teams.

8. *Automation*—Banner 9 comes with Banner Workflow, which allows tasks to be automated. During automation, tasks can occur at various modules as well as external applications. FNU has also procured JAMS workload automation software to run and closely monitor every job.

9. *Scalable*—FNU has procured the hardware technology that is scalable and allows Banner to grow as per FNU's requirement's growth.

10. *Self-Service*—Banner 9 comes with a self service portal which allows users access to a portal where they can perform most of the services themselves instead of visiting front office staff. It also comes with a mobile app server that allows access to Banner service as well as a student e-learning environment such as Moodle within the same app.

CONCLUSION

FNU has procured a very large set of modules for their ERP implementation. Upon completion, it is going to be Asia Pacific's largest Banner implementation. While FNU had the option to either develop the solution inhouse or have any external party develop it, FNU made the right decision to choose a proven ERP solution. Technology is developing at a very rapid rate and once applications are developed inhouse, it needs continuous support for its research and development for its evolution.

With forming a strategic alliance with Ellucian, FNU has placed itself on the international map and gets the opportunity to become one of the leading universities in showcasing digital transformation at this modern age. FNU rightly is prioritizing its focus on learning and teaching by outsourcing these kinds of activities.

RECOMMENDATION

- It is recommended that FNU maintains baseline implementation and performs any customizations using the standard Page Builder and other provisioned capabilities.
- It is recommended that FNU utilizes best practice for project management and change management to ensure the transition to the new system is very smooth.
- It is recommended that FNU strictly adheres to the scope of works to ensure project completion within the time. Failure to do so will

see the project continuing forever and will have huge financial implications.

- It is recommended that FNU closely monitors the cost and milestone deliverable to ensure any issues are highlighted and attended to at the earliest.
- It is recommended that FNU maintains a register for any customizations.

IMPLEMENTATION

- Since FNU has already started with the configuration of the system, it needs to ensure that data is clean before it is migrated to the new information system.
- FNU needs to perform independent tests and engage functional users in tests to ensure the system passes the expectations.
- Perform repetitive user training to ensure users are aware on how to use the system before go-live.
- Perform a phased rollout to ensure a small group of people are using the system and can be supported during the initial days before moving to the next module or next group of users.

REFERENCES

Deep, A., Guttridge, S., Dani, S., & Burns, N. (2008). Investigating factors affecting ERP selection in made-to-order SME sector. *Journal of Manufacturing Technology Management, 19*(4), 430–446.

CHAPTER 16

USAGE AND BENEFITS OF BANNER ERP SYSTEM AT A UNIVERSITY

Sam Goundar
The University of the South Pacific

Noneel Prasad
The University of the South Pacific

Dinesh Chetty
The University of the South Pacific

Rahul Prasad
The University of the South Pacific

Rayani Kumar
National Institute of Technology

Enterprise Systems and Technological Convergence, pages 291–304
Copyright © 2021 by Information Age Publishing
All rights of reproduction in any form reserved.

ABSTRACT

ERP systems play a vital role in an organization. However, the success of ERP systems is heavily dependent on the structure of the organization and the usage of the ERP system. The benefits of the ERP system implementation is very well reflected on the utilization of the ERP system by the organization. Our team's research is based on the implementation and usage of the Banner ERP system at a university in the South Pacific. The aim of this chapter is to explore the implementation and usage of the ERP Banner system and identify the benefits of it to the university. This chapter will also provide suggestions of ways in which the university could achieve more benefits from the banner system.

The introduction of ERP systems has provided a new direction for all the organizations around the world. With technological advancement at its peak in the 21st century, the increased research into how well ERP systems support the growth of business and organization has allowed ERP systems to make a stance amongst its users. Organizations implement ERP systems to channel their business process in such a way that will boost not only their performance in the market, but also enable them to grow steadily over the years.

The University of the South Pacific is the premier educational institution in the Pacific region. With twelve academic campuses situated over various island countries, the university currently accommodates for close to 25,000 students which will surely increase in the coming years. With the university setting its goals and objectives very clearly through its strategic plan 2013–2018 shows its commitment towards providing high quality education to its students and the students to be. The university has to rely heavily on the quality of the data stored within the premises for accurate analysis and making decisions.

This chapter focuses on the usage and benefits of the Banner ERP system at the University of the South Pacific. With the strategic plan of the university in place, the chapter also focuses on how the strategic plan has given rise to changes in data processing keeping Banner ERP system at the center. With changes in the pipeline for the data handling, the ability of the Banner ERP system to integrate with newer systems and plugins is also very well explored within the research paper.

The importance of this research lies in knowing what the current usages of the Banner ERP system are and the impact of the strategic plan on the ERP system. Exploring the changes to the university's information systems arising as a result of the strategic plan provides challenge to the Banner system in terms of integration. The flexibility of the ERP system to facilitate integration changes highlights its benefits to the university. The updated Delone and Mclean IS model provides insight to the critical dimensions of success along which the university's information systems and the ERP system are evaluated. The model also allows the research team to better understand how the ERP system is related to the university's information systems such as SOLS and Moodle.

Regardless of much focus on how the Banner ERP system works within the university and is linked with the information systems, the research team aims to identify the usages and the benefits of the Banner ERP system. These usages and benefits will be identified keeping in mind what USP's strategic plan requires and the ability of the ERP system to accommodate the changes and integration.

LITERATURE REVIEW

According to Abugabah and Sanzongi (2010) there have been numerous studies on ERP implementation and several related issues such as implementation procedures, business processes, and outcomes (e.g., Amoako-Gyampah & Salam, 2004; Hong & Kim, 2002; Mandal & Gunasekaran, 2002; Markus & Tanis, 2000; McAfee, 2002; Scott & Vessey, 2002; Somers, Nelson, & Regowsky, 2000; Sun, Yazdani, & Overend, 2005) but the research about ERP systems in higher education is still at the infancy stage. Higher education is the new big business and even though ERP research has neglected this area many universities have already implemented an ERP (Nielsen, 2002). The more the usage by the intended users at different levels in the company, the greater the likelihood that such a firm will gain competitive advantage which is one of the key goals of deploying an ERP system (Nwankpa & Roumani, 2014). ERP usage by appropriate users and their full involvement are one of the critical success factors for ERP systems and their implementation within an organization.

There are two main areas of user participation when a company or organization decides to implement an ERP system (Esteves et al., 2005). The first area is when a user participates in the stage of definition of the company's ERP system needs and the second area is when the user participates in the implementation of the ERP. ERP system misfits can easily be eliminated by having that percentage of user involvement during the selection and evaluation process (Noaman & Ahmed, 2015). User involvement at an early stage reveals a lot of crucial information and many problems can be identified at an early stage. It can identify if the ERP will require customization of various modules or provide a helping hand if business processes are required to be changed. There are issues that lead to users being discouraged from continually using the systems. These usage problems have been attributed to inadequate training, insufficient support for end-users, and severity of the implementation choice (Motwani, Mirchandani, Madan, & Gunasekaran, 2002; Nicolaou, 2004; Nwankpa & Roumani, 2014).

Study contends that those firms that facilitate ERP system usage after the initial ERP implementation are more likely to benefit from their ERP initiatives than firms that do not (Nwankpa, 2015). The successful implementation or adoption of technology by an organization must take into account the human and management issues.

Previous studies have identified many similarities between implementing ERP system software in educational institutes and in other organizations (Pollock & Cornford, 2005). As any challenges faced by companies, Higher education encounters all the same thus becomes important to study the implications and problems caused to address them accordingly. Large companies are not able to function properly today with the support of an efficient IT System. The computerization of all the areas of the company's operational results in the increase of its efficiency and effectiveness, and thus its competitiveness in the market (Agnieszka, 2017). More and more organizations are beginning to implement ERP systems because they are able to see the numerous benefits they bring along.

Shang and Seddon (2002) developed five dimensions of ERP benefits namely operational, managerial, strategic, IT infrastructure, and organizational. Our focus would be towards managerial looking into how the ERP system overtime has improved decision-making and planning and towards IT infrastructure as how ERP systems provide flexibility for current and future. According to Staehr (2010) managerial decisions throughout the ERP life cycle influence the extent of business benefits achieved during post implementation. A discussion made by Chou and Chang (2008) stated that performing two complementary tasks such as customization and organizational mechanisms improve ERP benefits. The paper focuses on a post implementation phase as firms have used ERP over a period of several years and the success of the initial stage does not necessarily lead to the benefits overall (Liang et al., 2007).

The usage and benefits of the ERP provide a competitive edge to USP and sets an example towards other universities in Fiji to invest in such technologies. Similar cases happen all around the world where universities begin to replace their legacy systems with the efficient ones by learning from others to improve their performance and learning services and finally to become more efficient in their operations (Marginson & Considine, 2000; Pollock & Cornford, 2001).

STATEMENT OF THE PROBLEM

Since the major aim of this research chapter mainly focuses on the usage and the benefits of the Banner ERP system, less focus has been on issues that need solving. Regardless of this, there were some major issues that were identified through the research work. These issues include Banner ERP system being underutilized due to unavailability of adequate resources, Banner ERP system data stored is not clean and all the information systems do not have a standard baseline for communicating and accessing the Banner ERP system.

RESEARCH QUESTIONS

The research chapter mainly focuses on the usage and the benefits of the Banner ERP system by the University of the South Pacific. The chapter focuses on the process flows of the USP and how the Banner ERP system fits into these process flows. Exploring the Banner system usages through interviewing the daily users has given a great insight as to how well the Banner ERP system is being used by the university. With the university's strategic plan set every 5 years, the university attempts to achieve its objectives and the goals that have been set out in the plan. The Banner ERP system being the centre of all the process flows then means that the changes that are laid out across the university impacts the ERP system as well. With major aims like achieving academic excellence through improved information quality, system quality, and user satisfaction, changes that are currently revolving around the Banner system are thoroughly being explored through this research.

The major aim of this research work has always been to focus on the usage and benefits of the Banner ERP system. Thus, less attention has been given by the research team to identify the issues in the process flows that need resolving. However, the use of the Delone and Mclean IS success model in the research paper has allowed the research teams to identify some of the issues that may be faced by the university using the ERP system. Since the model can be used to break down the processes and information system structure to gain a better understanding, it was noticed that the Banner ERP system is not utilized to its full potential. Current situation shows that the university is not using all the features of the Banner ERP system. One of the major reasons that were identified was that the university does not possess the appropriate resources to cater for the features that are currently left idle. Also, it was also identified that all the information systems that are being linked to the Banner system did not have a standard baseline for communicating with the Banner system. For this reason, there was a lot of data inconsistencies in the data facilitated by the ERP System. These are some of the issues related to the ERP system that have been identified by the ITS team and are trying to resolve as an attempt to meet the Strategic plan objectives.

When being compared with other research papers and journals, it can be said that this research paper does not have any new techniques or findings.

The research only explores the usages and benefits of the Banner system applied to the University of the South Pacific. The only unique thing that has been used in this research paper is the use of the updated Delone and Mclean IS success model to break down the usage of Banner ERP system. The research paper is applicable for getting information about how well the Banner ERP system can fit into an institution. The research paper will be able to provide assistance and information about the possible issues and problems that can arise while having the ERP system installed. The difference process flows and actions that need to be revisited and readjusted to fully utilize the Banner ERP system is something that this research paper can provide assistance with for information purposes. The research paper can also form a good source for case studies as well.

METHODOLOGY

Data Collection

For the purpose of research, the team planned to carry out interviews that were done with the banner system users at the University of the South Pacific. These users also include the IT staff who manage the ERP system also. On the same, the data was collected from online sources. These sources include previously researches done on ERP systems and organizations using the ERP system which provided base to our discussion and suggestions that the team has to provide.

Research Model

For the purpose of the research, the updated Delone and Mclean IS success model was used. The model seeks to provide a comprehensive understanding of the ERP system by identifying, describing, and explaining the relationships among six of the most critical dimensions of success along which information systems are commonly evaluated. These six dimensions of success that will be reflected on the banner system used by the university includes:

- *Information Quality:* Refers to the quality of the information that the system is able to store, deliver, or produce, and is one of the most common dimensions along which information systems are evaluated.
- *System Quality:* System quality indirectly impacts the extent to which the system is able to deliver benefits by means of mediational relationships through the usage intentions and user satisfaction constructs.

- *Service Quality:* Reflects on the quality of the services that the system will produce.
- *System Usage/Usage Intentions:* Intentions to use an information system and actual system use are well-established constructs in the information systems literature. In the IS success model system use and usage intentions are influenced by information, system, and service quality.
- *User Satisfaction:* User satisfaction directly influences the net benefits provided by an information system. Satisfaction refers to the extent to which a user is pleased or content with the information system.
- *Net System Benefits:* Reflects on the ability of the system to deliver is an important facet of the overall value of the system to its users or to the underlying organization.

RESULTS/FINDINGS

Research results indicate almost all of the modules being on the baseline without major modifications while accounts receivable is moving towards baseline (see Table 16.1).

To examine tasks carried out or are in progress to improve quality of information, systems, and services offered and maintained by USP, the following operational and IT infrastructure results came to light:

Operational Findings:

- slowly moving modules to baseline for quality improvement;
- having HelpDesk services available all around the campus;
- continuous business process re-engineering for process standardization;

TABLE 16.1 Module Usage of ERP Solution at USP		
	Baseline	
Module	Yes	No
Banner General	✓	
Student	✓	
Human Resources	✓	
Finance	✓	
Accounts Receivable		✓
Payroll	✓	

- brought in an Operational Data Store and Enterprise Data Warehouse;
- in process of integrating of a powerful business intelligence tool;
- running surveys such as total experience, academic course evaluation, graduation;
- destination;
- upgrading ERP system; and
- bringing in new ERP modules such as self service.

IT Infrastructure Findings:

- Using Nagios for IT, network, server, and application monitoring
- in progress of moving from AARNET STM 4 to 16 for higher bandwidth;
- working towards ITIL (information technology infrastructure library) compliance for service level agreement (SLA) benchmarks, and
- resource upgrade to cater for the ERP upgrade.

DISCUSSION

The research findings of the team strongly stress on the improvements and changes that the strategic plan requires to meet the objectives and the goals that have been set. With Banner ERP system already a major part of the university's business processes and decision makings. With new objectives and goals defined in the strategic plan, changes and upgrades related to the Banner ERP system and the information systems revolving around the ERP system is in the pipeline. The updated Delone and Mclean IS success model played an integral role in this research. The research model was used to break down all the business processes and the functionalities of the university to know more about how the university operates. Also the model allowed the team to learn more about the Banner ERP system, where it actually fits in the business processes and how well it is used in the university. The model also allowed the team to know more about the flaws in the business process that may have led to the underutilization of the Banner ERP System.

With the Banner ERP system being the center for all the data related to the university, staff and the students, different sections use a variety of information systems to execute their daily tasks and work. These information systems produce and process data which is not centralized or synchronized in time with the Banner ERP system. In this process of updating Banner, a lot of issues lay with unclean data in the ERP system. One of the major reasons identified for the unclean data is that the information systems are not structured or developed using a standard structure or the baseline. As a result, this only results in unclean data, but also affects the quality of the decisions made using reports derived from inaccurate data.

As an attempt by the university to achieve improved information quality through the strategic plan, the university management together with the necessary development team are currently working on adjusting all the information systems to them to have a standard baseline of accessing and processing information. Departments like the HR and the payroll of the university do not currently have their information systems aligned to have a standard baseline for accessing Banner ERP and processing. Having a standard baseline for the information contributes to achieving improved information quality for the university as well as better decision-making.

Business process re-engineering has always been associated with the ERP systems in one way or another. For the University of the South Pacific, the process flows are being revisited as an attempt to meet the strategic plan objectives. On the same, the process re-engineering phase is a major step towards improving the information quality of the university. Standardizing the business processes looks at the flow of the day to day tasks of the university keeping in mind that the businesses processes are very much connected to the Banner ERP system. Thus, changes in the business process and the flow would mean changes to the Banner ERP system. The changes in the business processes is also an attempt to maximize the usage of all the features of the Banner ERP system. Currently, the university's IT infrastructure is not adequate for all the major information systems and the plugins that are linked to the Banner ERP system. Maximizing the usage of all the features would mean a good return on the investment for purchasing very expensive applications by the ITS department of the university. With university's business processes re-engineered, benefits like productivity improvement, better performance control, cycle time reduction, and increased business flexibility. The quality of the information produced through these re-engineered processes will be improved. The university management will then be able to provide better services not only in an academic area but also other aspects through better analysis and accurate decisions for progress.

The university has now brought in Operational Data Stores (ODS) and Enterprise Data Warehouse (EDW) as an additional support for the Banner ERP System. The ODS system is very much used for carrying out operational reporting, controls, and decision-making for the organization. With the data that the information systems generate and use, the ODS makes an attempt to integrate all the data that is received from multiple sources which in this case are the various information systems of the departments. The main aim for this integration through the ODS is for reporting and analysis for decision-making. Thus, the management now gets an added advantage for more accurate analytical reports. One very important note to make for the ODS is that it incorporates actions such as cleaning, resolving redundancy, and checks against business rules and integrity as part of the integration process. This makes room for Banner ERP systems to facilitate cleaner data as well. With the ODS in place for better integration of data, the university's attempt to now achieve its objectives set through the strategic plan. This also adds to the standardization of the process flow re-engineering. With an attempt at achieving data integrity through ODS, benefits like better time management on the part of cleaning and resolving redundancy and flexibility on business process flow changes now seems achievable for the university. With all the data in the process of being centralized, it is now very much possible to explore the dashboarding capabilities of all the information systems and the data warehouses to ensure maximum uptime for all the systems. Exploring the dashboarding capabilities contributes towards achieving a better system quality. Any issues or problems with the university's system will be very much detectable and solved within a limited time frame. Maximizing the uptime of the systems would mean better customer service and user satisfaction.

User satisfaction is always the goal and objective for any organization or institute. At the University of the South Pacific captures users' feedback through various surveys that are run throughout the university. These surveys include total experience, academic course evaluation, and graduation destination surveys. These surveys form the baseline to the feedback on the services of the institute, the level of satisfaction that the current systems provide and improvements that can be brought about. Such surveys also form the base for the strategic plan objectives as well. The changes and the upgrades to the ERP system and the other information systems are triggered through such surveys and the decisions that are made using the survey data. With one of the basic aims to provide better customer service, the institute uses these surveys as a means to capture what exactly the students and the staff want from the university that will boost their academic and professional careers. The need for more surveys to be conducted within the institute would definitely mean a lot more changes and upgrades in the information systems as well. The changes such as process re-engineering, ODS, and EDW as well as ERP upgrades is an attempt to not only provide user satisfaction, but also to achieve information quality.

The Banner ERP system version that is used by the University of the South Pacific is Version 8. The management of the university is looking to upgrade the system to Version 9. For the upgrade to Version 9, the institute also needs to upgrade the necessary resources in order to ensure that the upgraded version of the ERP system works. The IT infrastructure needs to be looked at to ensure that Version 9 of Banner ERP system implementation would be possible to handle. The servers and the network in particular are the components that need to be upgraded as well. The upgrade of the ERP system is something the vendor will heavily engage in. The newer version of Banner ERP system brings with it a new look for the user interface. Together with that, the Banner system will cater for new tools and significantly improved capabilities. Banner 9 promises to allow for web-based mobility across all the devices and locations connected. Since the new Banner has modern functionality built into the application, the need to customize the Banner ERP will be minimized thus, less work on the part of the ITS officers. The version driven upgrades to the Banner system which often tend to cause operational disruptions from time to time are eliminated as the number of dependencies is reduced by the new upgrade.

With Banner 9 in place, the university will be affected in various ways. Reflecting on the effect on the students, the update streamlines all the processes making the modules and information systems mobile friendly. It also works to support multiple platforms. The Banner Version 9 also works to improve the response time of the data processing and retrieval. On the same, the faculty and the staff also will benefit heavily from the new Banner system. The system provides increased data integrity for all the data that is captured by the Banner system and also facilitates better analytics, boosting management decision-making and student retention. The upgrade makes information available at the fingertips of the staff, thus making student engagements during advising easier. The response time for the faculty and the staff will be improved using the new Banner ERP system. The upgrade to the Banner 9 can be seen as a major attempt to achieve improved system quality, information quality, system use, and user satisfaction.

CONCLUSION

Based on the research conducted, results indicate a significant amount of effort being placed in order for the university to maximize the use of the Banner ERP. Through continuous improvements, module by module USP is able to gain competitive advantages over their competitors and over the difficulties faced by the implementation and usage.

Results demonstrate that each module requires a lot of user involvement and support from top level management to make decisions of customization or business process engineering as the systems are not made specifically for one higher education environment like USP. The learning curve to take into account for any other university is that the implementation is much more convoluted than just straightforward mere acquiring the ERP system and hope for success to follow afterwards.

In brief, a lot of benefits have come to light as the core mission of the university is the advancement of knowledge and its people. The updated

Mclean and Delone model provided a comprehensive understanding of IS success and helped to classify the findings into information, system and service quality that the ERP system is able to help bring towards the university and linking the usage intentions and user satisfaction towards the overall benefits for USP itself.

The limitation to this study include:

- The results could be biased towards USP as information acquired were from the senior technical and management team of the university itself.
- User aspects have been absent due to the lack of user involvement during the research and the complexity of the higher education sector itself.

RECOMMENDATION AND FUTURE RESEARCH

The purpose of this research was to bring to light the usage and benefits of an ERP in USP and just like many similar research of ERP into higher education (Abugabah & Sanzogni, 2010), this chapter also lacks the user involvement research into details.

Higher education is persisting in this information system era and while people hate to say it but it's like running a business altogether. There are many reasons to motivate research in the higher education sector and this chapter suggests to put more effort and focus on user perspective during the studies being conducted as it was unable to do so thoroughly.

Student research alone does not provide that incentive for users thus unable to gain the results desired but through the help of senior management this could be possible. Typical papers focus more towards success and failure factors only while the directions should shift to elements such users, system quality, service quality, and how all these impacts of net benefits.

REFERENCES

Abugabah, A., & Sanzogni, L. (2010). Enterprise resource planning (ERP) system in higher education: A literature review and implications. *International Journal of Human and Social Sciences, 5*(6), 395–399.

Agnieszka, K. (2017). Advantages of using enterprise resource planning systems (ERP) in the management process. *World Scientific News, 89,* 237–243.

Amoako-Gyampah, K., & Salam. A. (2004). An extension of the technology acceptance model in an ERP implementation environment. *Information and Management, 41*(6), 731–745.

Chou, S.-W., & Chang, Y.-C. (2008). The implementation factors that influence the ERP (enterprise resource planning) benefits. *Decision Support Systems, 46,* 149–157. https://doi.org/10.1016/j.dss.2008.06.003

Esteves, J., Pastor, J., & Casanovas, J. (2005). Monitoring user involvement and participation in ERP implementation projects. *International Journal of Technology and Human Interaction, 1*(14), 1–16.

Hong, K., & Kim, Y. (2002). The critical success factors for ERP implementation: An organizational fit perspective. *Information & Management, 40*(1), 25–40.

Liang, H., Saraf, N., Hu, Q., & Xue, Y. (2007). Assimilation of enterprise systems: The effect of institutional pressures and the mediating role of top management. *MIS Quarterly, 31*(1), 59–87.

Mandal, P., & Gunasekaran, A. (2002). Application of SAP R/3 in on-line inventory control. *International Journal of Production Economics, 75*(1/2), 47–55.

Marginson, S., & Considine, M. (2000). *The enterprise university: Power, governance and reinvention in Australia.* Cambridge University Press.

Markus, M., & Tanis. C. (2000). *The enterprise system experience from adoption to success.* In R. W. Zmud (Ed.), *Framing the domains of IT management: Projecting the future through the past* (pp. 173–207). Pinnaflex Educational Resources.

McAfee, A. (2002). The impact of enterprise technology adoption on operational performance: An empirical investigation. *Production and Operations Management, 11*(1), 33–53.

Motwani, J., Mirchandani, D., Madan, M., & Gunasekaran, A. (2002). Successful implementation of ERP projects: Evidence from two case studies. *International Journal of Production Economics, 75*(1/2), 83–96.

Nicolaou, A. I. (2004). Firm performance effects in relation to the implementation and use of enterprise resource planning systems. *Journal of Information Systems, 18*(2), 79–105.

Nielsen, J. (2002). *Critical success factors for implementing an ERP system in a university environment: A case study from the Australian.* https://citeseerx.ist.psu.edu/viewdoc/download?doi=10.1.1.83.214&rep=rep1&type=pdf

Noaman, A., & Ahmed, F. F. (2015). ERP Systems functionalities in higher education. *Procedia Computer Science, 65,* 385–395. https://doi.org/10.1016/j.procs.2015.09.100

Nwankpa, J. (2015). ERP system usage and benefit: A model of antecedents and outcomes. *Computers in Human Behavior, 45,* 335–344. https://doi.org/10.1016/j.chb.2014.12.019

Nwankpa, J., & Roumani, Y. (2014). Understanding the link between organizational learning capability and ERP system usage: An empirical examination. *Computers in Human Behavior, 33,* 224–234.

Pollock, N., & Cornford, J. (2001). *Customising industry standard computer systems for universities: ERP Systems and the university as an 'unique' organisation.* https://www.researchgate.net/publication/3927117_Customising_industry_standard_computer_systems_for_universities_ERP_systems_and_the_university_as_a_'unique'_organisation

Pollock, N., & Cornford, J. (2005). *Implications of enterprise resource planning systems for universities: An analysis of benefits and risks.* The Observatory on Borderless Higher Education. file:///Users/karamiller/Downloads/Implications%20of

%20Enterprise%20Resource%20Planning%20_ERP_%20Systems%20for%20 Universities_An%20Analysis%20of%20Benefits%20and%20Risks_.pdf

Scott, J., & Vessey, I. (2002). Managing risks in enterprise implementations. *Communications of the ACM, 45*(4), 74–81.

Shang, S., & Seddon, P. B. (2002). Assessing and managing the benefits of enterprise systems: The business manager's perspective. *Information Systems Journal, 12*(4), 271–299.

Somers, T., Nelson, K., & Regowsky, A. (2000). Enterprise resource planning (ERP) for the next millennium: Development of an integrative framework and implications for research. In *Proceedings of the 6th Americas conference on information systems* (pp. 998–1004). Association for Information Systems.

Staehr, L. (2010). Understanding the role of managerial agency in achieving business benefits from ERP systems. *Information Systems Journal, 20*(3), 213–238.

Sun, A., Yazdani, A., & Overend, J. (2005). Achievement assessment for enterprise resource planning (ERP) system implementations based on critical success factors. *International Journal of Production Economics, 98*(2), 189–203.

CHAPTER 17

ANALYZING THE EFFECTIVENESS OF AN ERP'S ORDER FULFILMENT PROCESS

Sam Goundar
The University of the South Pacific

Dilule Stolz
The University of the South Pacific

Karen Aisake
The University of the South Pacific

Krishan Kumar
The University of the South Pacific

Jitendra Yadav
Indian Institute of Information Technology

Enterprise Systems and Technological Convergence, pages 305–323
Copyright © 2021 by Information Age Publishing
All rights of reproduction in any form reserved.

ABSTRACT

The purpose of this chapter is to investigate how an oil company's information system, STRIPES, has assisted in ensuring a competitive advantage for its customers through its operational capabilities. This system systematically examines the processes, from the point where the customer places their order to the time he receives their ordered fuel in their tank.

For this chapter, we will be applying the Delone and McLean information system success model in the context of operational order fulfillment in this oil industry. This study will rely on three research questions to allow us to explain the effectiveness and efficiency of this information system and provide us with a better understanding of how oil companies maintain its competitive advantage. The research methodology is a way of interviews and questionnaires for those that use this information system on a daily basis within the organization. A structured questionnaire was sent out to 50 operators within the organization which consisted of order fulfillment personnel and delivery analysts to terminal dispatchers and their respective supervisors. Of these, we received responses from 26 personnel. In total, we looked at four features which include quality of service, customer deliverables, flexibility of system use, and service for order fulfillment.

The information collection will be done by way of interviews and questionnaires for those within the oil company who use the information system as part of their daily task. Our data analysis showed that the users were generally satisfied with the information system STRIPES and indicated that it improved their processing time of their day to day operations.

Our chapter will assist researchers and students with better understanding of the operations capabilities of information systems with STRIPES.

STRIPES is the information system software used in this oil company. It was initially introduced in 2007 in some regions as a means to "stay up to date" with the ever-changing business environment. The organization realized that their information system was becoming aged and to ensure that the customers' (internal and external) demands were met, they needed to improve on this. These pressures have increased the interest in competitive priorities and operations capabilities among firms (Phusavat & Kanchana, 2007) and in the information systems required for effective management and decision-making (e.g., Sadeghi, Rasouli, & Jandaghi, 2016; Yang, Shi, & Yan, 2016). This information system is used by the operation function to monitor receipt of fuel into the bulk tanks along with shipments to end customers. It also looks at inventory controls, material balances, equipment measurement, and truck/fleet management, however these will be out of scope for this research chapter.

Our focus will be more around the process of supplying fuel to the end users—order fulfillment process. From the instant the customer places an order with the order fulfillment team, to when fuel reaches their tanks—ordering and dispatching. STRIPES has been implemented by this oil company to fundamentally transform their facilities and their business processes to enable step-change improvements, to allow for a competitive advantage.

Driven by their business methods, corporations set goals and objectives and implement action plans to attain these goals. In practice, we apply an operations management view with efforts that are related to areas such as information systems, marketing, and management.

The main purpose of this research is to obtain an insight into how the current system has been in operation, its integrity and whether its operation capabilities have changed over time.

For the above reason, this research will use the Delone and McLean IS success model, using the qualitative approach to further deduce information and collation of data. We hope to provide a broader and detailed insight into effectiveness, reliability, dependability, and competitiveness of the STRIPE processes and moreover, any step of change improvements.

Features used in the Delone and McLean IS success model are system quality, information quality, service quality, use, user's satisfaction, individual impact, and organizational impact.

We will look at four of the six as mentioned above which are information quality, service quality, user's satisfaction, and organizational impact. However, these dimensions are interrelated simultaneously to each other.

We hope to present a comprehensive and systematic literature review within the operations strategy space, with a selected target that identifies the operations capabilities.

Three problems that were identified with this STRIPES system are: delivery shipment number that needs to be auto-generated before the tanker is loaded, weekend back-up team not only looks after the Pacific region but also Australia and New Zealand. The team works from home, hence at times give priority to their area and not our Pacific region. New customer details are communicated via email and then the system database are populated.

Understanding information system success is an ongoing area of interest not only to researchers but also to practitioners and management stakeholders. Such understanding helps highlight the value of the system and can serve as a basis for subsequent decisions regarding such systems. There are various approaches to assessing the success of information systems (IS). The popular and most validated measure is the DeLone and McLean IS success model (D&M model). The D&M model was first propounded in 1992 and was updated with some modifications in 2003.

The D&M model has been applied and validated in a number of IS studies. For instance, it has been tested and validated in studies assessing the success of e-commerce systems, knowledge management systems, e-government systems, and much more.

LITERATURE REVIEW

According to Chuang and Lin (2017), e-service capability and service innovation orientation increases information-value offering to customer relationships and organizational performances. This is all enabled through having an information system. In today's world, one of the major trends that is changing society and businesses, both internally and externally, is being able to have digital information. Chuang and Lin (2017) introduced a resource-based perspective that looked at technology, human and business resources to develop an e-service capability into the overall business process. This research analyzed aspects affecting information-value contributions in e-service systems and the resulting outcomes in customer relationship performances and organizational performances. This study validated that the resource-based perspective and innovation strategy can be linked to model the interactions between e-service capability, service innovation orientation, and information-value offerings (Chuang & Lin, 2017). There is broad understanding among creators, analysts, advisors, and scholars in the field of the board that advancement is the focal ability for all associations keen on augmenting the open doors for achievement in the 21st century (Pereira & Fernandes, 2018).

Sansone, Hilletofth, and Eriksson (2016) conducted a systematic investigation of operational capabilities within the operations strategy area. The outcome of their research was to enable researchers and other organizations to expand on their understanding of critical operations capabilities. This investigation was done by way of literature reviews. Several research papers were looked at to provide a picture of the various studies that had already taken place in the field of operations capabilities. A number of operations capabilities were identified and included in a conceptual framework. This conceptual framework became the output of this research on operational capabilities. There were a total of seven highlights that were distinguished during the writing of the different articles officially distributed and these included cost, quality, conveyance, adaptability, administration, development, and condition. These basic tasks abilities give extra help to managers and associations intending to build up an activities methodology. Essentially, what this exploration gave was an establishment to directors and associations to use to build up their activities technique while remembering their associations destinations. Over the long haul, a superior and more profound understanding and sharing of information in regards to focused supremacy and tasks abilities can affect an associations achievement emphatically.

Another examination was directed to break down the impact of the data framework concerning the association's execution and business methodology. From a resource based point of view, the investigation saw how to help an inventive data framework methodology and a traditionalist data framework technique to give ease and separate business procedures. The after effects of this investigation from the Spanish sustenance industry uncovered the adequacy of inventive data frameworks methodologies in associations with minimal effort business techniques. To separate, imaginative data framework techniques neglect to reward the dangers of development in showcasing errands and in this way in business methodologies that depend on image separation. It was additionally discovered that the connection between data framework procedure and business methodology that are reliant on inventive separation is vague, anyway for the sustenance business the imaginative data framework technique was counterproductive.

The researchers concluded by providing guidance on strategic decision-making for developing information systems in organizations according to the organization's goals. According to Cram, Brohman, and Gallupe (2016), many publications focus on three information systems processes which include managing information systems development, managing information system outsourcing, and managing security. Though, there is an emergence of information system processes and technologies with distinct control challenges, there is a need to cogitate the wider applicability of past control insights. This research chapter integrates existing information system control concepts and associations into a comprehensive information system control model. This model is applied to emerging information system processes to guide future research and practice. There are five control measurements that have been recognized through the survey of 65 powerful data framework control-related diary papers. These were then combined into a solitary, coordinated model, and connected to past data framework control discoveries to the difficulties of rising data frameworks by representing a progression of related proposals.

From this research, it was found that the current information systems control research is increasingly applicable and relevant to tomorrow's emerging information system opportunities and challenges (Cram & Wiener, 2018).

Therefore information security remains a critical activity within today's organizations in light of continued data breaches, systems outages, and malicious software (Cram, Proudfoot, & D'Arcy, 2017; Ghafir et al., 2018). Although outside factors (e.g., external hackers, natural disasters) pose a significant threat to the security of an organization's information and technology resources, the actions of employees are often viewed as being a greater security risk (Willison & Warkentin, 2013). Hence, efficiency and its implementation mechanism have been the general management and the core content of the traditional public administration research. With the evolution and the development of public administration research, combined with the availability of the increasingly rich content, the concept of efficiency has often been used in different context (Han & Sun, 2016).

Though the effects of digitalization on organizations has been studied separately but there has been very little research done on the overall "big" picture of the effects. However, the digitalization of society and business is marching forward at an ever-increasing speed, calling for more converged research on the phenomenon (Oksanen, et al., 2018).

Information system is one of the important points which lead to the success of an organization, especially an organization that requires management and financial processing. The success of the information system is also important not only for organizations to improve their efficiency and productivity, but also for developers who are responsible for enhancing and improving the systems (Aboaoga, Aziz, & Mohamed, 2018).

A recent study reported that most organizations experienced an operational disruption, such as failure to ship product or close the books, lasting beyond one month while an IS was implemented or updated (Panorama Consulting Solutions, 2014). Specialized frameworks for generation are progressively computerized, which implies that they need to work dependably. In this way, the quickly extending idea of upkeep, where individuals would state that keeping up a procedure that permits the administration of the specialized condition and unwavering quality during the whole life cycle of the framework. Customarily, upkeep has been considered as a help work, non-gainful, and not a center capacity enhancing business.

However, it has been noticed that many manufacturing industries have used various approaches to improve maintenance effectiveness (Medaković, & Marić, 2018).

This hole is a key issue since advances in innovation bring about rising authoritative procedures that have not been utilized or experienced previously. Alongside these new innovation-based procedures comes the requirement for new controls, which drive execution towards authoritative destinations. Where research does not clearly articulate the most effective approaches to design and implement controls in these new processes, organizations are at an increased risk of investing in promising new IS initiatives that fail to live up to performance expectations (Cram et al., 2018).

Swamidass and Newell (1987) defines operations strategy as the effective use of operations strengths as a competitive weapon for the achievement of business and corporate goals. Corporate strategy leads to business strategy and subsequently to operations strategy. Driven by their business strategies, firms set goals and objectives and implement action plans to achieve these goals. Management IS is a concentrated reflection of modern management modernization and the modernization is a comprehensive concept that is the science and the technology management system in people's ideology and behavior habits of modern fusion (Zhu & Gao, 2015). Powerful administration data framework is the cutting edge of broad thoughts and techniques, current association framework and propelled PC innovation and the natural solidarity of the advanced individuals, and that will be the most recent specialized and the administration aftereffects of the dynamic and the age of the idea of dynamic.

Data frameworks had changed and improved business forms and the exchange of data. They have made business increasingly effective by encouraging a ceaseless access of data. Data frameworks empower sharing of data and offer access to new types of working, for example, home working, and new types of associations. Data frameworks reshape the authoritative procedure and not the other way around. Data efficiencies identify with time and cost investment funds produced using data frameworks. Organizations are investing huge sums of money in IS projects expecting to get positive benefits and business turn around. However, most organizations are failing to get a favorable return on investment and to derive maximum business value from IS investments (Mondo & Musungwini, 2019). Many business leaders and strategy scholars agree that the ability to effectively manage information and knowledge within an organization has become very important and provides a basis of a competitive advantage. The strategic management discipline has long sought to elicit the sources of sustainable competitive advantage and there is a significant body of research focusing on this objective and so IS management field has exerted great efforts in the same direction, there are recent researches arguing that information technology (IT) alone is unlikely to be a source of sustainable competitive advantage as it is easily to be replicated by competitors. Hence, strategic IS capability pioneers the beginning of a new era of IS management, in which organizations can continuously derive and leverage value through information (IS) that is implicitly embedded within the fabric of the organization.

Vital data (IS) capacity is a perplexing gathering of IT-related assets, information and abilities rehearsed through hierarchical procedures and engaging the association to use IS/IT resources for wanted destinations. To put it plainly, the IS ability is installed inside the texture of the association. Data has risen as a specialist of joining and the empowering influence of new intensity for the present association's in such powerful worldwide commercial centers. Business drifts in the associations of the 21st century have risen around provider and client connections, worldwide correspondences, learning the executives, focused insight, social development, and systems administration dependent on the Data Framework (IS). It has been understood that the absence of key arrangement between Data Framework (IS) and authoritative techniques has been oftentimes announced as a significant issue in overviews of business administrators and IT chiefs. Particularly, the hole among IT and business methodologies has been every now and again announced in creating nations. Hence, for the purpose of this study to enhance the strategic role of IS in the effectiveness and efficiency of the strategic design, the researcher developed a model proposing a positive relationship between three constructs: strategic IS capability as an independent variable, strategic design as a mediating variable, and organization's competitiveness as a dependent variable (Ibrahim & Abou Naem, 2019).

Delone and McLean (2016) wrote a monograph which suggested that researchers and practitioners face a daunting challenge when assessing the "success" of information systems. The aim of this monograph was to deepen the understanding of the researchers and practitioners of the multifaceted nature of IS success measurement which is driven by the ever-changing role and use of information technology. Delone and McLean (2016) in their monograph covered the history of information success measurement along with recent trends and future expectations for information system success measurement. They additionally distinguished the basic achievement factors that upgrade data framework achievement and gave an estimation and assessment direct for professionals. The result of this exhaustive investigation of data frameworks achievement estimation was intended to further improve the estimation practice among analysts and managers.

According to Guha and Kumar (2017), in the age of big data, consumers leave an easily traceable digital footprint whenever they visit websites online. This digital age has organizations capturing the digital footprints of their customers to understand and predict consumer behavior.

Rezvani, Dong, and Khosravi (2017) proposed that organizations face substantial challenges in capturing value from their investments in strategic information systems. In like manner, supervisors in any association are a compelling wellspring of inspiration to shape the post-appropriation demeanors and practices of clients and the achievement of their separate data frameworks. This data framework writing was centered fundamentally around the job of senior administration and notional clarifications of the job of managers in advancing proceeded with utilization of data frameworks. Taking a gander at transformational authority hypothesis and the data framework duration (ISC) model, this examination conjectures a theoretical model which separates the impact components by means of which various kinds of administration practices impact the accomplishment of data frameworks. The information that was gathered approved this speculation. The specialists additionally discovered that transformational authority practices of directors' impact the clients' valuations of fulfillment and evident handiness. This investigation takes into account different enquiries about to progress on the job of administration practices of managers considering the estimation of data frameworks. The examination likewise recommends compelling methodologies for advancing proceeds with use of mission basic frameworks, for example, venture frameworks and including an incentive from firms' IT speculations.

While the use and cost of the board data framework (MIS) have ended up being incredibly recognizable, little thought has been paid to assessing and conferring system sufficiency. Appraisal of system sufficiency is inconvenient as a result of its multi-dimensionality, its quantitative and abstract points, and the various, and consistently conflicting, evaluator viewpoints. This article gives a blueprint of what structure suitability means and how it should be evaluated. It is the first of two articles to appear in consecutive issues of the MIS Quarterly. Starting with the significance of structure ampleness, this article examines evaluation of system reasonability to the extent a hypothetical movement of system targets. The hierarchy is used to discuss problems in, and recommendations for, evaluating system effectiveness, and to compare MIS evaluation approaches (Hamilton & Chervany, 1981).

The second article characterizes and compares the evaluator viewpoints on system effectiveness for decision makers in several functional groups involved in MIS implementations—user, MIS, internal audit and management. Effective management IS are the modern management ideas and methods, modern organization systems and advanced computer technology and the organic unity of the modern people, and that will be the latest technical and the management results of the dynamic and the generation of the concept of dynamic.

Ten years prior, it was exhibited as the Delone and McLean data frameworks (IS) achievement model as a structure and model for estimating the complex dependent variable in IS exploration. Numerous exchanges were made on the significant IS achievement investigating commitments of the most recent decade, concentrating particularly on research endeavors that apply, approve, challenge, and propose upgrades to our unique model. In view of our assessment of those commitments, we propose minor refinements to the model and propose a refreshed Delone and McLean IS achievement model. Talk will be on utility of the refreshed model for estimating web based business framework achievement. Finally, we make a series of recommendations regarding the current and future measurement of IS success (DeLone & McLean, 2003).

The measurement of data frameworks (IS) achievement or viability is basic to our comprehension of the worth and adequacy of the Information system the executives activities and IS speculations. From that point forward, about 300 articles in refereed diaries have alluded to, and utilized, this IS achievement model. The wide ubiquity of the model is solid proof of the requirement for a thorough system so as to incorporate IS look into discoveries. The D&M IS achievement model, however, distributed in 1992, depended on hypothetical and observational IS research directed by various specialists during the 1970s and 1980s. The jobs of IS have changed and advanced during the most recent decade. Additionally, scholastic investigation into the estimation of data framework adequacy has advanced over a similar period.

RESEARCH QUESTIONS

1. What are the operations capability features?
2. What are the operations capabilities?
3. How has the features and operations capabilities changed over the years?

METHODOLOGY

The methodology that was applied by this study was the Delone and McLean IS success model. We used this model to acquire information and determine conclusions about the effectiveness and efficiency of the information systems, termed as STRIPES by the Oil company.

- *System quality:* We investigate the different inputs and characters of the information system. In this research we look in the ease of use, its flexibility, the system features, and response time.
- *Information quality:* We look at the characteristics of the system's output. This research paper further sees the output of information on the operational side of things with its correctness, timeliness of information collected, and its usefulness generated by the oil company system in use.
- *Service quality:* We look in the back up team with its quality in support of the information system. Here we examine the technical team and its responsiveness, the system inbuilt, and other reliability of the system.
- *Intention to Use or Use:* This feature was around how the information system is used. In order to get a better picture of how this is determined, we looked at the actual usage of the information system and to some extent the frequency of use. The aim to utilize or utilize is an elective measure to use for some other setting, contingent upon the idea of the data framework. Since most associations have a data framework set up which should be utilized for business activities, this exploration evaluated the helpfulness recognition.
- *User satisfaction:* For any data framework to be fruitful, this is a significant element to be estimated, frequently estimated by generally client fulfillment. This is evaluated in this examination by catching by and large client fulfillment with the oil business' data framework.

- *Organizational Benefits:* This is another feature that is equally important for a successful information system. Net advantages of the data framework comprise the degree to which a data framework adds to the accomplishment of the organization.

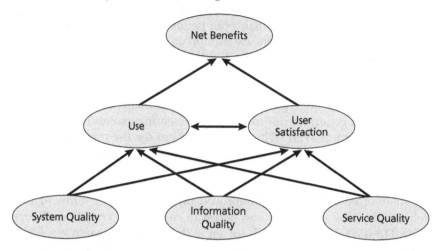

Figure 17.1

- Positivity affects system quality to use.
- Positivity affects system quality to user satisfaction.
- Positivity affects information quality to use.
- Positivity affects information quality to user satisfaction.
- Positivity affects service quality to use.
- Positivity affects service quality to user satisfaction.
- Positivity affects user satisfaction.
- Positivity affects perceived net benefit.
- Positivity affects user satisfaction to perceived net benefit.

As highlighted in our abstract we had decided to look at four features which were information quality, service quality, user satisfaction, and organizational impact while using the Delone and McLean information system success model. We found that all six features are interrelated and work simultaneously as shown in Figure 17.1.

RESULTS

From our three research questions, we developed a questionnaire to provide us an insight to how the IS is used within this organization. A structured questionnaire was sent out to 50 operators within the organization from five different markets, that is Fiji, Australia, New Zealand, Thailand, Papua New Guinea, and New Caledonia which consisted of order fulfillment personnel and delivery analysts to terminal dispatchers and their respective supervisors. Of these, we received responses from 26 personnel. Of the 26 we had interviewed five personnel from the Fiji market.

An analysis of our questionnaire can be found in Table 17.1 and represented in Figure 17.2 shows the assumption on the acceptance of the information system used by the operators of the organization in all areas from quality of service, customer deliveries, flexibility of the system use, and the service for order fulfillment is effective and efficient.

On information quality, the operators agreed that the information system, STRIPES, generated information in a timely manner and that data was correct (See Figure 17.3). Whereas 80% did not see the usefulness of the data generated as they were using STRIPES in its operational sense rather than in an analytical sense.

With regards to net benefits, the operators understood that using the information systems STRIPES improved their workflow in terms of fuel delivery, this also allowed for easy access to customer information (Figure 17.4). However, 79% noted did not agree that STRIPES system was being fully utilized with regards to communication amongst workers as listing of a new customer details are communicated via email then the system database is populated.

Figure 17.5 shows that while STRIPES is reliable when providing information when needed at 100%, 75% confirmed that the weekend backup team does not always respond on time within the shortest time possible. During the weekends, the backup team looks after other regions such as

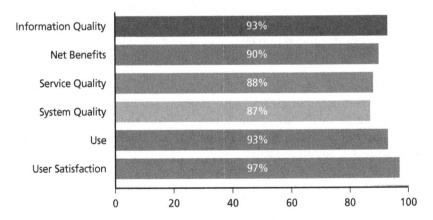

Figure 17.2 Features of ratings.

TABLE 17.1			
Features	**Total**	**%**	**Average**
Information Quality	**451**	**347**	**93%**
I trust the information output of STRIPES	122	94%	
STRIPES generates information in a timely manner	130	100%	
The data generated by STRIPES is useful	104	80%	
The data generated by STRIPES is correct	130	100%	
Net Benefits	**597**	**459**	**90%**
STRIPES facilitates easy access to customer information	130	100%	
STRIPES use will cause improved decision making	127	98%	
STRIPES will enhance communications among workers	103	79%	
STRIPES will help overcome the limitations of paper-based system	107	82%	
Using STRIPES will cause an improvement in fuel delivery	130	100%	
Service Quality	**459**	**353**	**88%**
STRIPES can be relied on to provide information as when needed	130	100%	
The output of STRIPES is complete for work processes	116	89%	
The overall design in place is adequate to support STRIPES	115	88%	
There is adequate technical support from backup team	98	75%	
System Quality	**451**	**347**	**87%**
I find it easy to get STRIPES to do what I want	104	80%	
I find STRIPES easy to use	130	100%	
Learning to use STRIPES was easy for me	87	67%	
STRIPES is flexible to interact with	130	100%	
Use	**484**	**372**	**93%**
I find STRIPES useful in my job	116	89%	
Using STRIPES enables me to complete tasks more quickly	120	92%	
Using STRIPES has improved my job performance	125	96%	
Using STRIPES has made my job easier	123	95%	
User Satisfaction	**378**	**291**	**97%**
I am generally satisfied using STRIPES	123	95%	
I am satisfied with the functions of STRIPES	130	100%	
STRIPES has eased work processes	125	96%	
Grand Total	**2,820**	**2,169**	**91%**

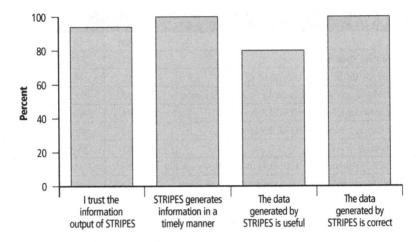

Figure 17.3 Information quality ratings.

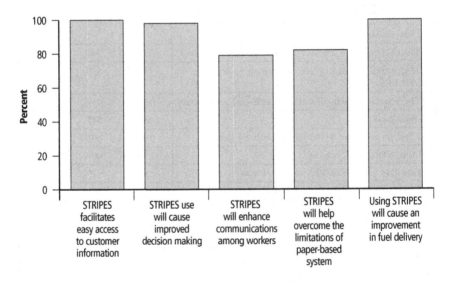

Figure 17.4 Net benefits ratings.

New Zealand, Australia, PNG, and Fiji. In most cases the Fiji team is having to wait for their responses as they tend to look into their regions first.

For system quality 100% agreed that the STRIPES system is user friendly, however 67% disagreed as they were new to using the STRIPES system (see Figure 17.6).

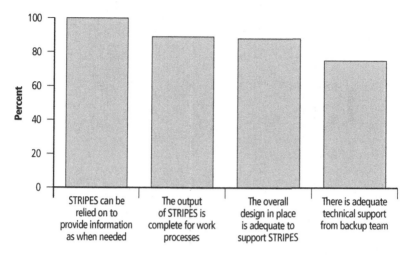

Figure 17.5 Service quality ratings.

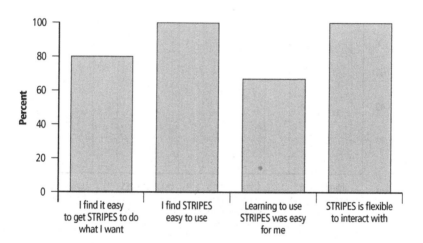

Figure 17.6 System quality ratings.

User satisfaction, overall 97% agreed that the STRIPES system eased the work processes, they were satisfied with its functions and in general they were satisfied (see Figure 17.7).

Use feature, overall 93% agreed that the STRIPES system assisted in their daily jobs in completing tasks more quickly, this also improved their job performances and that STRIPES was very useful in their work line (see Figure 17.8).

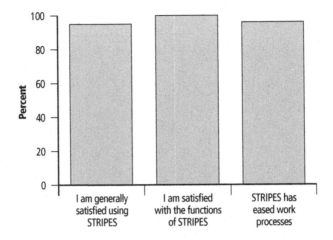

Figure 17.7   User satisfaction ratings.

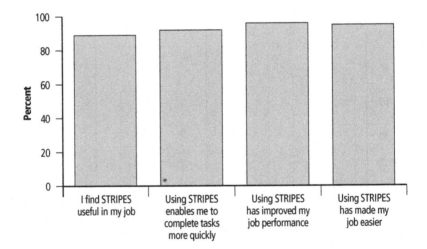

Figure 17.8   Use ratings.

DISCUSSION

Our research confirms that the Delone and McLean IS success model in the oil industry is valid. Our findings give credibility to the model's constructs and provide an interrelationship within the six features discussed as part of the model. Since this is the case, the model shows that the information systems used by this oil industry is an acceptable one resulting in a fit for use and we can validate its effectiveness and efficiency to measure the success of the information system.

As shown in Figure 17.1, we see that there is a connection between each of the features highlighted as part of the Delone and McLean information system success model. We identified that there is a direct connection between the system quality, information quality, and service quality with its use. There is also a relationship between these features with the user satisfaction feature.

System quality has a positive effect on use. Similarly, information quality and service quality both have positive impacts on the use. These features in turn have a similar positive impact on user satisfaction. Having said this, the use of the information system and the user satisfaction go hand in hand as they are interconnected with each other. The use and user satisfaction showed up as high and acceptable under the data analysis especially because of the high degree to which the information systems functionalities have been integrated with each other. The high level of use and user satisfaction results in a positive effect in net benefits.

We also found that the efficiency of the information system decreased the cycle of time for processing customer information which led to better decision making by management. This enabled the management team to provide a better customer service with the resources that were available with minimum disruption to the overall performance of the organization.

As discussed in the findings, shipment number has to be generated to enable a delivery, the weekend backup support team is not always reliable, and the customer set-up initiation is done via emails prior to being entered into the system (i.e., system not being fully utilized). While the system is acceptable and user friendly, there are areas that we feel needs to be improved as mentioned above.

With this research, it does contain some limitations. The survey conducted included mainly operators and we only received 52% of the questionnaires that we sent out. We also did not take into consideration the other users of this information system hence our data is purely based on one STRIPE user and that being this organization.

CONCLUSION

In conclusion, this chapter has validated the Delone and McLean information system success model in the framework of an oil industry. In the data analysis, we find that STRIPES is acceptable by its users and has a number of advantages within its functionality which makes it an efficient system. The system quality, information quality, and service quality have a positive effect on user satisfaction and use. Use and user satisfaction in turn have a positive influence on organizational benefits.

RECOMMENDATIONS

For further research, data collection has to be from multiple users of STRIPES to enable a better understanding of how the information system could be utilized. Recommended organizations should identify the competitive advantage and strategic value that they can gain through an information system, such as eliminating losses through effective use of systems and tools by allowing the user to effectively use the system.

REFERENCES

Aboaoga, M., Aziz, M. J. A., & Mohamed, I. (2018). Information system success framework based on interpersonal conflict factors. *International Journal of Electrical and Computer Engineering, 8*(5), 3740–3746.

Chuang, H., & Lin, H. (2017). Performance implications of information-value offering in e-service systems: Examining the resources-based perspective and innovation strategy. *Journal of Strategic Information Systems, 26*(1), 22–38.

Cram, W. A., Brohman, K., & Gallupe, B. R. (2016). Information systems control: A review and framework for emerging information systems processes. *Journal of the Association for Information Systems, 17*(4), 216–266.

Cram, W. A., Proudfoot, J. G., & D'Arcy, J. (2017). Organizational information security policies: A review and research framework. *European Journal of Information Systems, 26*(6), 605–641. doi:http://dx.doi.org/10.1057/s41303-017-0059-9

Cram, W. A., & Wiener, M. (2018). *Perceptions of control legitimacy in information systems development.* Information Technology & People.

Delone, W. H., & McLean, E. R. (2003). The DeLone and McLean model of information systems success: a ten-year update. *Journal of Management Information Systems, 19*(4), 9–30.

Delone, W., & McLean, E. (2016). information systems success measurement. *Foundations and Trends in Information Systems, 2*(1), 1–116. http://dx.doi.org/10.1561/2900000005

Ghafir, I., Saleem, J., Hammoudeh, M., Faour, H., Prenosil, V., Jaf, S.,..., Baker, T. (2018). Security threats to critical infrastructure: the human factor. *The Journal of Supercomputing, 74*(10), 4986–5002.

Guha, S., & Kumar, S. (2017). Emergence of big data research in operations management, information systems, and healthcare: Past contributions and future roadmaps. *Production and Operations Management, 27*(9), 1724–1735.

Hamilton, S., & Chervany, N. L. (1981). Evaluating information system effectiveness-Part I: Comparing evaluation approaches. *MIS Quarterly, 5*(3), 55–69.

Han, Y., & Sun, R. (2016). Research on public management efficiency improvement method based on parallel database-oriented optimization management information system. *Revista Ibérica De Sistemas e Tecnologias De Informação, E*(5), 425–436.

Ibrahim, A. A. A. E., & Abou Naem, A. E. H. M. (2019). The impact of strategic information system and strategic design on organization's competitiveness: a field study. *Academy of Strategic Management Journal, 18*(1), 1–12.

Medaković, V., & Marić, B. (2018). A model of management information system for technical system maintenance. *Acta Technica Corviniensis-Bulletin of Engineering, 11*(3), 85–90.

Mondo, L., & Musungwini, S. (2019). Developing a change management model for managing information systems initiated organisational change: a case of the banking sector in Zimbabwe. *Journal of Systems Integration, 10*(1), 49–61.

Oksanen, J., Kuusisto, O., Toivanen, M. B. L., Mäntylä, M., Naumanen, M., Rilla, N.,..., Valkokari, K. (2018). *In search of Finnish creative economy ecosystems and their development needs: study based on international benchmarking.*

Panorama Consulting Solutions. (2014). *ERP report: A Panorama Consulting Solutions research report.* Author.

Pereira, E. T., & Fernandes, A. J. (2018, July). *Are the most innovative SMEs the most competitive ones?* Paper presentation at the Theory and Applications in the Knowledge Economy Conference, Poznan.

Phusavat, K., & Kanchana, R. (2007). *Competitive priorities of manufacturing firms in Thailand.* Industrial Management & Data Systems.

Rezvani, A., Dong, L., & Khosravi, P. (2017). Promoting the continuing usage of strategic information systems: The role of supervisory leadership in the successful implementation of enterprise systems. *SSIS. International Journal of Information Management, 37*(5), 417–430.

Sadeghi, S., Rasouli, N., & Jandaghi, G. (2016). Identifying and prioritizing contributing factors in supply chain competitiveness by using PLS-BWM techniques (case study: Payam shoes company). *World Scientific News, 49*(2), 117–143.

Sansone, C., Hilletofth, P., & Eriksson, D. (2017). Critical operations capabilities for competitive manufacturing: A systematic review. *Industrial Management & Data Systems, 117*(5), 801–837. http://dx.doi.org/10.1108/IMDS-02-2016-0066

Swamidass, P. M., & Newell, W. T. (1987). Manufacturing strategy, environmental uncertainty and performance: a path analytic model. *Management Science, 33*(4), 509–524.

Willison, R., & Warkentin, M. (2013). Beyond deterrence: An expanded view of employee computer abuse. *MIS Quarterly,* 1–20.

Yang, Z., Shi, Y., & Yan, H. (2016). Scale, congestion, efficiency and effectiveness in e-commerce firms. *Electronic Commerce Research and Applications, 20,* 171–182.

Zhu, C., & Gao, D. (2015). Improved multi-kernel classification machine with Nyström approximation technique. *Pattern Recognition, 48*(4), 1490–1509.

CHAPTER 18

ANALYZING THE EFFECTIVENESS OF CRM IN A BANK

Sam Goundar
The University of the South Pacific

Aishal Singh
The University of the South Pacific

Charles Robinson
The University of the South Pacific

Esther Singh
The University of the South Pacific

Shelyn Dass
The University of the South Pacific

Enterprise Systems and Technological Convergence, pages 325–347
Copyright © 2021 by Information Age Publishing
All rights of reproduction in any form reserved.

ABSTRACT

The current study aims to find out the effectiveness of customer relationship management (CRM) in banking. It intends to determine the efficiency of how CRM works from a staff and customer perspective. This research is important since CRM has become a leading goal of marketing of every organization. Its outcomes will allow comprehensive understanding of how effective CRM is in this part of the globe. Balanced Score Card research model was utilized. All the statistical and theoretical data was analyzed through strategy maps and action plans. It was focusing on the four perspectives of financial, customer, internal, and knowledge growth. Once the data is collected through questionnaires and interviews, focus was made based on sub questions reflecting the four perspectives. This study will help test the efficiency and effectiveness of CRM systems used in banks. Thus allowing room for improvements and further sustainability. The study will provide comprehensive knowledge on how CRM could be best used for productivity and efficient running of banks.

According to the financial institution whose key role is to provide its client with banking and financial services, it is essential that the customer is given the power and option to choose the preferred service. Client's loyalty is not generally based on a particular brand but rather linked to personal loans, commercial loans, or other kinds of legitimate or contracted understanding. Many of the customers commonly prefer to be connected and maintain a relationship with a particular financial services provider. It is common for many customers to maintain financial services relationships with various other banks and financial service providing companies. Similarly, to business organizations, banks must take into account plans and practices which would provide enhancement initiatives enabling to promote and achieve customer retention and at the same time attract new potential customers to their brand. However, to achieve this, banks need to identify their marketing area, focus on resource development, and convert these resources to effective and efficient service and make it readily available to the customer. Over the changing time people have become well versed, stringent, demanding, and knowledgeable on how to carry out tasks and activities which were mostly handled only by banks thus this has enhanced them to choose between different institutions. With progressive nature of electronic communication technologies, banks are better enabled and more capable to reach out to their clients and potential customers, resolve their issues and concerns, create interest to purchase products and services offered by the bank, awakening a feeling of loyalty, and have continuous business interactions with their customers (Sharifi, Rezghi, & Nasiri, 2014).

Customer relationship management (CRM) is a strategized execution by financial organizations to strengthen the value of their brand and help in the identification and understanding of the customer's needs to provide and create accurate and specific information which contributes towards adding value to the banks' customers. CRM systems provide essential elements which can help to break down and achieve to deliver the clients with the best required services based on the client's preferences. This allows banks to monitor and implement strong relationships and a bond with beneficial customers and be able to point out products and services most applicable to the customers' needs (New Signature, 2014). In the survey done by Rostami, Valmohammadi, and Yousefpoor (2014), the findings acknowledge that the four aspects of CRM system consisting of service quality, service components, service accessibility, and management of customer grievances helps organizations achieve greater customer satisfaction.

This research will highlight customers' expectations towards the banks' services and products in the sense of competitiveness banking services and the common shortfalls faced by both the clients and the bank itself in terms of CRM. These constantly developing economic factors causes competition and taking care of the competition does not leave much room to target new clients. This research will also highlight the effectiveness of the current CRM in place in this ever changing digital era to assist banks with customer retention and achieving customer satisfaction. According to Al-Safi, Al-Safadi, and Al-Mudimigh (2012) the balance scorecard (BSC) is an effective measurement taken into consideration to measure the effectiveness of the performance of newly implemented business practices. This provides managers with an insight of how beneficial or how unproductive the implementation of new business practices have been from the study of the four perspectives: financial, customers, internal business processes, and innovation and learning. Feedback from both customers and banks was analyzed and the effectiveness of the current CRM in place was utilized and recommendations for further improvements were made.

LITERATURE REVIEW

CRM, is the practice of organizing comprehensive data about each customer and prudently managing all customer dealings in order to exploit customer loyalty (Kotler & Keller, 2006) Also, CRM emphasizes on handling liaison between a business and its existing and potential customer base. Customer knowledge is required to build a good relationship with customers. It is used in obtaining and constantly appraising knowledge on customer essentials, incentives, and behavior over the period of the relationship (Gebert, Geib, Kolbe, & Riempp, 2002). CRM solutions can deliver the groundwork for sustainable progress and allow organizations to endure and flourish in these unreliable times (Ruchi, 2014). According to Hendriyani and Auliana (2018), in the age of digitalization, technology is steering businesses to transform their platform procedures into digital progression for accomplishing sustainable collaborative objectives. Prevailing customer relationships propagate in prominence as organizations pursue a cost-effective way to cultivate corporate extension. Adding on, Herawaty, Tresna, and Liany said that CRM is an essential approach in business that assimilates internal procedures and roles with all peripheral networks to generate and appreciate worth for target consumers profitably. It is important through CRM that cooperation with individual customers is anticipated to be able to produce a condition that does not harm any group or a win-win solution (Ruchi, 2014). The ordinary businesses lose more than 20% of their customers yearly merely by being inadequate in attending to customer relationships. In some businesses this seepage is as great as 80%. The cost, in both circumstances, is astounding, but few industries actually comprehend the consequences (Tawinunt, Phimonsathien, & Wanno Fongsuwan, 2015). Customer satisfaction is vital towards CRM. Tseng (2016) identified that companies must continually exceed customer expectations in order to deliver adequate services and improve service excellence. Firms ought to expand their understanding concerning the customer and take hold of every prospect of networking with the customers.

Generally portraying, Hendriyani and Auliana (2018) stated that "a firm should make a strategy for gratification and importance for customers" (p. 2). Numerous welfares could be gained when executing CRM such as directing to grow client satisfaction, customer loyalty, and organization benefit (Al-Arafati, Kadir, & Al-Haderi, 2019). Also, excellent customer service is vital to cultivating associations with customers, and an improved relationship with one's customers can eventually lead to superior customer retention, customer loyalty, and more notably, lucrativeness (Tawinunt, Phimonsathien, & Wanno Fongsuwan, 2015). CRM is an essential scheme in businesses that assimilates internal procedures and roles with all peripheral links to generate and understand value for target consumers advantage. With CRM, relationships with individual customers are anticipated to be able to form a condition that does not harm any group or a win-win resolution. A satisfied customer is more likely to return than an unsatisfied customer. It helps to maintain existing customers and attract new ones (Maggon & Chaudhry, 2018). They also stated that the organization should be sensitive and receptive to changing needs of the customer. Consumer loyalty is evident when meaningful relationships between consumers and companies will exist.

The quality of customer relationships has a positive impact on bank performance (Najafi, Rezaei, & Rodi, 2017). It is essential that the surveyed banks improve service superiority, features, and admission level beforehand to encounter and be compelled to handle customer grievances (Rostami, Valmohammadi, & Yousefpoor, 2014). CRM propagated from demand on various processes to customer service.

Adding on, it is built on sales communications and rigorous data dispensation. With additional influence of advertising and customer coordination values, CRM progresses to embracing increased problem solving and personalized services. Nevertheless, the crucial customer relationship administration standard is to construct customer loyalty and lifetime support (Liew, C-B.A, 2008). According to Tawinunt, Phimonsathien, and Wanno Fongsuwan (2015), there must be disposition to aid customers and offer speedy service; the familiarity and politeness of staffs and their skill to motivate trust and assurance as well as their capability, courteousness, reliability, and safekeeping; and caring and personalized focus that the firm provides to its customers including access, communication, and listening to the customer. The output quality is the significant determining factor of customer satisfaction of application of CRM system, and it controls the relationship between the independent variable which is top management support and the dependent variable which is customer satisfaction of application of CRM structure (Al-Arafati, Kadir, & Al-Haderi, 2019). Tawinunt, Phimonsathien, and Wanno Fongsuwan (2015), have stated that components such as education and training play important roles as well. Performance assessment helps in compelling supportive performance in affiliation authority or in familiarizing relationship marketing matters and program organizations. Deprived of suitable performance assessment to measure CRM acts, it could be problematic to make choices about care, modification, or dissolution of CRM plans (Hasanian, Chong, & Gan, 2019).

CRM advertising and promotional tactics which are direct mail, social communication, special treatment, and physical rewards, play significant roles in constructing customer relationships (Lam, Cheung, & Lau, 2013). Customer worth is intrinsic in (or linked to) the usage of certain products or services, and customer value is observed by customers, instead of being accurately determined by sellers or other investors. Furthermore, these sensitive processes characteristically include a trade-off amongst what customers receive such as quality, benefits, and services; and what they sacrifice, such as value, opportunity cost, and up-keeping and learning cost (Wang, Lo, Chi, & Yang, 2019). Integrate diverse new knowledge from internal and external environments in order to develop new products and services for customers. CRM process includes four parts: knowledge discovery, market planning, customer interaction, and analysis and refinement (Tseng, 2016). Knowledge for customers, knowledge about customers, and knowledge from customers should be identified to CRM strategies. CRM requires strong integration of business processes which involve customers (Gebert et al., 2002). Delivering superior customer value is now recognized as one of the most important factors for the success of any firm now and in the future because it has a significant impact on the behavioral intentions of customers and because it has an important role in providing managers with insights into how to achieve superior CRM performance (Wang, Lo, Chi, & Yang, 2019). In the survey done by Rostami, Valmohammadi, and Yousefpoor (2014), results show that the four factors of CRM system, that is, service quality, service characteristics, level of service access, and handling complaints have a positive influence on customer satisfaction. Performance evaluation assists in relationship authority or in adapting relationship marketing objects and program structures. Without relevant performance evaluation to assess CRM actions, decision-making about maintenance will continue to be difficult to achieve, altering or terminating CRM plans (Hasanian, Chong, & Gan, 2015). Quality services based on customers had a positive impact on the quality of customer relationship (Najafi et al., 2017).

Digitalization causes companies to alter their platform to be digital so customers would have 24-hour access to companies via online service (Hendriyani & Auliana, 2018). Technology as a tool which is used in the form of CRM plays a key role in the industry and is something which increases in importance each year. Service quality acts as a criteria and goal to help with enterprises establish their baselines to acquire and then retain their customers (Tawinunt, Phimonsthien, & Fonsuwan, 2015). According to Henning Gebert (2005) operational, analytical, and collaborative CRM practices should be implemented. CRM requires activities to design interfaces that allow customers at customer interaction points for example web-self-service. IT investment pre-arrangements in social CRM context: For instance, regarding the expenses information is needed for IT investment decision in terms of IT expenses, that is, all IT related factors such as compatibility of a social CRM—module to current technology (infrastructure, software, APIs) and all expenses which come up with IT associated project implementations (Pflegger, 2015). E-marketing takes advantage of the electronic medium to perform marketing activities with the purpose of finding, attracting, winning, and retaining customers (Samanta, 2009). Yao (2011) has discovered that IT investment has a positive moderation effect on the CRM contentedness—customer achievement link. Technology aspects have a crucial part to play in CRM. This appears to exist because a technology can aid accelerate and advance human components and processes in CRM activeness (Herawaty, Tresna, & Liany, 2019). According to Chen and Ching (2004) electronic CRM assimilates sales, marketing, and service strategies which constitutes increasing value proposition for customers. Enabling organizations to recreate a conservative one-to-one relationship with customers along mass-market productiveness from merchandising to millions of customers. The research findings also indicated that with the implementation of e-CRM marketing efforts will profound customer loyalty. The advantage is that an electronic CRM has a rewarding outcome (quality of service, quality relationships with customers), and the bank (Najafi, Rezaei, & Rodi, 2017).

In conclusion, the special features of a service cause that service to be different in comparison to other competitors in the market which also increases the chances of more customers to be interested towards the bank and will eventually create their loyalty towards the organization. Creativity and innovation must be applied to create a specific characteristic for bank services and achieve those characteristics before others (Rostami, Valmohammadi, & Yousefpoor, 2014). The CRM's success is chiefly urged on by the performance and user acknowledgement of the technology firms initiate in an attempt to develop client knowledge and manage indulgence (Tawinunt, Phimonsthien, & Fonsuwan, 2015). According to Rostami, Valmohammadi, and Yousefpoor (2014) business organizations initial focus must be on service quality before availing these services to consumers in a way that could be easily obtainable and user friendly to customers and convincing for customers to use bank the services provided again in future. Another way of viewing customers is that customers are agents or the reason for changes which need to be incorporated into the organizations culture.

OBJECTIVE

The definitive goal of this research is to develop an effective CRM system in Australia and New Zealand Banking group (ANZ) in Fiji, which could otherwise be used holistically in other organizations. CRM is a method to manage a company's collaboration with current and prospective customers. The objective of the existing study is to provide an in depth review of literatures and business practices in relation to CRM and provide a theoretical structure for CRM. Predominantly, the study has the following sub objectives:

1. To examine current ANZ practices and researches in regards to CRM.
2. To investigate issues in relation to CRM in ANZ bank, Fiji.
3. To outline solutions and future sustainable prospects related to CRM in ANZ bank, Fiji.

The outcome of this study was valuable to the business organizations as well as related software providers in evolving better practices and tools for CRM.

METHODOLOGY

The framework which was used in this research was Balance Scorecard (BSC; see Figure 18.1). It manages and plans strategically in aligning business activities in relation to strategies and vision of the company, helps in

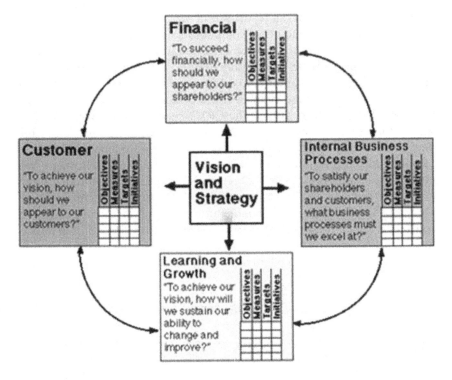

Figure 18.1   The Balanced Scorecard Framework.

communicating internally and externally, and helps in monitoring the company's performance against organizational strategic objectives. This framework was established by Dr. David Norton and Dr. Robert Kaplan in the 1990s. It is a collection of measures taken which enables managers to attain the organization's performance viewed in a balanced perspective. BSC contains financial measures that determine the outcomes of approaches which are taken. Also, it complements the measures taken in regard to finance with the operating measures for customer satisfaction, processes done internally, and organization's learning and growth actions. These strategic measures are used to drive future financial performance in the future. It enables executives to view the business from four separate perspectives:

1. financial,
2. customers,
3. learning and growth, and
4. internal business processes.

There are four perspectives which consider four parameters. These are goals, measures, targets, and initiatives. Goals emphasize what achievements are needed in order to be successful in terms of CRM, measures are the parameters used to know if it is a success, targets are the quantitative value used to determine the effectiveness of the measures taken, and initiatives are the strategies adopted to meet our goals.

Evaluation methods used were; entering data in excel format as illustrated in Figure 18.2. The green color indicates on target, red indicates needs help, orange indicates caution, and white indicates no data. A number of CRM strategies were identified and evaluated. Primary and secondary data was used to achieve objectives of this research. Secondary data was collected through accessing journals, books, and articles. Primary data collected was collected through interviews with staff and questionnaires using 50 customers. Interviews provided in-depth information about the relationship between variables in the research. Questionnaires provided customers' views and this assisted in analyzing the attitude and behavior towards CRM. Consent was obtained from the manager and their identity and data collected was kept confidential.

Research was commenced upon the lecturer's approval. In order to clearly articulate our strategy our research was further broken down into the following phases:

Phase 1—Secondary Research
Phase 2—Primary Research (using questionnaire surveys and interviews)
Phase 3—Analysis and Research Write Up
Phase 4—Presentation

RESULTS AND FINDINGS

Objectives

1. *Finance:* To ensure the bank has more customer retention and attraction is achieved with less expenditure and investments in this area.
2. *Customer:* Gaining customer loyalty and attracting new customers through the means of excellent and reliable customer services provided by the bank. also to ensure product quality, customer experience, price, and time are continuously improved for better customer service experience.
3. *Internal business processes:* To ensure the company policies are followed accurately and measures are taken to meet customer relationship management.
4. *Learning and growth:* Learn and improve in order to achieve customer relationship effectiveness.

Balanced Scorecard Template

Perspective	Objective	Measure	Q1 Actual/Status	Q2 Actual/Status	Q3 Actual/Status	Q4 Actual/Status	Year-To-Date Total Status Target	Initiatives
Financial	Objective 1	Measure 1	$0.00	$0.00	$0.00	$0.00	$0.00 $0.00	
	Objective 2	Measure 2	$0.00	$0.00	$0.00	$0.00	$0.00 $0.00	
	Objective 3	Measure 3	0.00	0.00	0.00	0.00	0.00 0.00	
		Measure 4	0.00	0.00	0.00	0.00	0.00 0.00	
		Measure 5	####	####	####	####	#### ####	
		Measure 6	####	0.00	####	####	#### ####	
Customer	Objective 4	Measure 7	$0.00	$0.00	$0.00	$0.00	$0.00 $0.00	
	Objective 5	Measure 8	$0.00	$0.00	$0.00	$0.00	$0.00 $0.00	
		Measure 9	0.00	0.00	0.00	0.00	0.00 0.00	
		Measure 10	0.00	0.00	0.00	0.00	0.00 0.00	
Internal Business Processes	Objective 6	Measure 11	$0.00	$0.00	$0.00	$0.00	$0.00 $0.00	Initiative 1
	Objective 7	Measure 12	$0.00	$0.00	$0.00	$0.00	$0.00 $0.00	
		Measure 13	0.00	0.00	0.00	0.00	0.00 0.00	
		Measure 14	0.00	0.00	0.00	0.00	0.00 0.00	
	Objective 8	Measure 15	####	####	####	####	#### ####	Initiative 2
		Measure 16	0.00	0.00	0.00	0.00	0.00 0.00	Initiative 3
		Measure 17	####	####	####	0.00	#### ####	
		Measure 18	####	0.00	####	0.00	#### ####	Initiative 4
	Objective 9	Measure 19	####	####	####	####	#### ####	
		Measure 20	####	0.00	####	####	#### ####	
Learning & Growth	Objective 10	Measure 21	$0.00	$0.00	$0.00	$0.00	$0.00 $0.00	Initiative 5
	Objective 11	Measure 22	$0.00	$0.00	$0.00	$0.00	$0.00 $0.00	Initiative 6
	Objective 12	Measure 23	0.00	0.00	0.00	0.00	0.00 0.00	Initiative 7
		Measure 24	0.00	0.00	0.00	0.00	0.00 0.00	Initiative 8
		Measure 25	####	####	####	####	#### ####	

Figure 18.2 Balanced scorecard template.

MEASURES

1. Finance
   1.1 Allocating funds for training and development
   1.2 Customer information system
   1.3 Community projects
   1.4 Advertisements
   1.5 Corporate social events Customer and staff social relationship building
   1.6 Branded merchandise giveaways
   1.7 Consultations
2. Customer
   2.1 Branded merchandise giveaways
   2.2 User friendly apps
   2.3 24/7 customer service call center
   2.4 Over the counter customer services
   2.5 Customer security and privacy
   2.6 E-banking
3. Internal business processes
   3.1 Customer advocate
   3.2 Customer satisfaction survey
   3.3 Customer advocacy program
   3.4 Meetings with customers
4. Learning and growth
   4.1 Skill assessments
   4.2 Team training
   4.3 Strategy awareness program
   4.4 Leadership and motivation programs
   4.5 Organization culture development
   4.6 Improved information system

According to the balanced scorecard method (see Figure 18.3) it is found that referring to its financial perspective measures 1.1, 1.2, 1.3, 1.4, and 1.7 is "on target" except for measures 1.5 and 1.6 which is regarded as "caution" which means more focus allocation of finance needs to be made towards customer and staff relationship building and promotional materials.

Referring to the customer perspective as shown above, measures 2.2, 2.4, and 2.5 are on target. Measures 2.1 and 2.3 need improvements whereas measure 2.6 which is labeled "needs help" requires immediate attention.

Internal business processes have revealed measure 3.1, 3.2, and 3.3 are being carried out well. Measure 3.4 is regarded caution because meetings are targeted only to corporate customers only and private individuals are neglected.

Under learning and growth all five measures taken were on target.

Balanced Scorecard

On Target / Caution / Needs help

Perspective	Objective	Measure	Actual Status	Initiatives
Financial	Objective 1	Measure 1.1	81.00%	Strategic funding is alocated for training and development
		Measure 1.2	83.00%	implementation of continuous upgrade of IS
		Measure 1.3	82.60%	strategic funding is allocated for community projects
		Measure 1.4	88.70%	continuous media presence
		Measure 1.5	49.60%	limited customer and staff relationship building
		Measure 1.6	48.90%	to promote brand name at a low cost advertising expenditure
		Measure 1.7	90.00%	personalized solutions
Customer	Objective 2	Measure 2.1	52.90%	promote branding and achieving customer satisfaction
		Measure 2.2	81.30%	user friendly apps
		Measure 2.3	49.80%	24/7 customer service help centre
		Measure 2.4	86.30%	over the counter customer services
		Measure 2.5	89.00%	customer security and privacy
		Measure 2.6	20.89%	Pacific ANZ app for all smart devices limited to internet connectivity
Internal Business	Objective 3	Measure 3.1	89.89%	allocate role of a customer advocate
		Measure 3.2	90.10%	continuos customer survey
		Measure 3.3	89.70%	development of customer advocate
		Measure 3.4	52.30%	meetings to corporate customers only
Learning & Growth	Objective 4	Measure 4.1	89.33%	Regular skill upgrading
		Measure 4.2	94.21%	adequate / relevant CRM training
		Measure 4.3	88.96%	adoptation to business culture
		Measure 4.4	91.47%	awarding systems
		Measure 4.5	86.33%	continuos upgrade with time market demand

Figure 18.3 The Balanced Scorecard Measures.

DISCUSSION

Financial Aspects ANZ Considers to Maintain and Improve Customer Relation Management

Finance is a very critical aspect of any organization. We have tried to gather information in regards to how ANZ uses and organize the utilization of funds to provide them with exceptional service and competitive advantage in regards to their service and processes over their competitors towards their staff, clients, prospective clients, and stakeholders.

Training and Development (Measure 1.1)

ANZ provides training and development to their staff to attain skill in the areas of leadership, customer focus, digital marketing, innovation, process optimization, and technology advancement to help enhance them with strategic capabilities towards achieving their business targets.

Customer Information System (Measure 1.2)

ANZ Bank in Fiji allows consumers to self-service with the availability of 24-hour helpline. It provides its clients with an exceptional user friendly customer information system where they have access to the extent where the customers can view their bank statement and execute local and international transfer of funds. The customer information has been continuously improved and updated over the past years at ANZ. It has evolved from just being available to corporate business clients to providing the same services to person clients.

Community Projects (Measure 1.3)

ANZ bank is involved in various community projects to show their involvement and contribution towards developments for the communities of Fiji.

Advertisement (Measure 1.4)

The bank spends a substantial amount of money to advertise their products and services to existing clients and prospective clients. Some of the forms of advertisement by the bank are billboard advertisements, online advertisements, and media advertisements.

Customer and Staff Relation Building (Measure 1.5)

According to the findings of the questionnaire, it was found that ANZ organizes corporate events which targets building better relationships and understanding, internally, amongst its staff, and also greatly focuses on creating and building a good relationship between the bank and its corporate clients. Some of their incentives include team bonding exercises, hosting and sponsoring of corporate events and social events for staff.

Promotional Material (Measure 1.6)

ANZ invests in acquiring and providing its clients with promotional materials to promote and support the bank's products and services for advertisement purposes. Promotional materials also help greatly reaching out to potential clients.

Consultations (Measure 1.7)

ANZ also creates personalized customer experiences by providing the clients with consultations of finances and how the clients could go about with their business and personal banking dealings. These consultations are not just focused at the current clients but the bank also makes initiatives to target potential future clients by going to business houses to discuss the bank's products and services.

Customer

Branded Merchandise Giveaways (Measure 2.1)

According to the research, ANZ bank rewards loyal corporate customers with branded merchandise during promotional giveaways. Promotional giveaways are a cost effective mode of advertising as it reaches out to a mass number of people and at the same time, winning customers' loyalty. Increase in brand recognition is achieved at lower cost and has a lasting impact on the customers, for example, customers utilize branded umbrellas for many years. Many non-commercial customers are eager to collect branded merchandise as well and feel left out of this opportunity as non-corperate customers are not part of these merchandise giveaway promotions.

User Friendly Apps (Measure 2.2)

ANZ customers can access bank services via user friendly apps which can be assessed instantly, provided the customer has access to the Internet. The features on the app are easy to use and are compatible on any smart device, it takes only a few seconds to login to accounts, customers can carry out a number of tasks via ANZ banking app; users can transfer funds, pay bills, check account balance, study recent transactions, and so on. However, there are times when the mobile Internet app is not available and multiple attempts to login into the account refreshes the app; customers are required to go through a longer process of signing into the account.

Customer Service Call Centre (Measure 2.3)

Customers have the option of 24-hour customer service; customers have 24-hour access to the customer service at ANZ headquarters, most issues encountered by the customers are resolved over the phone. According to the research finding, customers prefer calling to the customer service call center as customers do not have to stand and wait in long queues to be served; the issues are resolved promptly and is available 24/7, the only drawback is that this free calls service is only available for landline callers and a charged service for mobile callers. This method of customer service promotes intimacy, and awakens a sense of reliability and trust among the customers towards the bank as the customers feel that the bank considers its customers important and has made such services available to the customers.

Over the Counter Customer Services (Measure 2.4)

Over the counter customer services is crucial for any organization, at ANZ, front desk customer service is the first impression of the bank. Customers have the option of arranging appointments with customer representatives at the ANZ bank to avoid waiting in long queues. The friendly customer representative provides customers with satisfactory customer's services. During this one on one interaction with the customer, the customers are informed about the products and services provided by the bank which may be applicable to the customer's needs. Few customers were disappointed with the performance of the bank according to the findings of this research, reason for this disappointment was occasions where appointments were arranged and confirmed with the customer service representative but upon the customer's arrival the customer representative was out of the office or was not available for the agreed time. Customers were not informed of cancellation of appointments or unavailability of the customer service representative. This had an adverse impact on the customers as the customers did not feel important or valued by the bank. Few unsatisfied customers also raised concerns on the time spent waiting in long queues to be served by the customer service representative, the reason for this delay according to the customers is few number of customer service staff available to serve the large number of customers. According to new customers who had applied for new cards were informed that ANZ will advise customers once card and pin which are to be picked up. ANZ failed to inform few of the new customers and the customers only found out that their cards were ready for pickup upon following up with the bank themselves. There were even cases where banks had shredded the new cards with pins due late pickups, which made customers wait for another few months for a new card to arrive.

Customer Security and Privacy (Measure 2.5)

As per this research, the customers of ANZ are confident with the customer security and privacy of data and personal information. According to the long-term customers of ANZ there has been no incident of any security breaches to their account to date and customers totally rely on ANZ for protection and safeguarding of customer information and data. Most customers are not aware of the measures taken by ANZ to protect customers' data and information from cybercrimes.

E-Banking (Measure 2.6)

This research reveals that, according to ANZ customers who use Internet banking, they find ANZ Internet banking efficient as a number of tasks can be performed as long as Internet connection is available. Some of these task/services include paying bills, transferring funds, viewing account statements, and other. According to the customers, to be able to use Internet banking, some training on the usage of these advanced features are required. Some customers suggested short instructional videos on proceeding with login and setting up security questions will be helpful to customers who intend to sign up for Internet banking. E-banking has its limitations as there are often times when due to weak connections login to accounts is not possible and at times few customers end up being locked out of their accounts which is a hassle. One-time login options, choice of security questions to answer, notifications of wrong password entered via email and SMS, and so forth, are among suggestions from the customers to improve the e-banking experience for its customer. An interesting feature of Internet banking is that ANZ puts up a max of 3 promotional advertisements of products and services which may be of interest to the user. These advertisements enable customers to learn about new products and services offered by the bank.

Internal Business Processes

Customer Advocate (Measure 3.1)

According to research, it was gathered that ANZ Bank, either it be a branch or a headquarters, have an employee who has a distinguished role as a "customer advocate." This person manages customer complaints and complements. The purpose of this role is to make it easier for customers when assisting in their complaints and ensuring that it does not arise again. This position has a great responsibility in ensuring that complaints and complements are escalated within effective timeframes and fair outcomes are achieved. Also an advocate has influence in organizations operating systems, decision-making, and processes. In general, the customer advocate provides a "voice" for customers. All staff are educated on the role of a customer advocate.

Customer Satisfaction Survey (Measure 3.2)

Customer satisfaction surveys is an important process by which the banks are able to identify the strengths and weaknesses of customer service provided by each individual of the bank. This does not only shed importance to customer service but determines the productivity, skill, and knowledge level of each employee who somehow or the other serves customers. Here the bank sends out customer feedback forms to the customers through bank tellers or even via email. The sole purpose of these surveys are to understand the customer satisfaction levels, with each bank experience, product or service. The customer advocates collect these data and convert them into various rating scales. These variations in ratings are measured over time and a much comprehensive understanding is created. Here there is a clearer picture to whether customer expectations are met or not. When the positive and negative customer perceptions are identified, actions are taken accordingly to improve customer relations.

Customer Advocacy Program (Measure 3.3)

This is a functional program in ANZ Bank. This program has been implemented to create a culture which promotes customer-focus and service. Persistent service is emphasized towards customer needs.

Meetings With Corporate Customers (Measure 3.4)

ANZ Bank ensured that they devote time and effort in communicating with its customers. There are regular meetings with corporate customers.

These meetings are usually via Skype or face-to-face. The results showed that regular meetings allowed adaptation and growth in customer service and established strong customer relations. With this approach, there is increased focus on relationships. Marketing also occurs through this since organizations success is shared and through good relationships, the customers begin recommending products and services to others.

Learning and Growth

In the learning and growth perspective of the balanced scorecard learning and growth perspective, intangible business aspects of the business are focused on skills of our team and our culture.

The questions related to this perspective is: How can the organization learn and improve in order to achieve its vision in terms of CRM effectiveness? The measure taken to conquer this was done by executing skill assessment, team training, strategy awareness programs, leadership and motivation, organizational culture development, and improving information systems.

The three themes for the learning and growth perspective of the balanced scorecard are Measure 4.1, Measure 4.2, and Measure 4.3 below. Learning and growth perspective are focused on: employee capabilities, managing information system capability themes, and strategy awareness and motivation.

Employee Capabilities (Measure 4.1)

Look at the objectives in the internal perspective. Does your team have enough skills to achieve those objectives? Formulate respective goals in the learning and growth perspective: Skills assessment and team training. Skill assessments are conducted within the company to upskill staff to grasp the new ideas implemented in activities related to CRM. At times, skills assessment is done as on the job training. Assessment will be conducted to review how much is learned after the idea presentation is done. The same manner applies to team training. This is done to upgrade our customer service platforms, for example, staff who deal with customers face to face (customer service officers, loan officers, outreach team members, call center staff, etc.).

Information System Capability Theme (Measure 4.2)

In this theme, information systems are explored in our organization for the strategic needs to be executed effectively. The formulated goals are to improve the information system capabilities. Conducting training for information systems in terms of CRM. Mainly focusing on eCRM for example Internet banking and website usage for information dissemination and online helpline systems. As new information is introduced regarding CRM, the staff are to be trained to adjust to new or changed processes in regards to CRM. Also refresher training is conducted to refresh training that was conducted before. Refreshers are done for essential IS implementations.

Strategy Awareness and Motivation Theme (Measure 4.3)

Few relevant motivational and alignment themes are addressed in this theme. The goals for this theme can be formulated as: strategy awareness program, leadership and motivation, and organizational culture development. Strategy awareness program is done for staff and newcomers. Organizational culture in terms of CRM strategies is focused on more and staff are given training to acquire the cultural knowledge of the organization. Leadership and motivational staff are practiced fully as the organization is conducting awards nights. CRM catalysts are identified and given awards. It also gives a staff a motivational push to CRM implementation in ANZ.

CONCLUSION

The finding of this research shows the following implications: firstly, according to financial perspective ANZ banks strategic funding is used for the following; training and development, upgrading of customer information system, community projects, advertisements, corporate social events, branded merchandise giveaways, and consultations. Secondly, according to the customer perspective the measures taken are: branded merchandise giveaways promotions, implementing e-banking such as designing user friendly apps compatible on smart devices for easier access, providing 24/7 call center services to customers for instant solutions to problems encountered by customers, providing over the counter customer services for face to face consultations, ensure customer security and privacy to protect customer data and customer information from cybercrimes. Moreover, through internal business processes perspective ANZ offers customer advocate roles committed to escalating and resolving customer praises and grievances in a timely manner, conducting customer satisfaction surveys to analyze customer feedback and implement relevant changes, implementing customer advocacy program to create employee awareness on customer priority and conducting regular meetings with corporate customers for gaining customer loyalty. Finally, the last perspective is learning and growth which includes the following measures: skills assessment amongst employees, regular team trainings conducted, employee refresher awareness programs, motivational programs to ensure employees are constantly motivated to offer efficient and excellent customer services, and emphasizing on continuous organizational culture development for better customer experience.

RECOMMENDATION AND FUTURE RESEARCH

We recommend more emphasis on customer and staff relationship building. Research showed that currently priority is given to corporate customers.

Financial budget should be extended whereby non-corporate (personal) potential customers are included in these social events. Only corporate clients are entitled to branded merchandise giveaways. It is recommended that a budget should be planned in a way where promotion is inclusive of personal customers as well to promote low cost advertising for better CRM.

24/7 customer service help center is available but it benefits only to the landline users as it is a free call service. It is a charged service for mobile callers. The bank should work providing free call services to both landline and mobile callers as there is an increase in mobile users which would promote a sense of customer importance. For e-Banking there needs to be partnership with network providers like Vodafone or Digicel for better Internet banking. This will enhance customer satisfaction.

Regular meetings with corporate customers is evident. Personal customers' needs to be inclusive of these meetings. Equal focus needs to be made to both corporate and personal customers. This is to gain customer loyalty regardless of their financial status.

The above recommendations need serious consideration to enhance CRM. Implementations of existing services within ANZ overseas banks in order to provide uniform customer services globally.

Majority of the research papers done on CRM are based on overseas organizations especially in developed countries. There is a need for more research within the pacific zone. This will allow other banking organizations to improve their services and relationship with customers. A detailed research should be conducted on the existing information system in place in banking organizations for CRM.

APPENDIX

Questionnaire A

The purpose of this questionnaire is to analyze the effectiveness of customer relationship management in the bank.

Please answer the following questions:

Name: _____

Age: _____

Gender: _____

Marital Status: _____

Occupation: _____

(kindly select the option most relevant to you)	Strongly Disagree	Disagree	Neutral	Agree	Strongly Agree
1. I am satisfied with the frontline customer services.					
2. I am satisfied with the electronic banking services provided by ANZ bank.					
3. I often participate in customer evaluations conducted by ANZ bank.					
4. ANZ bank makes an effort to find out my banking needs.					
5. I am confident in the banks security and user authentications.					
6. I am part of promotional and social events organized by ANZ bank.					
7. My concerns are escalated and resolved in a timely manner by ANZ bank.					
8. I am aware of ongoing promotions of services and products provided by ANZ bank.					
9. My business is important to ANZ bank.					
10. Is there room for future improvements? If yes, please state the improvements.					

Questionnaire B

The purpose of this questionnaire is to analyze the effectiveness of customer relationship management in the bank.

Please answer the following questions:

Name: _____

Age: _____

Gender: _____

Marital Status: _____

Occupation: _____

(kindly select the option most relevant to you)	Strongly Disagree	Disagree	Neutral	Agree	Strongly Agree
1. Ample funds and resources are allocated for training and development.					
2. The customer information system in place is up to date and frequently upgraded.					
3. My bank is involved in a number of community projects.					
4. Enough funds are allocated for advertisements of products and services to customers.					
5. Social corporate events are conducted regularly.					
6. All grievances raised by customers are escalated and resolved ethically and efficiently.					
7. Customer satisfaction survey is regularly conducted.					
8. All employees are aware of customer advocacy program.					
9. Regular meetings are conducted with corporate and personal customers.					
10. Customer service skills are assessed regularly.					

REFERENCES

Al-Arafati, A., Kadir, K. A., & Al-Haderi, S. (2019). The mediating effect of output quality on the relationship between top management support and customer satisfaction on the implementation of customer relationship management system in public sector. *Academy of Strategic Management Journal, 18*(2), 1–11.

Al-Safi, A. M., Al-Safadi, L., & Al-Mudimigh, A. (2012). CRM scorecard: CRM performance measurement. *International Journal of Networked Computing and Advanced Information Management, 2*(1), 1–14.

Chen, J. S., & Ching, R. K. (2004). An empirical study of the relationship of IT intensity and organizational absorptive capacity on CRM performance. *Journal of Global Information Management, 12*(1), 1–17.

Gebert, H., Geib, M., Kolbe, L., & Riempp, G. (2002). Towards customer knowledge management. In *Proceedings of the 2nd International Conference on Electronic Business* (ICEB 2002).

Hasanian, G., Chong, C. W., & Gan, G. C. (2015). Application of knowledge management factors on customer relationship management process. *Library Review.*

Hasanian, G., Chong, C. W., & Gan, G. C. (2019). Application of knowlegde managemnet factors on customer relationship management process. *Application of Knowledge Management, 64*(8), 583–595.

Hendriyani, C., & Auliana, L. (2018). Transformation from relationship marketing to electronic customer relationship management: A literature study. *Review of Integrative Business and Economics Research, 7,* 116–124.

Herawaty, T., Tresna, P. W., & Liany, I. L. (2019). The effect of customer relationship management on customer loyalty (Study at Crown Hotel in Transikmalaya). *Review of Integrative business Econimics Research, 8*(3), 150–156.

Kotler, P., & Keller, K. L. (2006). *Marketing management 12e.* New Jersey.

Lam, A. Y., Cheung, R., & Lau, M. M. (2013). The influence of internet-based customer relationship management on customer loyalty. *Contemporary Management Research, 9*(4).

Liew, C.-B. A. (2008). Strategic intergration of knowledge management and customer relationship management. *Journal of Knowledge Management, 12*(4), 131–146.

Maggon, M., & Chaudhry, H. (2018). Exploring relationships between customer satisfaction and customer attitude from customer relationship management viewpoint: An empirical study of leisure travellers. *FIIB Business Review, 7*(1), 57–65.

Najafi, A., Rezaei, S., & Rodi, A. D. (2017). The effect of electronic customer relationship management on customer relationship quality: Evidence from Mellat Bank of Arak City. *Journal of Economic & Management Perspectives, 11*(3), 539–548.

New Signature. (2014, September 9). CRM for banking: A few special considerations. *New Signature.* https://newsignature.com/articles/crm-for-banking-a-few-special-considerations/

Pfleger, L. (2015). The business case of IT investments for social customer relationship management. *Journal of Improving Firm Processes, Strategies and Success using Social Media, 75*(6), 369–382.

Rostami, A. R., Valmohammadi, C., & Yousefpoor, J. (2014). The relationship between customer satisfaction and customer relationship management system: A case study of Ghavamin Bank. *Journal of Industrial and Commercial Training, 46*(4), 220–227.

Ruchi. (2014). Customer relationship management: A customer retention strategy. *International Journal of Management research & Review, 4*(5), 624–631.

Samanta, I. (2009). The Impact of e-Customer relationship marketing in hotel industry. In M. D. Lytras, P. Ordonez de Pablos, E. Damiani, D. Avison, A. Naeve, & D. G. Horner (Eds.), *Best practices for the knowledge society: Knowledge, learning, development, and technology for all* (pp. 484–494). Springer.

Sharifi, Z., Rezghi, M., & Nasiri, M. (2014, October). A new algorithm for solving data sparsity problem based-on Non negative matrix factorization in recommender systems. In *2014 4th International Conference on Computer and Knowledge Engineering* (ICCKE; pp. 56–61). IEEE.

Tawinunt, K., Phimonsathien, T., & Fongsuwan, W. (2015). Service quality and customer relationship management affecting customer retention of longstay travelers in the Thai tourism industry: A sem approach. *International Journal of Arts & Science, 8*(2), 459–477.

Tseng, S. M. (2016). Knowledge management capability, customer relationship management, and service quality. *Journal of Enterprise Information Management.*

Wang, Y., Lo, H. P., Chi, R., & Yang, Y. (2019). An integrated framework for customer relationship management. *Managing Service Quality, 14*(2), 169–182.

Yao, H.-I. (2011). Effectiveness of customer relationship managemnet on customer satisfaction in commercial bank in Taiwan. *Contemporary Management Research, 7*(2), 105–116.

CHAPTER 19

HUMAN RESOURCES MANAGEMENT SYSTEM FOR INTEGRATION AND PRODUCTIVITY

Sam Goundar
The University of the South Pacific

Ashish Lata
The University of the South Pacific

Christopher Siga
The University of the South Pacific

Pritika Singh
The University of the South Pacific

Sainimelia Damuni
The University of the South Pacific

Salome Baleivanualala
The University of the South Pacific

Shelvin Senik
The University of the South Pacific

Enterprise Systems and Technological Convergence, pages 349–368
Copyright © 2021 by Information Age Publishing
349

ABSTRACT

The focus today has passed from administrative management tasks to becoming a strategic partner of the overall organization strategy, largely with the strong support of information technologies evolution in this field of knowledge.

Two systematic analyses have been carried out to identify the problems. This included an interview and chat with current system users through which it was reported to management. The second one was analyzed through the audit report from the external auditors. The auditor's report highlighted that few of the documents were missing from employee files and recommended the HR division to maintain e-copies of documents. This case study has identified reporting, retrieval of employee documentation, and system integration as the major concerns that need to be resolved.

The ways that we are going to resolve the issues identified include:

- Identify the current challenges presented by the current system in use.
- Determine available opportunities to compare it with other software to gain competitive advantage.
- Recommend the university to have a suitable HR information system that can enable to address the above concerns.

This case study will help improve efficiency and effectiveness of the HR functions by way of integration. An integrated HRIS system will therefore enhance the university to align its strategic goals. Nagendra and Deshpande (2013) revealed that organizations need to integrate HRIS functions with other business functions. The study revealed that HRIS needs to offer more intelligent capabilities to increase the effectiveness of HR planning.

In this case study, we will provide an overview of some applications of technology in functional areas of human resources management (HRM) within the university with references to literature based on management information systems. Our case study adds to the discussion of the use of the Delone and Mclean IS success model. The IS success model identifies the relationship among six critical dimensions of IS success and these are information quality, system quality, service quality, system use/usage intentions, user satisfactions, and the net system benefits (Delone & McLean, 2003).

The model illustrated in Figure 19.1 was created by William H. Delone and Ephraim R. McLean in 1992. They presented an information system (IS) success model as a framework and model for measuring the complex-dependent variable in information system research. The authors a decade later, in 2003 in response to feedback received from other scholars working in the same area further refined this. The reason to use this model for our case study is because it has been considered to be one of the most influential theories in the IS research.

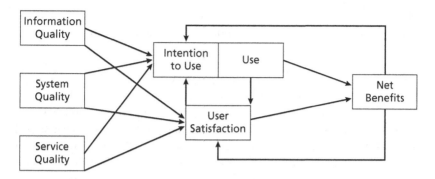

Figure 19.1 DeLone & McLean Model of IS success. *Source:* Delone & McLean, 2003.

Technology acceptance model (TAM) is also applicable in our case study. This case study uses the TAM to explain the utilization of HRIS in the university under study. In 1986, Fred Davis introduced the TAM, a model that was specifically designed to understand user acceptance towards information systems and or technologies of change (see Figure 19.2).

In our case study investigation, the problem-oriented approach was used which involved the following activities:

1. Identify whether there are problems and opportunities in the information systems that we are going to investigate on.
2. Develop or evaluate alternative system solutions.
3. Select suitable solutions or recommendations that meet our requirements.

The case study is based on primary data collected through a structured questionnaire from the HR personnel of 21 out of 30 employees of the HR division. The data collected was analyzed using the Microsoft Excel spreadsheet. We further supported our case study with published works allowing the team to evaluate and provide commendation on the systems overall validity and dependability.

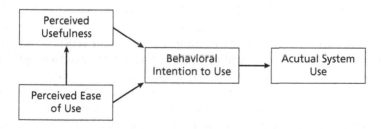

Figure 19.2 Technology acceptance model. *Source:* Davis et al. (1989); Venkatesh et al. (2003).

The results indicate that there are critical issues with the current HRIS in terms of reporting, integration, and document management.

BACKGROUND

The university was established in January 2010. Fiji has three publicly known universities with the university under study being one of the universities. It has five colleges, with over 20,000 students and approximately 2,000 employees. The university operates its core business from over 12 different locations while most support services operate as centralized hubs. HR manages all its processes from one location. To support the functions of HR, there are multiple systems in place such as PayGlobal, employee self-service (ESS), online recruitment system, personnel requisition system (PRF), and the performance management system (PMS). At this stage it is important to note that all systems operate independent to each other without any form of integration.

The recruitment system, PRF and PMS are in-house developed systems that have been designed and adopted to be specific to the university process. PayGlobal and ESS on the other hand are off the shelf HR products that are in place to support the payroll, employee details, and minor personnel management processes for HR. This study focuses on the use of the PayGlobal system at this university. It will discuss the challenges and problems existing with current HR information systems. The lack of integration of these systems have hindered and delayed work outputs.

Similar to the university setting HRIS has been adopted into many areas of the HR process and many different areas have also been researched on HRIS among various industry types. It has been noticed that many organizations tend to ignore the value that HR systems adds to the HR processes. Organizations are not able to foresee the importance of the HR system while small organizations often find the HR system costly to adopt. In many instances, employers tend to take action on the HR needs when they have failed instead of taking proactive action. Organizations with such circumstances, normally are not able to forecast the actual needs of the firm.

In the context of higher education accurate data on people for reporting becomes essential for strategic human resource decisions. This determines the reason on why human resource information systems (HRIS) need to be established and extensively used in higher education systems to support the underlying education processes, practices and most importantly the human resource needs (Trim, 2003). It has been noticed that this normally is not the case and systems are used to mainly reduce administrative workload at all levels of HR. Many organizations tend to focus more on the short-term need of systems without being able to use systems for strategic level decisions.

The case study is important as it attempts to understand the need for a system and whether it is able to efficiently support the needs of the HR department in a university setting. This study will be significantly relevant to universities in Fiji as it attempts to identify the level of HRIS adaptation and may also be beneficial to the senior management team for decision-making.

PROBLEM STATEMENT

This case is analyzed using the problem-oriented approach. The problem-oriented approach is applicable to real life situation cases. Our case study will identify all the problems with the current information systems at the human resources division. Finally, the recommendation and action plan will be specified.

The three major problems identified at the university were:

1. *Reporting and analysis of employee information:* Preparing reports is currently managed manually. Data from PayGlobal is dumped into excel and reporting and analysis is then carried out manually. It is time consuming and costly to produce reports, whereby a staff is allocated just to prepare reports. The types of reports requested from external parties such as Fiji Higher Education Commission, banks, FRCS, and FNPF are delayed because of the delay in reports being prepared. Internal reporting or HR analytics in relation to HR functions such as talent management, employee engagement, performance, retention to ensure decision-making is also delayed due to the system unable to perform these analytics.

2. *Document management:* Document management is another issue with the current software. The HR system is unable to store documents due to the size limits. In order to retrieve documents, HR staff have to refer to employee personal files which is very time consuming keeping in mind the huge number of employee files being kept by the HR division. Currently there is no electronic filing system that is needed to support HR files which can be accessed remotely for convenience. Manual record keeping is risky in cases of natural disasters. It also increases the university's cost such as printing of documents and storage.

3. *Lack of system integration between departments:* System integration is also a problem with the current HR system. Not all modules of the HR systems are used with PayGlobal software. The linkage between one department to another is weak. Passing off information from one department to another is managed manually. Most of the processes are managed manually, example processing of allowances of employees.

LITERATURE REVIEW

Considering increased competition nowadays, businesses strive to gain competitive advantage, increase their economic indicators, work productivity and efficiency, reduce costs and get other benefits through implementation of integrated information systems. By improving internal processes and financial performance of the company, the general business performance could be influenced by the deployment of such information system. (Lipaj & Davidaviciene, 2013, p. 1)

One of the key issues of successful business is human resources management and that the process is under great influence of modern information technology. HRIS are systems used to collect, record, store, analyze and retrieve data concerning an organization's human resources, but it is not merely reduction of administrative procedures. (Dorel & Bradic-Martinovic, 2011, p. 2)

Considering this framework, this chapter aims to study the use of HRIS in improving HR operations. Particularly, it focuses on the need of HRIS in the performance of HRM functions at the lowest possible cost and also at a fast rate, which pose increased challenges for HR professionals. (Chauhan, Sharma, & Tyagi, 2011, p. 1)

This study examined the impact of the adoption of electronic HRM on the HRM function and how much it has affected to change the role of HR managers. In addition to that, it was intended to study the level and types of technologies that are used in HR in Sri Lanka and the drivers of adoption of technology in the Sri Lankan context. There were several reasons for driving organizations towards the adoption of e-HRM in Sri Lanka and the most common of which was the desire to be the leading edge. (De Alwis, 2010, p. 2)

Drawing on process theory, this study examines the process of Information System (IS) implementation by explaining how factors of information system implementation influence each other and how interactions among them produce results. Based on one successful case and two unsuccessful cases, we develop the process model of IS implementation, by which the process of IS implementation and the dynamics of IS success can be explained. (Hee-Woong & Pan, 2006, p. 2)

However, there is no accepted or over all framework that arrange the important aspects of effective HRIS in a way helping to assist HRIS success, the single available options are by looking through the lens of well-known theories and models of IS success, by which the success of HRIS can be usefully assessed. The study, then, develop and validate a multidimensional HRIS systems success model based on the IS success theories: the technology acceptance model, User satisfaction and DeLone and McLean information system success model. The study argues that using user satisfaction as surrogate indicator for measuring the success of HRIS has some theoretical difficulties, in similar vein, using TAM alone may not be sufficient to adequately capture the full meaning of effectiveness or the success of HRIS; this study posits that

HRIS success is a joint function of system and information characteristics and acceptance. (Shibly, 2011, p. 1)

Owing to the revolution of Information Technology, Human Resource Information Systems is of profound significance in managing Human Resources in the contemporary globalized knowledge economy. The number of organizations gathering, storing, analyzing, and distributing human resources data using Human That influence adoption of HRIS or any Information Systems through a thorough literature study and consolidate them under four major factors namely Technological, Organizational, Environmental and Psychological. (Anitha & Aruna, 2013, p. 1)

The Human Resource Information Systems as a function of IS are also become inevitable for organization, because they know that their human resources are one of the most important factor in their success, therefore to implement a human resource information system in their human resources will help the organizations reach their goals easily. (Buzkan, 2016, p. 1)

According to Hendrickson (2003),

Human Resource Information System is the technological backbone of Human Resources. While all of human resources practice is affected by information technology, human resource information systems (HRIS) and HRIS administration comprise a distinct, supporting function within HR. Contemporary HRIS is an organizational boundary spanner that must meet the needs of a number of organizational stakeholders. Not all HRIS are created equal, nor do they need to be. Different size firms in differing operational contexts require HRIS that meet their specific needs and remain cost-effective. Information technology will continue to have a significant impact on HR applications in all organizations. Firms will also continue to change the process of HRIS development. The use of portal technology will affect HRIS delivery. As custodians of the organization's human capital, the HR function may become integrated and immersed in the design and acquisition of knowledge management systems. (p. 6)

Owing to the revolution in information technology, the face of the contemporary workplace has changed and systems have been made more effective by introducing new techniques. Majority of the organizations have understood the importance of information storage and retrieval. The authors focused on how modern technology is helping in ensuring effectiveness of HR functions. Human Resource Information System (HRIS) is an opportunity for organizations to make the HR department administratively and strategically participative in operating the organization. The main objective is to understand the extent to which HRIS is being used in increasing the administrative and strategic functions of the HR department. A survey of 18 HR Managers from various private corporations operating in Lahore, Pakistan showed that HRIS is positively used as a tool to achieve greater administrative efficiency by adding value in the department. (Sadiq, Fareed, Khurram, & Mujtaba, 2012, p. 3)

As stated in the findings from a paper by Ramezan (2010), "The integrated system seemed to be producing efficient and effective feedback amongst the users at the Iranian oil company due to its efficiency" (p. 1).

The similar sentiments are shared by Halawi (2005) who "discovered that there is a strong relationship between knowledge quality, service quality perceptions, intention to use, user satisfaction and knowledge management systems success after utilizing the Delone and McLean IS model to assess the information system in a knowledge-based organization" (p. 1).

The research conducted by Wiblen, Grant, and Dery (2010) "presented a complete survey of an organization's decision to transition from their trademarked stand-alone HRIS system to an integrated vendor system. The study showed how the transition eventually led to reshaping of the organizations understanding of the talent requirements in both human resources and information technology (IT) functions and resulted in a new approach to the management of talent" (p. 1).

The study by Arvidsson, Holmstrom, and Lyytinen (2014) highlights

> the strategic intent of the Information System in a paper mill. The authors developed a multi-dimensional view of IS strategy, conceptualizing three key challenges in the IS strategy process to explain how and why a paper mill despite successfully implementing a strategic production management system, failed to produce intended strategic change. This outcome is called strategy blindness, organizational incapability to realize the strategic intent of implemented, available system capabilities. The researchers identified three salient factors that contribute to strategy blindness that is mistranslation of intent, flexibility of the IT artifact and cognitive entrenchment, and discuss how they affect strategic implementation process. (p. 2)

> Human Resource Management (HRM) has experienced significant changes from administrative management responsibilities to becoming a strategic associate of the overall organization plan. Fast shifting markets, industries, and services require managerial environments capable of constant adjustment with new ideas and reduced time-to-market. HRM has been strained to take up new logics and most HR managers must forget old habits and ways of thinking but should facilitate organizations to define their strategies and build programs to develop their human capital. Quality of HRM is a key success factor for organizations. HRIS allows us to respond more quickly to changes and to needs of decision-making, budget control and global analysis. Information systems have been a valuable tool for HR managers to facilitate HR processes and practices hence qualified HR professionals have a special role in order for effective operation of the system. (Silva & Lima, 2018, p. 5)

> As a nurturer and caretaker of the workforce, the HR department would, in turn, need to undergo fundamental changes, moving beyond its traditional responsibilities of personnel administration and employee advocacy to play a central role in helping companies fulfil their highest-level business goals. If

HR did not become more tightly linked with strategic and economic objectives, the reasoning went, its ability to make an adequate contribution to the bottom line would be undermined. (Connolly, Mardis, & Down, 1997, p. 1)

2.0 FINDINGS

Analysis of the Problems

The HR department of the university uses PayGlobal and ESS to manage employee data. The two systematic analyses were carried out to identify the existence of the problems:

1. *Interview and Chat With Current System Users*—After talking to the current users, it was revealed that users are unable to generate reports through the system. Secondly there is no provision for e-copies of the documents. Finally, there is no system integration between HR and payroll therefore restrictions on getting data on time for decision-making. These concerns are the usual obstacles that are brought to the attention of the senior management group by the other senior stakeholders of the university such as the deans and the directors. This case study will refer to these concerns as managerial issues.
2. *The Internal Audit Findings*—The internal auditors have reported on missing documents on few of the personal files and have recommended to keep e-copies of the documents for easy retrieval to resolve the issue of document management.

The following have been the issues which enabled HR to identify potential problems:

1. The deadlines for report submission such as qualification report to Fiji higher education and annual report data were delayed by HR and not submitted on time. This resulted in seeking for extension for report submission.
2. In order to retrieve documents, staff of HR has to follow a lengthy procedure which requires forms to be endorsed by three parties before a personal file can be retrieved. Decision-making is delayed as well.
3. HR is unable to generate data due to rules being set up in the current system which delays processing of the transaction in relation to pay and benefits.

Data Analysis

It is seen from the responses from 21 HR staff of this university, that most of them, that is 95.24% have agreed that there is a need to have an upgraded and integrated HRIS (see Table 19.1, Figure 19.3). Secondly, all have agreed that retrieving e-copies of the documents from the current HRIS is not possible, which delays work processes and decision-making.

Even though the analysis shows where 38.10% have agreed that the internal and external information is well managed, there are still challenges in getting .pdf copies of the documents, integration, and reporting.

TABLE 19.1	Data Analysis	
Concerns	Statement	% Agree
1	The internal and external information is well managed by the current HR system.	38.10
2	The current HRIS is able to analyze and match demand for internal users.	23.81
3	The current HRIS is able to analyze and match demand for external users.	14.29
4	The reports required by stakeholders is provided in a timely manner.	28.57
5	Current system helps in decision-making.	42.86
6	The copies of documents are readily available on the current HRIS.	0.00
7	Your HRIS is linked to other departments to share information.	4.76
8	There is a need to have an upgraded integrated HRIS.	95.24

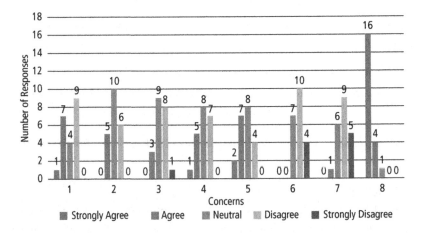

Figure 19.3 The important role of HRIS in the organization.

Only 21.81% of the HR staff participating in the survey agreed that the current HRIS is able to analyze and match demand for internal users. While 14.29% agreed that the current HRIS is able to analyze and match demand for external users. The major issue is reporting to external parties. These include reporting as follows:

- *Fiji higher education commission:* Quarter operating grant report is needed to enable the university to be eligible for grants. This report is critical to the university as it may have financial implications, which can affect the budget of the university. This includes reporting on staff qualification, the minimum qualification requirements, and staff to student ratio per college. Separate systems are used to compile this report that is time consuming and at times delays report submission.
- *Fiji commerce and employers federation (FCEF):* Annually analysis needs to be done to successfully upload data to participate in the online survey conducted by FCEF. Separate analysis is carried out manually which is very time consuming and hectic.
- *The Association of Commonwealth Universities (ACU) surveys:* This data is provided to ACU annually for their benchmarking exercise. The requirement of the report is not managed by the current HRIS, instead analysis is done manually and updated online.

Finally, to sum up, our findings highlight that there is a direct need to upgrade or implement an integrated HRIS in the university. Human resource has grown significantly in the last few decades therefore, to collect, record, store, manage, timely retrieval and decision-making, an integrated HRIS is needed to increase the universities' competitive advantage, produce variety of HR related reports, and shift the focus of HR from the processing of transactions to strategic HRM.

Analysis in Relation to Delone and Mclean Model

This case study is guided by the updated Delone and Mclean model to analyze the university's HRMS for integration and productivity. Using the six dimensions of the Delone and Mclean model, we have analyzed the data collected through the questionnaires and related these with the six dimensions of the model. The constructs of this case study is further explained using the six dimensions as follows:

1. *Information quality:* This study relates to the university's systems in terms of timeliness, accuracy, reliability, and trustworthiness. Our

case study uses information quality in terms of correctness, usefulness, and timeliness of the information generated by the university's current information system in use.

2. *System quality:* This looks at the desirable characteristics of an information system. By ensuring the characteristics of the current information system used by the university, this study aims to review the systems ease of use, system features, accessibility of information, and response time.

3. *Service quality:* This represents the quality of the support that the users receive from the IS department and IT support personnel and assessed by using service quality dimensions, such as assurance and responsiveness by the systems support department, as well as the provision of user training. Service quality was measured by examining the technical support in place for users of the university's information system, the network infrastructure in place, and the reliability of the system.

4. *Intention to use:* This involves the assessment of how the information system is utilized by the users. The case study assesses the actual usage and the frequency of use of the university's information system. It also reviews the information gathered from the perspective of perceived usefulness.

5. *User satisfaction:* This is considered one of the most important measures of the system's success, often measured by overall user satisfaction. It was assessed in the study by capturing overall user satisfaction with the university's current information system. User satisfaction directly influences the net benefits provided by an information system. User satisfaction can be defined as the consumer's fulfillment response and judgment regarding product or service features that provide pleasurable levels of consumption. Many past studies demonstrated IS user satisfaction as a mediating variable at various IS domains. "User satisfaction is a strong indicator to measure whether an information system is accepted or not. In the context of this study, IS user satisfaction is conceptualized as the attitude towards computer application that results in a pleasurable level to the user in terms of information system quality and information quality. User satisfaction remains an important means of measuring our customers' opinions of our e-commerce system and should cover the entire customer experience cycle from information retrieval through purchase, payment, receipt, and service" (DeLone & McLean, 2003).

6. *Net benefits:* This dimension is regarded as the most important measure of IS success and tends to provide the extent to which an IS contributes to the success of various stakeholders. This included

both positive aspects that were specific to our case study and negative aspects that were drawn from the responses from the users of the current HR system for the division of human resources.

Our case study is also guided by TAM. The TAM model aims to identify how the individual's perception affects the intentions to use the information technology as well as the actual usage (Davis, 1986). It includes the two main factors and these are the perceived usefulness that will enhance the job performance and the perceived ease of use; that is, how difficult will it be to use the system? In comparison to the current HRIS, the users feel that the system does not enhance their job performance since the job requirements are not met. Users are unable to generate reports in a timely manner and have difficulties in retrieving documents.

DISCUSSION

The three major problems in the division of human resource's HRIS are the following:

Reporting and Analysis of Employee Information

Reporting and analysis of employee information was seen as one of the problem areas that needs improvement for better decision-making. The current practice does not allow HR to generate reports based on the requirements of the users. This has been seen as an example of inefficient and irritable reporting.

The alternative solution to this problem is to upgrade or implement a new HRIS that enables HR to generate reports in a timely and efficient manner. The new HRIS will allow HR to analyze the data related to HR functions like recruitment, talent management, employee engagement, performance, and retention to ensure better decision-making. In the world today, human resources has moved to a higher level thus in order for the university to compete with other competitors of the same deliverables, we need to improve our service deliveries through better HR software. With automation, the system will allow reports to be generated pro-actively.

Document Management

Currently the HR division of the university is managing its employee records manually. This includes documents such as employee contracts,

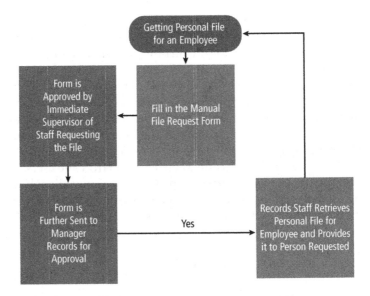

Figure 19.4 The manual process.

interview documents, CV, certificates, payroll documents, police and medical reports. In order to retrieve any documents from a personal file of employees, the requester follows a lengthy process as outlined in Figure 19.4.

The alternative solution to the problem identified above is to have a HRIS that has the document management capabilities. There will be few manual tasks and higher efficiency levels with document management. It will also reduce storage costs, have more document security and legal compliance. Based on Fiji's legislative requirements, it is recommended to keep manual documents for at least 7 years and discard manual copies as years pass by.

Some of the drawbacks with the new HRIS can be:

- Systems can be vulnerable to hacking where sensitive data could fall into wrong hands.
- Prone to viral attacks.
- Non-retrieval of e-copies of documents during power outages or technical glitches.

Lack of System Integration Between Departments

Based on the current HRIS, there is lack of system integration between payroll, applicant tracking, workforce, and learning management. Certain reports required by HR cannot be facilitated due to lack of system integration between HR and payroll. For example, while preparing budgets to be presented in HR meetings; HR staff need data to analyze. However, they need to get this from payroll, which is time consuming, and delays preparation of the HR budgets for better recruitment decisions.

We do note that there are some obstacles with system integration and this deals with security issues. However, systems need to be designed to prevent unauthorized access to sensitive and confidential data and the unintended publication of such information.

To sum up, in order to resolve the above problems, there are two possible solutions:

1. To continue using the current HR system but upgrading it to a new version where issues in regards to reporting, document management, and integration can be resolved. This may incur additional cost to the university apart from the annual license fee for the current HRIS.

2. There is a need for the university to implement an integrated management software looking at the amount of transactions that takes place daily, the huge number of students and staff. The integrated HRIS will help getting accurate data, no more data redundancies, efficient reporting, and promoting competitive advantage. This may be even more costly than compared to the solution above.

CONCLUSION

To conclude, the different systems that exist in the university are not user friendly. It creates an unstable environment. The users of the HRIS should acquire a better understanding of the need to have an updated and integrated HRIS despite facing the barriers and challenges upon implementation. Improved accuracy, quick access to information, and cost reduction are some of the benefits as identified through the literature review. The university needs real-time analytics, reporting and it is possible through the implementation of new HRIS. It is evident that the university has direct competition with other universities in Fiji. Thus IT plays a very vital role in assisting the university to gain the competitive advantage. In today's world, every department including HR is being assessed on their abilities. The university may encounter challenges in terms of user acceptance to the new HRIS. This can be overcome by providing trainings to all HRIS users and creating awareness on the benefits arising from the new HRIS in terms of efficiency, effectiveness, and reducing labor efforts.

RECOMMENDATION

Out of the two possible solutions, our proposed solution is to implement an integrated HRIS, which will have one common platform and provide HR users with real time integration, document management, and reporting intelligence. The new proposed HRIS will also provide more rich functionalities in excess to process and systems through various platforms. This will have long-run effects on the university.

However, to address the current problems, the HR division needs to upgrade their current systems and allow management and the ICT team to find possible integrated systems with consultation with HR.

IMPLEMENTATION

In order for HR to have the new HRIS implemented, this needs to be supported by the top management. The inception of the idea needs to be realized, agreed upon, and this has to be treated as an investment for the university.

TABLE 19.2	Proposed Automated HRIS Capabilities	
HR Applications	**Current System Capabilities**	**Proposed Automated HRIS Capabilities**
Recruitment and Selection	Stand-alone system—In house built	Internet recruiting, e-recruitment to be integrated with HRIS.
Training and Development	Manually managed—Paper based	Integrated HRIS to allow to track education, qualifications, and skills of the employees.
Payroll Administration	Manual time entry; Plus an off the shelf software purchased (PayGlobal software)	Electronic time clock to be integrated with HRIS and automation of pay process.
Benefits Administration	Manually managed	The new HRIS to track benefit eligibility and allowing benefits to be inputted and triggered to payroll with ease.
Compensation Management/ Administration	Manual plus HR stand-alone system is used (PayGlobal software)	The new HRIS allowing employees to review information online for their compensation claims.
Performance Appraisal	Stand-alone system—In house built	The new HRIS allowing to have an online application of performance appraisal and allowing reviews to be made readily available.
HR Planning	Manually managed	HRIS to track and monitor the workforce and retain talent.

Since implementing a new HRIS is costly and may lead the university to purchase one standalone ERP to support the core functions of the university which includes student services, finance, and HR. Feasibility study needs to be conducted outlining scope, future benefits, cost estimations and the value added to the university as a whole. Both the HR and IT team should be part of the project in order to implement the new HRIS.

The barriers or challenges that the university needs to consider while implementing the new HRIS are:

- cost of setting up and maintaining a HRIS can be high,
- lack of support from the top management and IT department,
- time management,
- insufficient financial reports, and
- the new system can be inconvenient if users fail to accept the new HRIS.

APPENDIX
MIS433: Management Information Systems

Topic: Analyzing Human Resources Management System for Integration and Productivity Questionnaire

We are interested in your assessment of the current Human Resources Information System and would like you to take a few minutes to complete this questionnaire. All information collected will be kept confidential and will only be used for research purpose only.

1. The internal and external information is well managed by the current HR system.
   ☐ *Strongly Agree* ☐ *Agree* ☐ *Neutral* ☐ *Disagree* ☐ *Strongly Disagree*

2. The current HRIS is able to analyse and match demand for internal users.
   ☐ *Strongly Agree* ☐ *Agree* ☐ *Neutral* ☐ *Disagree* ☐ *Strongly Disagree*

3. The current HRIS is able to analyse and match demand for external users.
   ☐ *Strongly Agree* ☐ *Agree* ☐ *Neutral* ☐ *Disagree* ☐ *Strongly Disagree*

4. The reports required by stakeholders is provided in a timely manner.
   ☐ *Strongly Agree* ☐ *Agree* ☐ *Neutral* ☐ *Disagree* ☐ *Strongly Disagree*

5. Current system helps in decision making.
   ☐ *Strongly Agree* ☐ *Agree* ☐ *Neutral* ☐ *Disagree* ☐ *Strongly Disagree*

6. The e-copies of documents are readily available on the current HRIS.
   ☐ *Strongly Agree* ☐ *Agree* ☐ *Neutral* ☐ *Disagree* ☐ *Strongly Disagree*

7. Your HRIS is linked to other departments to share information.
   ☐ *Strongly Agree* ☐ *Agree* ☐ *Neutral* ☐ *Disagree* ☐ *Strongly Disagree*

8. There is a need to have a upgraded integrated HRIS.
   ☐ *Strongly Agree* ☐ *Agree* ☐ *Neutral* ☐ *Disagree* ☐ *Strongly Disagree*

9. Do you have a set of reports that you provide regularly to stakeholders?

10. In what format do you produce reports?

11. How often are the reports produced?

12. How long does it take you to generate a report from time of the request?

13. How do you retrieve documents, which are required for analysis and decision-making?

REFERENCES

Anitha, J., & Aruna, M. (2013). Adoption of Human Resource Information System in Organisations. *Journal of Management, 4*(2), 5–16.

Arvidsson, V., Holmstrom, J., & Lyytinen, K. (2014). Information systems use as strategy practice: A multi-dimensional view of strategic information system implementation and use. *Journal of Strategic Information Systems, 23*(1), 45–61.

Buzkan, H. (2016). The role of human resource information system (HRIS) in organizations: A review of literature. *Academic Journal of Interdisciplinary Studies, 5*(1), 133–138.

Chauhan, A., Sharma, S. K., & Tyagi, T. (2011). Role of HRIS in improving modern HR operations. *Review of Management, 1*(2), 58–70.

Connolly, T. R., Mardis, W., & Down, J. W. (1997). Leading companies are linking HR and strategy but many companies following suit are realizing the path is not without its bumps. *American Management Association, 86*(6), 10–16.

Davis, F. D. (1986). *A technology acceptance model for empirically testing new end-user information systems: Theory and results* (Doctoral dissertation). MIT Sloan School of Management.

De Alwis, A. C. (2010). The impact of electronic human resource management on the role of human resource managers. *E+M Ekonomie a Management, 13*(4), 47–60.

Delone, W. H., & McLean, E. R. (2003). The DeLone and McLean model of information systems success: A ten-year update. *Journal of Management Information Systems, 19*(4), 9–30. https://doi.org/10.1080/07421222.2003.11045748

Dorel, D. D., & Bradic-Martinovic, A. (2011). *The role of information systems in human resource management.* https://mpra.ub.uni-muenchen.de/35286/1/Chapter_2 _draft_The_Role_of_Information_Systems_in_Human_Resource_Management .pdf

Halawi, L. A. (2005). *Knowledge management systems' success in knowledge-based organizations: An empirical validation utilizing the Delone and Mclean IS success model.* https://www.semanticscholar.org/paper/Knowledge-Management-Systems' -Success-in-An-the-and-Halawi/3d8a4c61a2300180998f3b79ca6753420566 6241

Hee-Woong, K., & Pan, S. L. (2006). Towards a process model of information systems implementation: The customer relationship management. *Database for Advances in Information Systems, 37*(1), 59–76.

Hendrickson, A. R. (2003). Human resource information systems: Backbone technology of contemporary human resources. *Journal of Labor Research, 24*(3), 381–394. https://doi.org/10.10007/s12122-003-1002-5

Lipaj, D., & Davidaviciene, V. (2013). Influence of informations systems on business performance. *Mokslas: Lietuvos Ateitis, 5*(1), 38–45.

Nagendra, A., & Deshpande, M. (2013). Human resource information systems (HRIS) in HR planning and development in mid to large sized organizations. *Procedia–Social and Behavioral Sciences, 133*, 61–67.

Ramezan, M. (2009). Measuring the effectiveness of human resource information systems in national iranian oil company an empirical assessment. *Iranian Journal of Management Studies, 2*(2), 129–145.

Sadiq, U., Fareed, A., Khurram, I., & Mujtaba, B. G. (2012). The impact of information systems on the performance of human resources department. *Journal of Business Studies Quarterly, 3*(4), 77–91.

Shibly, H. A. (2011). Human resources information systems success assessment: An integrative model. *Australian Journal of Basic and Applied Sciences, 5*(5), 157–169.

Silva, M. S., & Lima, C. G. (2018). *The role of information systems in human resource management.* https://www.intechopen.com/books/management-of-information -systems/the-role-of-information-systems-in-human-resource-management

Trim, P. (2003). Strategic marketing of further and higher educational institutions: Partnership arrangements and centres of entrepreneurship. *International Journal of Educational Management, 17*(2), 59–70.

Venkatesh, V., Morris, M. G., Davis, G. B., & Davis, F. D. (2003). User acceptance of information technology: Toward a unified view. *MIS Quarterly, 27*(3), 425–478.

Wiblen, S., Grant, D., & Dery, K. (2010). Transitioning to a new HRIS: The reshaping of human resources and information technology talent. *Journal of Electronic Commerce Research, 11*(4), 251–267.

Printed in the United States
by Baker & Taylor Publisher Services